"Vernon Whaley and
Pastor's Bible Class at Tho[mas Road Baptist Church for two and]
one-half years. They have c[ome to the table with a wealth of]
practical qualifications to [write this book. They know]
people, they know music, they know God, and they have put it all together in the Pastor's Bible Class. In addition to that, Vernon leads special music/worship events at Thomas Road Baptist Church.

"There is a second reason why they are qualified to write this book. They are both scholars in several disciplines, and they not only understand the nature of academic pursuits but also have excelled in writing this book on the history of worship.

"But thirdly, Vernon Whaley is the chairman of the Liberty University Center for Worship that involves the graduate and undergraduate preparation of music leaders at Liberty University. Dr. Towns is dean of the School of Religion in which these musicians study. Together they have made the Praise and Worship Institute the fastest growing of all schools of Christian music in America. More than 900 students study in the graduate and undergraduate programs. These students do more than just excel in the classroom and in music. They are involved in practical projects and local church ministries, serving the Lord in many different ways. It is a great honor and privilege to endorse this book because I endorse the men who wrote it, the ministry they represent, and what they have accomplished for God."

Jonathan Falwell
senior pastor, Thomas Road Baptist Church

"It is fitting that Elmer Towns and Vernon Whaley should be the ones to take on such an expansive tome as *Worship through the Ages*. Elmer is long-time dean of the School of Religion at Liberty University and the consummate teacher of the Great Awakenings. Vernon is a key architect of one of the largest and most successful worship programs in the world at Liberty University's Center for Worship. Together, they are committed to understanding the substance of worship, the history of worship, and the key biblical characters who live out the story of worship—and to communicating that in a way that actually ignites worship in their readers.

"Passion for worship is obvious as Elmer Towns and Vernon Whaley give us a guided tour from Genesis to Revelation and through the most defining Awakenings and movements in the history of the church. Inclusion of the latter half of the twentieth century corrects an often-missing element in God's worship story. With equal parts history, theological perspective, biographical insight, and cultural anthropology, Elmer Towns and Vernon Whaley ignite longing and prayer for the next Great Awakening."

Chuck Fromm, publisher, *Worship Leader* magazine

"*Worship through the Ages* is informative and inspirational. The book is a great teaching tool concerning authentic worship of our awesome God that inspires me to know God more intimately and serve Him more passionately. It's absolutely a must-read for anyone who desires to lead church worship in any capacity. My life is richer and my ministry is stronger because of this great work. Thank you, Dr. Whaley and Dr. Towns, for this powerful read!"

Babbie Mason
recording artist/songwriter/author

"I've known for several years this book was coming, and I've hardly been able to wait. No one knows church music like Vernon Whaley; no one knows church work better than Elmer Towns. Combine their efforts on a biblical foundation, add some incredible charts, tell some great stories, relate some colorful history—and you've got *Worship through the Ages*. This book will intrigue, inform and inspire you. And it'll encourage you to pray afresh: 'Revive us again; fill each heart with Thy love; / May each soul be rekindled with fire from above.'"

Robert J. Morgan
pastor, conference speaker, author

"Every worship leader needs to know the inspiring stories behind the great spiritual awakenings. *Worship through the Ages* not only tells those stories but also provides insights into the innovations each movement brought to the practice of worship. Each chapter will whet your appetite for God to bring revival to your church, your community, and the world."

Rory Noland
director of Heart of the Artist Ministries

"I recommend *Worship through the Ages* for pastors, worship leaders, and students. It will help Christians understand why they use the music they do, what it will accomplish, how God has used music in the past, and what is the biblical basis for music ministry. *Worship through the Ages* is a valuable contribution to the churches, as we think together about how to worship well."

Ed Stetzer
author, *Subversive Kingdom*, www.edstetzer.com

Worship through the Ages

How the Great Awakenings Shape Evangelical Worship

Nashville, Tennessee

Worship through the Ages

Copyright © 2012 by Elmer L. Towns and Vernon M. Whaley

All rights reserved.

ISBN: 978-1-4336-7257-6

Published by B&H Publishing Group
Nashville, Tennessee

Dewey Decimal Classification: 269
Subject Heading: WORSHIP—HISTORY \ PUBLIC WORSHIP \ RELIGIOUS AWAKENING

Scripture quotations marked CEV are taken from the Contemporary English Version, Copyright © 1995 American Bible Society. All rights reserved.

Scripture quoations marked ESV are taken from The Holy Bible, English Standard Version Copyright © 2001 by Crossway Bibles, a division of Good News Publishers.

Scripture quotations designated (NIV) are from THE HOLY BIBLE: NEW INTERNATIONAL VERSION®. NIV®. Copyright © 1973, 1978, 1984, 2011 by Biblica. All rights reserved worldwide.

Scripture quotations marked NCV are taken from the New Century Version. Copyright © 1987, 1988, 1991 by Thomas Nelson, Inc. Used by permission. All rights reserved.

Scripture quotations marked NKJV are taken from the New King James Version. Copyright © 1982 by Thomas Nelson, Inc. Used by permission. All rights reserved.

Permission has been received to quote freely from and use *The 10 Greatest Revivals Ever: From Pentecost to the Present* © 2000 by Elmer L. Towns and Douglas Porter.

Printed in the United States of America

1 2 3 4 5 6 7 8 9 10 11 12 • 17 16 15 14 13 12
VP

To the Worship Students of Liberty University

Every generation of Liberty University students has recognized what God is doing in the world, in the church, and in their hearts. They have dedicated themselves to ministry with the view of doing what God is doing.

Down through the centuries, God has used young men and women—college-age students—to usher in his great awakenings. In the early days at Liberty University, God poured out revival on the students at Liberty, and they became a part of the awakening of the 1970s.

In recent days, God is again stirring hearts to worship him in spirit and in truth. Not only do Liberty students worship God in convocation and many other places; God has called together a great multitude of students to prepare for ministry at Liberty University's Center for Worship. They not only study worship but also prepare themselves to go out and lead worship after graduation. It is to these students that we dedicate this volume for *the glory of God and the testimony of Jesus Christ.* . . . And, may God magnify their task as they lead this next generation to worship.

Contents

FOREWORD by Mike Harland ix

INTRODUCTION 1

CHAPTER 1: Worship in the Old Testament, Part 1 9

CHAPTER 2: Worship in the Old Testament, Part 2 25

CHAPTER 3: Pentecost: A New Expression of Worship
(AD 30–100). 43

CHAPTER 4: Christianity Sweeps across the Greco-Roman
World (AD 100–500) 65

CHAPTER 5: The Middle Ages (the Dark Ages) (500–1500) 83

CHAPTER 6: Reformation (1517) 99

CHAPTER 7: The Awakening in Europe and America
(1727–1790). 113

CHAPTER 8: The Camp Meeting Awakenings (1780–1820) . . . 131

CHAPTER 9: The Sunday School and Charles Finney Revivals (1820–1850) 159

CHAPTER 10: The Laymen's Prayer Revival (1857–1890) 179

CHAPTER 11: The Welsh Revival (1904–1906) 201

CHAPTER 12: The Azusa Street Revival (1906–1908) 219

CHAPTER 13: The Revivalists and Great Evangelistic Campaigns, Part 1 (1890–1935) 235

CHAPTER 14: The Revivalists and Great Evangelistic Campaigns, Part 2 (1935–1960) 263

CHAPTER 15: The Baby Boomer Revival, Part 1 (1965–1985)... 293

CHAPTER 16: The Baby Boomer Revival, Part 2 (1965–1985)... 315

CHAPTER 17: Moving toward a Twenty-First-Century Great Worship Awakening 341

EPILOGUE 367

APPENDIX: Worship through the Ages Time Line 375
NAME INDEX 383
SUBJECT INDEX 389

Foreword

I love stories. Whether they come from a great book or conversation, a well-made film or a song, stories inspire and challenge and give us perspective on life. We learn who we are by the stories our families tell about us. And we define our lives for others by the stories we tell about ourselves.

That's why *Worship through the Ages* is such an important book. It contains a very important story—our story.

"Those who don't know history are destined to repeat it" is an often-used quote attributed to Edmund Burke, a British statesman who lived in the 1700's. Interestingly, it is also often attributed to George Santayana, an author who lived from 1863 to 1952. It seems that in the effort to remember a great quote about the importance of history, we can't actually remember who said it. Someone dropped the story somewhere. Yet the sentiment of the quote rings true.

Saying that worship has changed throughout human history is stating an obvious fact. Across cultures and belief systems, the worship of God and his son, Jesus Christ, has taken on many forms and expressions. During the vast metamorphosis of church practice in our worship, a few profound lessons have emerged along the way. That's why this story is so important.

For many, there is a significant gap in the history of worship in the Christian church. We are well versed in the biblical record of how God was worshipped by his people. We see the acceptance of Abel's sacrifice and the rejection of Cain's in the opening scenes of time as the learning begins. We watch the construction of a tower in Genesis 11 and the response of God to this self-proclaiming monument of humanity. We cringe as Abram offers his own son and rejoice when God provides a substitute. We tremble as Aaron builds an idol for the children of Israel just beyond the Red Sea and beneath the mountain of God. We are thrilled when David sings and cry when Job suffers yet still worships.

And when the sky opens up with the angelic announcement of Messiah's birth, the worship crescendos to unprecedented dynamics. We watch closely as Jesus goes to the temple and prays in the garden. We mourn at the tomb and rejoice at the resurrection. We sing with Paul and Silas in jail and fill with anticipation as John writes the concluding chapters from the isle of Patmos. And the whole time, we are learning about worship.

The next season of development in our worship theology begins when our own story of faith is born. But then our growth is limited to our own experiences—the church we grew up in or the ministry that we are involved in now. But what if we could look inside the ways God has moved in the hearts of his people throughout the history of the church? What if we could hear those stories and see those great moves of his Spirit among his people? What could we learn about worship?

It's true that the biblical text is all we need to develop a solid theology of worship. In no way does this book suggest that we should build our theology based on the experience of others. That would be dangerous ground.

But the Bible does model for us time and time again that God's people are to remember what he has done and to celebrate God's goodness.

In 1 Chronicles 15 when the ark of the covenant returns to Jerusalem, David sings a glorious psalm of thanksgiving. Verses eight and nine read, "Give thanks to the Lord, call upon His name; proclaim His deeds among the peoples. Sing to Him; sing praise to Him; tell all His wonderful works!" (HCSB). In Ps 71:18 it says, "Even when I am old and gray, God, do not abandon me. Then I will proclaim Your power to another generation, Your strength to all who are to come" (HCSB).

God wants us to tell our stories.

In the modern day, we have more stories to tell from the history of the church, but less people are telling them. At times we approach our way of worship as if it were something we discovered. With this volume, Towns and Whaley help us gain perspective on the grand narrative of God's story. And when we reflect on the ways the hand of God has moved among his people throughout history, we are suddenly thrust back into the reality that God has always moved among his people and the great worship of his name always takes front and center.

At this point our hearts become troubled. For as we look inside the wonder of these great moves of God throughout history, we are painfully reminded that none of us have ever experienced anything like it in our lifetimes. This is true, despite the progress (at least that's what we call it) that our churches have made in their worship expression. We have more music, more energy, more expression, and more hands in the air—and all the while our impact on this culture gets smaller and smaller. We have seen worship, but have we seen revival?

Perhaps the lesson here flows directly from the heart of God. In his infinite love for us, God doesn't want us merely to have better worship—God wants us to have him. The apostle Paul's ultimate goal in life, expressed so well in Phil 3:10 (HCSB), was not to "worship God more deeply," but to "know Him and the power of His resurrection and the fellowship of His sufferings."

When God's people come to the place of seeking him, and not just an experience with him, then our faithful God has promised to move in and take over. What follows then is what real worship is all about. We seem to have it backwards: we tend to think if we will worship him in the right ways, he will send revival. But this story tells us the exact opposite is true: if we will seek him, he will revive our hearts and we will find him. And when we find him and see him in his awesome glory, we will worship him.

We need to hear this story. And in the hearing, we need to be reminded that unless we seek him with all our hearts, our worship will be only empty religion.

May God move in his people in fresh ways and write a new chapter of awakening and worship into our story.

Mike Harland
Director, LifeWay Worship

Introduction

As a child growing up in a Presbyterian church, I (Elmer) had to learn the children's catechism. I would sit in the swing on the front porch as my mother asked me the questions:

"Who made you?"
I answered, "God."
Then she would ask, "What else did God make?"
I would answer, "God made all things."
Then we came to the "big" question, "What is the chief end of man?"
To which I always replied, "The chief end of man is to glorify God and enjoy him forever."

Enjoy him forever? Yes, God created us to enjoy him. How do we do this? We enjoy God as we learn more about him, which makes us want to spend time *with* him. The more we understand about God, the more we want to worship him. In the process, God reveals more of himself to us. He has done this through the ages.

Though Elmer learned as a child that the chief end of man is to "glorify God and enjoy him forever," I'm not sure I (Vernon) was ever taught to enjoy God during my formative years. I was taught to serve God, to love working for God, to pray to and depend on him, and to reach out to an unsaved world with the good news of Jesus Christ. I was not taught how to enjoy God.

It was not until the summer of 1988 that I began to discover the heart of Christian worship. I realized that if I was ever going to enjoy God, I must learn how to be honest in my worship of him—free from selfish agendas, ulterior motives, and hidden desires to be a famous musician, minister of music, publisher, or arranger. By this time, I had served as a minister of music in evangelical churches for more than sixteen years and had already taught church music at a Bible college for six years. I am not sure I had ever known in my heart the thrill of genuine worship. Over a three-year period, though, God made some deep and serious changes in my heart. In May 1986, my grandmother died. In May 1987, my mother-in-law died on an operating table at Baptist Hospital in Nashville, Tennessee. Finally, in May 1988, my father died suddenly of a heart attack, I lost my job, and I began to realize for the first time what it means to be totally broken in spirit.

I am not sure I understood before that time the meaning of King David's statement, "The sacrifice God wants is a broken spirit. God . . . will not reject a heart that is broken and sorry for sin" (Ps 51:17 NCV). God got my attention. I was finally at a point in my walk with him where my self-centered ego was crushed, and the Holy Spirit began to teach me how to worship. Over the next four years, I learned how to enjoy him and thrill at the wonder of being honest in my worship before his throne.

What Is Worship?

We struggle for words to describe *worship* of our all-powerful, all-sufficient, all-knowing, ever-present God. After all, he alone is omnipotent, omniscient, and omnipresent.[1] It is impossible to express sufficiently our love, reverence, respect, devotion, adulation, adoration, and veneration of the *Ancient of Days*. We struggle to find adequate words because the God we worship is beyond our comprehension.

Such a God is not required to establish a relationship with human beings. He is self-sufficient and complete. He doesn't need us to *help him do his job better.* He is *Elohim*: the God Most High—the all-powerful creator,[2] the God of heaven,[3] the Holy One,[4] and the righteous sovereign.[5] Through his infinite wisdom,[6] he formed us in his image and placed within us the desire to know him, walk with him, fellowship with him, and love him supremely—the desire to worship.[7]

He did not give us this desire to worship so that he could have his inner needs met. Jesus said that "true worshippers shall worship the Father in spirit and in truth: for the Father seeketh such to worship him" (John 4:23 KJV). We worship him because God is actively seeking true worshippers. Our God *seeks us* because he loves us and desires to establish a living, vibrant relationship with his best creation—man and woman. This is where worship begins.

From conception, God loves us with an everlasting love. Daily, he reveals himself as sustainer, giver of life, provider, companion, and caregiver for all creation. He displays his ability to work everything for our joy seamlessly and in perfect harmony. What he does for us is an act of his free will. Why? Because he loves us.

The God of the universe reveals himself by showing us his power, plan, and purpose for life. He does this so that we will know him, worship him, and enjoy him forever. When we glorify his work and proclaim his wonders, we testify of the greatness of our everlasting God.

How then do we define *worship* of this God? True worship is not measured by the songs we sing; by the atmosphere, space, or environment we create in which to worship; by the number of Scriptures we read; or by the technology we deem important for facilitating worship. Worship is not determined by our preference for praise band, pipe organ, orchestra, or acoustic instruments. It is not defined by vocal selections (a cappella or with accompaniment) or by a musician's instrumental skill. In fact, musical expressions may not be essential for biblical worship at all.

Jesus' statement is the best definition of worship. Our Lord called his definition the greatest commandment: "Love the Lord thy God with all thy heart, and with all thy soul, and with all thy mind, and with all thy strength" (Mark 12:30 KJV). Worship of God motivates us to change the way we live, because . . .

Worship is *formational*—shaping us as fully devoted followers of Christ.

Worship is *transformational*—changing us from old to new, dead to living. This kind of worship is what we experience every time we enter the presence of God. He changes us from the inside out.

Worship is *relational*—strengthening our bond with Christ (our upward relationship) and with other people (our horizontal relationship).

Worship is *missional*—demonstrated by our commitment to love our neighbor, tell our story about God, and take the gospel to the nations.

Worship is *reproducible*—motivating us to teach and train others to worship in spirit and in truth.

Sometimes our worship is measured by *repentance*—confessing our sins, asking for forgiveness, and determining to do that which is right and good. At times, true worship is measured by new insights we learn about God as we look into his face and the things of earth *grow strangely dim*.[8]

True worship always involves the believer responding to God's revealed truth by:

Obeying him!
Magnifying him!
Serving him!
Seeking him!

Following him!

Loving him!

Lifting him up!

Proclaiming his wonders!

If the "what" of worship is love of and devotion to God, what is the "how" of worship? Jesus gives us one answer in John 4 when he says we worship the Father "in spirit," referring to the work of the Holy Spirit in our lives. When we worship "in spirit," we yield to the Holy Spirit, we are led by the Holy Spirit, and we submit to the Holy Spirit's work in our lives. Worship *in spirit* also involves our emotions, our inner feelings, our passions, our motives, our ambitions, and the deepest desires of our hearts—all totally dedicated to honoring Jesus.

The second "how" of worship involves *truth*. Jesus said that we worship the Father in "truth." Our public and private worship must be guided by God's Word.

Biblical worship encompasses our heart's desire, our love for God, and our commitment to worship in spirit (our emotions) and in truth (our intellect). This kind of worship has been a part of every great spiritual awakening in history.

Through the centuries, there have been periods of great encounter with God. We often call these periods *revivals* or *Great Awakenings*. During these periods of awakening, new methods, styles, processes, and techniques of worship emerge. Sometimes God's people emerge from awakenings expressing their love for him in completely new ways. Through awakenings, lives are always changed, communities are transformed, families are restored, and people turn from wickedness to righteousness.

About *Worship through the Ages*

Worship through the Ages tells the story of how worship developed through these Great Awakenings. It documents how, through the ages, God moved in mysterious ways to make himself known to man. With each awakening, paradigm shifts emerged in private and public expressions of worship.

The focus of this book is not worship methodology or instruction for planning worship services. This book is not *prescriptive*. It is *descriptive* of the worship practices throughout the church age as related to the Great Awakenings. It tells a story, and in the process documents trends, methods, and essential personalities involved in worship.

The Organization of *Worship through the Ages*

This book is a tool for Bible study groups, Sunday classes, worship leaders, praise teams, pastors, and students of worship in high school, college, and seminary classrooms. It is not an exhaustive treatment of Christian worship, Great Awakenings, or church history.

Most historians agree that there have been at least four major, worldwide Great Awakenings. While we include these awakenings in our study, our examination also includes other spiritual renewals that have impacted Christian history. Our story begins with Genesis and concludes with the Praise and Worship Awakening of the late twentieth and early twenty-first centuries. The study includes: (1) an overview of Old and New Testament worship; (2) the Great Awakening at Pentecost; (3) the Awakenings of the early Christians; (4) the Awakening of the Reformation, 1500–1650; (5) the Awakening in England and America, 1727–1790; (6) the Camp Meeting Awakening, 1790–1820; (7) the Sunday School and Charles Finney Awakening, 1820–1850; (8) the Laymen's Awakening, 1857–1890; (9) the Welsh Revivals,

1904–1906; (10) the Azusa Street Awakening, 1906–1908; (11) the Early Evangelistic Meetings, 1900–1935; (12) the World War II Awakening; (13) the Jesus Movement, 1960–1985; and (14) the Praise and Worship Awakening, 1985–2000). Then, in the epilogue, we provide a short overview of how worship innovations and new paradigms have shaped the worship we enjoy today.

Each chapter includes: (1) an overview of the cultural, political, and religious events that led to the awakening; (2) the story of the awakening; (3) a list of strategic personalities who helped change worship practices during the awakening; and (4) explanation of the new worship paradigm established during the awakening.

At the End of the Day . . .

Our goal for this book is fourfold: first, we want to tell the story of worship so that our sovereign Lord is magnified and exalted. We want to glorify God for what he has done in our lives and in the lives of thousands of believers through the ages. We are instructed to "tell the nations of his glory; tell all people the miracles he does." Why? Because "the Lord is great; he should be praised at all times" (Ps 96:3–4 NCV).

Second, we want to bless readers with the stories, biblical truths, and worship principles collected in this book. Perhaps you too will weep as you learn how deeply many of our brothers and sisters in Christ sacrificed in order to advance worship. Perhaps you too will be amazed at the work of God's Spirit during some of the most desperate times in human history. Perhaps you will join us as we celebrate God's use of ordinary people to accomplish extraordinary things.

Third, we want to enrich worship today by helping believers understand the history of worship. We will learn together why evangelicals worship the way we do today and why various denominational groups express worship differently.

Fourth, we want to equip readers to analyze future changes in worship. By identifying and appreciating innovations to evangelical worship in the past, we will be able to better comprehend and accept changes that will certainly come in the future.

Maybe as you read *Worship through the Ages,* God will speak to you, as he has to us, about how his love of mankind is revealed in his plan for worship. We hope you will stand in wonder, as we have, at God's provision of redemption through the Lord Jesus Christ, which enables all of us to become worshippers of the King of kings. And perhaps, while tracing God's plan for *Worship through the Ages,* you too will glorify God and enjoy him forever.

Notes

1. Gen 18:14; Pss 33:9; 115:3; 139:7–12; 147:4–5; Jer 23:23–24.

2. Gen 1:1–3; Deut 10:17; Pss 57:2; 68; Mark 13:19. *Elohim* is the Hebrew word for *God*. It is the plural of "El"—The Strong One. God is the all-powerful creator of the universe. God knows all and is everywhere present at all times (Nathan Stone, *Names of God* [Chicago: Moody, 1987], 11–17). For a complete list of the names of God, including the names of Jesus and the Holy Spirit, see Elmer Towns, *The Names of the Holy Spirit* (Ventura, CA: Regal Books, 1994).

3. Josh 2:11.

4. Josh 24:19.

5. Gen 18:25; Ps 7:9–12.

6. Prov 8:22–31.

7. Is 43:7.

8. From "Turn Your Eyes Upon Jesus" by Helen H. Lemmel, © 1950 by New Spring, a division of Brentwood-Benson Music Publishing, Inc.

CHAPTER 1

Worship in the Old Testament, Part 1

This is the story of Christian worship—not Hindi worship, Islamic worship, or the worship of man. This is the story of how the God of Israel moves and works through the ages to make his will and purposes known. In one sense, this is a documentation of God's work for each generation as he makes himself known to man. The immediate human response to God's revelation is always worship. Christian worship, as we know it in the evangelical community, is deeply rooted in the past. Much of what we believe today about worship and many of the practices we employ in our worship traditions were derived and shaped by the events, leaders, teachings, theology, and even worship traditions of the Old Testament.

Worship before the Creation of the World

"In the beginning God created the heavens and the earth" (Gen 1:1 CEV). The word *heavens* is an all-inclusive term that refers to the atmosphere, the stratosphere, and the abode where God lives. While it includes all we can see with the naked eye, it also includes God's throne in heaven and the angels who live in heaven to worship God. Before the world was shaped and formed, God created worshippers and a place where worship would reside.

"Where were you when I made the earth's foundation? Who marked off how big it should be? Who stretched a ruler across it? What were the earth's foundations set on, or who put its cornerstone in place while the morning stars sang together and all the angels shouted with joy?" (Job 38:4–7 NCV).

God asked these questions of Job and revealed that the very first act during God's creative process inspired worship. The angels worshipped God for his mighty acts. They worshipped him for the beauty of his creation. They worshipped him in his holiness.

Because worship is about God and not about the worshipper, the angels were given a *free choice* to exercise their worship. One angel, the mightiest and most spectacular of them all, Lucifer, chose not to worship God (Isa 14:12–15). Instead, he wanted to ascend into heaven to exalt himself above God's throne, above the stars, above the angels of God, and above the clouds, to "be like the Most High" (Isa 14:14 NKJV). Because Lucifer turned praise and adoration upon himself, God judged him, saying, "But you were brought down to the grave, to the deep places where the dead are" (Isa 14:15 NCV). The angels who followed Lucifer were likewise judged.

What of the angels who chose to continue worshipping God? Today, they serve at God's pleasure. They sing around God's throne, "Holy, holy, holy" (Isa 6:3). Night and day they worship him, saying, "Holy, holy, holy is the Lord God Almighty. He was, he is, and he is coming" (Rev 4:8b NCV). The Bible says that these angels number as many as the stars in heaven.

Worship and Creation

With each stroke of his mighty paintbrush, our great God created a masterpiece for all to enjoy. He called his creation, "good."[1] He created an environment so wonderful, so natural, so perfect that he chose to walk on the earth in the cool of the day and take pleasure in all that he had created. He chose to fellowship with his best creation, man and woman.

Deep inside the heart of man, he created a desire for worship. Absolutely nothing would ever satisfy humans but worship of the living Lord. Men and women, however, would not have access to Heaven as did the angels. They would be limited to one of the tiniest of all planets—Earth. They would move one step at a time. They would be limited to human flesh that needed to sleep, eat, and grow.

Human beings were the crown of God's creation, created in his image. "You have made him [man] a little lower than the angels, and You have crowned him with glory and honor" (Ps 8:5 NKJV). "In the image of God He created them. He created them male and female. God blessed them and said, 'have many children and grow in number. Fill the earth and be its master'" (Gen 1:26–28 NCV).

The fellowship between God and man continued each day. "They heard the voice of the LORD God walking in the garden in the cool of the day" (Gen 3:8 KJV), they had fellowship with him, and they enjoyed his presence.

Soon the rebellion of Lucifer also found its way into man's and woman's heart. Adam and Eve broke their relationship with God by openly disobeying his commands. For the first time they felt guilt, need, burden, restlessness, and shame, and the penalty for this sin was death.

Even so, God still wanted a vibrant relationship with his best creation. He desired to dwell with those he loved. He wanted them to know him and desired to have communion and fellowship on a level reserved only for best friends and comrades.

Adam and Eve still had a deep desire and eternal need to worship God, to love him, and to enjoy his presence in their lives. What was the solution to this dilemma? God provided a way for man and woman to worship and for the penalty of death to be satisfied. Thus began what we know today as Christian worship.

In the Old Testament dispensation, man and woman expressed their love to God by making sacrifices. (Much more about these sacrifices later, but for now, they included animals, grain, songs, service, love, and surrender.) The sacrifice God wanted most, though, was that which came from contrite, remorseful, and repentant hearts. God was looking at the motive of worshippers. He was not at all interested in people "going through the motions" of worship. He was looking for worship from men and women who were genuine in their love for him. So, who were these worshippers? The next section will offer a quick overview of some of the early worshippers, and we will see how they expressed their love and devotion to God.

Strategic Personalities in Old Testament Worship

Cain and Abel

These young men were the sons of Adam and Eve, our first parents. Their story about acceptable and unacceptable worship is recorded in Genesis 4. Apparently, they had distinct personalities, but both brought gifts of sacrifice to the Lord.

Cain, the older brother, was a farmer. He tended the fields and grew grain, vegetables, and fruit. I suspect, like many older brothers, Cain was a bit of a know-it-all. Abel, on the other hand, tended the flocks of the field. He was a shepherd.

The Bible does not give record of the quality, value, or preparation process of Cain's gift. However, God "did not accept Cain and his gift" (Gen 4:3–5 NCV).

In response, "Cain became very angry and felt rejected" (v. 5 NCV).

So, the Lord asked Cain, "Why are you angry? Why do you look so unhappy? If you do things well, I will accept you, but if you do not do them well, sin is ready to attack you" (vv. 6–7). God's invitation for Cain to present an acceptable sacrifice went unheeded. Cain lured Abel to a field and killed him. God reacted by cursing the very object Cain worshipped the most—his work with the ground. God told Cain that even though he would expend great effort to plant and tend crops, they would not grow well. Cain and his family were cursed to wander around on the earth as nomads. After God dealt with Cain and his sin, the Bible states, "Men began to call on the name of the LORD" (Gen 4:26 NKJV).

Jabal, Jubal, and Tubal-Cain

According to Gen 4:16–22, Cain's great-great-great-grandson, Lamech, had two wives. The first wife, Adah, had a son by the name of Jabal. He became the first person to live in tents and raise cattle. The second wife, Zillah, had two sons. Jubal was the first person to play the harp and flute, and his brother Tubal-Cain was the first to make tools out of bronze and iron. These three sons represented the three components of Old Testament worship: (1) animals for burnt sacrifices, (2) musical instruments for the accompanying "sacrifice of praise," and (3) tools for preparing the sacrifice.

Jabal	Jubal	Tubal-Cain
Animal breeder and farmer	Maker of musical instruments	Maker of tools of bronze and iron

Enoch

This was the son of a man named Jared. The Bible says that Enoch walked with God. Apparently, his fellowship with God was sweet. His love for God was genuine. His worship of God was sincere, and his focus on God was deliberate. Enoch walked with God for 365 years until one day he could not be found "because God took him" (Gen 5:24 NCV).

Noah

God saw the wickedness of man and decided to judge the earth with a flood, but Noah found grace in the eyes of the Lord (Gen 6:8) because Noah walked with God and worshipped him (Gen 6:9 NCV). This is the same word used in describing the relationship Enoch had with God. Both men *walked* with God.

Noah did everything God commanded him (Gen 6:22; 7:5). He was obedient. Noah built an ark for the salvation of the eight in his family, and they were delivered from God's judgment inside it. Immediately after exiting the ark on the top of Mount Ararat, "Noah built an altar to the Lord. He took some of all the clean birds and animals, and he burned them on the altar as offerings to God" (Gen 8:20 NCV).

This is the essence of worship. Noah and his family magnified, praised, and thanked God for saving their lives. When "the Lord smelled a sweet savor . . ." (Gen 8:21 KJV) (the aroma coming from the sacrifice), he received the sacrifice with great joy.

People of Babel

Genesis 11 tells the story of misguided worship. Like the worship offered by Cain, these people refused to revere God. "As the people moved from the east, they found a plain in the land of Babylonia and settled there" (Gen 11:2 NCV). They used bricks instead of rocks and stones to build a city and tower. "We will become famous. Then we will not be scattered over all the earth," they said (Gen 11:4 NCV). Apparently, at this place called "Babel," men and women decided to congregate and build a ziggurat for their own pleasure and worship. God responded and said, "Let us go down, and there confound their language. . . . So the LORD scattered them abroad from thence upon the face of the earth" (Gen 11:7–8 KJV). Again, we see the consequences of misguided, self-centered worship.

Abraham

God instructed 75-year-old Abram to leave the land of Ur, along with his 65-year-old wife, Sarai. (At that time, he was still using the name Abram—later changed by God to Abraham.) Together, they committed themselves to obeying and worshipping God.

Abram is introduced as the son of Terah and brother to Nahor and Haran. He was a family man devoted to caring for his brothers and sisters. Sarai is introduced as Abram's childless half sister. Apparently, Sarai was a strikingly beautiful woman, full of grace and charm, even at 65.

It is with Abraham that worship of the Lord was established as a formal, intentional act:

1. *Abraham worshipped by obeying God.* When Abram received the call from God to move from Ur to Canaan, his immediate and forthright response was obedience. He heard God's promise and determined in his heart to obey.[2] The call was to "leave your country, leave your relatives, leave your father's family and go to the land I will show you."[3] Abram obeyed. Obedience is at the heart of worship. Obedience was already in Abram's heart.[4]

2. *Abraham built an altar and established a location for worship of the Lord.*[5] Every time God revealed himself to Abraham, his immediate

response was to build an altar and worship. By so doing, he remembered God's provisions, promises, and special manifestations.

God appeared to Abram and said, "I will give this land to your descendants." In response, Abram built an altar "to the LORD, who had appeared."[6]

Abram worshipped when returning to Canaan after living in Egypt during famine and drought. Again, he built an altar.

God protected Abram—in spite of his lying about Sarai out of the fear of man. What was Abram's response? He built an altar at Bethel and worshipped.[7]

Abram traveled from Shechem to the mountain east of Bethel, set up a tent, and built another altar to the Lord. He worshipped God there.[8]

When Lot, Abram's nephew, saw there was much water in the Jordan Valley and chose to claim the best, greenest land for himself, God spoke.[9] Abram chose to live in the land of Canaan. There, he built an altar and worshipped.

Abram worshipped after God commanded him to look to "the north and south and east and west" and see all that was given to his descendants forever. God told Abram, "If anyone could count the dust on the earth, he could count your people." Abram moved his family and all his belongings to Mamre at the city of Hebron in Canaan. There he built an altar to the Lord and worshipped.[10]

3. *Abraham observed special posture for worship.*[11] In Gen 17:17, Abraham bowed face down and listened to the Lord.

4. *Abraham paid a tithe.* In Gen 14:20, Abram worshipped after the Lord granted victory in battle by giving a tithe back to God. As Abram returned home, he met Melchizedek, king of Salem. It is obvious that Abraham recognized him as more than an average king or priest. Melchizedek gave Abram this blessing:

Abram, may you be blessed by God Most High,
the God who made heaven and earth.
And we praise God Most High,
who has helped you to defeat your enemies.[12]

In response, Abram gave to Melchizedek a tithe (10%) of all the gold, silver, cattle, and other spoil brought back from battle.

5. *Abraham worshipped by saying, "Here I am."* Genesis 22 provides the most famous account of Abraham hearing God's voice and responding, "Here I am." God told Abraham to take his only son, Isaac, to Mount Moriah for the purpose of offering the boy as a sacrifice. When they arrived at the foot of the mountain, Abraham instructed the servants to wait. He and Isaac would return from the mountain, he said. Abraham took Isaac, the son that he loved, up the mountain. Together they built an altar to the Lord. Abraham then tied Isaac's hands and feet, placed him on the altar, and drew his knife to kill him. Just then, an angel of the Lord called out, "Abraham, Abraham." Again, Abraham answered, "Here I am," and the angel told him not to harm Isaac. Abraham looked up and saw a male sheep caught in the bushes by its horns to use as a sacrifice. Abraham grabbed the sheep, killed it, and offered it as a whole burnt offering to God. Isaac was saved and Abraham named the mountain The Lord Provides. The angel responded by reaffirming God's covenant to make of him a great nation, to bless him and his descendants.

6. *Abraham worshipped before doing the work of ministry.* The first time the term *worship* is used in the Bible is in Gen 22:5. Abraham worshipped *before* taking Isaac to the mountain. He proved himself faithful to God at Mount Moriah and in so doing demonstrated a key to acceptable worship: coming to God with a genuine desire to live in a holy manner before Him.

7. *Abraham offered praise at the confirmation of covenants.* Abraham was a man of great faith. Through Abraham, God estab-

lished his own unique, peculiar nation. God made a covenant with Abraham (Gen 12:1–3). Each time God confirmed this covenant, Abraham built an altar, offered sacrifices, and worshipped.

Moses

Raised in the home of an Egyptian, Moses was perhaps the most significant Old Testament leader for the people of Israel. The events in his life were surrounded by worship of the living Lord. Indeed, he led the children of Israel in worship of the Lord, Yahweh.

Defining moments in his life were marked by personal encounters with the living Lord. God spoke to Moses in the desert through a burning bush, instructing him to confront Pharaoh, the ruler of Egypt. Moses demanded that Pharaoh let God's people go so that they could worship the true God, Yahweh, in the wilderness (Exod 5:1). Pharaoh was incredulous: "I know not the Lord, neither will I let Israel go" (Exod 5:2 KJV).

Moses repeated his request: "We pray thee, three days' journey into the desert, and sacrifice unto the Lord our God; lest He fall upon us with pestilence, or the sword" (Exod 5:3 KJV). Pharaoh refused, and in spite of ten plagues that God sent on Egypt as a curse, Pharaoh's heart grew increasingly hard and stubborn. After the tenth plague, the death of every firstborn throughout Egypt, Pharaoh gave the Israelites their freedom to worship Yahweh. In the process, Moses proved that Yahweh could defeat Pharaoh and the false gods of the Egyptians. God used Moses to lead the Israelites out of Egypt for the purpose of providing freedom to worship.

Moses encountered God again at Mount Sinai. There he received the Ten Commandments as the foundation for Israel's new identity as a nation. Three of the commandments addressed the issue of worship: The First Commandment dealt with the *focus* of Israel's worship, "I am the Lord thy God. . . . Thou shalt have no other gods before me" (Exod 20:2–3 KJV).

The Second Commandment focused on the *method* of worship, "Thou shalt not make unto thee any graven images" (Exod 20:4 KJV). The word *graven* means "carved." The Second Commandment plainly forbade revering any physical representation of God.

The Fourth Commandment established a specific *day of the week* for worship, the seventh day, the Sabbath (Exod 20:8–11 KJV).

During this encounter at Mount Sinai, the Lord gave Moses instructions concerning (1) assembly for worship, (2) instruments of worship, (3) methods of worship, (4) laws for living, (5) laws for giving, (6) laws for property, relationships, and fairness, (7) the yearly feasts, (8) the Sabbath, (9) correct worship times, and (10) the tabernacle.

He also gave Moses instructions regarding construction and use of the tabernacle, a "holy tent" where the children of Israel would worship. The Lord desired a holy place where he could live among his people. To that end, he provided instruction for building (1) a table, (2) a lampstand, (3) the entrance of the holy tent, (4) an altar for burnt offerings, and (5) the courtyard of the holy tent. He also gave instruction regarding oil for the lamp, clothing for the priests, appointment of priests, daily sacrifices, and a tax for the tent of meeting.[13] When the tabernacle was complete, Moses, the leadership, and the people were ready to dedicate the tent to God.

Then a cloud covered the tent, and the glory of the Lord filled the tabernacle so that Moses was not able to enter. When the cloud was taken up, the children of Israel continued on their journey. Whenever the cloud returned to the tabernacle, they were to remain stationary until it was taken up. The cloud of the Lord was upon the tabernacle by day, and fire was upon it by night (Exod 40:34–38). The presence of

God filled the tabernacle, and people knew the Lord was there because they could see his glory.

Joshua

After serving for 40 years as Moses' assistant, Joshua led the people into the Promised Land. God promised to help Joshua, just as he did with Moses. Each time God did something miraculous, Joshua built an altar to the Lord and worshipped. Joshua was faithful to lead the people in remembering the goodness of the Lord and commanded the men of Israel to erect an altar of twelve stones when crossing the Jordan River. He also worshipped the "Captain of the Lord's Army" (thought by some to be Jesus) before going to battle at Jericho.

King David

Long considered one of the greatest examples of worship, David had a unique and powerful relationship with God. In fact, God commended him for being a "man after my own heart." David was famous for his focused, unrestrained worship of the Lord, and he organized a system of worship for the entire Jewish nation to follow. David led his people as a worshipper of the Most High God. He wrote most of the Book of Psalms. Even during the time when seeking God's forgiveness for murder and adultery, David declared: "Lord, let me speak so I may praise you, the sacrifice God wants is a broken spirit . . . God, you will not reject a heart that is broken and sorry for sin" (Ps 51:15,17 NCV).

The Prophets

The prophets often condemned Israel for its hypocrisy in worship. While the people retained the outward forms of temple worship, they did not give their best to God and mixed worship of Yahweh with that of the heathen gods. Many offered God their worst animals as sacrifices and even participated in adultery and public idolatry. They also did not keep the Sabbath. So God carried away his people into Babylon (2 Chr 36:21).

Each of the prophets, in his own unique voice, taught about authentic worship and *obedience*. In short, to obey the word of the Lord is better than anything.

The prophets taught that:

1. *When we see God, we are always made aware of our own sin.* Once we see our sin in comparison with God's awesomeness, we seek forgiveness and restoration as a first act of worship.
2. *God wants us to demonstrate our worship by living righteously for him.* Isaiah 1:16 encourages us to "wash [ourselves] and make [ourselves] clean." We are told to stop doing evil things.
3. *God will not accept our worship while we foster social injustice, neglect the fatherless, or ignore the poor, disabled, and elderly.*
4. *We are to do good, seek justice, help orphans, punish those who hurt others, and stand up for the rights of widows.* (Isa 1:16–17 NCV)
5. *God's people are to show their love for God by loving those less fortunate.*
6. *God is most glorified when he sees his work grow and develop in our lives.* As we worship, we *experience* his comfort, peace, direction, and love. Through our worship, he gives us the opportunity for fellowship with him and to trust him.
7. *When we worship the God of Hope, we bring glory due his name:*

    I am the Lord.
    That is my name.
    I will not give my glory to another;
    I will not let idols take the praise that should be mine.
    (Isa 42:8 NCV)

Ezra

Ezra was a priest who led a large number of people back to Jerusalem after the Babylonian exile. He was given the responsibility of rebuilding the temple, teaching worship traditions, and transcribing Scripture from the ancient papers. He assisted Nehemiah in rebuilding the walls around Jerusalem and helped to reestablish worship practices.

Nehemiah

After the Israelites returned from Babylon to Jerusalem, Nehemiah led them to rebuild the walls around the great city. Nehemiah 8 records a most impressive worship service at the reading of the Scripture:

> Ezra opened the book in full view of everyone, because he was above them. As he opened it, all the people stood up. Ezra praised the LORD, the great God, and all the people held up their hands and said, "Amen! Amen!" Then they bowed down and worshiped the LORD with their faces to the ground. (Neh 8:5–6 NCV)

When Nehemiah finished rebuilding the walls, he dedicated them with music. The Levites throughout the land were asked to come to Jerusalem to assist in the ceremonies. They were to take part in the joyous occasion with their songs of thanksgiving and with the music of cymbals, lyres, and harps. They used musical instruments prescribed by David, the man of God. Two choirs gave thanks as they led a procession to the temple of God where they took their places. Other worship leaders and musicians accompanied Nehemiah (Neh 12:27–42).

Summary of Worship Innovations

In the Old Testament, God established a purpose, place, people, and plan for worship. Beginning with creation, his mighty acts inspired worship.

Worship practices in the Old Testament were first somewhat primitive and simple. People worshipped God on high places (mountains) or near the doors of tents. The head of the family worshipped God as a representative for his whole family. Abraham, Isaac, Jacob, Joseph, Moses, Joshua, and a host of faithful men and women worshipped God in genuine love and adoration. There seemed to be no sharp distinction originally between private worship and public worship.

God used strategic people as facilitators of worship. Moses introduced the tabernacle as the dwelling place of God. King David instituted worship structure. Solomon, his son, built a temple in which all the nations of the world could know Yahweh. Worship in the tabernacle and in the temple was highly organized and included a complex system of rituals, sacrifices, and feast. Worship was led exclusively by priests, and the musicians assisting in worship were part of the tribe of Levi.

In the next chapter, we will see how worship that began in the garden, continued through the historical periods of the Old Testament, was proclaimed by the prophets, and was explained by the psalmist. We will see how worship is structured, organized, and presented by faithful people with hearts of love for the Most High God.

Notes

1. Gen 1:10,12,18,21,25,31.
2. Gen 12:1–9; 15:7; Acts 7:2–4; Heb 11:8–12.
3. Gen 12:1 (NCV).
4. Abraham obeyed the call, left his country, and trusted God to do what he had promised (Heb 11:8,11).
5. Abraham, Isaac, and Jacob built altars throughout Canaan to mark the sites where God manifested himself to them under various names (Gen 12:7–8; 13:14–18; 28:10–22). Sacrifice was offered only at those sites. This demonstrated that God owned the land and that he would give it to his people

at the appropriate time. (David Peterson, *Engaging with God: A Biblical Theology of Worship* [Winona Lake, IN: IVP Academic, 2002], 25).

6. Gen 12:7.
7. Gen 12:10–20.
8. Gen 13:3.
9. Gen 13:8–13.
10. Gen 13:14–18.
11. Gen 17:3,17; 18:1–5,13–16,22–33.
12. Gen 14:19–20 (NCV).
13. See Exodus 26–31 for complete instructions regarding the tabernacle.

CHAPTER 2

Worship in the Old Testament, Part 2

God has always used people as the primary means of carrying out his plans. Each time God reveals himself in the Old Testament, the immediate response by men and women is worship in various forms. God is honored when we purpose to worship privately and publicly, and establish places for worship.

In our last chapter, we learned about the people God used. We learned that his plan for worship began before the foundation of the world. We discovered how he reveals himself in creation, why he desires our worship, and how worship developed during the Old Testament years.

In this chapter, we are going to observe how worship was practiced, what methods were used in worship, and the pattern for worship in the Old Testament.

The Practice of Old Testament Worship

Two types of worship are described in the Old Testament. The first is spontaneous worship—often done in private. The second is more formal and professional—normally done in public. Professional priests expressed for the people a response to God through specific acts of worship, including: serving, singing, reading Scripture (the Torah) publicly, shouting, sacrificing, and sharing.[1]

The worship experience was highly sensory. It appealed to the eye with use of visible symbols such as altars, candlesticks, and vestments.

Worship was also appealing to the ear through the use of music performed by the priests. According to Donald P. Hustad, "The belief that music affects human behavior was common. And, for that matter, has persisted throughout Scripture times and . . . in history."[2]

Worship appealed to the nose (smell). This included the smell of incense and the burning of animal flesh during the sacrifice. Because the taste of the meal was part of the peace offering, it also appealed to the tongue.

Music

The most significant use of music in the Old Testament is in praising God. Old Testament music accompanied work, worship, merrymaking, and war. Music was used to inspire prophets, enthrone kings, celebrate the harvest, and to help in officiating weddings and funerals. In 2 Kgs 3:14–16, Elisha the prophet used music to proclaim God's judgment. While a harp was being played, the Lord gave Elisha power.

Worship music was also used in dirges, lamentations, and incantations. According to Hustad, "Musical sound was frequently associated with a sense of the presence and power of God."[3]

Worship could be a time of loud exultation: "Blow the trumpets in times of gladness. Sound them again at your annual festivals and at the beginning of each month to rejoice over your burnt offerings and peace offerings. The trumpets will remind the Lord your God of His covenant with you. I am the Lord your God" (Num 10:10 ELT).[4]

Other significant examples of musical practices in the Old Testament include: (1) a family party for Jacob in Genesis 31, (2) a celebration at the crossing of the Red Sea by Moses and his sister in Exodus 15, (3) Moses' prayer song before his death (Deuteronomy 32), (4) Joshua and Gideon using trumpets at the time of battle, (5) the welcome of Jephthah in Judges 11:34, (6) the triumph of David in 1 Sam 18:6, (7) David singing praise songs for battle and devotion to the Lord, (8) Solomon using music in worship at the dedication of the temple (2 Chronicles 5–6), (9) the choir preceding the army of God when Jehoshaphat goes into battle, (10) Isaiah using song to encourage the worship of Jehovah (Isaiah 42), (11) Jonah singing a song of thanksgiving from the belly of the great fish (Jonah 2:9), and (12) the song of the three Hebrews in the furnace (Daniel 3).

Singing

Apparently singing was accompanied by the clapping of hands, shouting, and making melody.[5] Exodus 15:1–21 describes the first recorded instance of singing praise to the Lord. The song is a narrative of thanksgiving led by Moses and his sister Miriam after the Israelites crossed the Red Sea and were delivered by God from the Egyptians. The presentation was both instrumental and vocal, involved both men and women, and was accompanied by expressive movement.

The Old Testament reveals that God's people have long used music to express their joy, gratitude, praise, adoration, sorrow, sadness, determination, and dedication. Singing is mentioned more than 100 times in the Old Testament. Musicians are present in Old Testament public worship more than 50 times.

Instruments of Song

Singing was often accompanied by instruments (e.g., Ps 81:2). Old Testament instruments can be grouped into three basic categories:

1. *Percussion.* This includes cymbals, sistrums (shakers), castanets, timbrel or tabret, drums, and bells. Cymbals include *Meziltayim*

(1 Chr 15:16; 2 Chr 5:13) and *Zelzelim* (Ps 150:5). The historian Josephus describes the Zelzelim as large bronze plates played with both hands. The Sistrum, a shaker or rattling instrument, includes the *Shalishim* (1 Sam 18:6) and *Mena'an'im* (2 Sam 6:5). Drums are called *Toph* and are probably something akin to the tambourine. Bells include the *Pa'amonim* (Exod 28:33–34) and *Mezillot* (Zech 14:20).

2. *Winds.* The family of wind instruments includes pipes or organs, horns, and trumpets. They are most often identified as *Ugahb* (Ps 150:3). They are categorized as horns, trumpets, and pipes. The Bible refers to horns as *Keren* (Lev 4:7; 1 Chr 25:5), *Shophar* (Exod 19:16; Ps 81:3), and *Yobel* (Lev 25:9; Josh 6:5). The Old Testament word *Hazozerah* (Num 10:2) refers to the trumpet. This term *trumpet* is not the same as that used for the Feast of Trumpets in Lev 23:23–25. This word is literally a "memorial of shout" rather than a call for trumpets. Pipes also fall into the wind family of instruments. These include two instruments: the *Halil,* which has a wailing or moaning type of sound (Jer 48:36), and the *Nahilah,* which is referred to in Psalm 5.

3. *Strings.* Used most often in the Old Testament, this type of instrument includes harps, psaltery, lute, and guitar. The *Kinnor* is related to the Kithara or lyre (Ps 43:7; Gen 4:21). The *Nebel* is used twenty-seven times in Scripture and the *Asor* is used three times in Psalms. The *Sebbeka* is a string instrument used in Nebuchadnezzar's court and is probably identified more with heathen worship. The *Pesanterin* is a dulcimer prototype while the *Kathros* or *Kithros* is a four-string type of lute or lyre.[6]

Banners

Banners in worship were used to represent ideals and aspirations, evoke emotions and devotion, and unify people under one purpose. There were three strategic purposes for banners in Hebrew life: (1) they were used to designate the location of a group, in particular each of the twelve tribes of Israel; (2) banners were lifted up in the time of victory; and (3) banners served as a rallying point for the congregation. The banner marked the center of attention, place of hope, and central location for thanksgiving.

Dance

Interpretive movement was used to show victory, joy, adoration, and admiration of God. Not much is known about the technique for dance in Old Testament worship. Men and women did not dance as partners, and presentations were void of sensuality.

Sacrifices

As we have already discovered, sacrifices were part of Old Testament worship from the very beginning. Cain and Abel brought sacrifices to God (Gen 4:4). Noah offered sacrifices to the Lord. Abraham, Isaac, Jacob, and Joseph also offered sacrifices.

God told Moses, "On the first day of the seventh month, you will call the people to a sacred assembly" (Lev 23:24 ELT). The main purpose of a sacrifice was for worship of the Lord. "The people must worship God with the sacrifice of their hands, presenting offerings unto the Lord by fire" (Lev 23:25 ELT). All of Israel was required to offer sacrifice.

At Sinai, Moses received instructions on how the people should worship God with sacrifices. A sacrifice was a prized material object that a worshipper offered to God to establish or maintain a relationship with him. The motives for offering sacrifices varied, but generally the sacrifice expressed faith in God and repentance from sin.

Three requirements surrounded all sacrifices: (1) Every offering must belong to the one making the sacrifice; (2) The sacrifice must be greatly valued in the eyes of the one making the offering to God; and (3) The sacrifice must be greatly valued in the eyes of God—the one receiving the sacrifice.

God directed his people to offer five different sacrifices (Leviticus 1–6) of meat or produce from the field. The animals allowed for sacrifices were oxen, sheep, goats, and pigeons. Permitted produce included items such as wine, oil, corn, and grain. Such sacrifices could also take the form of meal, dough, and cakes.

1. *The Sin Offering (Lev 4:1–35; 6:24–30)*. The sin offering was for sins unconsciously or unintentionally committed. Through it, the worshipper confessed his sins. This offering was either for the whole nation of Israel or for an individual.

2. *The Trespass (Guilt) Offering (Lev 5:14; 6–7)*. The trespass offering was a special type of sin offering where a person could make restitution to one against whom he had sinned. If the sin was against God, the worshipper was required to confess his sin and make the matter right, and his sin was forgiven by a guilt offering. This offering was always a lamb. Whereas with the sin offering blood could be poured or sprinkled on the sacrifice, with the trespass offering the blood was not sprinkled but poured over the surface of the altar.

3. *The Burnt Offering (Leviticus 1)*. This offering was wholly consumed by fire on the altar, while in the previous offerings only the fat portion of the sacrifice was burned up. The purpose of this offering was to satisfy Jehovah by signifying an entire consecration of the worshipper to him.

Sometimes the burnt offering was called the "continual" burnt offering because of the frequency with which it was offered to God. It was also called the "whole burnt offering" (Ps 51:19 KJV) because no part was left for the worshipper to eat, and no portion of the offering was designated for the priest.

This was the sacrifice to keep Israel in proper covenant relationship with God, and it was offered every day in the morning and in the evening. On special feast days, more than one lamb was offered to God. This was the only sacrifice that a non-Israelite was permitted to offer God in worship (Lev 17:8; 22:18–25).

4. *The Peace Offering (Leviticus 3).* This sacrifice did not deal with sin. It was an offering to express gratitude, thanksgiving, or fellowship with God. The peace offering was not offered at any set time, except Pentecost (Lev 23:19–20). It reflected the spontaneous worship of God (Lev 19:5).

The peace offering included the "wave" offering, in which the priest stood and waved the offering to God in commitment before taking it home to eat. It is also called the "heave offering" because grain could be tossed in the air symbolically to offer the sacrifice to God. Sometimes the offering was taken home and eaten by the priest. At other times, it was eaten in the sanctuary by the worshipper and the priest (Lev 7:15; Deut 12:1,17).

5. *The Meal Offering (Lev 2:1–16; 6:14–18).* This was not an animal offering, but as the name suggests, it was an offering of flour, unleavened bread, cakes, waffles, or ears of grain that were roasted. Only a portion of this offering was given to God in worship. The rest was kept for the priest, who ate it in the holy place or took it home to his family. Many times the meal offering accompanied the sin or trespass offering (Lev 6:16; 10:12–13).

The drink offering was not an independent offering to God, but was given in conjunction with a meal offering or peace offering. It did not accompany the sin or trespass offering, and it consisted of wine that was poured out on the altar—probably upon sacrificial meat before it was burned.

Besides these offerings, God was offered twelve loaves of showbread that were renewed on a regular basis. Oil was offered to God to fill the tabernacle's seven lamps every morning (Lev 24:1–9). The worshipper could also bring incense for the Altar of Incense that was renewed every morning and evening (Exod 30:1,7; 40:26–27).

Fasting to the Lord

The Jewish worshipper honored God by fasting and feasting. Fasting was the discipline of not eating and giving of oneself to prayer, confession of sin, and seeking God's favor. Every Jewish worshipper fasted on the Day of Atonement: "On the tenth day of the seventh month of each year, you must go without eating to show sorrow for your sins" (Lev 16:29 CEV). Food was kept from the body, reflecting an inner hunger for God in worship, sacrifice, and dedication.

Feasting to the Lord

God required the Jews to feast during special times of worship. These feasts were fixed by God (Leviticus 23). Later, two more were added, i.e., the Feast of Lights (Hanukkah) on the twenty-fifth day of Kislev (roughly our modern month of December) and the Feast of Purim, observed on the fourteenth and fifteenth of Adar (roughly our modern month of March).

1. *The Passover or the Feast of Unleavened Bread.* The Jews celebrated this feast on the fourteenth day of the first month of their religious year, i.e., Nisan (approximately the time of April). This feast commemorated their deliverance from Egypt and the establishment of their nation by blood redemption. It lasted seven days (Lev 23:5–8), and all types of sacrifices were offered according to the needs of worshippers and the dictates of God. This feast was eaten by the family to express fellowship with one another and worship of God.

2. *The Feast of Firstfruits (Lev 23:9–14).* This feast was celebrated one day after Passover, and worshippers pledged to God that they would

give him the first of their crops. This pledge was made by offering to God some of the firstfruits that they had grown.

3. *The Feast of Pentecost (Lev 23:15–22).* This feast was celebrated 50 days after Passover on the sixth day of the month of Sivan (approximately June). Worshippers made the "wave offering," indicating that they were giving to God a portion of what they had earned from their work. This feast lasted one day at the end of the wheat harvest. The amount of the offering was not specified, but the people were exhorted to give the Lord an offering of their firstfruits.

4. *The Feast of Trumpets or New Moon.* This feast was held on the first day of the seventh month (roughly our modern October). Trumpets were blown, calling the workers to come away from the harvest fields because their work for the year was complete. During this feast, the Law was read publicly and the people fellowshipped together with meals and worship of God.

5. *The Day of Atonement.* This was called a feast, but in practice it was a fast (see above) celebrated on the tenth day of Tishri (roughly October). On this day the high priest confessed all the sins of the people and entered the holy of holies on their behalf with the blood of reconciliation. The people identified with this solemn act by expressing sorrow for sins and begging for God's mercy and forgiveness.

6. *The Feast of Tabernacles or Booths.* This was the last of the feasts commanded by God, and it began five days after the Day of Atonement (Lev 23:34–44). This feast lasted seven days and marked the completion of the harvest. During this festival, the people lived in booths or tents outside their homes to remind them how their forefathers wandered in the wilderness and lived in booths for forty years. There were numerous sacrifices made during this feast. The whole week was a time of eating and fellowship.

The various feasts were spread throughout the year to remind Israel regularly of their relationship to God and how they should worship him in different ways on different occasions.

Old Testament Worship in the Tabernacle

God desired to dwell among the Israelites. He wanted to have fellowship with them and be able to communicate with them. So he gave detailed instructions for constructing the tabernacle. It was to be a moveable "tent of meeting" (Exodus 25–40; Hebrews 9–13). The tabernacle and its courtyard were constructed according to a pattern set by God, not by Moses.

We study the tabernacle to understand the steps the Lord laid out for a sinful people to approach a holy God. It was built in approximately 1440 BC and was the place where God dwelled with his people for 400 years. It was used from the time of the exodus until the time of King Solomon, when the permanent temple was built. The tabernacle was the center of the Israelite camp, with the twelve tribes camped around it in a special arrangement.

Music and worship in the tabernacle were not as well defined as they would be subsequently in the temple. Because of the nomadic life generally associated with early Hebrew culture, worship music prior to King David's reign was probably unstructured and little more than the ringing of cymbals, the blowing of trumpets, and spontaneous noise-making. Such music was performed by nonprofessional men and women and took the form of vocal solos, small ensembles, congregational singing, choral singing, instrumental offerings, and dance accompanied by voice or instrument.

Pattern of Organization for Old Testament Worship in the Temple (King David)

Hebrew music during the reigns of King David and King Solomon included strategic and well-planned times of worship in the temple. King David is credited with structuring music for temple worship. Notably, 10 percent of the people serving in temple ministries were musicians. David appointed 4,000 members of the 38,000-member tribe of Levi to serve as professional ministers of music and singers. Their responsibilities were *"to raise sounds of joy"* (1 Chr 15:16 ESV, italics mine) with musical instruments.

All the musicians were part of the tribe of Levi. They were set apart for the service of the King of kings. King David appointed Chenaniah the leader of song (1 Chr 15:22). Heman was appointed the leader of all those who sang to the Lord (1 Chr 15:19). Jeduthun was the leader of all those who led worship with cymbals and percussion instruments (1 Chr 25:1–7).

Chenaniah—Lead Worshipper		
Heman led all singers	Jeduthun led all percussionists	Asaph led worship education program

Asaph was responsible for the training of musicians. He was the director of "the center for worship" and helped organize a curriculum for equipping leaders of worship. Each musician in the tribe of Levi was required to complete a five-year training period in music and worship. Asaph designed the curriculum and appointed instructors from the tribe of Levi to help.[7] He served as director of music on the day King Solomon dedicated the temple and the glory of the Lord filled the house (2 Chr 5:11–7:3). Asaph wrote twelve of the 150 psalms. His descendants were the musicians in charge of worship during the time Jehoshaphat went into battle with the choir leading the army (2 Chronicles 20). One of Asaph's grandsons brought the king a message from the Lord. It was the descendants of Asaph who led Nehemiah and the children of Israel out of exile back to the city of Jerusalem.

The choir consisted of at least 12 male singers. They were required to be part of the tribe of Levi and complete a five-year training period in music and worship. These musicians were set apart for service, sanctified with a clean heart, and were between the ages of 35 and 50. They were paid for their services, provided housing, and treated like other religious workers.[8]

While it was mandated that choirs have a minimum of 12 members, it was not unusual for large, well-rehearsed choirs to lead in the celebration of great events and significant worship times. Solomon's choir numbered 4,000 (1 Chr 23:5). Zerubbabel's temple choir consisted of 200 singers (Ezra 2:65), and Nehemiah's temple choir included 245 men and women (Neh 7:67).

Worship in the Psalms

God provided a hymnal of praise for his people in the book of Psalms. From the time of David, the psalms played an integral part in Hebrew worship. The psalms are a poetic dialogue between God and man that was set to music. They offer songs to accompany the offering of sacrifices. Psalms, performed by the temple musicians, were sung when the temple of Solomon was built, and they described man's relationship with God.

The book of Psalms is divided into five sections, also referred to as "books":

1. Book I: Psalms 1–41
2. Book II: Psalms 42–72

3. Book III: Psalms 73–89
4. Book IV: Psalms 90–106
5. Book V: Psalms 107–150

These five divisions correspond to the first five books of the Old Testament, the Pentateuch, written by Moses. In the collection are: (1) psalms of praise, (2) psalms of history, (3) psalms of penitence, (4) psalms of imprecation (cursing of enemies), and (5) messianic psalms (prophecies regarding the coming of Christ as Messiah). The psalms include more than 175 references of praise to God for his greatness, justice, wonders, compassion, mercy, grace, righteousness, goodness, sovereign care, salvation, and protection.

What can we learn about worship from the psalms?

1. *The psalms teach us to worship reverently in God's presence.* Reverence is an attitude of the heart, not necessarily reflected by the volume of our words or the movement of our feet. Reverence is sensitivity to God's presence and awareness of his intimate fellowship with us.

2. *The psalms teach us to worship God with praise.* More than twenty psalms offer praise for all God has done in creation, sustaining our lives, saving us, and protecting us. There is great praise in Psalms 33, 34, 40, and 42.

3. *Many psalms teach us to achieve intimacy with God through worship.* The sons of Korah cried out, "My soul longeth, yea, even fainteth for the courts of the Lord; my heart and my flesh crieth out for the living God" (Ps 84:2 KJV). They also worshipped God, saying, "Blessed are they that dwell in thy house. Blessed is the man whose strength is in thee" (Ps 84:4–5 KJV). The sons of Korah declared, "A day in thy courts is better than a thousand. I had rather be a doorkeeper in the house of my God than to dwell in the tents of wickedness" (Ps 84:10 KJV).

4. *Many psalms teach us to delight in worshipping God.* Moses, the author of Psalm 91, savors God's presence when he says, "He that dwelleth

in the secret place of the Most High shall abide under the shadow of the Almighty" (Ps 91:1 KJV).

5. *The psalms teach us to express great love and appreciation in worship.* In Psalm 119, each verse expresses gratitude for the Word of God that gives guidance in life. For through the Word of God, people find joy, holiness, and direction for their lives.

6. *The psalms teach us to express faith in divine providence as we worship God.* The psalmist expresses great faith in God's guidance, protection, and providence. In Psalms 65 and 121, the psalmist expresses gratitude to God for his continued care.

7. *The psalms help the worshipper find refuge in God.* God is called a rock, a stronghold, and the One who protects his people. In Psalms 46, 61, and 62, the psalmist rejoices that God looks after him, protects him, and is the strength of his life.

8. *The psalms teach us to conquer our foes through worship.* In Ps 18:31–42 (NCV) the psalmist says,

> Who is God? Only the Lord. Who is the Rock? Only our God. God is my protection. . . . He trains my hands for battle so my arms can bend a bronze bow. . . . I chased my enemies and caught them. I did not quit until they were destroyed. I crushed them so. . . . You gave me strength in battle. You made my enemies bow before me. You made my enemies turn back, and I destroyed those who hated me. . . . I beat my enemies into pieces, like dust in the wind. I poured them out like mud in the streets.

Again, in Psalm 44:5, the psalmist exalts God for victory in worship when praising the name of the Lord. In Ps 138:1–3 (NCV), we are given an example of how thanksgiving, worship, and praise meld into a testimony of victory: "Lord, I will thank you with all my heart; I will sing to you before the gods. I will bow down facing your holy Temple, and I will thank you for your love and loyalty. You have made your name and your word greater than anything. On the day I called to you, you answered me. You made me strong and brave."

Then, in Ps 144:1–8 (NCV), we see further evidence of God's response to us when we put our trust in him: "Praise the Lord, my Rock, who trains me for war, who trains me for battle. He protects me like a strong, walled city, and he loves me. He is my defender and my Savior, my shield and my protection. He helps me keep my people under control." God promised his people victory when they trusted him.

9. *The psalms teach us to confess our sins in worship and ask for God's forgiveness.* Models of confession are found in Psalms 32, 78, 95, and 106. Along with confession, worshippers are to seek forgiveness and return to fellowship with God. In Psalm 51, David, who had committed murder and adultery, pleads for God's forgiveness and cleansing.

10. *The psalms teach us to have passion in worship.* The sons of Korah say, "As the hart panteth after the water brooks, so my soul longeth after God" (Ps 42:1 KJV). They go on to say, "My soul thirsteth for God, the living God, when shall I come and appear before God?" (Ps 42:2 KJV).

11. *The psalms instruct us to sing praise to the name of the Lord* (Ps 7:17).

12. *The psalms instruct us to make music skillfully and on a variety of instruments* (Psalms 33; 150).

The Intertestamental Period

The Synagogue and the Jewish Home

The practice of meeting in synagogues began among Jews who were exiles in other lands—perhaps during the captivity in Babylon (c. 600 BC). Because the traditional sacrifices of animals and other materials could only be offered at the temple, the emphasis in synagogues was on the sacrifices of praise and prayer, instruction in the Old Testament Law

(The Torah) and the Prophets; interpretations and exhortation based on the readings, and, a basic liturgy of set blessings.[9] Worship theologian Allen Ross contends that "the basic traditions of the worship of ancient Israel were carried forward but with significant new developments and a different spirit."[10]

Synagogues became the center of educational and social life for their members, and they eventually were established worldwide—wherever there were enough Jews to support their activities. Synagogue worship was fully developed and used in the Holy Land and throughout the Hellenistic world during the lifetime of Jesus and the early years of the Christian church.[11]

Synagogue worship was essentially a service of the Word and prayer. The service was congregational, involving a rabbi and a group of laypersons that often participated in the readings, prayers, and open discussions. Synagogue worship followed the Hebrew calendar, including: (1) observance of the annual cycle of feasts and festivals, (2) a cyclical schedule of Scripture readings using a Hebrew lectionary, and (3) prayers according to the seasons.[12]

It was during the 400 silent years between the Testaments that the Jews built synagogues as gathering places in which communities could worship. Of primary importance to synagogue worship was the teaching of the Word of God. During those years when there were no prophets, the faith of Israel became increasingly institutionalized. Whereas during the Old Testament period the Jews were mostly illiterate, during the intertestamental period they became a reading people. This helped preserve Jewish identity while other cultures disappeared. Religious literature was written and revered in the synagogue until the traditions, comments, and interpretations recorded in the Talmud, Midrashim, and Cabala were considered as authoritative as the Scriptures on which they commented.

Sects began forming within Judaism, including the Sadducees and Pharisees. For 400 years, God did not speak to his people. While they had a record of what God had already said, divine instructions were increasingly ignored.

Summary of Worship Innovations

We learned in the previous chapter that God established a purpose, place, people, and plan for worship. We learned in this chapter that worship practices in the Old Testament developed in two stages. The first stage was highly organized, centering on the tabernacle and the temple. Worship during this stage was led by priests, assisted by Levites, and included a complex system of rituals, sacrifices, and feasts. Singing, playing of instruments, dance, reading of Scripture, shouting, clapping, and banners were all a part of the Old Testament worship tradition.

The second stage began during the exile, when God was worshipped through the synagogue. The word *synagogue* comes from the Greek, meaning "gathering place" or "place of assembly." The synagogue brought God's people together for instruction, fellowship, and worship. When twelve Jewish families lived in any area, they were required by law to build a synagogue and come together for instruction and worship of God on the Sabbath day.[13] This second stage greatly differed from worship in the temple. Whereas temple worship was centralized in Jerusalem, synagogues were found wherever there were twelve Jewish families. In the temple, the emphasis was upon establishing a relationship with God through sacrifice. The synagogue's emphasis was upon instruction and worship.

God did not abandoned his people during the 400 years of silence. He was silent, but he was about to speak as loudly and clearly as he would ever speak to any people. But this time he would speak through his son Jesus! "When the fullness of the time was come, God sent forth his Son, made of a woman, made under the Law, to redeem them that were under the Law, that we might receive the adoption of sons" (Gal 4:4–5 KJV). "In these last days God has spoken to us through his Son" (Heb 1:1–2 NCV).

In the next chapter, we will see how full and unreserved access to God may be realized through the person of Jesus Christ. We will learn how Jesus ushers in an innovative paradigm for worship as a new covenant is established between God and man.

Notes

1. Donald P. Hustad, *Jubilate II: Church Music in Worship and Renewal* (Carol Stream, IL: Hope, 1993), 131.

2. Ibid., 133.

3. Ibid., 140–41.

4. ELT marks translation by Elmer Towns.

5. Hustad, *Jubilate II*, 134.

6. Lecture by Armenio Suzano at the Musikseminar by Bibel Mission, Niedenburg, Germany, June 3, 2011.

7. John F. Wilson, *An Introduction to Church Music* (Chicago: Moody, 1965), 24.

8. Vernon M. Whaley, *Understanding Music and Worship in the Local Church* (Wheaton: Evangelical Training Association, 2002), 31–32.

9. Allen P. Ross, *Recalling the Hope of Glory* (Grand Rapids: Kregel Academic, 2006), 356–60.

10. Ibid., 357.

11. Hustad, *Jubilate II*, 141–43.

12. Andrew Wilson-Dickson, *The Story of Christian Music* (Minneapolis: Fortress, 1992), 22–23.

13. See W. E. Bind, *Expositionary Dictionary of New Testament Words* (Lynchburg, VA: Old Time Gospel Hour, 1978), 1113.

CHAPTER 3

Pentecost: A New Expression of Worship (AD 30–100)

It began on a mountain outside Jerusalem. Jesus asked the eleven disciples to meet him there. They did—all of them, together. The events that followed changed worship forever. The disciples were talking to Jesus about the things to come. Suddenly, Jesus said, "When the Holy Spirit comes to you, you will receive power. You will be my witnesses—in Jerusalem, in all of Judea, in Samaria, and in every part of the world" (Acts 1:8 NCV).

At that moment, Jesus began to ascend to heaven. When he finished talking, he simply left the disciples standing on the hillside. He was lifted up—in the air—into the clouds. He was gone!

Suddenly, two men wearing white clothes stood before the disciples. They said, "Men of Galilee, why are you standing here looking into the sky? Jesus, whom you saw taken up from you into heaven, will come back in the same way you saw him go" (Acts 1:9–11 NCV).

Jesus told his beloved disciples to trust him. He promised to always be with them. And the disciples took Jesus at his word. They saw the risen Christ. Each disciple, in his own way, committed himself to telling the good news to anyone willing to listen. Christians still met in buildings, but now the Most High God chose to dwell in the physical body of each believer. He chose to make his temple the hearts of men, women, boys, and girls. That experience forever transformed the disciples.

The Introduction of the Church—an Awakening to Be Remembered!

When the day of Pentecost came, all the disciples were together in one place. One hundred twenty believers gathered in an upper room for prayer, which transformed them both inwardly and outwardly. Previously, they saw Jesus in his resurrected body.

They saw him.

They touched him!

They fellowshipped with him!

They worshipped him.

Yet Jesus told his disciples that he must go away. If he did not leave, the Comforter would never come (John 16:7). After Jesus entered heaven, all things were ready for the Holy Spirit to be poured out upon his disciples. Did the disciples prepare for that inauguration? Yes indeed, they prayed!

Jesus promised they would have new power. "I will pray the Father, and He will give you another Helper, that He may abide with you forever—the Spirit of truth, whom the world cannot receive . . . but you know Him, for He dwells with you and will be in you" (John 14:16–17 NKJV). They had not yet *experienced* the Holy Spirit! Certainly, they remembered the promise that the Spirit would come. So they were praying for the coming of the Comforter, the Holy Spirit.

Suddenly a noise like a strong, blowing wind came from heaven and filled the whole house. Something like flames of fire that were separated stood over each of the 120 in attendance. They were filled with the Holy Spirit—God himself entered each person in the room. God had a new temple in which to dwell. God himself came in the person of the Holy Spirit and entered the heart of every man and woman in the building.

Immediately, they were filled with the Holy Spirit. All 120 received power. This was the power promised by Jesus in Matt 28:18–20 and Acts 1:7–8. Instantly, the Holy Spirit gave them authority to speak in other languages and they attacked the dark, evil kingdom of Satan with the Word of God.

It was the celebration of the Jewish holiday, Pentecost. Thousands of Jewish citizens were in Jerusalem from every country in the world. They heard this loud noise of Spirit-filled believers. Soon, a crowd assembled. They were all amazed because each one heard the disciples speaking in his own language. They said,

> "Look! Aren't all of these people that we hear speaking from Galilee? How then is it possible that we each hear them in our own languages? We are from different places: Parthia, Media, Elam, Mesopotamia, Judea, Cappadocia, Pontus, Asia, Phrygia, Pamphylia, Egypt, the areas of Libya near Cyrene, Rome (both Jews and those who had become Jews), Crete, and Arabia. But we hear them in our own languages about the great things God has done! . . . What does this mean?" (Acts 2:2–12 NCV)

Peter stood in front of the entire crowd and quoted Joel 2:28-32 to explain what was happening: "God says: In the last days I will pour out my Spirit on all kinds of people. Your sons and daughters will prophesy. Your young men will see visions, and your old men will dream dreams and prophesy. At that time I will will pour out my Spirit . . . show miracles in the sky and on the earth. . . . Then anyone who calls on the Lord will be saved" (Acts 2:17–21 NCV).

Peter explained how Jesus from Nazareth was a very special man. "God clearly showed this to you by the miracles, wonders, and signs he did through Jesus." Peter continued,

> You all know this, because it happened right here among you. Jesus was given to you, and with the help of those who don't know the law, you put him to death by nailing him to a cross. But this was God's plan which he had made long ago; he knew all this would happen. God raised Jesus from the dead and set him free from the pain of death, because death could not hold him. Jesus is the One whom God raised from the dead. And we are all witnesses to this. Jesus was lifted up to heaven and is now at God's right side. The Father has given the Holy Spirit to Jesus as he promised. So Jesus has poured out that Spirit, and this is what you now see and hear. So, all the people of Israel should know this truly: God has made Jesus—the man you nailed to the cross—both Lord and Christ. (Acts 2:22–24,33–36 NCV)

Peter concluded by saying, "Change your hearts and lives and be baptized, each one of you, in the name of Jesus Christ for the forgiveness of your sins. And you will receive the gift of the Holy Spirit. This promise is for you, your children, and all who are far away. It is for everyone the Lord our God calls to himself" (Acts 2:38–40 NCV).

About three thousand people believed what Peter said, were baptized, and were added to the church that day. The Lord added daily to those who were being saved as they became worshippers of the Most High God (Acts 2:43–47 NCV).

Events Leading to the Awakening at Pentecost

Down through the centuries, there have been times of great revival, repentance, and turning back to God. These times are sometimes referred to as "Great Awakenings." Most of these *awakenings* are worldwide events that impact the community and culture in a powerful, life-changing way. Usually, thousands of people turn from sinful behavior to embrace righteousness and holy living. Broken lives are mended and crushed relationships are restored. Sometimes awakenings are years in the making and often in response to sustained and intense prayers for revival by God's people. At other times, the awakening comes quickly and unexpectedly. An awakening usually continues for an extended period of time.

Historians generally agree that the Christian church has experienced at least four *official* awakenings. In recent years, historians have articulated nine or ten periods in history when the Spirit of God moved on multiple communities and revival spread across the land and around the world.

Some believe that Pentecost, and the coming of the Holy Spirit, was a time of awakening. Others argue that it was the "coming of the church age," and because it was not a revival (at least in what is traditionally understood as a revival), it cannot be called a "Great Awakening." It is agreed that a miraculous event took place at Pentecost that changed the world and rocked the established religious norms of the day.

The awakening at Pentecost, described above, actually began weeks before when Jesus raised the cup at the Last Supper and introduced to his disciples the new covenant. It is important to remember that, as we begin our journey to document the relationship between the Great Awakenings and worship, New Testament worship begins and ends with the person of Jesus. Fully God and fully man, Jesus is the visible representation of our invisible God, Yahweh. He is God with us, Immanuel. He is Lord of lords and King of kings. He is the Son of God and the Son of Man. From before the foundation of the world, God planned that Jesus Christ, his only son, the Messiah, would serve as the mediator between himself and sinful man: Sinful man on one side, a perfect God on the other, and Jesus Christ in the middle.

Why is this so important? God's plan freed humanity to worship; no longer condemned in sin, no longer separated from God, no longer forbidden to worship God; forever justified by his work on the cross.

What changed? What is so important about the new covenant? The answer is Jesus!

As God incarnate, Jesus could do that which no one else could: redefine acceptable worship and establish the new covenant on which it was based.[1] Jesus changed the rules. Under his rules, we are no longer bound by Old Testament laws regarding sacrifice, worship practices, the Sabbath, and the temple. We worship in spirit and truth.

Because salvation comes through the substitutionary work of Christ on the cross, we are privileged to enjoy worship—free from the curse of sin, bondage of the law, and penalty of disobedience. Once we receive salvation through Jesus, he dwells in our hearts. Jesus becomes our worship leader. Jesus becomes our sacrifice, our Passover lamb, our propitiation, and our redeemer.

Jesus is the supreme worship leader through whom the new covenant is established. With the new covenant comes a change in our focus. All our worship is now focused on one person, Jesus. All the traditions, practices, prayers, sacrifices, and songs in the Old Testament point to Jesus.

Remember the temple veil? It was ripped when Jesus died. This action symbolized for all eternity the complete destruction of the barrier between God and man. No longer was the priest the only one permitted to come before God. Jesus' death made possible for *all* that which was *im*possible for Old Testament worshippers—*direct access to God*. This is the paradox of the ages: *even* those so full of hate and envy that they crucified the Son of God now have access to God. Christ's empty tomb stands as a monument to his conclusive victory over Satan.

Impact of the Great Awakening at Pentecost on the Church

What happened at Pentecost changed worship forever. It was a defining moment in history when God, the most high God of Abraham, Isaac, and Jacob, chose a new dwelling place. This was the beginning of the church age.

No longer is the center of worship a temple building. Followers of Christ can now worship God everywhere—in the streets, in the synagogue, on mountaintops, in caves, in homes and small buildings, and in prison. Most importantly, they can now worship Jesus in their hearts.

Strategic Personalities

Jesus, Peter, Paul, John, James, the disciples, and the early Christians served as strategic personalities during this first awakening. Each person or group made a contribution to the worship practices of the early church.

Jesus

We have already established the fact that Jesus is central to our worship. During the Last Supper, he proclaimed the gospel message that *the new covenant is based on the work of one person—himself.* Jesus became our tabernacle. His sacrifice on the cross for the sins of the world provided a new and personal way for humans to be made right before God. The Old Testament required sacrifice of an animal. Jesus became the eternal sacrifice through which came forgiveness of sin and a path to unhindered worship of God.

Peter

Next is Peter, seemingly an unlikely character to continue the work and ministry of Jesus. After all, he denied Jesus three times. God's ways often confound human reason. Peter became the foremost leader of the church. Peter announced the coming of the Holy Spirit on that day of Pentecost. Peter encouraged the persecuted believers to let the Holy Spirit perfect, establish, strengthen, and settle them in their worship of the Lord (1 Peter 5). In spite of some initial hesitation, Peter led the Jerusalem church in proclaiming the availability of the gospel to the nations. When they heard this, they praised God and said, "So God is allowing even those who are not Jewish to turn to him and live" (Acts 11:4a,18 NCV). Historians generally agree that Peter suffered martyrdom while in Rome during the persecution under Nero. It is believed that Peter was crucified upside-down.

Paul

Equally important to the success of the early church was the ministry of Paul, who considered himself an apostle to the Gentiles. The better part of his ministry was given to three missionary journeys and writing epistles to churches while he was imprisoned for the cause of Christ. Paul's instruction in Ephesians 5 and Colossians 3 to sing with psalms, hymns, and spiritual songs still serves as a guide for biblical worship today. It is generally agreed among historians that Paul was beheaded in Rome during the reign of Nero.[2]

John

John's contribution to worship is related primarily to his vision while exiled on the island of Patmos. His documentation of the "end times" in Revelation, the last book in the Bible, serves as a foreshadowing of worship in heaven while providing a model for our practices here on earth.

John, Peter, and Paul were actively engaged in preaching the gospel, establishing new churches, and nurturing young believers in all parts of Asia Minor. It is generally believed that following the visions at Patmos, John was a teacher in Ephesus until his death around AD 100.[3]

James

The apostle long considered the leader of the church in Jerusalem, James instructed Christians about worship practices in the epistle bearing his name. First, worshippers are to stop being double minded and seek God's wisdom in all things, according to James (James 1). Second, worshippers are to stop "playing favorites" (James 2). Third, worshippers are to call the elders of the church together for prayer and anointing the sick with oil (James 5). Historians agree that James was killed by order of the high priest in AD 62.[4]

The Disciples and Early Christians

The eleven disciples began meeting on a regular basis almost immediately after Jesus was crucified. Jesus told them to meet regularly to celebrate the new covenant provided through his death on the cross—to share the bread and cup. They assembled on Sundays to celebrate his resurrection and to remember him. There were also meetings on other days of the week for teaching and worship, especially on the Sabbath, usually in the synagogue.

The early Christians were Jewish and did not consider themselves part of a new religion. Rather, they considered their newfound faith in Christ a confirmation that the Messianic age had finally come. So it was natural that their worship reflected the synagogue. There were basically two groups of Jewish Christians: the Hebrews and the Hellenists. The former resided in Jerusalem. The Hellenistic Jewish Christians largely were dispersed throughout the Roman Empire and primarily spoke

Greek. They helped Gentiles accept Christianity as an alternative to traditional Roman pantheism.

Two significant events impacted early Christian worship. First, huge numbers of Gentiles joined the church. Thus, no longer was it considered necessary to follow the synagogue model. Believers were as prone to meet in homes, on hillsides, and in public places as in the local synagogue. Second, Christians dispersed throughout the empire. In the words of Justo González, "Nameless Christians . . . for different reasons—persecution, business, or missionary calling—traveled from place to place taking the news of the Gospel with them."[5]

Paradigm Shifts and Innovations by the Early Church

Early Jewish believers modeled their Christian worship on what they had experienced in the synagogue, adding the observance of the Lord's Supper. Much of the language of synagogue worship, as well as the choices of readings, were carried over into the early church. It is evident that the apostles continued to observe the Jewish festivals and were accustomed to following the Hebrew lectionary.[6] Eventually, the synagogue and the upper-room experiences were united in one two-part service on Sunday—celebrating the Eucharist (communion) and teaching the Word.

Celebrating the Eucharist

The Eucharist, or Holy Communion, is a way of proclaiming to the world the work of Christ's redemption. Through it, Jesus directs Christians' faith and worship toward his new covenant sacrifice. The upper-room experience became a turning point in worship. In the words of Alan Ross,

Jesus transformed worship for all time by giving believers something greater to remember in their worship—his body and his blood that was poured out for the sins of the world. Jesus the Messiah of Israel was fulfilling the Scriptures. Now, true spiritual worship would be in Christ.[7]

During the Last Supper, Jesus presented himself as the *living sacrifice, our Passover Lamb*. No longer would people need look to the sacrifice of an animal for atonement. Jesus is the permanent, once-and-forever sacrifice. Even so, for the Christians, "those early communion services did not center on the Lord's passion, but rather on his victory by which a new age had dawned."[8] The breaking of the bread was experienced with generosity and gladness of heart (Acts 2:46).

The Passover and Holy Communion

The Last Supper was structured much like the customary Passover meal, complete with Scripture recitations, prayers, songs, sharing of the cup, and breaking of bread. The Passover meal was a time of remembering Yahweh's deliverance of Israel from Egyptian slavery. It was a special time for families and loved ones to gather and celebrate God's goodness.

The Passover meal usually began with a blessing and the sharing of the first cup of wine, the *cup of sanctification*. This was followed by *The Hallel* (Psalms 113–116), usually sung by the entire group. Participants then shared a second cup of wine called the *cup of interpretation*. Food was then served. It included bitter herbs, unleavened bread, and lamb—reminders to Israel of the hardship of Egypt, the manna, and the Passover sacrifice. The meal was preceded by a prayer of thanksgiving by the leader. After the meal, another prayer was offered and a third cup of wine shared, the *cup of blessing*. The meal concluded with the singing of a second part of *The Hallel* (Psalms 117–118) and a fourth cup of wine, called the *cup of consummation*.[9]

At the Last Supper, Jesus led the worship service, using prayers as opportunities to explain the meaning of the bread and wine. Just as the Passover leader told the Old Testament story, Jesus explained the new covenant and gave the disciples promises for the future. In so doing, he established a worship liturgy that remains a model for believers today.

A Time of Cleansing

Sacrifices in the Old Testament often were preceded by a time of personal cleansing. The Last Supper was no exception. Jesus required that the disciples' feet be washed as a symbol of their spiritual cleansing. This cleansing, performed personally by Jesus, confirmed his role as leader of the meal.[10] Beyond that, he demonstrated his willingness to be the servant-savior prepared to take away the sins of the world and taught the requirement of humility, forgiveness, and service. Most importantly, he emphasized the importance of a clean heart when participating in the Lord's Supper. Later, the apostle Paul reminded the Corinthian Christians to "examine themselves" (1 Cor 11:27–29) before taking part in the Lord's Supper.

The Bread

The Hebrews understood that the Passover meal celebrated symbolically their release from bondage. For example, the unleavened bread represented the manna provided by God in the wilderness. Similarly, the Lord's Supper symbolically celebrates Jesus' broken body, given freely for the sins of the world. He told us to eat the bread in celebration of his sacrifice for us.

The Cup

Jesus presented himself to his disciples as the Lamb of God—the ultimate sacrifice. Jesus "took the cup, gave thanks and offered it" (Matt 26:27–28 ELT). Called *the cup of blessing*, he used its red wine to symbolize the shedding of blood. He knew his sacrificial death would forever transform the spiritual life and worship of his disciples. He knew this offering would establish peace between man and God.[11] He explained how his death was necessary to establish and restore communion, communication, and companionship of all people with God.

Jesus declined taking the fourth cup, the *cup of consummation*, with the disciples. This cup represented the fulfillment of his plan of redemption—heaven and eternal life. Jesus told his disciples, "I will not drink of this fruit of the vine again until that day when I drink it new in the kingdom of God" (Mark 14:25 NCV).

The Singing

Jesus and his disciples concluded the Last Supper by singing a hymn together. It was natural for the disciples to dismiss the meal with spontaneous praise and worship. In keeping with the normal Passover practice, and reflecting what they had just experienced together, the song was probably taken from Psalm 118. According to Ross, "Christians who use 'Hosannah' and 'Blessed is he who comes in the name of the Lord' in their worship liturgy are celebrating the fulfillment of the divinely inspired hymns used in Passover."[12] Sometimes sung completely and at other times in sections, this psalm is one of the *Hallel* songs thanking God for victory.

When Jesus and the disciples finished the song of praise, they left the upper room for the Mount of Olives and the garden of Gethsemane. Likewise, the early Christians would always end their time of communion with a hymn of worship and celebration.

Worship Practices in the Temple, Synagogues, and Homes

Christians met daily in the temple, synagogues, and homes. They preached, prayed, and worshipped—in the streets, as prisoners in jail, on ships in the midst of storms, in caves, and on hillsides. Their faith was very public.

They stayed busy with the tasks of *teaching* (doctrine), *sharing* (the good news; their testimonies; their possessions; their fellowship), *breaking bread* (meals; communion; feeding the poor), and *praying together* (prayers of thanksgiving; praise; worship; blessings; supplications). During the early days, following the awakening at Pentecost, there was great respect for God. Huge numbers of people became worshippers of Christ as the disciples, emboldened by the power of the Holy Spirit within them, shared testimonies, preached the gospel, performed miracles, and offered the unsaved an alternative to the hopelessness of idols and false teachers that was such a major part of their culture (Acts 2:41–47).

The New Model for Worship

The worship practices presented to the Roman believers by Paul were innovations that changed the complexion of church life during the first century. He described three worship practices for the early Christians.

First, *worship includes preaching.* In writing to the Roman believers, Paul categorized preaching the Word of God as a part of worship. "I am not ashamed of the gospel," he wrote, "because it is the power of God for the salvation of everyone who believes: first for the Jew, then for the Gentile" (Rom 1:16 NIV).

"The language here," writes David Peterson, "suggests that gospel preaching is necessary to bring about that obedience of faith through Jesus Christ which is the 'understanding worship' of the eschatological era." Peterson continues:

> Paul's "priestly" ministry was radically different because it was conducted out in the world, rather than in some sacred place. He clearly gives that ministry a novel significance when he describes

[preaching] as the means by which he worships . . . God. . . . Missionary preaching and the establishment of churches in the truths of the gospel can be described as fulfilling a God-given "liturgy" or service to the churches. At the same time, these vital activities can be regarded as specific and particular expressions of Christian "worship" or service to God.[13]

Heretofore, reading Scripture, singing songs, praying, and adoration of God had been the primary expressions of worship. With Paul, however, preaching of the good news was equally vital to the worship process (Rom 1:5,16; 12:1–8; 15:9,18; 16:19). This concept changed forever the role of the preacher from mere exhortation to worship.

Second, *worship is a lifestyle.* It involves living out one's Christian faith in front of a heathen, ungodly world. Worship involves *presenting our bodies* to God as living sacrifices. These sacrifices are freely given and involve love and devotion to God. The concept of sacrifices was certainly relevant to both Jewish and Roman culture. Paul said this sacrifice is a *living* sacrifice that includes the ambitions, thoughts, and intentions of the heart. Paul also suggested that worship of God involves *holiness.* Now that our bodies are the temple of God, it is important that he inhabits a clean, sanctified, and purified temple—a vessel fit for service. Holiness provides evidence of honest, genuine worship. Worship that is acceptable to God involves service. The very process of "offering the sacrifice," according to Paul, is a *spiritual act of worship.* David Peterson comments on the distinction between lifestyle worship and corporate worship:

> When Christians become preoccupied with the notion of offering God acceptable worship in a congregational context and thus with the minutiae of church services, they need to be reminded that Paul's focus was on the service of everyday life.[14]

Third, *worship is no longer defined by specific form or ritual,* but by a much more personal element—*spiritual gifts.* This diversification of worship according to individual gifts is a new concept because it encourages believers to recognize individual talents as treasures to be offered to the Lord:

> If a man's gift is prophesying, let him use it in proportion to his faith. If it is serving, let him serve; if it is teaching, let him teach; if it is encouraging, let him encourage; if it is contributing to the needs of others, let him give generously; if it is leadership, let him govern diligently; if it is showing mercy, let him do it cheerfully. (Rom 12:4–8 NIV)

Music Practices and Innovations

Little is known about the exact function of music in the early church's worship. Worship was no longer the work of professionals, ordained priests, cantors, and gatekeepers. The service was driven by lay worshippers who were committed to publically expressing their newfound faith in God. The Spirit-led worship mentioned in Eph 5:19; Col 3:16; and 1 Cor 14:26 retained three elements from the synagogue: (1) psalms and Scripture songs (often called hymns), (2) Scripture readings and sermons, and (3) discussion ("a lesson"). Worship in the early church was thoroughly social and congregational with all worshippers aware of their neighbors and of God as each person took part and perhaps assumed some role of leadership.[15]

There is little evidence of instrumental music in the first-century church. It could be that early Christians were influenced more by the heavy emphasis on vocal worship in the synagogue than by the predominantly secular use of instruments. Perhaps so much attention was placed on avoiding and surviving persecution that little time was given to developing opportunities for worship with musical instruments.

Paul's use of the Greek word *psallo* in Ephesians 5:19 may imply the use of musical instruments in worship. According to Armenio Suzano, *psallo* means "(1) to pluck off, pull out, (2) to cause to vibrate by touching, to twang, (2a) to touch or strike the chord, to twang the strings of a musical instrument so that they gently vibrate, (2b) to play on a stringed instrument, to play the harp, etc., (2c) to sing to the music of the harp, (2d) in the NT to sing a hymn, to celebrate the praises of God in song."[16]

W. Hines Sims offers the following observation about the use of instruments in the New Testament church:

> If God the Father recognized and received the praise and worship connected with singing and the playing of instruments in accepted forms all through the Old Testament, he also as God the Son and God the Holy Spirit in the New Testament endorses such use in the New Testament churches, for he is One and unchanging and cannot be incompatible with himself. The fact that instruments were an accepted part of worship in the Old Testament makes clear the thought that had God wished that churches not use instruments under the New Covenant, he would have, through the medium of his inspired writers, specifically said so.[17]

Summary of Worship Innovations

The revival on the day of Pentecost will never take place again. Pentecost was the beginning of the church and the introduction of the Holy Spirit to the world, and believers were indwelt by Jesus Christ as the "body" of Christ (Eph 1:23). While we cannot re-experience Pentecost, the tremendous power that came on Pentecost is available today. Just as the early church evangelized the Mediterranean world, we can accomplish great feats for Christ today. The same power is promised to us: "But you shall receive power when the Holy Spirit has come upon you; and you shall be witnesses to Me in Jerusalem, and in all Judea and Samaria, and to the end of the earth" (Acts 1:8 NKJV).

Pentecost set the standard for Christianity. This is how today's church should believe, worship, and practice faith in daily life. Pentecost set the standard for the divine transformation of lives so God's glory could be manifested in the church today. Pentecost was the greatest revival ever. Without it, none of the other revivals throughout history would have occurred.

So, what are the implications for our worship today? First, with the coming of the Holy Spirit's ministry, *believers begin to experience and enjoy God's plan for personal, private worship.* This involves understanding and experiencing "triune" worship. Believers are able to receive an understanding of worship from God, participate in worship because of the work of Jesus, and enjoy the privilege of experiencing worship through the ministry of the Holy Spirit. Why? Because the Holy Spirit (God himself) now resides in the believer. God no longer dwells in a cloud, a fire by night, tents, or buildings. God now chooses to dwell in the hearts of his best creation, men and women.

Our worship is no longer restricted by the traditions of the past, the activities we must perform, a location, or a building. Rather, we worship by knowing, loving, and enjoying the presence of God in our lives. The change from Old to New Testament worship is radical. It gives us opportunity to focus on the person who lives within us.

Second, *our worship services should center around four tasks: teaching, sharing, breaking bread, and praying.* The early church taught the good news, the gospel. They shared on two levels: communicating the good news of salvation through Jesus and distributing their wealth to one another.

Breaking bread involved taking communion—the cup and the bread. They prayed prayers of intercession—for people's healing, for the kingdom of God to be advanced, for protection, and for God's favor to be shown to them.

Third, *we should meet together for worship regularly.* Initially, the church met regularly in the synagogue and temple.

- "The believers met together in the Temple every day. They ate together in their homes happy to share their food with joyful hearts. They praised God and were liked by all the people. Every day the Lord added those who were being saved to the group of believers" (Acts 2:46–47 NCV).
- "In Iconium, Paul and Barnabas went as usual to the Jewish synagogue. They spoke so well that a great many Jews and Greeks believed" (Acts 14:1–2 NCV).
- "Paul went into the synagogue as he always did, and on each Sabbath day for three weeks, he talked with the Jews about the Scriptures. He explained and proved that the Christ must die and then rise from the dead. . . . Some of the Jews were convinced and joined Paul and Silas, along with many of the Greeks who worshipped God and many of the important women" (Acts 17:2–3a,4 NCV).

Fourth, *we should worship even when facing persecution and death.* It is important to keep in mind that some early Christians experienced severe and continual persecution.

- "They called the apostles in, beat them, and told them not to speak in the name of Jesus again. Then they let them go free. The apostles left the meeting full of joy because they were given the honor of suffering disgrace for Jesus. Every day in the Temple and in people's homes they continued teaching the people and telling the Good News—that Jesus is the Christ" (Acts 5:40–42 NCV).
- "Many of the believers were scattered when they were persecuted after Stephen was killed. Some of them went as far as Phoenicia, Cyprus, and Antioch telling the message to others, but only to Jews. Some of the believers were people from Cyprus and Cyrene.

When they came to Antioch, they spoke also to Greeks, telling them the Good News about the Lord Jesus. The Lord was helping the believers, and a large group of people believed and turned to the Lord" (Acts 11:19–21 NCV).

Stephen was executed when he stood and proclaimed the gospel. James, the brother of John, was killed by Herod Agrippa. Paul was imprisoned for his persistence in preaching the gospel. "Wherever they were scattered, they told people the Good News" (Acts 8:4 NCV). As they ran from cave to cave or village to village, they met for worship. Their worship times sustained them and helped their knowledge of Christ take root and grow.

Fifth, *we should encourage one another as we worship.* The early church encouraged one another in the Word of God. They spoke words of encouragement when living under the fear of persecution, and they were encouraged to seek God and understand his purpose in their lives.

- "The believers in Antioch put Paul into the Lord's care, and he went through Syria and Cilicia, giving strength to the churches" (Acts 15:40b–41 NCV).
- "When they came out of the jail, they went to Lydia's house where they saw some of the believers and encouraged them" (Acts 16:40 NCV).
- "Giving strength to the followers" (Acts 18:23 NCV).
- "Apollos . . . helped them very much" (Acts 18:27 NCV).
- "Barnabas was a good man, full of the Holy Spirit and full of faith. When he reached Antioch and saw how God had blessed the people, he was glad. He encouraged all the believers in Antioch always to obey the Lord with all their hearts, and many people became followers of the Lord" (Acts 11:23–24 NCV).

Sixth, *worship should become a part of our daily lifestyle.* Early Christians were encouraged to present their bodies as living sacrifices to God in worship through Christian service, caring for their brothers and sisters in the Lord, and expressing their talents and gifts in private and public worship.

Seventh, *worship should be multicultural.* On the day of Pentecost when worship broke out among the multitudes, people from many nations were present. With the coming of New Testament worship came focused endeavors to tell the good news to other nations. The gift of salvation is given to all who believe irrespective of their ethnic origin. Peter's encounter with the Holy Spirit through a vision prompted him to change his methodology in preaching and to speak favorably about Gentiles to the church in Jerusalem (Acts 10–11).

The early Christians were so convinced of God's love for the entire world that when some tried to divide Jews and Gentiles, James, the half brother of Jesus, stood up at the Council of Jerusalem and declared God's intention for "the rest of mankind" to seek Him, "even all the Gentiles" (Acts 15:16–17 NIV). The new church had a new worship of the heart, not the past outward forms of Levitical priests bringing sacrifices and performing temple rituals. The new church age was different from the rule-keeping ways of the old covenant.

Jerry Falwell said, "God is not impressed with buildings, budgets or programs; the only thing in this world that impresses God is people."[18] Jesus demanded willing service rather than mere outward conformity. Jesus took his movement out of buildings (temples and synagogues) and put his people on the streets. Now, the streets belong to God's people, and they preach in the marketplaces, homes, jails, or anyplace they go.

In the next chapter we will see how God sometimes uses famine, war, sickness, and even martyrdom to accomplish his purposes. We will see how Christianity swept across the Greco-Roman world and in the process introduced a new paradigm for worship.

Notes

1. Noel Due, *Created for Worship* (Downers Grove, IL: InterVarsity), 139.

2. Justo González, *The Story of Christianity, Volume 1: The Early Church to the Dawn of the Reformation* (New York: Harper-Collins, 1984), 27.

3. Ibid., 28–29.

4. Ibid., 31.

5. Ibid., 30.

6. Don Hustad, *Jubilate II: Church Music in Worship and Renewal* (Carol Stream, IL: Hope, 1993), 143–45.

7. Alan Ross, *Recalling the Hope of Glory* (Grand Rapids: Kregel, 2006), 405.

8. González, *The Story of Christianity*, 20.

9. Ross, *Hope of Glory*, 394.

10. Ibid., 391.

11. See ibid., 396–97. According to Alan Ross, the wine brought together three significant Old Testament passages: Moses confirming the old covenant with blood (Exod 24:8), Jeremiah prophesying about a new covenant (Jer 31:31–34), and Isaiah predicting the coming of a suffering servant who would be "wounded for our transgressions" (Isa 52:13–53:12).

12. Ibid., 403.

13. David Peterson, *Engaging with God: A Biblical Theology of Worship* (Downers Grove, IL: IVP Academic, 2002), 180–82.

14. Ibid., 187–88.

15. Ibid., 146.

16. Lecture by Armenio Suzano at the Musikseminar by Bibel Mission, Niedenburg, Germany, June 3, 2011.

17. W. Hines Sims, *Instrumental Music in the Church* (Nashville: The Sunday School Board of the Southern Baptist Convention, 1947), 16–17.

18. A familiar Jerry Falwell quote often heard while preaching from the Thomas Road Baptist Church pulpit, Lynchburg, Virginia.

CHAPTER 4

Christianity Sweeps across the Greco-Roman World (AD 100–500)

God sometimes uses famine, war, hardship, persecution, sickness, and government as means of bringing people to himself. This was especially true for Christians who lived during the first, second, and third centuries.

There were famous martyrs during this period. One by one, they faced a decision: "swear by the emperor and curse Christ, or die"—usually by fire, sword, or angry lions in a Roman arena. Thousands chose execution.

For example, Ignatius (AD 35–107) was an elderly bishop of the church at Antioch. A native Syrian and an "eyewitness" of the apostles, he was a friend of John, the beloved apostle. Ignatius was well over 70 years of age when arrested, tried, and condemned to die in Rome. While under guard on his final journey to Rome, he wrote several letters to churches in Asia Minor and urged the continuation of the church after his death.[1]

They loved not their lives!

> Ignatius said, "I would rather die for Christ than rule the whole earth. Leave me to the beasts that I may by them be a partaker of God. Welcome nails and cross, welcome broken bones, bruised body, welcome all diabolic torture, if I may but obtain the Lord Jesus Christ." Ignatius was thrown to the lions and eaten alive in AD 107 because of his faith in Christ.[2]

The Early Church in Transition

At first, Christianity was predominantly Jewish. By the beginning of the second century, however, it had become more multi-ethnic. While possessing Jewish roots, it was now a new and different faith. It took on Hellenistic characteristics as it entered the European world. However, it was not exclusively Hellenistic.

At Pentecost, people were in Jerusalem from all parts of the known world—including Mesopotamia, North Africa, and Turkey—and they took Christianity back to their homelands. In the first century, there were strong churches in Antioch and Damascus, and Christianity followed trade routes through the Tigris and Euphrates valleys.

Christianity spread to the northern shores of Africa—Carthage, Tunis, and Algeria. Out of this area emerged many early Christian writings.

Many Italians immigrated to Carthage, and the city became primarily Latin in culture and language. These immigrants were open to the Christian message. As a result, Carthage became one of the dominant centers of Christianity. By the end of the third century, there were more than 100 bishops in Northern Africa. Out of this area came the Christian apologists Tertullian and Cyprian.

By the end of the third century, Christianity was well established in Spain. Although early Christian writers indicate the churches had difficulty with idolatry and adultery, Christianity also grew in France. The most famous name associated with French Christianity is Irenaeus, even though he was from Smyrna in Turkey. Taught by the apostle John, Irenaeus moved to Lyons, France, and experienced a long, prosperous life. By AD 300, Christianity was firmly entrenched in northern France along the cities of the Rhine River.[3]

Armenia experienced mass conversions in the third century. It seems that the missionary Gregory, called "the Illuminator," was responsible for the nation turning to Christ. Gregory was born in aristocracy and became a Christian while in exile in Caesarea of Cappadocia. Initially, he endured much persecution, but he finally won King Tradt of Armenia to Christ. Many of the nobles throughout Armenia also were converted. As a result, the vast majority of the population turned to Christianity. Many of their pagan shrines became places of worship, and numerous pagan priests who were converted to Christianity later became leaders in the church. When they died, their sons took their places as leaders of Christianity. Gregory was appointed bishop at Caesarea and became head of the Armenian Church. Following his death, his descendants assumed leadership in the church.[4]

The Early Church and Culture

Most Christians in the early church came from society's underprivileged class—the dispossessed, slaves, and outcasts. Thus, some nonbelievers attacked Christianity as a movement of the uneducated and powerless, set on undermining the Roman Empire. Celsus, for instance, declared that it had "its chief hold among the ignorant." To the contrary, though, Christianity was not based on ignorance. Rather, those who became Christians were committed to learning and advancement, and the teaching of Christianity supported the government. As Christians gained education, they also gained social prominence.

From AD 100 to 316, the church was severely persecuted. One emperor even issued an edict against Christians.[5] As a result, a "tradition of martyrdom" developed within Christianity. Many who became Christians expected to be martyred because of their faith in Christ.

The believers' godly lifestyle often convicted pagans of sin. The fact that Christianity would not compromise with paganism fostered resentment among the Roman elite, and the Christian *culture* irritated political leaders. The reaction was persecution. In Rome, even members of one prominent family were executed for their faith.[6]

Some made false charges against Christianity. It was said that since both sexes met together at night, the church was guilty of polygamous intercourse. There were rumors that Christians regularly sacrificed infant children and consumed their blood and flesh. The fact that Christians called one another brothers, sisters, and loved ones, even when they barely knew one another, caused the cynical Romans to assume that relationships within the Christian community were immoral.[7]

Christians were falsely charged with treason, membership in a foreign cult, and the practice of magic. Since Christians refused to associate with the imperial worship of Caesar, they were viewed as hostile to the state. The government was hostile toward any rival of its emperor, and Christians called Jesus Christ their Lord and King. The price for faithfulness to Christ was persecution and sometimes death.

Persecution and Martyrdom of the Believers

Most historians recognize eight major periods of persecution, beginning under Nero in the 60s and ending under Diocletian in the early 300s. Nero was the Roman emperor from AD 54 to AD 68. He began his persecution of Christians to cover up a fire in Rome that many suspected him of starting in AD 64. About two-thirds of the city was destroyed. When some among the Roman elite suspected Nero of arson, he blamed *the Christians* for the crime and ordered them to be persecuted and killed.[8]

Many Roman citizens had little regard for Christians. They were offended by the Christian opposition to their pagan gods and believed Christians hated mankind.[9] Still, even some opponents of Christianity believed Nero's persecution went too far. The Roman historian Tacitus was one example. According to Tacitus:

> Before killing the Christians, Nero used them to amuse the people. Some were dressed in furs, to be killed by dogs. Others were crucified. Still others were set on fire early in the night, so that they might illumine it. Nero opened his own gardens for these shows, and in the circus he himself became a spectacle, for he mingled with the people dressed as a charioteer, or he rode around in his chariot. All of this aroused the mercy of the people, even against these culprits who deserved an exemplary punishment, for it was clear that they were not being destroyed for the common good, but rather to satisfy the cruelty of one person [Nero].[10]

There are many accounts of faithful, God-fearing men and women—old and young alike—who were killed because they named Jesus as their Lord. Consider Polycarp (AD 69–155), a younger contemporary and student of Ignatius. Born in Smyrna, he lived during the first generation after the apostles and was a disciple of the apostle John. According to one account, a mob of pagans shouted against Polycarp: "This is the father of the Christians, the destroyer of our gods, who teaches many not to sacrifice or worship." For this accusation, Polycarp was arrested, tried, and condemned to death. In making the death sentence, those in authority urged the old preacher to "respect his age,"

You will not be burned!

recant, and renounce his faith in Christ. He replied, "Eighty-six years have I served him [Jesus] and he hath done me no wrong. How can I speak evil of my king who saved me?" A fire was lit around Polycarp, but when, according to tradition, the flames refused to consume him, he was killed with the sword and his body thrown in the fire.[11]

The persecution under Emperor Diocletian was the last and perhaps the most severe official persecution by the Roman government. A decree was issued in 303 that ordered the destruction of church buildings, burning of sacred books, and demotion of any Christian from office or place of political power.[12]

The conflict between Christians and Rome continued until finally Christianity became the clear victor. Constantinus Chlorus, the father of Constantine, was governing Britain, Gaul, and Spain for Rome when the persecution broke out. He limited his persecution to tearing down some church buildings. The two men who were called emperors of Rome, Diocletian and Maximian, both abdicated their thrones in 305. At this point, Chlorus and another ruler named Galerius received the title Augustus. Through a complex series of political maneuverings, Chlorus' son Constantine was proclaimed Augustus by Roman troops. When Constantine defeated his rival Maxentius in battle, he became master of the empire.[13]

On the eve of Constantine's battle with Maxentius, he turned to Christianity. He later told his friend Bishop Eusebius, a reliable early historian, that as he was praying, he had a vision of a lighted cross (the Chi-Rho symbol that he put on his soldiers' shields) in the heavens bearing the words "Conquer by this." He later had a dream that God told him to use the same sign as a safeguard in all encounters with the enemy. In the ensuing battle, Constantine defeated his enemies at Milvian Bridge near Rome, took possession of the city, and established Christianity as an official religion of the empire.[14]

Many people wrongly state that Constantine made Christianity the sole religion of the empire. While he did make Christianity the "official" religion of the state, in reality he supported both paganism and Christianity. Yes, Constantine was a Christian, but he continued to hold the title *Pontifex Maximus*, the chief priest of the pagan state cult. When he died, the Roman senate, following long-established custom, declared that he was one of the gods. He also waited to receive baptism until he was on his deathbed. No one really knows whether Constantine was a Christian merely for political advantage or by conviction.

In either case, reforms under Constantine were many. The church was permitted to receive donations through wills. Sundays were placed in the same legal position as pagan feast days. The decisions of bishops' courts were respected by Rome, and bishops were allowed to carry out some official government functions. Constantine also kept Christian clergy in his home, and his children were instructed in Christian faith and practice.

Constantine built many large churches and gave money to bishops to do the same. He prohibited the repair of heathen temples that had been ruined and forbade any attempt to force Christians to participate in non-Christian religious ceremonies.[15]

With this newfound religious freedom, Christians experienced a significant shift in their worship practices. Robert Webber explains:

> The conversion of Constantine in the early part of the fourth century resulted in a significant worldview shift in the Roman Empire. A political world previously at enmity with the church was now courting the favor of the church and in the late fourth century decreed the church to be the only legitimate religion of the Roman world. This worldview shift put the church into a friendly environment where, with gifts of buildings in which to worship, the worship of the church shifted from intimacy to theater.[16]

Innovations to Worship Practices

Worship in the early church was simple and sincere. For the most part, public worship was structured loosely, relying on the bishop (overseer) or elder and deacons for spiritual guidance and accountability. Apparently, the organization of local churches varied from place to place. By the second century, three distinct positions of leadership emerged: bishop, presbyter—or elder—and deacon. According to historians, some local churches may not have been led by one bishop but by a group of leaders that were called "bishops" or "presbyters."[17]

During the times of the most extreme Roman persecution, Christians were considered an illegal, underground group not to be trusted. By Roman tradition, they were treated as a "menace," and "bore the marks of conspiracy." One historian writes that Romans saw Christians as:

> followers of a man executed for treason and obstinately refusing to acknowledge or sacrifice to the gods by which Roman civilization swore and which gave the emperor his divinity. In short, they were members of an illegal society which had to be stamped out.[18]

The church's opinion regarding popular forms of entertainment reinforced the perception that it was an enemy of Rome. Dancing, drama, and instrumental music were almost universally shunned by the early Christians. The Romans considered participation in dance, drama, and instrumental music marks of refinement and intellect and took offense at the position of abstinence held by most Christians. It was because of the association of these art forms with wickedness, corruption, decadence, and immorality of the pagans that the Christians resisted them.[19] In AD 111, Pliny the Younger, Roman governor of Bithynia and Pontus, characterized Christians not as criminals, but pacifists—honest and trustworthy. Pliny wrote the Roman Emperor Trajan about early Christian worship services:

> They were wont to assemble on a set day before dawn and to sing a hymn among themselves to Christ, as to a god, and . . . they pledged themselves by vow not to some crime, but that they would commit neither fraud, nor theft, nor adultery, nor betray their word, nor deny a trust when summoned; after which it was their custom to separate and to come together again to take food—ordinary and harmless food.[20]

In spite of the Roman army's best efforts to annihilate Christians, the church and the cause of the gospel continued to spread throughout the known world. Formal evangelism campaigns, as we know them today, did not exist. Rather, people heard about Christ in kitchens, shops, and living rooms. They heard about Jesus at the market and in places of business. Some brave teachers and philosophers held debates in their schools and won converts among the intellectual elite.[21] Still, the majority of converts were the fruit of the "anonymous" Christians whose witness—lifestyle worship—led others to follow Christ.

The Gathering Place for Worship—the Building

Because of the extreme threat of persecution, no emphasis was placed on the construction of huge, impressive buildings where Christians could meet for worship. They met in catacombs, caves, and private homes. Their emphasis was on spiritual community and the need to be a "pilgrim people" free from any attachments to this world.[22] Near the end of the second and the beginning of the third century, these "houses of the church"[23] became the main meeting places for believers, in part because they could not readily be identified as "Christian" buildings. Gradually, especially under the rule of Constantine, large buildings were built to accommodate worshippers.[24]

The Service of Worship

Christian worship in the second and third centuries reflected an attitude of service, sacrifice, and surrender, and in general was not based on a formal liturgy. It was Christians' custom to meet on the first day of the week (Sunday) because it was the day of the resurrection of their Lord. The meeting was a joyous occasion, including the celebration of communion. The tone was one of delight, joy, wonder, thanksgiving, and gratefulness—not sorrow, grief, or despair. In the beginning, communion was part of a communal meal. By the second century though, the "common meal" was abandoned, and the only eating in worship was the symbolic consumption of the elements.[25]

Among the first printed worship orders from the second century is the one in Justin Martyr's Apology to the Emperor Antoninus Pius, written around AD 150. Justin describes a typical Christian worship service as meeting in the "Christian Synagogue." There were two main parts to the service (liturgy). The order of service was extremely important and full of symbolism.

Part One: The Service (Liturgy) of the Word

> **Reading from the Scriptures:** Law, Prophets, Epistles, Acts, Gospels, Letters from Bishops
>
> **Psalms, hymns or spiritual songs:** sung by cantors between Scripture readings
>
> **Alleluias**
>
> **Sermon or Sermons**

Catechisms

Common Prayers: (mostly spontaneous)

Deacon's litany: for catechumens (new believers being trained in principles of discipleship) and those repenting and confessing sin

Dismissal of all by the faithful[26]

It was customary for everyone to stand during the reading of the Scriptures. Most believers did not own a copy of the Scriptures themselves, so public worship was the only time they had opportunity to learn the Bible. The reading could potentially be several hours in length. It was often a rather extensive presentation with significant times set aside for questions and answers by the believers.[27] Scripture was read from a rostrum, and people probably stood during prayers with hands and arms "stretched heavenward or folded on the breast as in ancient Jewish worship."[28] The "worship leader" was probably the bishop. Deacons were involved in reading the Scriptures, praying, collecting offerings, guarding the doors, maintaining order, and presenting the elements during communion.

Part Two: The Service (Liturgy) of Communion (the Lord's Supper)

Kiss of Peace

Offertory: giving of alms and gifts

Prayer of thanksgiving: including long spontaneous prayers followed by a common "AMEN"

Presentation of the bread and wine: given to the one presiding

Prayer over the elements: usually recounting the work of Christ, the power of the Holy Spirit, and the worthiness of God

Sharing of the Bread: the congregation

Sharing of the Common Cup: the congregation

Prayer of Benediction[29]

Three important characteristics of these early services should be mentioned:

(1) Prayers were not yet fixed, and the order of service (liturgy) was not so structured that free expressions of worship were prohibited.[30] (2) Only those who had been baptized were welcome at communion—including believers from other congregations. According to González, "Converts who had not yet received baptism were allowed in the early part of the service—the readings, sermons, and prayers—but were sent away come time for the communion proper."[31] (3) It was often the custom to gather for communion at the tombs of the departed faithful. This was especially true in the case of martyrs.[32]

At least two other events were important in early Christian worship: Easter and baptism. At first, the Christian calendar was simple, with every Sunday serving as a sort of Easter to celebrate Christ's resurrection. Fridays were given to fasting, sorrow, and penance. Sundays were days for rejoicing, fellowship, and joy. Once a year, Christians observed a very special day commemorating the resurrection, though there was disagreement over when the great day was to be celebrated.[33]

In addition to celebrating the resurrection, new converts were baptized, usually by immersion. Generally, baptism was administered once a year on Easter Sunday. Preference was that participants should be baptized in running water, which was termed "living water."[34] At the beginning of the ceremony, each candidate presenting himself or herself for baptism was asked three questions based on a document that today we call the "Apostles' Creed." These questions were to be answered by the new convert with, "I believe."

1. Do you believe in God the Father almighty?
2. Do you believe in Christ Jesus, the Son of God, who was born of the Holy Ghost and of Mary the virgin, who was crucified under Pontius Pilate, and died, and rose again at the third day, living

from among the dead, and ascended unto heaven and sat at the right of the Father, and will come to judge the quick and the dead?
3. Do you believe in the Holy Ghost, the holy church, and the resurrection of the flesh?[35]

Once the candidate answered in the affirmative, the bishop or deacon proceeded to baptize the new believer. González describes this baptism:

> It was customary for those about to be baptized to fast on Friday and Saturday, and to be baptized very early Sunday morning, which was the time of the Resurrection of Jesus. The candidates were completely naked, the men separated from the women. On emerging from the waters, the neophytes [new converts] were given white robes, as a sign of their new life in Christ. They were also given water to drink, as a sign that they were thoroughly cleansed, both outside and inside. Then they were anointed, thus making them part of the royal priesthood; and were given milk and honey, as a sign of the Promised Land into which they were now entering.[36]

Upon completion of the baptism ceremony, the congregation processed to its normal meeting place where the new converts had opportunity to partake of communion for the first time.[37]

Musical Practices in the Third and Fourth Centuries

Generally speaking, Christians in the first and second centuries sang psalms or Scripture texts, hymns of doctrine and faith, and spiritual songs. During the third and fourth centuries, the church saw a renewal of theology and evangelism through music.[38] The Gnostics and Marcionites used music to promote their false theology. Around AD 154, a teacher named Bardesanes and his son, Harmonius, wrote significant numbers of hymns that propagated a "brand of mystical astrology."

They used popular music as a means of communicating their lyrics, and much of the theology proved to be heretical. Their songs taught that Jesus was not equal to God in His divinity. To counter this trend, Ambrose of Milan wrote doctrinally pure hymns and in the process developed a simple, rhythmic, and syllabic chant that had strong appeal to the common person.

Worship was organized to meet the challenges of the growing congregations. The clergy, partly to control the spread of heretical hymns, took a more prominent role in the preparation and presentation of music for worship.

Methodology + Leadership

Summary of Events in the Early Church (AD 100–500)

Christianity began as an obscure movement—one among many in the Roman world. Its object of reverence, Jesus Christ, had been put to death by the Roman government. That same government tried first to contain Christianity and destroy it through persecution. The message of faith spread rapidly as the early Christians evangelized and educated the pagans. Not only did Christianity survive, but in the first half of the fourth century, it was adopted as the official religion of the Roman Empire.

Once the Emperor Constantine decreed (AD 313) that Christianity was legal and should be accepted throughout the empire, the church experienced unprecedented growth. Congregations grew so fast that it became impossible to train new pastors and deacons adequately before placing them in leadership roles. Bishops began writing down "acceptable worship materials" for the uneducated, but ordained, leaders to read. Citing the concern of heretical hymns, church leaders assigned all public singing in worship to the clergy.

In 410, the city of Rome was burned. In 476, the last of the Roman emperors was overthrown. The mighty Roman Empire crumbled. In response, bishops began to take on the role of politicians. A new nobility was created that included bishops and church leaders. The church formed a close bond with the state, and corruption followed soon.

In our next chapter, we will see how revival came to God's people during what historians call the "Dark Ages." This revival came in spite of the sinful and corrupt Roman Catholic Church, the mass slaughter of Christians by *the Muslims of Western Europe*, and *the Crusades* that followed. God once again saved his church through the lives of strategic individuals.

Notes

1. Justo L. González, *The Story of Christianity*, vol. 1 (New York: Harper One, 1984), 42–43.
2. Ibid., 44.
3. Ibid., 103–9.
4. Ibid.
5. Ibid., 36.
6. Ibid.
7. See ibid., 49–50.
8. See ibid., 33–35.
9. Ibid.
10. Ibid., 34–35.
11. Michael Collins and Matthew Price, *The Story of Christianity: 2000 Years of Faith* (New York: DK, 2003), 44–45.
12. See González, *The Story of Christianity*, 102–4.
13. Ibid., 107.
14. Collins and Price, *The Story of Christianity*, 58.
15. Ibid., 96.
16. Robert E. Webber, *Worship Old and New* (Grand Rapids: Zondervan, 1994), 95.
17. González, *The Story of Christianity*, 97.

18. Andrew Wilson-Dickson, *The Story of Christian Music* (Minneapolis: Fortress, 1992), 26.

19. Ibid., 28.

20. J. McKinnon, *Music in Early Christian Literature* (London: Cambridge University Press, 1986), 27, quoted in Andrew Wilson-Dickson, *The Story of Christian Music from Gregorian Chant to Black Gospel: an Authoritative Illustrated Guide to All the Major Traditions of Music for Worship* (Minneapolis: Augsburg Fortress, 2003), 28.

21. According to González, "Famous teachers, such as Justin and Origen, held debates in their schools and won converts among the intelligentsia. Even so, the early church worship centered on communion and only baptized Christians were admitted to its celebration" [services]. *The Story of Christianity*, 99.

22. Ivor Davidson, *The Birth of the Church: From Jesus to Constantine, AD 30–312*, Baker History of the Church, vol. 1 (Grand Rapids, MI: Baker, 2004), 287.

23. Ibid., 289.

24. See González, *The Story of Christianity*, 126–28.

25. Ibid., 93–94.

26. Webber, *Worship Old and New*, 96.

27. González, *The Story of Christianity*, 94–95.

28. Webber, *Worship Old and New*, 97.

29. This order is compiled from four accounts of third- and fourth-century communion services. Donald Hustad includes times of thanksgiving with improvised prayer (*Jubilate II: Church Music in Worship and Renewal* [Carol Stream, IL: Hope, 1993], 160); Davidson indicates that communion services were often held daily in the Western churches (*The Birth of the Church*, 284); González mentions a benediction with no description of the improvised prayers of thanksgiving (*The Story of Christianity*, 94); and Webber includes litany by the deacons, reservation of bread for the sick and absent, and psalms and hymns (*Worship Old and New*, 96–98). According to González, "although these were the common elements in a typical communion service, in various places and circumstances other elements could be added" (94). According to Hustad, by modern standards, the service would be considered theologically evangelical (162).

30. Webber, *Worship Old and New*, 98.
31. González, *The Story of Christianity*, 94.
32. Ibid., 95.
33. Ibid., 95–96.
34. Ibid., 96–97. Scholars are still not in agreement as to whether the early church practiced infant baptism.
35. González, *The Story of Christianity*, 63–64.
36. Ibid., 96.
37. Ibid.
38. Hustad, *Jubilate II*, 164–65.

CHAPTER 5

The Middle Ages (the Dark Ages) (500–1500)

During the Middle Ages, the church enjoyed its largest growth in history. By 1500 the cross was honored in all of Europe and much of North Africa and the Middle East. It was planted even on the shores of the Western Hemisphere in what is known today as North and South America.[1]

Yet there was a struggle between forces of evil that corrupted Christianity and forces of good that spread revival. Throughout the Middle Ages, the gospel was darkened in local churches, and the brightest lights shined in the monasteries of Europe.

For one thousand years (500–1500) there were a significant number of external developments that influenced the church—many of them related to the founding of Islam in Arabia in the early seventh century. Islamic armies occupied much of the Mediterranean world, including Palestine. The Crusades in the twelfth and thirteenth centuries were devoted primarily to freeing the Middle East from Islamic control, but the Ottoman Turks reestablished Islamic control in the fifteenth century. The most significant ecclesiastical development during this period was the division between Western and Eastern Christendom in 1054.

While there were no recorded times of worldwide revival during the Middle Ages, God still used his people to do his work for his purposes. For instance, **Girolamo Savonarola** (AD 1452–1498), an Italian priest who began preaching the same year that Martin Luther was born, challenged the corruption of both the church and the state from his pulpit in Florence. In vain, he tried to revive the Catholic Church from within the institution.

Under Savonarola's preaching, revival swept through Florence and transformed the city. Aristocrats tried to codify the content of his preaching into the laws for the city. Later, many other cities used his writings as the basis for a system of city government, and the laws that governed Florence spread throughout Europe. These laws included a just form of taxation, elimination of torture, statutes against gambling, and the institution of a court of appeals for those who were tried unjustly.[2]

Savonarola preached that all believers made up the true church, the body of Christ. He was best known, however, for preaching God's judgment upon sin. His Bible was covered with notes that came to him as he studied the Scriptures, and his sermons were expositions of the Word of God.

Savonarola had visions of the future and made predictions—some of which came true—and many feared him as a man of God. As a young man, his intense devotion to Jesus Christ became evident. He spent many hours in prayer, fasting, and kneeling at the church altar. His soul was deeply troubled by sin, worldliness, and the vice he saw in the church. He preached against luxury, splendor, and the wealth of the Medici family that ruled Florence. So passionate was his preaching that people would stagger out from his sermons dazed, bewildered, and speechless. Sometimes when he was preaching, people would break into tears and sob so loudly that the congregation could not hear the sermon.

He was such a popular preacher that people arrived at church five or six hours before the sermon just to get a seat. At times, men and women would climb the iron gate at the cathedral entrance and tie themselves there to sleep while they waited for him to come and preach. On one Christmas Eve while seated in the pulpit, Savonarola remained still for five hours in a trance as he fellowshipped with God. The people waited patiently during that whole time because they thought he was receiving a message from God. Some claim that his face illuminated as he sat waiting for his opportunity to preach.[3]

When Savonarola was transferred to the Duomo Cathedral—the largest church in Florence—he took the transfer and predicted that he would only be there for eight years, which proved to be accurate. He was very popular.

> People came along the streets, singing and rejoicing and listening to the sermons with such interest that when they were finished, the people thought he had scarcely begun. Savonarola seemed to be swept onward by a might not his own, and carried his audiences with him. Soon, all of Florence was at the feet of this great preacher.[4]

The Middle Ages—the Church in Transition

The Middle Ages began with the fall of the Roman Empire in 476 and continued until the beginning of the Renaissance and the Reformation in approximately 1500. This period saw the depopulation of the empire and de-urbanization due to the barbarian invasion of Franks from the north and the Islamic invasion from the south. North Africa and the Middle East, once part of the Eastern Roman Empire, were conquered by Islam, almost completely removing any influence of Western civilization and Christianity. The Middle Ages saw the establishment of feudalism, which was a return to an agriculturally based existence where people lived and worked on farms.⁵

Both the influence of Roman culture as well as the influence of the Greco-Roman culture dwindled during this period. The prominence of Greek philosophy waned, and the Roman law was not enforced. The new barbarian culture that replaced Roman culture was considered "lower" or even "primitive," and interaction between the empire's diverse regions disintegrated.

When a culture disappears, the religion associated with that culture also tends to die. This happened in North Africa and the Mideast, but it did not happen in Europe. In 496, Clovis, king of the Franks, was baptized. It was a landmark conversion of a Germanic invader coming into the Roman Empire. One Christian culture, therefore, passed and another Christian culture began.⁶

Following Constantine, Christianity became the new "state religion." Adherence to it was required in order to be a citizen of the region. The church developed new political elite with bishops and cardinals of the empire taking unprecedented control of huge regions and populations. There was growing unity between the church and the rulers of various parts of Europe.

As a result, the church grew more powerful politically, but weaker spirituality. Church leadership continued to compromise as the *true church* of Jesus Christ was engulfed by organization and outward pomp. Throughout the process, the clergy's focus on making disciples of Christ weakened, and was lost altogether in some cases, as ministers adapted to accommodate the unsaved masses. The church boasted of more converts, but there were few disciples of Christ.

[handwritten note: Parallels to the status of today's church.]

Strategic Personalities

Monasticism was an early response to the perceived corruption of the church. Becoming a monk was an individual response, and monks lived a solitary existence of seeking God. Anthony (250–356) is usually viewed as the first monk, but Pachomius (292–346) was the first to organize a monastery. He did so in Tadennisi, Egypt, with a dozen other monks. Soon, there were more than 7,000 monks living in Egypt and Syria.[7]

Benedict of Nursia (480–543) was so shocked by what he saw in the church that he moved east of Rome and lived as a hermit. In 529, he began what is known as the Benedictine Order with the founding of a monastery at Monte Cassino. Benedict's rule for life and discipline became the guide for monks throughout Europe and across the world. The monastery continued until it was destroyed during World War II.

Patrick of Ireland (389–461) lived during the age of the Church Fathers, but what he accomplished influenced the Middle Ages. He was born in AD 389, reared in comfortable Christian circumstances, and understood a smattering of Latin. At sixteen years of age, Patrick was captured by raiders, taken to Ireland, and for at least six years served as a slave there. He filled his nights and days with prayer and fasting, and dreams came to him. Once, he had a dream of a ship in a distant harbor, and he believed God was leading him to return to England.

When he arrived in England, he continued to have dreams, and it is said a vision came to him that was similar to the one at Troas calling Paul to Europe. The vision instructed Patrick to return and preach the gospel in Ireland. Many miracles are attributed to Patrick, but we are not sure how many actually occurred.

According to some accounts, when Patrick returned to the kingdom where he had once been a slave, the king rebuked him saying, "You know I must kill you." As the king reached for his sword, his hand was

Healed by faith (belief) in Christ.

paralyzed and he fell to the ground begging Patrick, "Pray for me." The king was immediately healed, and Patrick baptized him.

Among the best-known Irish Christians was a monk named Columba. **Columba** (521–597) was born in Donegal, Ireland. Very little is known about his early life. In 563, he and twelve of his followers sailed to Scotland where he established a center of missionary activity at Iona. His labors resulted in reaching the entire island with Christianity. He founded numerous monasteries in the Hebrides and on the Scottish mainland. From Iona, missionaries went all over Europe establishing churches and monasteries. Tradition states that Columba lived an ascetic life and compelled his monks to pattern their lives after his example.

Columba's last work was the transcription of Scripture. On the day preceding his death, he was busy transcribing the Psalms. As he finished transcribing words from Ps 34:10, "They who seek the Lord shall want no manner of thing that is good," Columba said, "I think that I shall write no more." The next morning, Sunday, June 9, 597, he was found dead before the altar in the church. So profound was the influence of Columba that for many generations, all the kings of Scotland were brought to Iona for burial beside their great apostle. One of Columba's students, Aidan (AD 651), followed his example and built a monastery on the island of Lindisfarne as a base from which he evangelized the people of Northumbria, Northern England.

In 909, Duke William of Aquitaine gave a charter to the Benedictine abbott **Berno of Baume** to establish a new monastery at Cluny in Eastern France. The monastery was free of all outside control. Berno and his immediate successor, Odo, were spiritual leaders, and many monasteries were reorganized to be like Cluny. The monks of Cluny were known for their financial integrity and sexual purity, becoming agents of social reform in their communities. By the tenth century, there were more than seventy monasteries throughout France under the control of the abbott of Cluny.

Anselm (1033–1109), **Bernard of Clairvaux** (1090–1153), **Thomas Aquinas** (1225–1274), and **Thomas à Kempis** (1380–1471) were among the Middle Ages' most important Christian figures. Some used songs as a means of communicating truth. Several wrote books of theology and poetry. Thomas Aquinas (1225–1274) defended Christianity using Greek—particularly Aristotelian—philosophy and science. Scholasticism, which attempted to bring Christianity into harmony with modern civilization, reached its apex in Aquinas. His emphasis on reason as the interpreter of truth had a lasting impact on Christian education.[8]

Francis of Assisi (1182–1226) was converted during an illness and led a reform movement in his native Italy. He preached a simple gospel of "Christ first, Christ last, Christ all and in all." During his lifetime, Francis preached across Italy and in places as remote as Spain and Egypt. He emphasized *congregational singing* and wrote hymns and songs in the language of the people set to popular melodies.[9]

The Franciscan Order was established in Italy by Francis of Assisi. It quickly became popular and in 1210 was chartered as an official order. Along with the Dominicans (an order of preachers), the Franciscans were the principal missionary movement of the day. About 1215, a young woman name Clare established a companion order for women named the Poor Clares.[10]

Around 1176, **Peter Waldo**, a rich merchant of Lyons, France, read the New Testament and was impressed with the claims of Jesus Christ. He sold all of his possessions and kept only what was necessary for the care of his family. He established a group known as "The Poor in Spirit" that was later called the *Waldensians*. This was a movement of laymen who preached the gospel far and wide until they were forbidden to do so by the pope. The pope decreed they could only preach when invited by the clergy. Because they refused to stop preaching, the Waldensians were excommunicated in 1184 and continued to exist underground.[11]

The *Waldensians* believed that people should have a Bible in their language and that the Scriptures were the final authority in matters of faith and practice. They went out two-by-two, following the example of Christ, establishing their own churches and appointing their own clergy.[12]

Two more strategic personalities need attention prior to moving into the events leading up to the Reformation:

John Wycliffe (1328–84) had a strong ministry among the academic community and ecclesiastical leaders in England. He called for the church to return to its biblical heritage. He condemned the church's temporal riches, citing the need to return to Christlike humility, and told church leadership that there was no biblical justification for their unbridled pride and materialism. Wycliffe condemned the sale of indulgences, mocked the doctrine of transubstantiation, and warned against the doctrine of papal supremacy. He also believed the music of the church had become too elaborate:

> In the old days, men sang songs of mourning when they were in prison, in order to teach the Gospel, to put away idleness, and to be occupied in a useful way for the time. But those songs . . . invite jollity and pride, and theirs lead to mourning and to dwelling longer on God's Law. A short time later vain trick began to be employed—*discant, contred* notes, *organum* and *hoquetus.*[13]

Wycliffe believed that everyone deserved the opportunity to read and hear the Word of God in their own language. Eventually, he was condemned as a heretic. In 1382, Wycliffe's disciples broke with the longstanding tradition of the Roman Catholic Church and translated the entire Bible into the English language.[14] Perhaps for the first time in a thousand years the whole Bible had been translated into a European language other than Latin. Although portions of Scripture had been translated into various vernacular languages, this was a new movement that laid groundwork for the Reformation.[15]

Armed with the Bible in their own language, a group of Wycliffe's disciples, called Lollards, went out two-by-two, taking the message of the gospel to villages throughout England. Each team of Lollards had a different portion of Scripture. They would remain at a village until they had read the entire portion to the inhabitants and explained its meaning. Then they would move on to another village. Early in the fifteenth century, it was estimated that half of the men in England embraced the teachings of John Wycliffe because of the Lollards. Over time, the term "Lollard" came to mean anyone dissatisfied with the church.[16]

John Hus (1370–1415) was influenced by the teachings of John Wycliffe and began preaching throughout Bohemia. Even though the books of Wycliffe were banned and burned in Prague, Hus preached the same truths from his pulpit. The masses flocked to hear him preach the Word of God. He also called for social reform in the nation.

Hus was persecuted and martyred for the cause of Christ on his fifty-sixth birthday. However, the truth of his preaching continued to resound among Bohemian brethren. Centuries later they fled for refuge to the estate of Count Zinzendorf (this became the starting point of the Great Awakening in Europe and America).[17]

Innovations in Worship Practices

One of the most important innovations in worship was the use of chant by Pope Gregory. He encouraged differing factions in the church to integrate the various Gallican, Ambrosian, Mozarabic, and Celtic liturgies into one "Roman structure" so that there would be uniformity in worship. The use of chant (singing one melodic line in unison) was drawn from the Jewish synagogue. Most, if not all, Gregorian chant has its origin in one of three types of music: cantillation—which are prayers, readings, and psalms; free composition;[18] and antiphons—which are short improvised phrases or refrains of Hallelujah inserted between verses from the Psalms.[19] Chant was taught and carried on throughout the following centuries.[20]

Though music was not the focus of Gregory's time as pope, it proved to be his most enduring legacy. As Andrew Wilson-Dickson notes, "Pope Gregory, a great diplomat, administrator and theologian, would probably be surprised to know that he is most widely remembered for the changes to the music for the Roman liturgy which took place during his papacy."[21]

The monastic tradition ushered in new forms of worship. **Benedict of Nursia** developed "The Rule," a system where he divided the day into (1) six hours of prayer, (2) five hours for manual work, and (3) four hours for the study of Scripture. In his "Rules," the six hours of prayer were divided into a daily round of services:

- Matins (morning)—before daybreak
- Lauds (praises)—at dawn
- Prime (at the first hour)—6:00 AM
- Terce (third hour)—9:00 AM
- Sext (sixth hour)–mid-day
- None (ninth hour)–3:00 PM
- Vespers (evening)–6:00 or sunset
- Compline (completion)–at the end of the day

The services were organized around the Psalms in such a way that all 150 psalms were sung every week. Prime, Terce, Sext, and None (the lesser hours) were much simpler and only lasted 20 minutes each. The order of service was as follows:

> Greeting
>   "The Lord be with you"—Priest
>   "And with your Spirit"—Congregation
> Hymn—everyone
> Scripture—chanted by reader
> Response—everyone
> Dismissal

Two types of music were generally sung during the Divine Office (another type of worship service under Benedict's Rule)—*modes* and *hymns*. Since there was no concept of the "key of a song," the monks developed a system called modes. Each mode was identified by its sequence of intervals. Most of the Gregorian chant, no matter how elaborate or complex, is based on one of the eight modes.[22] The second type of song used in the Divine Office was the hymn,[23] which could be Scripture, a paraphrase of Scripture, or based on a scriptural text or thought. Hymn lyric and melody were often improvised and freely composed.[24]

By the eleventh century, the hymn was used as a means for communicating theology—at times theology that was inconsistent with biblical truth. Many of these hymns contained "hidden messages" about God, creation, the relationship of man to the animal kingdom, and numerology.

To counter this practice, innovative hymn services were developed by the clergy that included the use of choir and vocal ensemble. For the first time in eight hundred years of Christian worship, the clergy sang chant in parts—polyphony.[25] (The use of a single line of melody is known as monody. Polyphony refers to multiple melodies sung together.) The principal melody was known as the organum. This was usually written down. Other complementary melody lines were composed and sung "against" the organum. These new chants were often very complex and ornate.[26]

The final innovation to worship during the Middle Ages was the development of written notation for music. For about a thousand years, Christian music was sung and passed on from generation to generation by oral tradition. Melodies had to be memorized. Guido D'Arezzo (995–1050) began to develop a system whereby singers could write down the music. He instructed singers to place above the words signs (neumes) that represented certain musical notes. Initially, there was no indication of the duration of notes, so interpretation of the songs differed considerably from congregation to congregation. Guido is credited with the invention of the "sol-fal" system of singing—shapes represented different pitches—and trained his young choirboys to differentiate between the tones and semitones used in each melody.[27]

According to Andrew Wilson-Dickson, "The importance of the development of notation cannot be stressed too strongly."[28] Notation allowed for the creation of music of different styles. Prior to its development, Christian music, like folk music, changed with the culture and times. With this invention, there was a way to codify the music and establish a musical heritage. It took many years for the "process to take hold," but in the end it provided a vehicle for communicating worship—even the worship we enjoy today.

Summary of the Middle Ages

The British Isles were largely untouched by these developments, and it was on the island of Iona that an Irish monk, Columba (521–597), established a significant educational center that was at once a monastery and a training ground for foreign missionaries. The monks practiced a new approach to the worship structure by introducing the service of Divine Office. They sang one-line melodies called chant. Later, chant was performed by male choirs (made up entirely of clergy members) and with multiple parts (polyphony). By the early eleventh century, musical notation had been invented and was being used in the worship service.[29]

What became of that Italian preacher noted at the beginning of this chapter, Girolamo Savonarola? He predicted that those who opposed him would die within a year. Three people died: Pope Lorenzo, the king of Naples, and Charles VIII, who invaded England from France. As King Charles advanced on Florence, Savonarola cried for the people to repent of their sins in order to save themselves from destruction. Savonarola went out to meet King Charles and begged him to spare the city. He told Charles that if he did not leave Florence, he would die. Charles retreated. The next king of France did invade Italy, not believing the pronouncement of Savonarola. He died.[30]

As a result of Savonarola's preaching, most of the hoodlums in the region exchanged the singing of filthy songs for hymns. The children went from house to house confiscating anything that people had acquired from carnivals and other venues of sinful entertainment, bringing them to the piazza to be burned. It is estimated that an octangular pyramid some 60 feet tall and 240 feet in circumference was burned because of the influence of Savonarola.[31]

Savonarola was not without his enemies. His many enemies among the aristocracy of Florence turned him over to the "religious authorities," and Pope Alexander IV excommunicated him for refusing to stop publicizing his prophecies. He was imprisoned and finally hanged in a public square in Florence.[32]

At the end of the Middle Ages some reformers ushered in a new dispensation of spiritual life. While the Renaissance brought academic freedom and renewed civilization to the masses, the Reformation brought spiritual freedom and the power of God to the masses. In the next chapter, we will see how these Middle-Ages reformers, John Wycliffe of England, John Hus of Bohemia, and Girolamo Savonarola of Italy—all bearing the light of the gospel—passed their mantle on to Martin Luther, John Calvin, Ulrich Zwingli, and John Knox and helped establish a series of new paradigms for worship.

Notes

1. Robert A. Baker and John M. Landers, *A Summary of Christian History* (Nashville: B&H, 2005), 290–91.

2. Elmer Towns and Douglas Porter, *The Ten Greatest Revivals Ever: From Pentecost to the Present* (Ventura, CA: Vine Books, 2000), 186–87.

3. Ibid., 189.

4. Ibid., 188.

5. Baker and Landers, *A Summary of Christian History,* 94–95.

6. Ibid., 69–70.

7. Towns and Porter, *The Ten Greatest Revivals Ever,* 178–80. The accounts regarding monasticism, Benedict of Nursia, Saint Patrick of Ireland, Columba, and Berno of Baume are taken from Towns and Porter.

8. Baker and Landers, *A Summary of Christian History,* 142–44.

9. Andrew Wilson-Dickson, *The Story of Christian Music: From Gregorian Chant to Black Gospel, an Illustrated Guide to All the Major Traditions of Music in Worship* (Minneapolis: Fortress, 1992), 139.

10. Towns and Porter, *The Ten Greatest Revivals Ever,* 179.

11. Ibid.

12. Ibid.

13. Wilson-Dickson, *The Story of Christian Music,* 55–56.

14. Ibid., 180–83.

15. Ibid.

16. Ibid., 180.

17. Ibid., 181.

18. Ibid., 38.

19. Ibid., 35.

20. Ibid., 31–32.

21. Ibid., 32.

22. Ibid., 34.

23. According to Augustine, a hymn is simply a "song in praise of God." This included songs where the lyrics were not necessarily Scripture—those closely based on a Scripture text. Andrew Wilson-Dickson, *The Story of Christian Music,* 35.

24. Ibid.

25. Ibid., 49.

26. Ibid.

27. Ibid., 44.

28. Ibid., 48.

29. Ibid., 47–48.

30. Towns and Porter, *The Ten Greatest Revivals Ever,* 181, 187–89.

31. Ibid.

32. Ibid.

CHAPTER 6

Reformation (1517)

In 1630, a relatively unknown minister named John Livingstone was invited to preach at an open-air communion service in the Scottish village of Shotts. Towns and Porter tell the story:

> John Livingstone rose to address the large crowd, reading from Ezekiel: "Therefore say to them, 'Thus says the Lord God: "You eat meat with blood, you lift up your eyes toward your idols, and shed blood. Should you then possess the land? You rely on your sword, you commit abominations, and you defile one another's wives. Should you then possess the land?"'" (Ezek 33:25–26).
>
> As Livingstone finished reading the text of Scripture, he challenged the congregation to "examine themselves" before taking part in the communion services. He then quoted Ezekiel 36:25–26: "Then I will sprinkle clean water on you, and you shall be clean; I will cleanse you from all your filthiness and from all your idols. I will give you a new heart and put a new spirit within you; I will take the heart of stone out of your flesh and give you a heart of flesh."
>
> During the communion and preaching, it began to rain lightly and people scattered to take cover. In response, Livingstone cried out, "If a few drops of rain so easily upset you, then what will

you do in the day of judgment when God rains down fire and brimstone upon those that reject Christ?"

In a moment, the power of God came down upon the crowd. People fell on their faces as if they had been "slain in the field of battle." Hundreds cried out to God in deep agony for their souls. By the end of the day, more than 500 people were converted to faith in Christ.[1]

Such was the spirit of revival during the days of the Protestant Reformation.

Moving toward the Reformation and Revival

Throughout the Dark Ages (AD 500–1517), the five key strongholds of Christianity were Jerusalem, Antioch, Alexandria, Constantinople, and Rome. By 1500, four of these were controlled by Islam as it conquered North Africa, the Near East, and parts of Eastern Europe. Only Rome survived, and biblical Christianity was obscured by political corruption among church leaders.[2]

From 1000 to 1350 Christianity won the formal religious allegiance of most of Northwestern and Central Europe. Christianity advanced into Russia and recaptured the Iberian Peninsula from Islam. Later, it moved forward into Iceland, Greenland, and North America. Small groups in Central, East, and South Asia professed belief as well, but Christianity's major strength and vitality was found in Western Europe.

Hostile invasions stopped, growth in commercial wealth occurred, and modern political states were born. Commerce revived, and Europe emerged from feudalism. Simultaneously, Islam and Buddhism, as well as Hinduism and Confucianism, grew in influence. Nevertheless, Christianity survived both the decline of its political protectors and the corruption of its own religious system. This period of resurgence was followed by another period of decline. Christianity's geographic frontiers shrank greatly. It vanished from most of Asia and parts of the Balkans. Moral decay spread throughout Western Europe.[3]

Meanwhile, in China, the Ming Dynasty replaced the Mongols and hastened the disappearance of Christianity there. Tamerlane, a fanatic Muslim, prosecuted extensive wars of conquest through Central Asia, Persia, Mesopotamia, and North India, causing the near end of Christianity in these areas.[4]

The Ottoman Turks took much of Asia Minor from its Christian rulers. In 1452 Constantinople fell before their advance. They swept into the Balkans and Eastern Europe, bringing Islam with them. The plague of "Black Death" devastated Europe. Absolute monarchs rose to power in the political states of Europe as the Holy Roman Empire declined. These monarchs exercised power over the churches in their domain.[5]

The Renaissance, with its pronounced humanism, undercut much of Christianity. The humanists believed that man could determine his own destiny, and they denied the existence of God and the supernatural. There was much scoffing at Christianity and much criticism of the church's structure.[6] By the end of the Middle Ages, the monasteries, clergy, and papacy were badly corrupted, and the worldview of many Europeans had changed.[7]

The Renaissance spurred the growth of individualism, and many immersed themselves in the study of logic, reason, mathematics, humanities, and the arts. Wealth was no longer controlled by feudal landowners, and new wealth emerged in trade centers across Europe, creating a middle class of bankers, traders, merchants and industrialists. Economic individualism stirred across the Western world, creating a desire for academic and creative individualism. People explored new dimensions of literature, the arts, music, and sculpture.

The main body of Christendom remained in Europe, and many Christian communities in Asia collapsed. There were advances in Spain and Russia, and some spiritual vitality was seen in the church in Russia. Additionally, widespread Christian mysticism existed in Europe. This was the period of Wycliffe and the Lollards, of Hus and the Hussites, of Savonarola—small indicators of explosive events to come. Other forces were coming on the scene: the Swiss Brethren, the Anabaptist movement in the Netherlands, the Brethren of the Common Life in Germany, the Pietists, and the Huguenot Revivals in France, which focused on obedience to Christ rather than mere political power.[8]

Overview of the Great Awakening—the Reformation

One individual, however, was used by God most prominently to break through the political and ecclesiastical mire—Martin Luther (1483–1546). Luther, an Augustinian monk of Wittenberg, challenged the Catholic Church's religious control over the Christian world. His challenge centered on the individual's freedom to exercise his conscience before God. Luther was bold to tell everyone, including Rome, that the just live by faith in Christ. On October 31, 1517, he posted ninety-five statements (or theses) on a church door in Wittenberg, publically challenging the pope and his authority over the church.

Luther believed that grace and the forgiveness of sins came through simple faith in Jesus Christ, not through meeting the demands of the church. He believed repentance from sin and faith in Jesus Christ were the only two essential elements for salvation. No person could simply buy his way to God through indulgences, pilgrimages, or membership in monastic orders. In Luther's mind, these were "spurious inventions of the Church to line its coffers."[9] Indeed, money from the sale of indulgences was used to finance the lavish building of St. Peter's Basilica in Rome. The Roman Catholic Church categorically rejected Luther's challenge.[10]

However, Luther's message generated support elsewhere. State rulers saw in Luther an occasion to free themselves from the oppressive economic and political control of the Roman Catholic Church. Following Luther's excommunication from the Catholic Church, Frederick, imperial elector of Germany, protected him and his followers from persecution. Luther's "desire for change was not motivated by politics but by sincere Christian conviction and the consequence of a balanced spiritual and family life."[11] By 1520, he was no longer trying to maintain any relationship with the "mother church." Later, he even called it the antichrist and publically burned a papal edict requiring him to submit to Rome.[12]

Strategic Personalities

Others appeared on the scene with Luther and preached against the same abuses of the Catholic Church and calling for a rediscovery of true Christianity and the true church.

Ulrich Zwingli (1484–1531), a young priest in Zurich, Switzerland, followed the example of Luther. Known as the "people's priest,"[13] Zwingli broke from the "organized Church of Rome" and established a Reformed church. In the process, he made substantial changes in worship by stripping away every practice that he believed could not be supported by Scripture.

His preaching was marked by scholarship, simplicity, conviction, and fervor.[14] In 1523, he published his Sixty-Seven Theses—a summary of his teaching. Citing the lack of scriptural support, he opposed the traditional fast during Lent. Zwingli also opposed transubstantiation, saint worship, pilgrimages, purgatory, statues, and even the Mass itself. He claimed that civil government should be under submission to Christ. He advocated the Scriptures, not church government or the pope, as the sole religious authority for life. He believed the church of Rome had departed from its "original purity" and was perverted. Finally, Zwingli believed the Lord's Supper was merely symbolic, and that Christ was not actually present in the elements.[15]

In 1536, **John Calvin** (1509–1564) published the *Institutes of the Christian Religion*, a theological treatise that became the foundation for a 1541 reformation movement in Geneva, Switzerland. Organizing the religious life of the city around his concept of model Christianity, Calvin believed Geneva was to be the "New Jerusalem." He argued that the new European trade cities should govern themselves under the direct authority of God—without the intervention of Rome. He said each person was to be a good citizen, submitting to proper government and paying taxes. The rulers of some cities went along with Calvin when they saw that the "Protestants" were obedient citizens who were productive in their private lives.[16] The church in Geneva, though not going as far as Zwingli, went beyond Luther in its rejection of Catholic worship practices.[17]

The Reformation extended to England when King Henry VIII decided to break with the Catholic Church because it would not grant him a divorce. He also wanted to get his hands on the wealth of the Catholic Church, which included extensive property holdings, and not be required to funnel money to Rome. Under Henry's reign, the Anglican Church (or the Church of England) retained many Catholic forms in worship rather than emulating the practices of reformers elsewhere in Europe. England shifted back and forth between Catholicism and Protestantism until Queen Elizabeth I stabilized England in the Protestant fold.[18]

John Knox (1514–1572) was educated at Glasgow University in Scotland, ordained into the priesthood in 1539, and became a reformer of Scotland. When Mary Tudor became queen over Scotland, he went into exile primarily in Geneva, where he learned doctrine and church polity from John Calvin. When he returned to his country, his preaching won many to the Reformed faith. Due to the numerous threats on his life, he left Scotland. The queen proclaimed him an outlaw and condemned him to death.[19]

Because the Roman Church had lost England and faced opposition in Scotland, it influenced France to send soldiers to Scotland to keep it in the Roman fold. In July 1560, though, the English army came to Scotland to help the Protestants. Knox hoped the wealth of the Catholic Church would come to the Reformed Church, but that hope was shattered by politicians who took it for themselves.

Knox wrote *The Book of Common Order, The Scots Confession of Faith,* and *The First Book of Discipline.* He prayed a famous prayer—"give me Scotland or I die"—and helped keep the Reformation strong in his country.[20]

Thirty Years' War (1618–1648)

One of the most important influences on worship in Germany was the **Thirty Years' War (1618–1648)**. Beginning as a Catholic-Protestant conflict, it quickly developed into a larger political, spiritual, and social conflict that at one time involved the entire continent of Europe. Many suffered extreme hardships during this time. Famine, poverty, and disease were the norm—especially in Germany.

During the war, Christian leaders opposed the established religious hierarchy and organized their own communities of believers. Most notable were the Anabaptists (meaning "rebaptizers"). They did not believe that the baptism of infants was biblical, and they limited the ordinance to adults who professed faith in Christ. They were persecuted by Catholics, Lutherans, and the Reformed Church, which resulted in their dispersal throughout Europe—especially to Switzerland, the Netherlands, and Moravia, Germany.[21]

Also important during the Thirty Years' War was a group known as the Pietists. Beginning in Frankfurt in 1647, their first leader was Philipp Jakob Spener (1635–1705). Spener believed that

> spiritual rebirth and the beginnings of a personal relationship with Jesus Christ were the prerequisite for Church membership, and . . . that the church's priesthood was not and should not be specially privileged.[22]

The main concern of this movement was to counteract the "arid scholasticism and cold formalism" that characterized the state Lutheran Church. Pietists encouraged small-group Bible study and prayer groups, and felt the chief goal in worship was edification of believers. Two major contributors to worship associated with the Pietists were the Moravian Brethren, under the direction of Nikolaus von Zinzendorf, and J. S. Bach.[23] Pietistic worship placed great emphasis on the transcendence of God and the need for repentance, conversion, assurance of salvation, and a personal relationship with Christ.[24]

Innovations to Worship

Prior to the Reformation, worship needed reform. Corruption was the norm for many clergy members—even in worship services. The simple services of the first century developed into complex ceremonies that were, of necessity, led by professional clergy. Worship historian Don Hustad suggests five areas of deterioration in the worship practices of the Roman Catholic Church.[25]

First, the preaching of the Bible was minimized. Though time was allotted for reading passages from the Bible—the Psalms, Gospels, and Epistles in particular—readings were often omitted in favor of stories about the lives of the saints. In some parishes, the priests were so poorly trained that they were not able to read Scripture.

Second, worship services were conducted in Latin, not a language spoken by common people. Consequently, the congregation became a passive observer.

Third, the communion service (Lord's Supper or Eucharist) became a priestly function. It was no longer viewed as a time of celebration, but as a time of mourning. The congregants focused on *seeing* the offering of sacrifice—not partaking of it themselves—and using the rosary for private prayers. Only the officiating priest was permitted to receive the bread and the cup. Most of the congregation received communion only once a year.

Fourth, the emphasis during the Mass was on Christ's death. Little attention was given to the resurrection or promises of the second coming.

Fifth, the Roman Catholic "Prayer of Thanksgiving" morphed into a long petition for God to receive offerings from the saints. As a result, many often feared that God would not accept their gifts.

Congregational singing was nearly eliminated in the Roman churches after the fourth-century Laodicean Council's decree: "If laymen are forbidden to preach and interpret the Scriptures, much more are they forbidden to sing publicly in church." Hustad also suggests four catalysts of change and innovation in worship: (1) the Lutheran Reformation, (2) the Calvinist Reformation, (3) the Reformation in England, and (4) the Free Church Reformation (which included the Separatists, Independents, Pietists, and Puritans).[26]

Luther's Innovations and Worship

Protestant congregational singing as it is known today began with Luther and the Reformation movement of the sixteenth century. As Hustad noted, "Luther is remembered as the individual who gave the German people the Bible and the hymnbook in their own language."[27]

The same conviction that motivated Luther's translation of the Bible into German also produced his desire for congregational songs. Indeed, his emphasis on the priesthood of *all* believers required that all be permitted to praise the Lord with singing. "Next to theology, I give the first and highest honor to music,"[28] he wrote. At the heart of Luther's worship philosophy was a desire for God's people to respond to him in their own personal song. "Let God speak to his people through Scripture," Luther wrote. "Let His people respond with the singing of their songs."[29]

Luther was a musician—equally gifted as a vocalist and a lutenist [guitarist].[30] He believed music to be of utmost importance in worship, and at times he used it to teach doctrine. In fact, Luther believed that he often won more converts through his singing than he did through his preaching.[31]

Two main types of Protestant worship music emerged from the sixteenth-century Reformation: Luther's German chorale and Calvin's use of the Psalter. Luther's songs, known as chorales, were popularized in Germany and Scandinavia. They were much less complicated than the polyphonic chant used by priests during pre-Reformation times. Most of his chorales for the congregation were unaccompanied unison melodies. The chorale paved the way for congregations and choirs to sing in four-part harmony—soprano, alto, tenor, and bass. Luther retained the use of choirs in the church service, in the Roman Catholic tradition.

Some consider Luther the *first evangelical hymn writer*—often composing tunes for his lyrics. His hymns served three purposes: (1) to demonstrate believer priesthood (theological), (2) to propagate Lutheran doctrine (pedagogical), and (3) to retain what he thought to be orthodox in the Roman Mass (eccelesiastical).[32]

There is no credible evidence that Luther used tunes sung in bars and pubs as source material for his hymns. Rather, he wrote in the style of secular German lyric poets. He also adapted texts and tunes familiar to his people from plainsong, sacred and secular folk-song melodies, and the Roman Catholic liturgy.[33]

Calvin's Innovations and Worship

Just as Luther placed the German chorale in an important worship role, **Calvin** brought metrical psalms to prominence. Calvin rejected any worship practice associated with the Roman Catholic Church. This included the use of organs, choirs, and *humanly composed* hymns.[34] He believed Christian worship should include only songs from Scripture—especially the book of Psalms. Thus, he rendered the psalms in metric poetry that could be sung to hymn tunes.

At one point, Calvin commissioned the French court poet Clément Marot to set all 150 psalms in meter. From this work, he completed and published the *Genevan Psalter* in 1562. These songs were sung in unison by the congregation and without any instrumental accompaniment.[35]

Calvin's worship philosophy included two complementary principles: (1) Keep the worship simple. Since music was to be sung by all the people, it needed to be kept accessible to all the people. Its beauty resided in its simplicity. (2) Worship should be modest. This applied to the presentation in particular. Since music was to be used for praising God, it should be offered with gratitude and reverence—not drawing attention to any person other than Christ.

The significance of Calvin's contribution to worship cannot be overstated. His books were used in England and the American colonies for decades following their publication. The metrical structure of the psalms in the *Genevan Psalter* followed the pattern of popular music, with several four-line stanzas sung to the same melody—always in unison.[36]

Worship historian Andrew Wilson-Dickson argues that the "three great Churches of Europe—Catholic, Lutheran and Calvinist—

demonstrated a triangle of dissension of which there are still echoes in every argument concerning [worship] and its music [today]."[37] Wilson-Dickson then quotes Lorenzo Bianconi's quip about the difference between the three groups: (1) The Catholic in church listens without singing, (2) the Calvinist sings without listening, and (3) the Lutheran listens and sings simultaneously.[38]

In Roman Catholic worship, there was no congregational participation. The clergy served as a mediator between God and his people. The Calvinists endeavored to go back to the early church and model the New Testament practice of singing songs from Scripture—mostly the Psalms. They believed Christian music and worship should conform to the pattern of the early church. The Lutherans sought to maintain a balance between worship like that of the early church and the expression of faith through new worship songs, like the music of Bach.[39]

The Reality of Congregational Singing

Although Luther had great concern for congregational singing, it was not until the end of the sixteenth century that hymn singing gained wide acceptance. Initially, the tradition of congregational participation in Christian worship did not take root. Most congregational songs were sung unaccompanied by musical instruments and in unison. The choir (if used at all) sang tunes with the melody in the tenor voice. While the organ was used in the service, it was not included during congregational hymn singing. By the end of the sixteenth century, hymns were written in four parts. Until that time, hymnal publications were designed for use by either congregation or choir—rarely, if ever, for both. Now, great attention was placed on keeping the harmonic structure of the hymn relatively simple so that it could be sung by congregation or choir.[40]

Summary of the Great Awakening

The Protestant Reformation was an awakening that gave people access to the Word of God. They were revived in their walk with God and became strongly individualistic in their approach to him, believing they did not need a priest to intercede for them.

Various attempts to reform the church characterized the period from 1500 to 1750, and each movement contributed something to the development of Christianity. Reformers ranged from Christian humanists to pietists, and from Protestants to Counter-Reformation Catholics.

The Great Awakening in Europe and America from 1727 to 1790 is the subject of our next chapter. The Reformation brought with it many exciting changes in the way people expressed their worship to God. Now, in this next awakening, we will see how God uses select people's creativity and unique hymn-writing gifts as a means of facilitating worship and bringing people unto himself.

Notes

1. Elmer Towns and Douglas Porter, *The Ten Greatest Revivals Ever: From Pentecost to the Present* (Ventura, CA: Vine Books, 2000), 136–37.

2. Ibid., 191.

3. Justo L. González, *The Story of Christianity* (New York: HarperOne, 1984), 342–61.

4. Ibid.

5. Ibid.

6. Andrew Wilson-Dickson, *The Story of Christian Music: From Gregorian Chant to Black Gospel, an Illustrated Guide to All the Major Traditions of Music in Worship* (Minneapolis: Fortress, 1992), 59.

7. Donald Hustad, *Jubilate II: Church Music in Worship and Renewal* (Carol Stream, IL: Hope Publishing, 1993), 181–86.

8. Towns and Porter, *The Ten Greatest Revivals Ever,* 181–84.

9. Wilson-Dickson, *The Story of Christian Music,* 60.

10. Ibid.

11. Ibid., 60–61.

12. Towns and Porter, *The Ten Greatest Revivals Ever,* 194.

13. Winkie Pratney, *Revival: Its Principles and Personalities* (Lafayette, LA: Vital Issues Press, 1994), 44.

14. C. George Fry and Duane W. H. Arnold, "Reclaiming Reformation Day," *Christianity Today,* October 22, 1982, 36.

15. Pratney, *Revival,* 45.

16. Ibid.

17. Towns and Porter, *The Ten Greatest Revivals Ever,* 136–38.

18. Ibid., 195–96.

19. Ibid., 136.

20. Ibid., 137.

21. Nanne van der Zijpp, "Moravians in the Netherlands," *Global Anabaptist Mennonite Encyclopedia Online* (1957), http://www.gameo.org/encyclopedia/contents/M6696.html; accessed May 21, 2012.

22. Wilson-Dickson, *The Story of Christian Music,* 97.

23. Hustad, *Jubilate II,* 204.

24. William J. Reynolds and Milburn Price, *A Survey of Christian Hymnody* (New York: Holt, Rinehart and Winston, 1963), 24–25.

25. Hustad, *Jubilate II,* 185.

26. Ibid., 186.

27. Ibid.

28. Robert Morgan, *Preacher's Sourcebook of Creative Sermon Illustrations* (Nashville: Thomas Nelson, 2007), 320.

29. Hustad, *Jubilate II,* 186–87.

30. Wilson-Dickson, *The Story of Christian Music,* 60.

31. Hustad, *Jubilate II,* 188.

32. Ibid., 186–88.

33. Wilson-Dickson, *The Story of Christian Music,* 62.

34. Hustad, *Jubilate II,* 186–88.

35. Reynolds and Price, *A Survey of Christian Hymnody,* 32.

36. Ibid.

37. Wilson-Dickson, *The Story of Christian Music,* 65.

38. L. Bianconi, *Music in the Seventeenth Century* (Cambridge: Cambridge University Press, 1987), 134.

39. Wilson-Dickson, *The Story of Christian Music,* 81.

40. Ibid., 62.

CHAPTER 7

The Awakening in Europe and America (1727–1790)

In our study of the Great Awakenings, significant attention is given to the study of the strategic times in history when God purposefully and passionately revealed himself to the world through times of revival and Holy Spirit movement. During each of these awakenings, a new paradigm for the practice of worship has emerged.

Most historians agree that the "awakening" in Europe and America from 1727 to 1790 is easily one of the first times in history when God used hymn singing and music expression as a means for introducing revival to his church. Although the First Great Awakening in Europe and America lasted only 50 years, it had an enduring influence on both church and society. The Moravians from Germany sent out more than 100 missionaries within 25 years and rejuvenated the foreign missions enterprise. In North America, David Brainerd, a young missionary, reached out to the native tribes around Crossweeksung, New Jersey. Families were strengthened as alcohol use declined, and hundreds of Indian men gave their hearts to Christ.[1]

This Great Awakening molded the moral character of the 13 colonies that were later organized into the United States. Fifty years later, when a French sociologist, Alexis de Tocqueville, toured America to determine the secret of its strength, he is alleged to have said, "America is great because America is good."[2] He saw the strength of America in its churches because they helped instill moral uprightness in the hearts of the people.

The Great Awakening in Europe and America (1727–1790) changed the character of churches. Many new congregations were led by pastors not trained in universities. John Wesley said that he would ordain a man who had "letters [could read and write], numbers [could count], and the Holy Spirit." Thus, Wesley used what have been termed "ploughboy preachers" to transform the world. These pastors, who lacked education but had the power of the Holy Spirit, helped transform society.

God allowed hymn writers to play a major role in this awakening. Calvinists produced liturgical hymns like those of Watts, while Pietists generated evangelical hymns like those of the Wesleys. According to Eskew and McElrath, "together these two types of classic hymnody *reformed the Reformation*."[3]

In America, a Congregationalist pastor named Jonathan Edwards (1703–1758) was a central figure in the Awakening. A graduate of Yale Divinity School, Edwards was an unwavering Calvinist who believed that every person desiring to receive eternal life in heaven must have a personal conversion experience.[4] Before preaching an important sermon he usually fasted and prayed for up to three days—always going without food and often without water. (The former is called a *fast* and the latter is called an *absolute fast*.)

In 1741, Edwards committed himself to a three-day, absolute fast to pray over a sermon he felt the Holy Spirit was leading him to preach— "Sinners in the Hands of an Angry God."[5] Once the sermon was written, he sought the power of God to deliver it. With a lantern in one hand and a fully written manuscript in the other, he read the sermon. Taking his text from Deut 32:35, "their foot shall slide in due time," Edwards told the congregation that they were like spiders in the hand of God being held out over the open mouth of hell. Only the grace of God kept them from being dropped into hell.[6]

In response, the power of revival swept the Enfield, Connecticut, church where he was preaching. People grabbed the pillars of the building, feeling they were being swept into hell. Women screamed. There were emotional outbursts throughout the congregation. Men wept as they repented of sin and sought to repair broken relationships with family members and neighbors. God used the brokenness of Jonathan Edwards to fuel the First Great Awakening in the New World.[7]

Overview of the Great Awakening

From 1517 to 1600, Reformation swept Northern Europe and England. Over time, however, churches that emerged from the Reformation needed reform and revival themselves. The theology and practices established by Zwingli, Calvin, Luther, and others had become *institutionalized* into programs, orders of worship, and large buildings. In many cases, passion for Christ degenerated into cold, established churches and ecclesiastical conflict. Andrew Wilson-Dickson provides an account of the condition in England during the concluding years of the seventeenth century:

> The Anglican Church was guilty of providing the outward image of worship, without being too concerned about the spiritual welfare of its congregations. The abject poverty and the pitiful quality of life for the masses were matters of no consequence for the very wealthy.[8]

It was the Age of Reason. Though Christian theology during the Reformation years was the foundation of much philosophy and intellectual discovery, within decades scholars pursued scientific explanations based solely on human senses without accounting for divine revelation.[9] They sought to create "an intellectual consensus for the view that the existence of God is unprovable."[10] Monarchs appointed bishops and *spiritual leaders* who often were nonbelievers or atheists. In Russia, Peter the Great appointed himself the head of the Russian Church. Many disregarded the pope's instructions regarding church practice in Spain, France, and Rome. In Austria, Joseph II issued more than 6,000 decrees directly impacting the religious life of the common people. "On the eve of the French Revolution," explain Price and Collins, "all but one of France's 130 bishops were aristocrats. The prime minister of France, although an atheist, was made archbishop of Toulouse and a cardinal."[11] Bishops in the Church of England were rarely religious, saintly, or devout men. Worship in the Lutheran and Catholic churches denigrated into religious ceremony void of substance or spiritual life.[12]

For the Christian church, the years from 1700 to 1790 became a *Period of Restoration*. The lightning of revival first struck in Germany at Herrnhutt. Then it crossed the Channel to England where John Wesley cried out, "The world is my parish." Finally, it crossed the Atlantic Ocean to America.

The Great Awakening in Germany

The Brethren of the Common Life spread over Europe through small home meetings. These believers were persecuted throughout Saxony and Germany but found a home and freedom at Herrnhutt, on the estate of Count Nikolaus von Zinzendorf. They saw themselves as the spiritual heirs of the Bohemian reformer John Hus. As they gathered to observe the Lord's Supper on a summer evening in 1727, the group experienced the presence of God so profoundly that they began a twenty-four-hour prayer meeting that continued for one hundred years. From that prayer meeting, hundreds of missionaries were sent to carry the gospel around the world.

The Great Awakening in America

Soon after the Herrnhutt revival, similar movements of renewal began breaking out in various parts of the United States. When the Moravians came to Georgia in 1732, they influenced John Wesley (1703–1791), an Anglican clergyman who planted a church in Savannah. Yet Wesley soon left Georgia a discouraged man. He wrote in his journal, "I came to Georgia to convert the heathen, but who will convert me?"[13]

Later, on May 14, 1738, Wesley was converted in a Moravian meeting at Aldersgate Street in London. Wesley wrote in his journal about the experience:

> In the evening I went very unwillingly to a society in Aldersgate Street, where one was reading Luther's preface to the Epistle to the Romans. About a quarter before nine, while he was describing the change which God works in the heart through faith in Christ, I felt my heart strangely warmed. I felt I did trust in Christ, Christ alone for salvation; and an assurance was given me that He had taken away my sins, even mine, and saved me from the law of sin and death.[14]

The Moravians also inspired Wesley and his brother Charles to sing. When the Wesleys returned to America, they brought to the new land their hymn traditions, choirs, and hymn writers.

The Great Awakening in England

At the University of Oxford, John Wesley and his friend George Whitefield (1714–1770) were members of the "Holy Club," a student group that read Christian classics and did charitable work among the poor. Charles Wesley (1707–1788) experienced conversion at Aldersgate a few days prior to his brother.

After graduation, the Wesleys and Whitefield began preaching across England in the established church, but they were not received well. The following February, when Whitefield found pulpits closing to him, he discovered an innovative way to reach the masses. While visiting his hometown of Bristol, England, he heard someone ask, "If [you] will convert heathens, why did you not go to the Colliers [miners] of Kingsworth [a nearby coal mining town where no church existed]?"

So on Saturday, February 17, 1738, Whitefield preached to about 200 coal miners in an open field. Within a month, more than 20,000 braved the cold weather to hear him preach, and thousands were converted.

Whitefield wanted to move to America to preach the gospel, and he needed someone to take over his ministry with the miners. He invited John Wesley to join him and take over the work, but Wesley was not inclined to preach in the open fields. On Sunday, March 13, Wesley wrote in his journal that he "could scarcely reconcile" himself "to the strange way of preaching in the field." He quipped, "I should have thought the saving of souls almost a sin if it had not been done in a church." When Wesley realized that Jesus himself preached in the open air, however, he was ready to do it. He wrote in his journal that he "submitted to be more vile and proclaim in the highways the glad tidings of salvation, speaking from a little eminence in the ground adjoining to the city, to almost 3,000 people."

Whitefield left England and made Savannah, Georgia, his home, establishing the well-respected Bethesda Orphanage. He traveled from Georgia along the Atlantic coastline, preaching in every colony until he had gone to the northernmost city in the colonies at that time. When people learned of Whitefield's appearance in their town, they would arrive before the evangelist by the thousands ready to hear him preach.

Wesley and Whitefield forever changed England and America through their innovative methods. The Church of England was the only official religion in England and many of the colonies during this era, but the Wesleys and Whitefield established dissenter churches that emphasized preaching, small accountability groups, and prayer meetings.[15] This new movement was called "Methodist."

Wesley remained head of the Methodists for more than 50 years and spent his life preaching in the fields, the streets, and Methodist preaching chapels. During his lifetime he traveled 250,000 miles preaching a total of 42,000 sermons. His activities are recorded in his *Journal* and letters. He died at the age of 88 and preached until the very month of his death.

Strategic Personalities

Many people who impacted worship during the European and American Awakening were ministers who also happened to be musicians.

Particular Baptist pastor **Benjamin Keach** (1640–1704) merits attention as a significant composer and writer of Christian hymns. While most of his ministry did not occur in the eighteenth century, he set precedent for the use of hymns in congregational singing, establishing a pattern for the century to come.

Throughout the 1600s, public singing from sources other than the Bible was considered by many to be heresy. Keach's hymns were viewed by many as devotional songs of "human composure." But in 1673, Keach "persuaded the majority of his congregation in Southwark to sing a hymn at the end of Communion, remembering the Gospel account of the Last Supper."[16] The practice was very controversial. Eskew and McElrath observe that "in view of the fact that Baptists at this time were generally opposed to such a practice, Keach's pioneering effort is all the more remarkable."[17]

Keach published *The Breach Repaired in God's Worship, or Singing of Psalms, Hymns and Spiritual Songs Proved to Be an Holy Ordinance of Jesus Christ* (1691). In 1691, he also published a collection of 300 hymns, *Spiritual Melody*.[18]

Long considered the "father of English hymnody," **Isaac Watts** (1674–1748) was a congregational minister who had a profound influence on England. A new era of congregational singing was established with his hymns. Eskew and McElrath contend that Watts provided "the confluence of Calvinist and Lutheran" song for worship:

> Lutheran hymnody and Calvinian psalmody—the two major streams of church song stemming from the Reformation—for generations had developed along parallel lines in England, Scotland, and Wales. Finally, in the early eighteenth century they converged and blended in the person and work of Isaac Watts.[19]

Watts was first a theologian and preacher. He believed the songs and hymns of the church "should express the gospel of the New Testament, regardless of the musical or literary form." He also believed that "Christian song should express the thoughts and feelings of those who sang rather than merely relate the experiences and circumstances of the psalm writers of the Old Testament."[20] Don Hustad makes the following observation about Watts and other early English hymn writers:

While renewal periods frequently have brought new forms of worship song, occasionally the process is reversed. New forms may come first, contributing to the spiritual health of the Christian community. Such a movement was the transition from psalm-singing to hymn-singing in English-language cultures, culminating in the work of Isaac Watts.[21]

Watts composed hymns that often captured the theology of his sermons. He possessed a unique ability to unite paraphrases of Scripture and devotional poetry. His philosophy for successful hymn writing included two key ideas. First, to engage in authentic praise, "Christian folk had to go beyond the mere words of Scripture to include original expressions of devotion and thanksgiving." Second, he believed that "if the Psalms were to be used in Christian worship, they must be renovated by giving them Christian content."[22]

Watts *modernized* the Psalter with the publication of *Hymns and Spiritual Songs* (1707). He integrated the concepts of New Testament praise and Old Testament psalm singing in his most significant work, *Psalms of David Imitated in the Language of the New Testament* (1719). Among his adaptations of psalms are "Jesus Shall Reign" (Psalm 72), "O God, Our Help in Ages Past" (Psalm 90), and "Joy to the World" (Psalm 98).[23] As Hustad observed:

> [His] hymns are not comparable to the simple, popular songs of many revival movements. He was one of the most brilliant men of his time, and, although he claimed that his verses were couched in "vulgar" (common vernacular) speech, they have been cherished by the church for almost three centuries. Watts has been said to combine most successfully the expression of objective worship with that of subjective devotional experience.[24]

Watts introduced into worship hymns of doctrine, devotion, and personal testimony. They were simple in meter and vocabulary with frequent use of repetition and parallelism—imitating the structural principles used in most psalms.

Most important to Watts was the presentation of Calvinistic theology in his hymns. For the first time, congregations sang about the glory and sovereignty of God, the security of election, and the atonement.[25]

Without doubt, Watts is the person who "most changed the course of English-speaking congregational praise."[26] He set the standard for all hymn writers to follow. Harry Eskew and Hugh McElrath aptly summarize traits unique to Watts's hymns:

Hymnody by Isaac Watts: Unique Traits in Form

1. It is simple in meter.
2. It is simple in vocabulary—predominantly Anglo-Saxon words, with preference for monosyllables.
3. It is striking in its opening line—tersely proclaiming the theme of the entire hymn like a headline.
4. It is frequent in its use of repetition and parallelism, following the structural principle of the Psalms.
5. It is often half-rhymed with liberal use of imperfect rhymes or assonances (similarity of two or more vowel sounds).
6. It is dramatic in its climax, usually expressed in a final stanza.[27]

> **Hymnody by Isaac Watts: Unique Traits in Content**
>
> 1. It is comprehensive in scope and cosmic background.
> 2. It is Calvinistic in theology: emphasis on doctrines dealing with the glory and sovereignty of God, depravity of human nature, security of the elect, and the all-sufficient atonement of Jesus Christ on the cross for the sins of humankind.
> 3. It is Christian in focus: Christ exalted and adored above all else as the very center of worship.
> 4. It is liturgical in purpose: inspired by the setting of public worship and conceived for the use of the people of the congregation in public praise.
> 5. It is scriptural in flavor: faithfully paraphrasing Scripture and masterfully incorporating biblical language, allusion, and thought.[28]

John and Charles Wesley were significant contributors to English hymnody as well. While Isaac Watts's songs focused primarily on the "transcendent character of God" (his power and awesome qualities that are beyond human understanding), the Wesley hymns stressed God's ability to identify with humans as a loving heavenly Father. Together, John and Charles Wesley wrote and translated more than 6,500 hymns. In general, John Wesley was the preacher and Charles was the composer. John's greatest contribution to English hymnody was the collecting, editing, publishing, and promoting of his brother's hymns.

Like Watts, John and Charles Wesley were careful to craft their hymns for congregational singing. Eskew and McElrath articulate six characteristics of the *form* of Wesley hymns and ten traits of their *content*.

Wesley Hymns: Commitment to Form

1. Rich in the variety of poetic meters. Wesley had superb mastery of at least twenty meters. They were not content to remain with the old psalm meters.
2. Constructed so that sound and sense coincide.
3. Wesley rarely fails to make the ends of his lines correspond with natural pauses in thought, thus making them very suitable for singing.
4. Bold and free in scriptural paraphrase. Rather than keeping strictly to a restatement of the original, Wesley makes imaginative comment on his scriptural passages.
5. Skillful in the mixture of Anglo-Saxon and Latin vocabulary.
6. Masterful in the use of the conventional eighteenth century literary devices—careful rhyme, repetition, anaphora (referring to a word or concept earlier sung with a different term), and chiasmus (opposite words are paired).[29]

Wesley Hymns: Commitment to Content

1. Replete with Christian dogma. Reflecting Moravian influence, Wesley is Arminian in theology.
2. Contain a body of experimental and practical doctrine.
3. Full of scriptural allusions.
4. Disciplined by biblical truth.
5. Expressive of passionate Christian experience.
6. Reflective of every mood of the Christian soul.
7. Full of joy and confidence.
8. Simple and smooth, speaking directly of important matters dealing with God and the souls of human beings.
9. Democratic in design and evangelistic in purpose.
10. Mystical, glowing with a luminous quality transfiguring history and experience.[30]

While Watts and the Wesley brothers dominated the landscape of hymn writers during this Great Awakening, there were other men and women who also made significant contributions to Christian worship. Some of these people are: John Rippon ("How Firm a Foundation"), John Newton ("Amazing Grace"), William Cowper ("There Is a Fountain Filled with Blood"), Philip Doddridge ("O Happy Day"), William Williams ("Guide Me, O Thou Great Jehovah"), Lady Huntingdon, Edward Perronet ("All Hail the Power of Jesus' Name"), Augustus Toplady ("Rock of Ages"), and John Fawcett ("Blest Be the Tie that Binds").

Innovations to Worship

According to Eskew and McElrath:

> Not until the arrival of the Methodists and Evangelicals in the mid-eighteenth century did compassion seem once more to return to Christianity, and with it came a renewed awareness of the need and the possibility of redemption, expressed in a great surge of hymns. With them returned the corporate expression of faith in God which lies at the heart of Christian worship.[31]

The Great Awakening in Europe and America (1727–1790) gave rise to a campaign by clergy in England and America to educate congregations in the art of singing. Many publishers of psalters and song books included long sections in their introductions explaining the fundamentals of music. Itinerate music teachers traveled from church to church hosting singing schools and selling psalters or hymn books. By the end of the century, more than 450 metrical psalters and 250 different hymn books had been published.[32] This caused some musical confusion because many of the books were published without written musical notation, and melodies to which the lyrics were set seemed to be in a constant state of change. Additionally, editors took great liberty to change texts to suit their own interests.[33]

By mid-century, hymns were consistently being used in worship—especially in rural and less aristocratic communities. Hymn writers strategically used hymns as a means for communicating theology and doctrine. For the first time, music was used as a tool for evangelism, as people began singing in public songs of personal experience—an important innovation to worship. Hymn writers of the seventeenth and eighteenth centuries were concerned with composing songs that expressed both doctrine and personal experience.

America and the Early Singing School

Beginning in the seventeenth century, those arriving in the New World from Europe brought with them the traditions and songs of the Old World. For Congregationalists and others of the Calvinist persuasion, this included metrical psalmody—especially among the English-, French-, and Dutch-speaking settlers. Among the German, French, and Scandinavian settlers, the chorale was an important musical tradition. Both metrical psalmody and chorales were sung without instrumental accompaniment.[34]

The establishment of singing schools among the early colonies had a major impact on congregational worship. Harvard-educated ministers sought to improve what they perceived as poor congregational singing, and they endeavored to teach their people to read music instead of singing by ear. In the process of learning songs, the early settlers learned doctrine, theology, and practical methods for leading worship.

In 1721, John Tufts, a pastor from Massachusetts, compiled the first singing-school manual: *An Introduction to the Singing of Psalm Tunes*. The book had two basic features: (1) an introduction to music theory (also called rudiments of music) and (2) a compilation of music with sacred texts for singing.[35]

By the end of the eighteenth century, singing-school textbooks were standardized in an oblong shape, and because most of their tunes had only one stanza of text, they were usually known as *tunebooks*. Singing-school books included metrical psalms, hymns, and noncongregational music—including fuging tunes and anthems by composers such as William Billings, William Walker, Oliver Holden, and Lewis Edson.

One benefit of the Singing School Movement was that it provided a platform for developing American composers and hymn writers. Singing schools also helped establish precedent for the use of indigenous folk melody and hymns in worship.

Summary of the Great Awakening

The Great Awakening in Europe and America (1727–1790) not only brought spiritual transformation to the churches of Europe and North America, it also brought musical renewal to the worship of God's people. Indeed, the Wesleys, drawing on the influence of the Moravians, brought a new song to the church. The theological descendants of Luther and Calvin translated their worship traditions to a new generation. Out of Calvin's tradition, for example, came a series of Psalters in French, including the *Genevan Psalter*, which was one of the first books of worship to be used in Colonial America.[36]

In the next chapter, we will see how God once again used revival to transform his people's worship during the early days of the United States of America. We will learn about the Camp Meeting revivals; the work of the circuit-riding preachers; the revivals in Kentucky, Tennessee, and Virginia; and the new approaches to worship that resulted. We will also learn about the outdoor meetings and the new commitment to multi-ethnic worship that deeply influenced the next Great Awakening.

Notes

1. Andrew Wilson-Dickson, *The Story of Christian Music: From Gregorian Chant to Black Gospel, an Authoritative Illustrated Guide to All the Major Traditions of Music for Worship* (Minneapolis: Fortress Press. 1992), 182–90.

2. Quote by Alexis de Tocqueville, think exist.com; available from http://thinkexist.com/quotation/america_is_great_because_she_is_good-if_america/10171.html; accessed April 5, 2011.

3. Harry Eskew and Hugh T. McElrath, *Sing with Understanding: An Introduction to Christian Hymnody* (Nashville: Church Street Press, 1995), 140–41.

4. Justo L. González, *The Story of Christianity*, vol. 2: *The Reformation to the Present Day* (New York: HarperOne, 1984), 228.

5. This sermon is among the best ever written and delivered by Jonathan Edwards, considered a classic and studied by American Christians and historians around the world. "Sinners in the Hands of an Angry God" provides a glimpse into the theology of the eighteenth-century Great Awakening in Europe and America.

6. Available at http://www.ccel.org/ccel/edwards/sermons.sinners.html.

7. Elmer L. Towns, *The Beginner's Guide to Fasting* (Ann Arbor, MI: Servant Publications, 2001), 126–27.

8. Wilson-Dickson, *The Story of Christian Music*, 110.

9. Empiricists endeavored to explain things on the basis of information received from their senses. French and German rationalists treated philosophy almost like a form of mathematics whereby everything could be reasoned from "first principles." Among the empiricists and rationalists were: John Locke (1632–1704), George Berkeley (1685–1753), David Hume (1711–1776), René Descartes (1596–1650), Baruch Spinoza (1632–1777), Emmanuel Kant (1724–1804), Voltaire (1694–1778), and Jean-Jacques Rousseau (1712–1778) (Michael Collins and Matthew Price, *The Story of Christianity* [Wheaton, IL: Tyndale House, 1999], 156.)

10. Ibid., 157.

11. Ibid., 163.

12. Ibid.

13. Elmer L. Towns, *Masters of the Faith* (Lynchburg, VA: Liberty Home Bible Institute, 1971), 41.

14. Ibid., 42.

15. It is because of their commitment to innovative methodology that the Wesley brothers were called "Methodists."

16. Ibid.

17. Eskew and McElrath, *Sing with Understanding*, 130.

18. Ibid.

19. Ibid., 131.

20. William J. Reynolds and Milburn Price, *A Survey of Christian Hymnody* (New York: Holt, Rinehart and Winston, 1963), 48.

21. Donald P. Hustad, *Jubilate II: Church Music in Worship and Renewal* (Carol Stream, IL: Hope, 1993), 205–6.

22. Eskew and McElrath, *Sing with Understanding*, 132.

23. Ibid., 133.

24. Hustad, *Jubilate II*, 206.

25. Eskew and McElrath, *Sing with Understanding*, 134–36.

26. Ibid., 135.

27. Ibid., 134.

28. Ibid.

29. Ibid., 138.

30. Ibid., 139.

31. Ibid., 110.

32. Wilson-Dickson, *The Story of Christian Music*, 111.

33. Ibid.

34. Ibid., 178.

35. Ibid., 179.

36. Reynolds and Price, *A Survey of Christian Hymnody*, 79–90.

CHAPTER 8

The Camp Meeting Awakenings (1780–1820)

Peter Cartwright, a strong, hardy, robust Methodist itinerant preacher, was ideally suited to evangelize over the rugged, independent folk of nineteenth-century Kentucky. His large, square shoulders and considerable strength were sometimes used to subdue the "rabble-rousers" in his meetings, and on many occasions he thrashed the worst rowdies who disturbed his preaching. His creed was to "love everybody and fear nobody." He saw nothing wrong with boxing a troublemaker so long as it was done in love and not revenge. Cartwright was converted in the "overflow" of the Cane Ridge Revival. He gave impetus to its further spread by becoming identified as one of its leaders.[1]

The Cartwright family moved from Amherst, Virginia, to Kentucky in 1785 to an area called Rogue's Harbor. The frontier spot had no school, no newspaper, and very little civilization. All the farmers were self-sufficient, eating what they grew and wearing what they wove from cotton or made from the skins of animals they killed. Cartwright described his early life: "I was a naturally wild, wicked boy and delighted in horse racing, card playing and dancing. My father restrained me little, though my mother often talked to me, wept over me, and prayed for me."

One day an itinerant Methodist preacher came through the encampment, staying at the Cartwright home and giving young Peter his first orientation to religion. When a camp meeting was held in his neighborhood, Cartwright said, "Scores of sinners fell under the preaching, like men slain in a mighty battle; Christians shouted for joy." Cartwright was not moved to conversion; in fact, he believed he could not be saved because he was a reprobate bound for hell.

Shortly after this, he returned to a home filled with drinking and dancing. He felt guilty when he got there, arose from his bed, and walked the floor, crying out to God. His mother was awakened by his prayers. Cartwright later recalled:

> All of a sudden my blood rushed to my head, my heart palpitated and in a few minutes I turned blind; an awful impression rested on my mind that death had come and I was unprepared to die. I fell on my knees and began to ask God to have mercy on me.[2]

Nevertheless, Cartwright failed to find salvation that evening. For the next three months, the young man searched long and fervently for God. Conviction of sin was so great, he was incapable of going about his chores; he could not seem to find pardon for his sins. When he heard about the great camp meeting, he attended and went forward with multitudes of weeping "seekers" to bow and earnestly pray for mercy.

It was there in his soul-struggle that Cartwright heard a voice saying, "Thy sins are all forgiven thee." Cartwright later described his reaction:

> Divine light flashed all around me, unspeakable joy sprang up into my soul. I rose to my feet, opened my eyes, and it really

seemed as if I were in heaven. . . . I have never for one moment doubted that the Lord did, then and there, forgive my sins and give me religion.³

The following year Cartwright was given an "exhorter's license" by the Methodist Church, recognizing the fact that he was already traveling and preaching to small groups.

The next year, the presiding Methodist elder gave him permission to form a circuit of churches in a new region of Kentucky. Cartwright protested, claiming that he was uneducated and an immature Christian. At length, Cartwright accepted the challenge and told God that he would go preach in a house, and if one soul were converted, it was evidence that he was called to evangelism.

That evening the greatest professing infidel in the area was present to hear him preach. Cartwright read for his text, "Trust ye in the LORD for ever; for in the LORD JEHOVAH is everlasting strength" (Isa 26:4 KJV). The infidel was soundly converted, joined the church, and became a leader in the church meeting in that house.

At age nineteen Cartwright was preaching with great unction and power, and his sermons were attended by marvelous manifestations of the Holy Spirit. "Often people were stricken down under an overwhelming conviction of sin," he observed. On one occasion, "the people fell in every direction, right and left, front and rear. It was supposed that not less than three hundred fell like dead men in mighty battle . . . loud wailings went up to heaven from sinners for mercy, and a general shout from Christians, so that noise was heard from afar off."⁴

Cartwright was a bold preacher of the gospel to unsaved people. One Saturday night he took lodging in an inn and, after the evening meal sat on the sidelines watching the people dance. A beautiful young lady came over, curtsied in front of him, and asked for a dance. Cartwright took the lady by the hand and led her to the middle of the floor, then announced to all in a loud voice, "I do not undertake any matter of importance without first asking the blessing of God upon it. . . ." Then he commanded the lady, "Let us kneel down and pray."[5]

Cartwright pulled her to her knees, then prayed loud and long, refusing to release her. Under the power of his prayers, some watching began to kneel, others ran out of the building, and a few sat still, unable to move. After the prayers, he preached a sermon and knelt down to pray again.

Cartwright continued praying and preaching until it was time to go to bed. The following day he preached a sermon, organized a Methodist society to meet in the inn, and took 32 into the new church. The landlord of the inn became the leader of the church.

Some criticized the emotional expressions known as "jerks" that were manifested in Cartwright's meetings, but they were manifested in all the great Cumberland revival meetings. Some said the "jerks" were purely nervous reactions caused by suggestion when others were seen barking. Others said it was the manifestation of the Holy Spirit.

Cartwright himself had the ability to sense when people were imitating the "jerks," and he dealt with them strictly. He even told the story of one man who, claiming to have the "jerks" but wanting to get rid of them, went to get a bottle of whiskey to "drink them off." As the man attempted to raise the bottle, a "jerk" more severe than any before broke his neck and he died.[6]

Such were the many wonderful and incredible stories of the Great Camp Meeting Revival. God did an unusual and incredible work in the lives of people during those years. What did God do to awaken to himself the generation at the beginning of our nineteenth century?

A Nation in Turmoil

To understand the significance of the Great Camp Meetings that sprung up across America, it is important to first see the events in context. In the years following the American Revolution, the United States experienced a long period of spiritual decline. Evidence of depravity was everywhere. The years of war took their toll on the church. The economy was in shambles. Church buildings had been burned. Farms were destroyed. Towns, by the scores, needed repair. Hundreds of clergy had died in battle, fighting the British alongside their congregants. While the new country won freedom from England, it lacked spiritual leadership.[7]

These conditions were complicated by the growing fascination of American intellectuals with European empiricism and rationalism. There was a rapid spread of secularism and deism among many. Deism denied the reality of God's intervention in the lives of people and rejected any notion of supernatural guidance or answers to prayer. Deists treated God as an "absentee landlord."[8] Deism taught that the Bible was myth, mostly allegory, and full of fables. Inspired revelation from God was thought to be nonexistent or irrelevant. Human reason determined good and evil. Man was exalted and God was ridiculed, mocked, denied, and scorned. Deism paid tribute to the supposed inherent goodness of man and incited lawlessness, self-indulgence, and immorality.[9] At one point, conditions got so bad in America that the French infidel and atheist Voltaire said Christianity would be forgotten in the new nation within three decades.[10]

America paid a price for its spiritual and moral decay. More than 15,000 of the 300,000 confirmed alcoholics in America died each year. Profanity was rampant, and women were afraid to go outdoors at night for fear of assault and rape. Bank robbery, fraud, infidelity, gambling, and licentiousness were commonplace.[11]

Revival chronicler J. Edwin Orr noted of American colleges and universities, "Christians were so few on campus in the 1790s that they met in secret, like a communist cell, and kept their minutes in code so that no one would know."[12]

As Christians became aware of the spiritual crisis on college campuses, their reactions were mixed. Many pious church members who lacked formal education were intimidated by those with formal degrees and did nothing. Others only prayed earnestly for the young men who had been sent off to the colleges to prepare for ministry.

One church historian wrote: "It seemed as if Christianity were about to be ushered out of the affairs of men."[13] The situation among many denominations was grim:

- Presbyterians publically deplored the nation's ungodliness but did little, if anything, to prevent rowdy behavior.
- Church attendance among Baptist churches was on the decline, and their few attempts at evangelism were feeble and ineffective.
- Since the death of Wesley, Methodists were losing more members than they were gaining.
- The Congregationalist Church of Lennox, Massachusetts, did not take in new members for nearly 16 years.
- Due to a lack of church business, the bishop of New York's Protestant Episcopal Church resigned and took a secular job.
- The Lutherans considered a merger with the Episcopalians. Both churches were desperate for members.
- John Marshall, chief justice of the United States Supreme Court, wrote to the Episcopal bishop of the Diocese of Virginia that "the Church was too far gone ever to be redeemed."[14]

What was the cure? How could any kind of spiritual antidote be applied to this dreadfully sinful disease? According to Orr, the cure came through a "concert of prayer."[15]

Indeed!

Meanwhile, across the Atlantic and little known to the desperate American pastors, God was already working in the heart of John Erskine of Edinburgh, Scotland. In 1784, convicted by the condition of his country, Erskine republished a work on revival by Jonathan Edwards, *An Humble Attempt to Promote Explicit Agreement and Visible Union of God's People in Extraordinary Prayer for the Revival of Religion and the Advancement of Christ's Kingdom*. The publication was made available to the churches of Great Britain, and their response was overwhelming. Entire denominations began to devote one Monday each month to prayer as "Prayer Unions" were formed all over the country. Soon, the power of God began to move across Wales. Once-empty churches in the British Isles were now packed, and thousands gathered in fields to hear the gospel. Thomas Chalmers along with Robert and James Haldane witnessed incredible church growth in Scotland. Ireland also experienced revival as the Methodists increased by thousands.[16]

Social reform followed. Anglicans fought for and won the abolition of the slave trade and the reform of Britain's wretched prisons.[17] In addition, God inspired one man to begin the Sunday School Movement.

Robert Raikes began the first Sunday school in Gloucester, England, in 1780, and the movement spread like wildfire. Essentially, Sunday schools taught children mathematics, reading, and writing in addition to providing religious instruction. Part of Raikes's intent with his Sunday school was to keep delinquents off the streets on Sunday.[18] The movement grew so rapidly that four years later, when John Wesley visited Leeds, England, he found 26 Sunday schools with more than 2,000 pupils taught by 45 teachers.[19]

By the mid-1780s, a Society for the Support and Encouragement of Sunday Schools throughout the British Dominions had been formed and more than 250,000 pupils were registered in Sunday schools. Later, the British Sunday School Movement would have a profound effect on America.

Events Leading to the Second Great Awakening

In 1794, a Baptist pastor named Isaac Backus called for clergy in every American Christian denomination to come together in prayer for revival, as the British had done before. A time was set. Prayer meetings convened every Monday at noon.

The Presbyterians of New York, New Jersey, and Pennsylvania joined this prayer movement. Francis Asbury signed on for the Methodist churches. Congregational, Reformed, and Baptist groups began to mingle in a network of prayer meetings. Soon the Moravians joined the movement and all of New England was praying at noon on Mondays for revival. In response, God began to pour his Spirit out on churches and ministries.

Revival began to take hold in New England, first among middle- and upper-class Anglicans. Spiritual renewal spread to the colleges. Revival first surfaced at Hampden-Sidney and Washington colleges in Virginia around 1787. It moved to Andover, Amherst, Dartmouth, and Princeton.[20]

God Uses a College President to Bring Revival

Timothy Dwight, who became president of Yale College in 1795, was among the best educated and most widely respected ministers of the day. As the grandson of Jonathan Edwards, he was familiar with the stories of the Great Awakening during the early and mid-1700s. More than just a man with knowledge, however, Dwight had caught something of his grandfather's passion for revival. Though an intellectual, he refused to believe that the pursuit of knowledge hindered faith in God.

The spiritual problems at Yale were serious. There was deep-seated disrespect for authority, and the students were caught up in deism, disregard for Scripture, and even atheism:

> Students found pleasure in nightly revelings that frequently included breaking tutors' windows and smashing bottles. Yale men regularly clashed with drunken townsmen in violent engagements where rocks flew and clubs flailed.
>
> Christian faith was unfashionable and reviled on campus. Voltaire became Yale's "prophet," and "reason" her watchword. Caught up in the fervor of the age, students renamed themselves after French philosophers, addressing each other as "Classmate Diderot" and "Sophomore D'Alembert," for example. Harvard had succumbed to rationalism long ago, and it appeared inevitable that Yale would follow suit. But for Dwight, it most likely would have.[21]

Recognizing the passion with which his students engaged in debate, Dwight challenged their thinking in a series of lectures that confronted aspects of the philosophy they had begun to embrace. Among his lecture topics were "The Nature and Danger of Infidel Philosophy" and "Is the Bible the Word of God?" In another lecture series, Dwight discussed various principles of deism and materialism.

In a forum that had long been sympathetic to rationalism, the college president's lectures convinced students that Christianity was intellectually credible. While many chose not to embrace the faith of their president, the student body came to respect him deeply and even to admire him. He preached the gospel of their forefathers in the language of their professors.

Dwight's initial ministry led to limited moral reform on the Yale campus, but it prepared the school for a more significant change. During a student revival in 1802, a third of the student body professed conversion. It was the first of several Yale College revivals under his leadership.[22]

Other campus revivals soon ensued. News of the movement at Yale sparked similar revivals on other campuses, and they all experienced a similar outpouring of the Holy Spirit. The "Infidel Movement" that some years earlier had gripped American colleges came to a quick end as students experienced God in a way that shattered their unbelief.[23]

The Cane Ridge Revival, 1801

The rugged men and women west of the Appalachian Mountains were not tempted by the lure of rationalist philosophy, but they experienced some of the same moral and spiritual problems that beset New England. According to historian Paul Dienstberger:

> What had arrived in the West was the biggest collection of law-breakers, whiskey drinkers, and the most uncontrolled lot in the world. Morals were non-existent. Few women were Christians and even fewer men admitted their faith. . . . The West was considered the most profaned place in all Christendom, and the only standards of judgment were the gun and "Lynch's" law, the rope. But, death and danger were daily threats from an arrow, or milk sickness, or even some wounded animal.[24]

One of the most infamous areas of this region was Logan County, Kentucky. It was known as "Rogues Harbor" because of lawlessness, gambling, drunkenness, and immorality. Residents of the community pledged to keep out any form of official law enforcement and civil order. A Presbyterian preacher named James McGready migrated to this community in 1796 from North Carolina and established himself as a strong preacher. According to Orr, his physical appearance also drew notice:

There was a Scotch-Irish Presbyterian minister named James McGready whose chief claim to fame was he was so ugly that he attracted attention. It was reported that people sometimes stopped in the street to ask: 'What does he do?" "He's a preacher." Then they reacted, saying: "A man with a face like that must really have something to say."[25]

McGready mourned with weeping over the evil so prevalent in the community. Upon arriving at the Muddy, Red, and Gasper River churches, he promptly set aside the third Saturday of each month for fasting and prayer, inspired by the prayer meetings of Northeastern Christians. McGready required the membership of the three churches to sign an agreement to pray at sunset on Saturday and at sunrise on Sunday:

> . . . we bind ourselves to observe the third Saturday of each month, for one year, as a day of fasting and prayer for the conversion of sinners in Logan county, and throughout the world. We also engage to spend one half hour every Saturday evening, beginning at the setting of the sun, and one half hour every Sabbath morning, from the rising of the sun, pleading with God to revive his work.[26]

In June 1800, at the Annual Red River Communion, more than five hundred people gathered from McGready's three congregations. Many traveled from as far away as sixty miles to attend. Because there were too many people for one man to serve, McGready secured five area pastors to help him administer communion and preach the Word. They included two brothers, John and William McGee, a Methodist and a Presbyterian respectively. Their sermons were simple and plainspoken, dealing with hell, heaven, and salvation for all who would believe. The meeting grew so large that they elected to move it outdoors. For three days, matters were orderly, serious, fervent, solemn, and sincere. Then a tangible sense of God's presence swept the congregation.[27] John McGee felt an irresistible urge to preach, and the people were eager to hear him. He began, and scores were converted.

So successful was the service that night that a second series of "sacramental meetings" was scheduled for late July 1800 at Gasper River. This was to be a four-day event with the main focus on reaching the lawless, depraved community with the gospel message.[28] This time, they expected large crowds. Since there were no buildings to accommodate the masses, McGready held his meeting in the forest. Congregants were told to come prepared to spend the night: "Bring your wagons and provisions." The people came. Frontiersmen drove horses and buggies from miles around. Making their wagons their home, they stayed for days.

Barton Stone, a pastor from Cane Ridge, Kentucky, was among those in attendance. So moved was he by the outpouring of the Holy Spirit, fervent prayer, confession of sin, and powerful praise services that he invited McGready to lead a meeting at Cane Ridge in August 1801. McGready agreed.

The attendance at Cane Ridge was greater than anyone expected. The meeting lasted from Friday to Wednesday, April 7–12, 1801. More than a thousand wagons were counted, and estimates of those in attendance range from 10,000 to 20,000.[29]

> Many went to Cane Ridge for religious reasons. Others made it an opportunity to gamble and carouse. Besides the pastor who had issued the original invitation, there were several Baptist and Methodist preachers. While some played and others drank, the pastors preached. A critic of the awakening later declared that, at Cane Ridge, as many souls were conceived as were saved. In any case, the response to the call to repentance was surprising and overwhelming. While some wept and others laughed uncontrol-

lably, others trembled, some ran about, and some even barked. The meeting lasted a week and since then many have been convinced that such gatherings were the best way to proclaim the gospel. After that time, when the words "evangelism" and "revival" were used, they evoked images of Cane Ridge.[30]

At the Cane Ridge Revival, a large "pen" was built near the "pulpit" similar to a cattle pen. However, it was not for animals. Tree logs were laid like pews within the pen so that those seeking salvation could go sit and cry out to God. While preaching was going on, there were dozens of people within the "pen" crying out for salvation or silently weeping their way to the cross. One observer describes a typical camp meeting this way:

> The glare of the blazing camp-fires falling on a dense assemblage of heads simultaneously bowed in adoration and reflected back from long ranges of tents upon every side; hundreds of candles and lamps suspended among the trees, together with numerous torches flashing to and fro, throwing an uncertain light upon the tremulous foliage, and giving an appearance of dim and indefinite extent to the depth of the forest; the solemn chanting of hymns swelling and falling on the night wind; the impassioned exhortations; the earnest prayers; the sobs, shrieks, or shouts, bursting from persons under intense agitation of mind; the sudden spasms which seized upon scores, and unexpectedly dashed them to the ground—all conspired to invest the scene with terrific interest, and to work up the feelings to the highest pitch of excitement. When we add to this, the lateness of the hour to which the exercises were protracted, sometimes till two in the morning, or longer; the eagerness of curiosity stimulated for so long a time previous; the reverent enthusiasm which ascribed the strange contortions witnessed, to the mysterious agency of God; the fervent and sanguine temperament of some of the preachers; and lastly, the boiling zeal of the Methodists, who could not

refrain from shouting aloud during the sermon, and shaking hands all round afterwards.[31]

The preaching at the Cane Ridge Revival was intense, hot, and moving. It was the opposite of worshippers gathering behind stained-glass windows to pray silently and listen quietly to a sermon. Another observer said:

> As the meetings progressed and the excitement grew more intense, and the crowd rushed from preacher to preacher, singing, shouting, laughing, calling upon men to repent, men and women fell upon the ground unable to help themselves, and in such numbers that it was impossible for the multitude to move about, especially at night, when the excitement was the greatest, without trampling them, and so those who fell were gathered up and carried to the meeting house, where the "spiritually slain," as they called them, were laid upon the floor. Some of them lay quiet, unable to move or speak; some could talk, but were unable to move; some would shriek as though in greatest agony, and bound about "like a live fish out of water."[32]

Wilson-Dickson quotes Ecroy Claxton's eyewitness account:

> The noise was like the roar of Niagara. The vast sea of human being seemed to be agitated as if by a storm. I counted seven ministers, all preaching at one time. . . . Some of the people were singing, others praying, some crying for mercy in the most piteous accents, while others were shouting most vociferously. . . . I stepped up on to a log. . . . The scene . . . was indescribable. At one time I saw at least five hundred swept down in a moment as if a battery of thousands had been opened upon them, and then immediately followed shrieks and shouts that rent the heavens.[33]

Soon the revival spread, spawning a movement. Thousands were saved at outdoor meetings across the South and West.

The Camp Meetings

About two years after the McGready meetings at Cane Ridge, people began referring to these outdoor gatherings as "camp meetings." Organizers hoped to duplicate the extraordinary working of the Holy Spirit experienced in Kentucky.

The meetings were a welcome time of fellowship for farmers. While they waited to harvest their fields, they gathered in great camps for community preaching, teaching, and renewal. Men would cut down all the low-hanging limbs of huge trees, leaving a canopy to protect the worshippers from the hot summer sun. People slept under wagons, and some brought tents.[34] Not only were the meetings meaningful spiritual events, they were social events, and in time became significant economic ventures.

Attendees cooked their meals over open fires, children played everywhere, and women visited with one another. Everyone gathered for preaching from 7 a.m. until dark. The pulpit was usually a platform nailed between two trees. The meetings were simple: enthusiastic singing from the heart interspersed between sermons of an hour's duration or more.[35] Evangelism was a vital part of the camp meetings.

In time, meetings became more structured and "spontaneity gave way to formal well-organized meetings bordering on military regimentation."[36] Sermons were scheduled and announced ahead of time. Meetings were held at 10 a.m. and 6 p.m. Attendance at all services was required. Meals were shared. A 10 p.m. curfew was enforced and "law enforcement committees" established rules to prevent theft and "courtship offensives."[37]

Baptists and Methodists embraced the camp meetings. Eventually, these gatherings developed into periods of revival. Baptists preferred to host the meetings in their church buildings while Methodists continued to embrace the large outdoor meetings. It became central to their strategy for church fellowship and evangelism. By 1811, more than 400 camp meetings had been organized. In time, tents were replaced by cabins, and camp meeting sites became retreat centers and vacation spots for frontier families.

Circuit-Riding Preachers

Circuit-riding preachers were critical to the success of camp meetings. Baptists and Methodists were eager to present the gospel to the settlers of the American frontier as "simply as possible," and they were willing to use preachers with little education. These bi-vocational preachers fueled phenomenal Baptist and Methodist growth during the early 1800s. When seeking to establish a new territory, the settlers were usually accompanied by a Baptist or Methodist circuit rider.

During the American Revolution, 243 Methodist churches were registered. By the War of 1812 there were more than 5,000 Methodist churches. Never had there been such an explosion of church planting and outreach. Brave Methodist circuit riders traveled across the newly established United States planting churches, preaching the gospel, and winning men and women to Jesus Christ.

Typically, these Methodist preachers were not college educated. Feeling a call from God to leave their occupations as farmers, shoemakers, carpenters, shopkeepers, and blacksmiths, they were known as "plough boy preachers." They never read their sermons as did the Anglicans and Congregationalists. Rather, they exhorted the people passionately from the Bible using anecdotes, illustrations, and analogies from everyday life.

Benjamin Franklin is said to have refused church attendance at Congregational and Presbyterian churches because the sermons put him to sleep, but attended street meetings to hear Methodist evangelists move him to tears. Franklin is quoted as saying, "I never take any money in my pockets to hear them, because they motivate me to donate it all."[38]

These circuit-riding preachers ended their sermons with an appeal to kneel in repentance before God. The circuit-rider preachers had learned to preach passionately by listening to passionate preachers. It was not their oratory that captivated the audience, but it was their power with God. Asbury once told his preachers, "Feel for power, feel for power."[39] It is said that the people loved circuit-rider preachers because they "made them feel." Because so many people fell to the ground in conviction under their preaching, they were called "holy knock 'em down" preachers.[40]

Known as the "wild man" preacher, circuit rider John A. Grande traveled the South. He once said, "I would sing a song or pray or exhort a few minutes, then the fire would break out among the people and the slain of the Lord everywhere were many."[41] Crowds followed him from one preaching point to another, "singing and shouting along the way." Circuit-riding preachers used cabins, taverns, tobacco barns, stables, and schools—any place they could find to preach the gospel. On many occasions, someone would donate a plot of ground and they would build a chapel, giving stability and presence to the Methodist Movement.

Strategic Personalities

The camp meetings were known for intensely emotional and personal encounters with God. In its early years, men like Archibald Alexander, Adoniram Judson (first missionary to Burma), and Samuel J. Mills were influenced by the Great Awakening. In the end, thousands of people all around the world were contributors to and influenced by the awakening on one level or another. Seven strategic people were used by God in a significant way to advance the kingdom during this awakening.

Dr. Timothy Dwight (1757–1817), grandson of the famous revivalist Jonathan Edwards, was president of Yale College (now Yale University) from 1795 to 1817. Dwight is credited with rescuing Yale College from the heretical teachings of deism, popular at the height of the Age of Reason and Enlightenment. He specifically "refuted the popular arguments [about] the reliability of Scripture and submitted his reasons for believing it to be the revelation of God." A gifted orator and speaker, he laid the foundation for the institution to establish a divinity school and college of law. During Dwight's tenure as president, the Lord blessed Yale with several seasons of revival. He developed a theology for revival and, unlike his grandfather, preached and supported the doctrine of free will.[42]

Nathaniel William Taylor (1786–1858) developed revivalist theology at Yale College. Mentored by Timothy Dwight, he pastored the First Church of New Haven (1812–22) and later served as the first professor of theology at the newly established Yale Divinity School.

Bishop Francis Asbury (1745–1816) was a longtime Methodist preacher from England. Asbury joined Thomas Coke in establishing the Methodist Episcopal Church. Originally sent to the United States in 1771 to head up the Methodist Church, Asbury visited every state, preached 17,000 sermons, ordained nearly 4,000 ministers, presided over 224 conferences, and stayed in 10,000 homes.[43] Tradition holds that Asbury traveled from Maine to Georgia, crossed the Appalachians 60 times, and wore out six horses. He never married. Asbury has been called the "Johnny Appleseed of the Gospel."[44]

Peter Cartwright (1785–1872) was a close friend to Asbury. He too was a circuit-riding preacher. Cartwright traces his conversion experience to the 1801 Cane Ridge meeting. In Cartwright's words, "It was there that I saw the divine light." Cartwright fiercely opposed slavery and preached against it at every opportunity. A preacher, traveling evangelist, and church planter for 60 years, during his time of service he baptized nearly 10,000 converts; preached 15,000 sermons; and debated Shakers, Mormons, and Abraham Lincoln—his opponent in the 1846 Illinois Congressional election.[45]

Bishop Richard Allen (1760–1831) was an African American who began preaching on the Methodist circuit in 1781. He was a freed slave who resided in Philadelphia. He was instrumental in establishing the African American Episcopal Church. He served the Philadelphia AME Church from 1816–31, which by 1820 had grown to a congregation of about 7,500 members. Richard Allen organized, assembled, and printed a hymnal documenting the hymns, songs, and spirituals sung by African Americans during the dark years of slavery.

James McGready (1763–1817) is considered one of the chief architects of the Cane Ridge Awakening (Camp Meeting revivals) of 1801. Born in Pennsylvania in 1763, he was a graduate of Log College (later renamed Jefferson College) and was personally mentored by its renowned founder and Bible scholar James McMillian. McGready was the first Presbyterian to pastor west of the Allegheny Mountains. In 1796, he left western North Carolina and moved to Logan County, Kentucky, to pastor three struggling churches (also known as societies). It was at the Gasper River Church that God began to stir in the hearts of people the need for revival. He was instrumental in seeing that the Cane Ridge Revival meetings were organized and executed according to established protocol. James McGready is considered the founding father of the Cumberland Presbyterian Movement.[46]

Barton Stone (1772–1844) was born in Port Tobacco, Maryland. He grew up attending the Church of England and was later influenced by and served in Baptist, Methodist, and Episcopal churches. He attended Guilford Academy in North Carolina. It was there that he sat under the teaching of Presbyterian minister and professor James

McGready. Stone was an important innovator during the Cane Ridge Awakening and was official host to the outdoor event at Cane Ridge, Kentucky. It was during the Cane Ridge meetings that Stone revealed that "faith is the only prerequisite for salvation." He was brought before the Presbyterian synod, accused of being an Arminian, and expelled from the denomination.[47]

Innovations in Worship

The camp meetings codified several important innovations in worship—especially for evangelicals. First Fourth Fifth, *public display of emotions* was rarely, if ever, seen in the strict Presbyterian, Congregationalist, and Baptist churches of the early colonies. The awakening at Gasper River Church and later at Cane Ridge provided opportunity to freely express worship, repentance, and sorrow for sin—even publicly.

Second, *evangelicals began to demonstrate their love for God through bodily movement and vocal expression.* Partly through the influence of African Americans attending camp meetings and services at Cane Ridge, shouting, clapping, dancing, and a variety of physical expressions of worship were permitted and even encouraged.

Third, *there was an adaptation and moderation of the traditional Calvinistic theology that drove earlier awakenings.* The 1727–1790 Great Awakening was driven by Calvinistic theology and included a strong emphasis on the intellectual aspect of Christianity. Believers had to know and cognitively understand what God wanted them to do, then obey in everyday life. This awakening, however, was driven by theology that emphasized emotions. Individuals had to "pray through" until they felt salvation in their souls. For instance, Peter Cartwright, a rugged Methodist itinerant preacher, prayed every night for two or three hours for more than two weeks searching for salvation until his mother prayed with him and he found his "peace" with God.

This greatly impacted worship services. The shift in theological emphasis opened doors for people to seek forgiveness of sin and publically invite Jesus to reside in their hearts. Congregants were invited to come to the front of the church after a sermon and respond to the messages.

Third, *meetings were held outdoors.* Circuit-riding preachers had been holding spontaneous services outside for decades. It was especially common for groups of believers to break out in song while walking or traveling with one another to church meetings. What made these outdoor meetings different was the attention to detail, setting up large meeting tents, grouping the meeting area in rows with split logs for pews, constructing a roughly hewn pulpit platform for preaching, and building a "pen" to which people could go during times of confession and repentance.

Third, *camp meetings provided opportunities for multiethnic worship.* Large numbers of African Americans (slaves at the time) attended these meetings and testified of conversion experiences. Their times of worship were enthusiastic, passionate, fervent, and exciting. Often, their wholehearted expressions of praise would drown out the preaching nearby.

> During the Great Awakening that spread from New England to Kentucky, millions of pioneers shouted, danced, barked, and jerked, getting release, entertainment and, incidentally, salvation. . . . Slaves attended these services and were profoundly influenced. They combined the revival hymns of eighteenth-century England with an African song style and created our greatest national music. . . . The first songs slaves sang on this continent were probably those sturdy eighteenth-century English [Isaac Watts and John Newton] hymns depicting amazing grace, Jordan's stormy banks, and fountains filled with blood.

Traditionally a leader would recite the line, after which the congregation sang in a slow, languorous manner called long or common meter, which allowed for intricate embellishments by each singer.[48]

Sometimes white men and women would join the black congregants in singing. Many took these newly learned songs back to their white churches in the city. At times, the celebration included leaping, singing, and dancing "after the order of David before the Ark."[49] According to Wilson-Dickson:

> The final moments of camp meetings literally broke down the barriers that kept blacks and whites apart. Joint worship followed with a free exchange of Christian music in a final march around the camp.[50]

Sixth, *folk music and spirituals were used as source material for worship*. In North America, all music genres used in worship trace their heritage to the early eighteenth-century singing school. These singing schools were accepted methods of music education for worship and were taught by itinerate music teacher/preachers who taught people how to sing in church. Singing schools often grew into large social events where families could gather for fellowship, build community, and participate in worship. With the singing school came a huge body of source material for worship.

Prior to the nineteenth century, almost all American congregations used music by Watts, the Wesley brothers, and other European hymn writers as source material. The songs were handed down by oral tradition or people learned the songs as they were transcribed and written down in shaped notes. Unique to this American tradition was music notation originally based on a four-shape note system. Later, in 1847, it was changed to a seven-note system that is still used in parts of America today. An entire body of literature was developed around this system of note reading that expressed a personal faith in God and encouraged congregational singing. The lyric was in ballad style, of simple language, and mainly concerned with salvation of the sinner. Interestingly, the African American community also adopted and adapted shaped-note singing to their times of worship:

> Another tradition found in the black fold church during this period was that of shape-note singing . . . for the singers sang "by note" rather than "by rote." They read music from *The Sacred Harp*. . . . They indulged in their special kind of singing when they gathered together for social entertainments in the community. The tradition included country festivals, where singers met for sessions lasting one or two days, and annual conventions or festivals that involved a large area of the state. A typical singing group might include as many as 500 people, who sat in a semicircle with the leader in the center. In addition to singing sessions, the activities . . . included classes conducted by teachers who received licenses to teach after passing examinations administered by the convention. . . . Often black communities had their own *Colored Sacred Harp;* it not only contained the old favorite hymns found in the white *Sacred Harp* but also hymns written by members of the community. . . . The repertory did not include spiritual or other kinds of folk songs.[51]

Music and worship styles of the camp meeting were primarily based on folk melodies of the Appalachian Mountain regions of the United States. The most common style trait of this tradition is the use of a modal melody based on a five-note (pentatonic) and other gapped scale. The refrains of these songs were of significance to their success. Sometimes refrains were simply added to an existing, well-known hymn. At other times, new songs were written for use in this style.[52]

Summary of the Great Awakening

The Great Awakening of the 1700s shaped the character of the emerging nation, but the Great Awakening of the camp meetings renewed and energized the church. This awakening combated deism. It turned many back to core religious and spiritual values, long held by Christians in the American colonies. Alcoholism, gambling, and prostitution abated. The abolition movement received a huge boost that lasted until the 1860s.

There was significant growth in church membership during this awakening. Methodists were the greatest beneficiaries of this surge, with more than 6,000 people added to their rosters during the first two years of the nineteenth century. Over the following decade, membership among both the Methodists and Baptists surged to more than 10,000. The Cumberland Presbyterians and Disciples of Christ were established as a result of the Cane Ridge revival meetings.

Overseas, the Great Awakening spurred births of the British and Foreign Bible Society, the Religious Tract Society, the Baptist Missionary Society, the Sunday School Movement, the London Missionary Society, and the Church Missionary Society. The modern missionary movement was born. Baptist missionary William Carey took the gospel to India. Adoniram Judson took the same message to Burma, and British evangelicals sent chaplains to their prison colonies in Australia. Samuel Marsden, one of those Australian chaplains, became the first to preach the gospel to the Maoris of New Zealand.

The successes of the camp meeting awakening set the stage for the very popular Sunday school revivals. In our next chapter, we will see how these Sunday school revivals changed the way families worship in private and public.

Notes

1. The account of Peter Cartwright recorded in Elmer Towns and Douglas Porter, *The Ten Greatest Revivals Ever: From Pentecost to the Present* (Ventura, CA: Vine Books, 2000), was originally told to Elmer Towns by J. Edwin Orr during a lecture series at Liberty University, Lynchburg, VA, in the late 1970s.

2. Ibid., 84.

3. Ibid., 84–85.

4. Ibid., 84.

5. Ibid., 85.

6. Ibid., 86.

7. Michael Collins and Matthew Price, *The Story of Christianity: 2000 Years of Faith* (Wheaton: Tyndale, 1999), 184.

8. J. Parnell McCarter, *Thy Kingdom Come: A Sketch of Christ's Church in Church History* (Jenison, MI: J. Parnell McCarter, 2004), http://www.puritans.net/curriculum/Thy%20Kingdom%20Come%20II/chapter62; accessed July 14, 2011.

9. Ibid.

10. Elmer Towns and Douglas Porter, *The Ten Greatest Revivals Ever*, 73.

11. McCarter, *Thy Kingdom Come*, http://www.puritans.net/curriculum/Thy%20Kingdom%20Come%20II/chapter62; accessed July 14, 2011.

12. Ibid.

13. Ibid.

14. Ibid.

15. Ibid.

16. Tony Cauchi, *The Second Worldwide Awakening of 1792*, http://www.revival-library.org/catalogues/1792ff/index1792.html; accessed July 14, 2011.

17. Ibid.

18. *Bicentennial Sunday School Bible*, Analytical Study Edition [KJV], Elmer Towns, ed. of Sunday School notes (Nashville: Regal, 1976), n.p. in Sunday school section.

19. Towns and Porter, *The Ten Greatest Revivals Ever*, 94.

20. Ray Shelton, *History of Revivalism*, http://www.fromdeathtolife.org/chistory/revival.html; accessed July 15, 2011.

21. Stephen J. Ahn, JE '96 Boston: The Yale Standard Committee, Yale University © 2001. http://yalestandard.com/timothydwight; accessed July 10, 2011.

22. According to Stephen J. Ahn and the Yale Standard Committee © 2001: "Another revival visited the campus in 1808. . . . In 1812–13 another revival came in which almost one hundred students gave their hearts to Christ. A fourth came in the spring of 1815, this one sparked by a group of students who gathered at 3:30 every morning to pray for the campus. One of the students was a convert from the previous revival, and later remembered these cold winter mornings of prayer as among the happiest of his life. Another student, who could not keep all the blessings he received to himself, happily carried a contagious faith to the Dartmouth campus, where afterwards, a revival ensued." http://yalestandard.com/timothydwightandyale.aspx; accessed July 10, 2011.

23. Towns and Porter, *The Ten Greatest Revivals Ever*, 61–63.

24. Paul R. Dienstberger, *The American Republic: A Nation of Christians* (Ashland, OH: Paul R. Dienstberger. 2000), chap. 4, http://www.prdienstberger.com/nation/index-people.htm; accessed July 15, 2011.

25. J. Edwin Orr, "Before the Great Awakening," reprinted from *The Role of Prayer in Spiritual Awakening* at http://www.revival-library.org/leadership/ra_prayer.php; accessed July 15, 2011.

26. Richard Beard, *Brief Biographical Sketches of Some of the Early Ministers of the Cumberland Presbyterian Church* (Nashville: Southern Methodist Publishing House, published for the author, 1867), 7–17, http://www.cumberland.org/hfcpc/McGready.htm; accessed July 18, 2011.

27. Porter and Towns, *The Ten Greatest Revivals Ever*, 79.

28. The following account is taken from Garrison and DeGroot, 1958, and posted to the Disciples of Christ website: http://www.cccdisciples.org/BStone.html; accessed July 15, 2011: "The Great Western Revival was a tidal wave of religious interest and excitement which began in about 1800, reaching its crest in 1803, and then gradually diminishing as it merged with the normal stream of evangelism. Its principal expansion fields were in Tennessee and Kentucky. On Sundays of May and June 1801, there was a succession of Great Western Revival meetings at churches in the region around Lexington, Kentucky. At the last three meetings, the attendance ran to 4,000 for the first,

8,000 for the second, and 10,000 for the third, according to contemporary estimates. The 'May communion appointment' at the Concord Church, of which Stone was a member, brought together between 5,000 and 6,000 people of various sects and many preachers of different denominations."

29. Ray Shelton, *History of Revivalism,* http://www.fromdeathtolife.org/chistory/revival.html; accessed July 15, 2011.

30. Justo L. González, *The Story of Christianity,* vol. 2: *The Reformation to the Present Day* (New York: Harper One, 1984), 245–46.

31. Ibid., 80–81.

32. Ibid., 81.

33. Andrew Wilson-Dickson, *The Story of Christian Music: From Gregorian Chant to Black Gospel* (Minneapolis: Fortress Press. 1992), 192.

34. Porter and Towns, *The Ten Greatest Revivals Ever,* 79.

35. Ibid.

36. Dienstberger, *The American Republic,* chap. 4, http://www.prdienstberger.com/nation/index-people.htm, accessed July 15, 2011.

37. Ibid.

38. Porter and Towns, *The Ten Greatest Revivals Ever,* 79.

39. Ibid.

40. Ibid.

41. Ibid.

42. Stephen J. Ahn, JE '96 © 2001 The Yale Standard Committee, http://yalestandard.com/timothydwight; accessed July 16, 2011.

43. Ibid.

44. Dienstberger, chapter 4, http://www.prdienstberger.com/nation/index-people.htm; accessed July 15, 2011.

45. Ibid.

46. Beard, 7–17, http://www.cumberland.org/hfcpc/McGready.htm; accessed July 18, 2011.

47. From Garrison and DeGroot, © 1958 and posted to the Disciples of Christ website: http://www.cccdisciples.org/BStone.html; accessed July 18, 2011.

48. Anthony Heilbut, *The Gospel Sound* (New York: Proscenium Publishers, 1985), xv–xx.

49. Christopher Small, *Music of the Common Tongue* (London: Wesleyan University Press, 1983), 156, quoted in Wilson-Dickson, *The Story of Christian Music,* 193.

50. Wilson-Dickson, *The Story of Christian Music,* 193.

51. Eileen Southern, *The Music of Black Americans: A History* (New York: W. W. Norton, 1983), 447–48.

52. William J. Reynolds and Milburn Price, *A Survey of Christian Hymnody* (New York: Holt, Rinehart and Winston, 1963), 91.

CHAPTER 9

The Sunday School and Charles Finney Revivals (1820–1850)

Titus Coan was a missionary to Hawaii during the decades of the 1830s and 1840s. God laid on the heart of this man a hunger and desire to tell the gospel story to a people group devoid of truth. They had never known the delivering power of the Holy Spirit. In 1836, Coan witnessed God working in the lives of people in Hilo, Hawaii. It was a remarkable working of God that spread across the waves to the rest of the Hawaiian Islands like wildfire. Coan told God's story.

Waimea, Hamakua, Kohala, Kona, and the other islands of the Hawaiian group were deeply moved by the gospel. Initially, many who worked among the Hawaiians considered them "so debased in mind and heart that they could not receive any true concept of the true God, or of spiritual things."[1]

As the movement continued, Hawaiians came to faith in large numbers. Christianity was demolishing the power of pagan religion. Thousands were finding freedom in Christ. Coan himself was convinced the movement was of God, not unlike revivals he had experienced in New England. "I had seen great and powerful awakenings under the preaching of Nettleton and Finney," he wrote. "And like doctrines, prayers, and efforts seemed to produce like fruits among this people."[2]

Occasionally, Coan witnessed physical manifestations not unlike those he had seen in the New England revivals. People would tremble as he explained the gospel, then fall helplessly to the floor.

While Coan was preaching on "Repentance Toward God and Faith in the Lord Jesus" to a large crowd gathered in an open field, a man who had been listening intently suddenly burst out in prayer, "Lord, have mercy on me, I am dead in my sins." Coan described what happened:

> His weeping was so loud, and his trembling so great, that the whole congregation was moved as by a common sympathy. Many wept aloud, and many commenced praying together. The scene was such as I had never before witnessed. I stood dumb in the midst of this weeping, wailing, praying multitude, not being able to make myself heard for about twenty minutes. When the noise was hushed, I continued my address with words of caution, lest they should feel that this kind of demonstration atoned for their sins, and rendered them acceptable before God. I assured them that all the Lord required was godly sorrow for the past, present faith in Christ, and henceforth faithful, filial, and cheerful obedience.[3]

At that point, concluded Coan, "calm came over the multitude, and we felt that the Lord was there."[4]

Overview of the Great Awakening

As the 1790–1820 Great Awakening began to spread across America, it was interrupted by the War of 1812. Much of America's energy was turned toward repelling British invaders in Washington and New Orleans. The White House was burned. There was the immediate threat of reoccupation by British troops, and it seemed as though America turned its attention away from revival to national survival.

Even though the clouds of war hovered over the new nation, God was still at work. Stories like the one above in Hawaii were told all around the world—in the British Isles, Sweden, Switzerland, France, Holland, Africa, Asia, and the Pacific. Revival was real and God was changing lives.[5]

In America, people still met in large numbers, especially in rural America, and the Spirit of God continued to make himself known at camp meetings and "brush arbors" all over the Western Carolinas, Eastern and Middle Tennessee, Kentucky, and Western Virginia. The Baptists and Methodists fully embraced the camp meeting and "brush arbor" format for special revival services. Their congregations were much more rural and often less intellectual than the Presbyterian and Congregationalist counterparts in New England. The Baptists and Methodists eventually developed the camp meetings into periodic revivals. These revivals became an important part of social life on the frontier.[6] Apparently, as these stalwart champions moved west, there was no shortage in preachers and evangelists among the Baptist and Methodist congregations:

> ... both Methodists and Baptists achieved rapid growth ... they were willing to present the message as simply as possible, and to use preachers with little or no education. While other denominations lacked personnel because they had no educational facilities on the frontier, Methodists and Baptists were willing to use whoever felt called by the Lord. The Methodists vanguard were lay preachers, many of them serving an entire "circuit," ... The Baptists made use of farmers or others who made a living from their trade, and who also served as pastors of the local church.[7]

As the government grappled with the survival of the new nation and the threat of war increased, God poured out his Spirit in yet a different but equally meaningful way on this nation. This time, revival came through the children and the Sunday School Movement.

In 1817, the American Sunday School Union (ASSU) was founded in Philadelphia to promote the establishment of a new medium of Christian education for children. Its purpose, as stated in the ASSU constitution, was:

> To concentrate the efforts of Sabbath School societies in different portions of our country; to disseminate useful information; to circulate moral and religious publications in every part of the land; and to endeavor to plant Sunday Schools wherever there is a population.[8]

This was an extension of the Sunday School Movement begun at Gloucester, England, in 1780 by printer, newspaper editor, and businessman **Robert Raikes** (1735–1811). Raikes saw the desperate need of the low-income children working in factories from sunrise to sunset. He sought to meet their physical, social, emotional, and spiritual needs through Bible teaching. It was his conviction that the parents of these children were "totally abandoned themselves, having no idea of instilling into the minds of their children principles to which they themselves were entire strangers."[9] "The world marches forth on the feet of little children," Raikes once remarked.[10] He believed that society, and the prison population, for that matter, could be changed by reaching the children with the gospel. He fed, clothed, educated, and trained hundreds of children on Sunday from 10 a.m. to 2 p.m. His basic foundation was to teach students to read the Word of God. The Sunday school gave an open Bible to the children.[11] In time, transformation of these children was dramatic and radical. Children discontinued their swearing and cursing. The crime rate dropped in Raikes's hometown and county. In 1786, "the magistrates of the area passed a unanimous *vote of thanks* for the impact Robert Raikes and his Sunday school had upon the morals of the youth of that area."[12] In the same way, God began using the Sunday school in America.

In 1830, the president of the American Sunday School Union, Francis Scott Key (author of the American National Anthem), challenged the annual ASSU convention with the vision of what he called "The Mississippi Valley Enterprise." Key reported that there were 4 million unconverted souls between Pittsburgh and Denver. He envisioned establishing within two years a Sunday school in every town in the frontier between Pittsburgh and the Rocky Mountains, an area of 1.3 million square miles. The anticipated budget for the project was $40,000.

Key called for 80 Sunday school missionaries to go and establish a Sunday school in every hamlet to reach the Midwest for Jesus Christ. He was active in enlisting many in the enterprise, including members of Congress, a justice of the Supreme Court, and his friend Sen. Daniel Webster. The outreach lasted 50 years: 61,297 Sunday schools were organized with 407,244 teachers and 2,650,784 pupils. A million books were placed in Sunday school libraries and 80 to 100 missionaries were employed each year in the project. A total of $2,133,364.13 was ultimately invested in the missionary project.[13] Many of those Sunday schools became Methodist and Baptist churches, and to this day account for the conservative bent of America's Midwest.[14]

Stephen Paxson was one of the American Sunday School Union's most well-known and dedicated missionaries. He was born with a speech impediment and was later nicknamed "Stuttering Stephen." Paxson had little formal schooling, but when he was thirty years old, his daughter, Mary, begged him to attend Sunday school and help her win a prize. He obliged. When he arrived, he was pressed into service to teach a class of boys. They read the Scripture, and he asked questions out of a book. Embarrassed that the Sunday school students knew more about the Bible than he did, Paxson read the Bible and eventually was converted. Wishing to minister in some capacity, he began to organize Sunday schools in his spare time. He became a missionary with the American Sunday School Union and traveled throughout Illinois and adjoining states.

His horse is said never to have passed a child without waiting for Paxson to stop and give out the gospel. In a leather-bound book carried with him wherever he would go, Paxson recorded the names of more than 83,000 children recruited for Sunday school.[15] He often returned east to raise money for libraries that would be used to establish Sunday schools. The sophisticated audiences alternately wept and laughed as he spoke, never heeding his grammatical mistakes. They gave liberally, becoming a part of founding Sunday schools in log cabins, tobacco barns, taverns, and dance halls. Paxson was credited with founding 1,314 new Sunday schools in more than 20 years of labor.

In nineteenth-century America, the Sunday school experienced phenomenal growth. From fewer than 100,000 children in 1824, Sunday school enrollment increased to more than 600,000 by 1831 and 3,250,000 by 1875. Church historians and Christian education experts agree that the "Sunday School did as much to 'tame the west' in the early days of [American] history as just about anything else. It also had an impact on the spread of Christianity westward."[16]

The Finney Revivals

Charles Grandison Finney (1792–1876) was a lawyer from Adams, New York, who was known for his atheism and antagonism toward evangelical Christianity. However, on October 10, 1821, he left his law office and climbed a hill across the street where he prayed from early morning until noon. Returning to his office, he announced that he had been converted.

Many people were surprised and suspicious, but he abandoned his law practice to preach the gospel across America. Finney was ordained by the Presbyterian Church in 1824, and a dozen years later aligned himself with the Congregational Church—primarily because of his preaching practices and shift in theological perspective.

Throughout his ministry, Finney used his skills as a lawyer to persuade congregations to make decisions for Christ. He was known as a powerful, emotional preacher who attracted great crowds. Whatever the population of the town, it was said that he could double it by his popularity and powerful preaching. Finney gave an invitation at the end of sermons for people to come and kneel and pray, to repent and receive salvation.

Finney's most remarkable revival occurred for five months at the Third Presbyterian Church in Rochester, New York, in 1830. As he preached, people would begin crying out for salvation, interrupting the sermon. Because Finney felt the contents of the sermon were important, he instructed the ushers to take the "repentant one" out to an after-meeting where he or she could pray for salvation.

Eventually, however, Finney had the backs of the first three pews of the auditorium removed, leaving three benches that he called "the mourners' benches." He instructed people not to cry out during his meetings, but to listen intently to the Word of God. He promised that at the end of his sermons he would invite people to come forward to the mourners' benches and seek salvation. They could remain in the church after the sermon for hours, as they "prayed through" to find salvation. This produced a major dispute with the pastor of the First Presbyterian Church, who felt Finney's style alienated his parishioners.

When Finney arrived in a new city for a crusade, often the elders in the host church would not allow him to remove the backs of their pews to form a "mourner's bench." As a result, he would place chairs across the front of the auditorium in front of the platform and invite people to come and pray for salvation. These chairs were called "the anxious seats."

Finally, Finney went to a Methodist church that had an altar where the congregation came to receive communion. Thereafter, Finney called his invitation the "altar call." Though others had called for response at the end of gospel sermons, Finney popularized the idea of an invitation at the end of a sermon where people could come forward to pray specifically for salvation.

One of Finney's more controversial practices was the remodeling of church sanctuaries. When confirming his availability for a series of meetings, Finney would often inform the trustees of the host church that they needed to remodel the pulpit area of their building. Telling them that "the present location of seats and pulpit does not fit our new and necessary mode of worship," he would instruct them to dispense with the church balconies and split chancel. Then, he would construct a platform across the front and place a pulpit in the middle to make certain the preaching remained the central focus of the services. Box pews were replaced by "simple pews" to allow room for people to respond to the invitation.

Finney also popularized "protracted meetings." He would continue to hold services and minister as long "as the revival season lasted." Campaigns would continue night after night, as long as the Holy Spirit was "blessing" and the people were responding to the invitation. This resulted in protracted meetings that would extend weeks on end.

Later, Finney recorded his techniques in *Lectures on Revival*. He already was at the center of controversy over many of the "new measures" (methods or techniques) that he employed. Some of his critics charged that he manipulated people, rather than letting the gospel do its work in people's hearts.

Finney justified his strategies by pointing out their success in turning people to Christ:

> God has established no particular measures to be used. We are left in the dark as to the measures which were pursued by the apostles and primitive preachers. . . . The appropriate means could bring revival to God's people [through] prayer, repentance, tarrying, and seeking God. I said that a revival is the result of the right use of the appropriate means, the means which God has enjoined for the production of a revival. Otherwise, God would not have enjoined them. But means will not produce a revival, we all know, without the blessing of God. No more will grain when it is sown produce a crop without the blessing of God. It is impossible for us to say that there is not as direct an influence or agency for God, to produce a crop of grain, as there is to produce a revival.[17]

According to one estimate, Finney's Rochester revival spread to 1,500 towns and villages through New England. Respected preacher Lyman Beecher said, "That was the greatest work of God and the greatest revival of religion that the world has ever seen in so short of a time." He estimated that more than 100,000 people had been converted and added to the churches in a single year through the revivals sparked by Finney.

Music and Worship Innovations

The Sunday School Movement and Finney revivals are not without significant innovations in music and worship. With the Sunday School Movement came an impressive number of Sunday school songs. These simple, easy-to-sing songs were especially effective with children. They were primarily for use in Sunday school meetings, personal or private devotions, and as part of individual, family gatherings. Ideally, the lyric and melody of the Sunday school song emphasized three phases of religious thinking: (1) the joys of heaven, (2) the love of Christ for the person singing, and (3) satisfaction gained in living the Christian life.[18]

Sunday school song lyric was subjective and set in common, everyday English. Little emphasis was placed on social issues such as feeding the poor, reaching the nations, or the growing abolitionist movement. Harmonic emphasis, melody, and musical style appealed to children and adults alike. The melody lines were rhythmically uncomplicated and harmonic language kept simple. The form reflected the verse with refrain style used with many of the camp meeting songs.[19] Perhaps the best-known song from this huge body of literature is "Jesus Loves Me," written by composer, music teacher, pianist, piano maker, and publisher William Bradbury.

The Finney revivals were equally innovative. In the words of Robb Redman, "the significance of Finney's approach to worship is hard to overstate."[20] Worship was purely pragmatic for Finney. Even so, he secured **Thomas Hastings** (1784–1872) as music evangelist for his meetings. Hastings was a leading music teacher, conductor, and composer of the day. He published "Finney Songbooks" and followed a new, unique-to-Finney, creative worship order.

Hastings may have been the first to establish a "clearly defined evangelistic music ministry."[21] Evangelistic Finney called his approach to worship the "new methods" and used songs with a simple and familiar melody and lyric.[22] According to historian Robb Redman:

> As Finney developed it, revival worship is characterized by emphasis on preaching. Other elements, such as prayer, reading scripture, and congregational singing and choral music (often

known as "preliminaries"), are secondary elements and should be related thematically to the sermon to prepare the audience for the message.[23]

Three aspects to Finney's worship should be noted: (1) Finney's "new measures" created a new, indigenous form of worship. He thoroughly contextualized worship and embraced musical and communication styles. (2) Finney's pragmatic approach to worship provided freedom over traditional practices by established denominations and conservative churches—particularly the larger congregations in the Eastern American seaboard. (3) Finney almost single-handedly inverted worship and evangelism. Heretofore, pastors believed that worship was primary and evangelism was a by-product. Finney believed the exact reverse—everything is done for the singular purpose of evangelism. In spite of its controversial implications, especially with the Presbyterians, this approach to revivalism quickly spread among Protestant churches.[24]

Regional Changes in Music and Worship. Around 1820, a division between Northern and Southern traditions in musical instruction began to impact the worship practices in the evangelical church. The sheer number of migrants moving to the United States after 1790 challenged music publishers to change their practices. These European migrants brought with them a round-note notational practice and hymn tradition based on slower harmonic rhythm, parallel thirds and sixths, and the more common major keys.

A movement called the *Reformed Branch* or *Progressive Movement* soon emerged in the Northern regions of the country. This movement encouraged music instruction and aided in the establishment of church and public school music, music conventions, choral societies and festivals, summer music schools, music normal institutes, and the publication of all types of music. In many ways, the movement itself was inspired by the revivalism, secular folk music, and Sunday school songs already part of the American landscape.

The dominant figure in this reform movement and leading composer was Lowell Mason. Mason advocated hymn tunes in a devotional style characterized by simplicity and dignity. Songs were generally set to original tunes or secular melodies suitable for the new urban revivalism of evangelist Charles G. Finney.

Counter to this movement was the *Character Notation Movement*. This approach to music instruction was more conservative, gave preference to maintaining the traditions taught by the old eighteenth-century singing school movement, and was adopted as a method of choice by Southern churches.

Prior to the Civil War, the impact of urban influence from the North was increasingly felt upon the rural, shape-note hymnody of the South. Heretofore, all shape-note songbooks were based on a four-shaped-note practice. Now, a new type of shaped-note tradition, developed around 1841, used a new seven-shape version for music notation. The strength of this approach to music instruction was in teaching students to sing and play in any key—of particular value to those using the folk tunes of Appalachia as a primary resource material for worship.

Even so, the seven-shape tune books included smaller portions of indigenous folk hymns and larger portions of European music. By the end of the century, musicians usually associated with the *Reformed Notation* Movement also composed music for the *Character Notation* Movement.

In context, the Southern shape-note gospel hymnody has been largely rural or small town. The nineteenth-century singing school and use of shape notes in worship has been basically for Southern church tradition rather than part of mass revivalism.

Western European Developments (1830–1850). While the events and changes in Europe had little if any direct impact on the revivalism of 1820–1850, musical practices and source material for hymn singing certainly had a growing impact on church worship in the American Northern regions. Changes in methodology certainly reflected the wave of Protestant Liberalism and the European intellectual elite.[25] As a result, European hymn writers during the nineteenth century were more influenced by a renewed interest in the classics. They were often more interested in intellectual and creative fulfillment than in the emotional expression of theological tenets.

A new religious movement known as the *Oxford* or *Tractarian Movement*[26] began in England during the 1830s. The Oxford emphasis was a reaction to the many "indifferent" and "careless worship services conducted by the more independent and non-conformist congregations."[27] According to Don Hustad's analysis in his landmark book *Jubilate II: Church Music in Worship and Renewal*, the Oxford Movement . . .

> brought back much of the pre-Reformation tradition into a number of British churches—reviving the ancient Greek and Latin Hymns (in English translations), Gregorian chant, and an increased use of symbolism (in vestments, furnishings, and liturgical action). This Anglican "counter-Reformation" or "counter-Evangelicalism," coupled with the commitment to liberal theology by another group of scholars, resulted eventually in the development of three Anglican parties in the 19th century . . . The Anglo-Catholics . . . Low church adherents . . . and the Broad Churches.[28]

Each of these parties represented a strategic and notable commitment to specific theological tenets. Thus, hymns written during this time are generally classified as follows:

(1) *High Church Hymns.* Writers of these hymns were Anglicans who resisted what they saw as a drift toward Rome. Even so, they were the closest to Roman Catholic theology. They were concerned with preserving the integrity of liturgical practices and traditions and looked with great disdain to the emotionalism associated with the evangelical.[29]

(2) *Evangelical or Low Church Hymns.* Writers of these songs and hymns often expressed a concern for the spiritual and social welfare of individuals. They rejected the Oxford Movement in general and remained strongly evangelical in preaching and worship style.

(3) *Broad Church Hymns.* These were written by those who represented the liberal and modern factions in the Anglican Church. They tend to be "moderate in liturgy but liberal in theology, emphasizing social, rather than personal, salvation."[30]

One other notable hymn type or style should be mentioned: The *Dissenting Hymns* were written by those in the Presbyterian, Methodist, and Baptist congregations. These groups had broken away from the established state church in England. Worship and the singing of hymns reached a new level of spiritual vitality during this period of time.[31]

As one can imagine, reaction in the West to the Protestant Liberalism of Europe was swift and decisive. Most viewed the movement a "threat to the very core of the Christian faith."[32]

Strategic Personalities

In addition to **Charles Finney** and those affiliated with the American Sunday School Union itself, strategic personalities having impact on worship practices during this period include, but are not limited to: William B. Bradbury, Thomas Hastings, George Root, William Doane, Charles Converse, J. G. Towner, , Lowell Mason, and Stephen Foster, American composer of "My Old Kentucky Home," "Jeanie with the

Light Brown Hair," "Beautiful Dreamer," and "Oh Suzanna." Each of these musicians made contributions to the body of literature eventually known as Sunday school song.

Influence of Lowell Mason. **Lowell Mason** (1792–1872) was more of an educator and publisher than a writer of Sunday school or gospel songs. He was a banker by day and musician by night and weekend. He was a gifted organist and author-composer of hymns such as "My Faith Looks Up to Thee," "From Greenland's Icy Mountains," and the "official arrangement" in most hymnals of "Joy to the World" by Isaac Watts.

In 1833, Mason cofounded the Boston Academy of Music. In 1838, he was named the first superintendent of public school music in Boston. Mason, along with William Bradbury and Thomas Hastings, developed the first programs of music education in public schools.[33] He was influential in developing the Eastern singing schools and often associated with well-known church musician-teachers. Mason and Bradbury traveled and studied in Europe and advocated the use of "scientific music" and helped establish the *Reformed Notation Movement*. Most notable is Mason's influence over many of the composer-music educators of the day, including: George Root, Thomas Hastings, and William Bradbury. Through a series of eight music books specifically published for church-sponsored singing schools, Mason successfully merged the popular singing style of the era with the theology and mission of the evangelical church. Lowell Mason wrote more than 1,600 "religious works" and is often called the "father of American church music." While there is little evidence that Mason himself was an *evangelist* or *revivalist*, he certainly had a profound influence on others who were clearly identified with the movements.

Summary: Paradigm Shifts and Innovations

Innovations in worship established by the Sunday School Movement opened the door for more radical changes by evangelists and itinerate Bible preacher-teachers. New, easy-to-sing songs were introduced for use in private devotions, Sunday school meetings, and family gatherings. Song lyrics were set in everyday English. Harmonic language was simple, and melodic lines were kept rhythmically uncomplicated.

Characteristics of American worship music include: (1) an emphasis on national hymns spurred on by a new sense of patriotism; (2) emphasis on songs promoting worldwide missions; (3) songs representing the different seasons, especially Christmas; (4) emphasis on hymns of devotion to Jesus; (5) emphasis on songs about the afterlife—especially folk and gospel hymnody; and (6) a new emphasis on songs reflecting a growing concern for social issues.

Perhaps this Great Awakening is best known by the writings of Charles Finney, *Lectures in Revival*. This book has been used by many church leaders as a textbook for revival and successful evangelism. Finney's "new measures" served as a catalyst for ushering in a "new worship service" that placed emphasis on evangelism over worship of God. Finney's contributions to worship innovations include: (1) inventing and establishing the *public invitation* or *altar call;* (2) "praying a revival down" whereby all persons may answer the gospel call of their own "free will"; (3) participation in "protracted meetings"; (4) relating to the surrounding community by developing and introducing indigenous forms of worship based on the community around him; (5) employing a worship leader (Thomas Hastings) and allowing him to establish a clearly defined evangelistic music ministry; (6) reversing the role of worship and evangelism (evangelism is primary, worship is secondary); and (7) renovating the platform of a church and placing the pulpit in the middle of the room, thus elevating preaching to an unprecedented place of significance and importance.

Finney believed that church leadership had a responsibility of reaching out with "new measures" to win lost people to Christ. Salvation was simply a relationship of a lost sinner to the gospel, and those who called upon Jesus for salvation could be born again.

As incredible as the revivals in New England and the rural areas of America were, God was not limiting his work to just one area. People around the globe were telling their story. As they told their own personal story about what God had done in their lives, God moved in the hearts of hundreds of people and they too became followers of Christ.

J. Edwin Orr once observed: "There have been instances in the history of the Church when the telling and retelling of the wonderful works of God have been used to rekindle the expectations of the faithful intercessors and prepare the way for another awakening."[34]

Such is the story of William Chambers Burns. God used his testimony to stir the hearts of those gathered in Kilsyth, Scotland. So the retelling of his story by carriers of revival around Scotland sparked revival fire throughout the land. In the process, God used the young preacher to turn Scotland upside down for Christ.

As Burns's popularity as a revivalist in Scotland peaked, he shocked those around him with the announcement that he was off "to preach the gospel to those who had never heard the precious name of Jesus!" He then went to China as a missionary to tell the story again.

The following entry in Burns's journal shows why God used him:

> Many who do come into the secret place, and who are God's children, enter it and leave it just as they entered, without ever so much as realizing the presence of God. And there are some believers who, even when they do obtain a blessing, and get a little quickening of soul, leave the secret place without seeking

more. They go to their chamber, and there get into the secret place, but then, as soon as they have got near to him, they think they have been peculiarly blessed, and leave their chamber, and go back into the world. Oh, how is it that the Lord's own people have so little perseverance? How is it that when they do enter into their place of prayer to be alone, they are so easily persuaded to be turned away empty?[35]

"Instead of wrestling with God to pour out his Spirit," Burns concluded, "they retire from the secret place without the answer, and submit to it as being God's will."[36]

Though used by God to bring revival to Scotland, Burns's real passion always remained the evangelization of the lost. On one occasion, he explained his life purpose in this statement: "The longing of my heart would be to go once around the world before I die, and preach one gospel invitation in the ear of every creature."[37]

While Finney preached in Rochester and some large cities in northern New York, for the most part the growth of the Industrial Revolution proved to be a barrier to Christianity. The large cities grew, and no one seemed willing to tell the story. No one seemed to find the key to winning the large cities to Christ until a group of laymen started a prayer meeting that shook New York City into a spirit of revival. A straightforward evangelist named Dwight L. Moody came along at what seemed like the end of this revival, and a new awakening in the late 1800s was sparked as he began to tell his story.

Notes

1. Elmer Towns and Douglas Porter, *The Ten Greatest Revivals Ever: From Pentecost to the Present* (Ventura, CA: Vine Books, 2000), 104–9.
2. Ibid.
3. Ibid., 107.
4. Ibid.

5. Ibid., 116.

6. Justo L. González, *The Story of Christianity*, vol. 2: *The Reformation to the Present Day* (New York: Harper Collins, 1984), 246.

7. Ibid.

8. Al Maxey, *Raikes' Ragged Regiment: Reflecting on the Sunday School and Non-Sunday School Movements*, 2005, http://www.zianet.com/maxey/reflx184.htm; accessed July 26, 2011.

9. Ibid.

10. Ibid.

11. Elmer L. Towns, preface, "The Bicentennial History of the Sunday School," in *The Holy Bible: Bicentennial Sunday School History, Analytical Study Edition* (Nashville: Regal, 1980).

12. Ibid.

13. Daniel G. Reid, coordinating ed.; Robert D. Linder, Bruce L. Shelley, and Harry S. Stout, consulting eds., *Dictionary of Christianity in America* (Downers Grove, IL: InterVarsity Press, 1990), s.v. "Key, Francis Scott."

14. Towns and Porter, *The Ten Greatest Revivals Ever*, 116.

15. *Dictionary of Christianity*, s.v. "Paxson, Stephen."

16. Maxey, *Raikes' Ragged Regiment*.

17. Towns and Porter, *The Ten Greatest Revivals Ever*, 102–3.

18. Smith Creek Music, 2001, http://www.smithcreekmusic.com/Hymnology/American.Hymnody/Gospel.hymnody/Sunday.School.songs.html; accessed June 30, 2011. `

19. Ibid.

20. Robb Redman, *The Great Worship Awakening: Singing a New Song in the Postmodern Church* (San Francisco: Jossey-Bass, 2002), 8.

21. Donald P. Hustad, *Jubilate II: Church Music in Worship Renewal* (Carol Stream, IL: Hope Publishing, 1993), 230.

22. Ibid.

23. Redman, *The Great Worship Awakening*, 7.

24. Ibid., 8–9.

25. González, *The Story of Christianity*, 256.

26. The Oxford Movement produced an important hymnal known as *Hymns Ancient and Modern*.

27. Harry Eskew and Hugh T. McElrath, *Sing with Understanding: An Introduction to Christian Hymnody*, 2nd ed. (Nashville: Church Street Music, 1995), 152–60.

28. Hustad, *Jubilate II*, 218.

29. Ibid.

30. Ibid.

31. Ibid.

32. González, *The Story of Christianity*, 256–57.

33. Eskew and McElrath, *Sing with Understanding*, 188–91.

34. Quoted in Towns and Porter, *The Ten Greatest Revivals Ever*, 9.

35. Towns and Porter, *The Ten Greatest Revivals Ever*, 9–10.

36. Ibid.

37. Ibid.

CHAPTER 10

The Laymen's Prayer Revival (1857–1890)

It was 9 p.m. on an unusually warm Sunday night, October 8, 1871. Bells blared as firemen on wagons rushed to the scene of a barn ablaze. Through a series of miscommunications, they went to the wrong address and were delayed in their efforts to extinguish the inferno. Wind whipped across the plains and through the Midwestern metropolis, feeding the flames at times to 100 feet or more. In just 30 minutes, the fire leaped across fields, consumed a church, and marched through city blocks. Hundreds tried in vain to contain the fire. The alarm was sounded for citizens to flee, and more than 80,000 residents ran in panic through the streets toward the nearest bridges and water.

Most of the city was built with wood. Even sidewalks were made of pine and various kinds of timber. Just weeks prior to the blaze, the *Chicago Tribune* warned of impending disaster—criticizing the city leadership for ignoring fire codes and allowing merchants and immigrants to erect "shabbily constructed shanties."[1] Conditions were ripe for the "perfect fire."

The fire lasted until Tuesday, October 10, when a rainstorm helped smother the remaining flames. In the end, an area about four miles long and one mile wide was destroyed—including the center of Chicago's business district. Hotels, newspapers, major businesses, and government buildings were annihilated. More than 100,000 people were left homeless.[2] Many left Chicago, never to return.

The Chicago Fire had a profound effect on two influential communicators of the gospel—D. L. Moody and Ira D. Sankey. The alarm bells on the night of October 8 interrupted Moody's preaching right at the point of invitation. People ran out the door, and Moody did not extend his customary invitation for salvation. Of the 300 people who were killed in the fire, several attended Moody's service. His huge "Tabernacle" lay in ashes. What seemed like devastation beyond imagination, though, turned into opportunity for revival and confession of sin. Strange as it may seem, God used the events in Chicago to help propel revival fires that actually began 14 years earlier with a group of faithful New York laymen.

Overview of the Great Awakening

In New York City, the Fulton Street Church (Dutch Reformed) hired Jeremiah Lamphier as a missionary to work among the city's unreached people. Not knowing how to begin, he organized a noon prayer meeting for businessmen. He printed invitations and flyers and distributed them to as many as would take them.[3]

Initially, no one showed up at the appointed time, but approximately twenty minutes later one person arrived. A few minutes later someone else came. In all, six people attended that first prayer meeting. Lamphier challenged them to fast and pray and give an hour to intercession for revival. When they sacrificed meals, prayer intensified and God began to work. Another room was opened up as the meetings expanded, and soon the church's auditorium was filled.

In February 1858, George Bennett of the *New York Herald* was standing at his second-floor window looking at the street below when the clock on the steeple chimed 12 noon. He saw men running from their shops, dashing madly down the street, but some were running in the opposite direction of the others. Puzzled by what he saw, he sent reporters to find out "why the men are running." The reporter responded, "The men are running to follow the exhortation of Jesus who said, 'Could you not pray with me one hour?'" (see Matt 26:40).

The *Herald* gave extensive coverage to the prayer meetings, first reporting 2,000 attendees, then providing daily headcounts. *The New York Tribune* devoted an entire issue to the laymen's prayer meeting in April 1859. As a result, the news traveled quickly by telegraph throughout America. Similar prayer meetings began along the Eastern seaboard, taking up the challenge, *Could you not pray with me one hour?* Many factories began to blow the lunch whistle at 11:55 a.m. to allow workers time to dash to the nearest church to pray for one hour. At 1:05 p.m., the whistle blew again to signal the time for employees to resume work.

In areas where factories were located away from churches, factory owners raised tents where the workers could pray, beginning the tradition of revival tents. In contrast with earlier revivals that emphasized preaching, this time prayer was the focus of the movement. The prayer meetings did not have leaders, nor did they have preachers. Prayers were informal. Anyone could pray, lead in a song, or give a five-minute word of testimony. Many times men rose and cried out for salvation as intercessors gathered around them.

The Laymen's Prayer Movement was driven by concerts of prayer—unified times when churches prayed together. Just as people enjoy musical concerts, organizers figured, God enjoys the prayers of his followers gathered in concert.

Within weeks, noon prayer meetings emerged in Boston; Baltimore; Washington, DC; Richmond; Charleston; Savannah; Mobile; New Orleans; Vicksburg; Memphis; St. Louis; Pittsburgh; Cincinnati; Chicago; and hundreds of smaller towns and rural areas. In four months, a revival of prayer had spread across America.[4]

> The majority of the churches in most denominations experienced a new dimension of prayer. The *Presbyterian Magazine* reported that as of May there had been fifty thousand converts of the revival. In February, a New York Methodist magazine reported a total of eight thousand conversions in Methodist meetings in one week. The Louisville daily paper reported seventeen thousand Baptist conversions in three weeks during the month of March. And according to a June statement, the conversion figures stood at 96,216—and still counting. All but two of the youth in one high school were saved. A similar event took place in Toledo, Ohio. These are just brief examples of what was happening constantly all across the nation.[5]

The spirit of revival continued into the decades following the Civil War. Among the notable personalities of this movement was Dwight L. Moody, a former boot salesman from Boston.

The Story of Dwight L. Moody (1837–1899)

Dwight L. Moody was born on February 5, 1837, the sixth of nine children, and reared on a small New England farm. At age four, his forty-one-year-old alcoholic father died. One month later, his widowed mother gave birth to twins.

Dwight had four years of formal schooling. He went to the local school periodically from about ages six to ten. By that time, he was considered old enough to work and was needed to help feed his family.[6] On his seventeenth birthday, he went to Boston to get a job with his uncle in a shoe store. One of the conditions set by his uncle for the job was that young Dwight would attend church each week. A Sunday school teacher, Edward Kimball, took interest in the young man and soon led him to a saving knowledge of Christ.[7]

In 1856, he moved to Chicago to work for another uncle in a shoe store. While in Chicago, he established himself as an energetic and innovative communicator of the gospel with a deep love for children. His passion to reach lost children became so great that he started his own Sunday school in an abandoned freight car, later moving it to a vacant saloon. Moody began a new method of evangelism called "The Gospel Wagon," a forerunner of the Sunday school bus. He would go to the slums of Chicago, pick up children in his horse-drawn wagon, and take them to the abandoned saloon where he taught them the Word of God.

By 1859, his Sunday school became the largest in Chicago and he was elected president of the Illinois Sunday School Association. Sunday school became so popular that there was a local Sunday school organization in every county from Illinois to the Atlantic Ocean. Massive Sunday school conventions attracted thousands and motivated teachers to reach children for Jesus Christ and teach them the Word of God.

When Moody assembled an Illinois convention, he declared, "This [meeting] so far is dead, we will not start until God sends us revival." So he dismissed the meeting to convene small prayer groups to ask the Lord for revival. Among the attendees was H. J. Heinz, who said, "I'd rather be known as a Sunday school man, not a ketchup man." Also in attendance was John Wanamaker, owner of the famous Wanamaker Department Store in Philadelphia, who later became postmaster general of the United States and superintendent of the three-thousand-student Sunday school at Immanuel Church in Philadelphia.

In 1860, at age 23, Moody devoted himself to full-time Christian work, preaching the gospel to Union soldiers during the Civil War. Upon his return to Chicago, he engaged in successful Sunday school ministry through the Young Men's Christian Association (YMCA). Moody's early evangelistic efforts included noon prayer meetings, organizing a church, open-air preaching, ministry to the homeless, and building the ministry of Chicago's YMCA, especially during the years between 1865 and 1871.[8]

Moody began pastoring the congregation that is today called The Moody Church. In the summer of 1871, he began preaching a series of sermons on biblical characters, and it was so successful that by the fall he was preaching to the largest crowds he had ever encountered.

Next, Moody preached a six-week series on the life of Christ, "From the Cradle to the Cross." On Sunday evening, October 8, he completed his fifth sermon in the series, "What Then Shall I Do with Jesus which Is Called Christ?" As the service was coming to a close, the invitation was interrupted by the sound of fire wagons rushing to the Great Chicago Fire. Moody dismissed the crowd, saying, "The next Sabbath we will come to Calvary and the Cross and decide what to do with Jesus of Nazareth."

The crowd never reassembled. That evening the fire brought death and devastation. The city was in ruins. Moody's Tabernacle lay in ashes. "What a mistake," Moody said years later. "Not giving the invitation was one of the biggest regrets of [my] life. I have never dared give an audience a week to think of their salvation since."[9]

Moody had a large sign printed over the back door of his auditorium, "You Can Be Saved Now!" Then he preached a sermon titled, "Instantaneous Conversion,"[10] explaining that people could be saved immediately by accepting Jesus Christ as Lord and Savior. Moody adopted the concept of "praying through" and allowing people to "tarry at the altar" until they found salvation. True to his word, never again did Moody preach a sermon without giving a public invitation to receive Christ at the conclusion, no matter how large or small the attendance. Because of the Chicago Fire, Moody's ministry was forever marked by purposeful soul-winning.[11]

After the fire destroyed Moody's Tabernacle, he traveled broadly raising money to rebuild it. Eventually, the travel and stress took their toll on Moody physically, emotionally, and spiritually. Two ladies in his church sensed the problem. So they sat regularly in the front row of the church praying for him. When he asked for whom they were praying, the ladies answered, "We have been praying for you." Moody objected, urging them to pray for the unsaved. They refused and claimed he needed something he did not have, "the power of the Spirit."

As spring of 1872 turned into summer, Moody sensed the need for a break from ministry—something he would not receive if he remained in America. He thought that if he went to England, where he was not well known, he could rest and study under the British Bible teachers he so admired. In New York City, on the way to England, Moody's life was changed. He confessed:

> I was crying all the time that God would fill me with His Spirit. Well, one day, in the city of New York—oh, what a day!—I cannot describe it, I seldom refer to it; it is almost too sacred an experience to name. Paul had an experience of which he never spoke for fourteen years. I can only say that God revealed Himself to me, and I had such an experience of His love that I had to ask Him to stay His hand. I went to preaching again. The sermons were not different; I did not present any new truths, and yet hundreds were converted. I would not now be placed back where I was before that blessed experience if you should give me all the world—that would be as the small dust of the balance.[12]

When Moody arrived in England, a pastor friend asked him to preach in his church. Initially, Moody did not want to preach, but he consented and preached the next Sunday. On that morning, he felt like he was preaching to one of the coldest congregations he had ever encountered. The people evidenced little interest in the gospel. Moody felt his time was wasted and was sorry he had committed to preach in the evening service. Determined not to disappoint his pastor friend, though, he decided to go ahead and preach.

A lady who heard Moody preach that morning went home and told her bedridden sister that she had heard him and that he would preach again in the evening.[13] "God has heard my prayers," the sick woman cried out. She told her sister not to bring lunch or disturb her for the rest of the day. She would fast and pray for the evening service.

That evening, there was a different spirit in the meeting. According to Moody's biographer, "It seemed, while he was preaching, as if the very atmosphere was changed with the Spirit of God. There came a hush upon all the people and a quick response to his words, though he had not been much in prayer that day, and could not understand it."[14]

At the end of the meeting, Moody directed all those who wanted to become Christians to stand. To him, it looked as though the whole church stood. He thought the people did not understand what he was saying. He told those who wanted to become Christians to make their way to "the inquiry room." So many crowded into the room that extra chairs had to be brought in. Neither Moody nor his pastor friend had ever witnessed the Lord move on an audience with that kind of power and conviction.

He stayed in the country several months, preaching the gospel and leading evangelistic campaigns. In 1873, he returned to England with song leader and evangelist Ira D. Sankey. The two men traveled much of Europe preaching and singing the gospel. The evangelistic campaigns in England laid the foundation for a successful career for both men as evangelists in Europe and America.

The Story of Ira D. Sankey (1840–1908)

Ira David Sankey was born in Edinburg, Lawrence County, Pennsylvania, August 28, 1840. The son of a prominent state senator, banker, editor, and member of Abraham Lincoln's Internal Revenue Service collection staff, Sankey served the Union army during the Civil War from 1860 to 1862. He married Fanny V. Edwards on September 9, 1863, and worked as an agent with the IRS. He began his work as a *singing evangelist* with Moody in the spring of 1871. Moody chose Sankey as his song leader on a trip to the Indianapolis YMCA convention because he was impressed with Sankey's ability to communicate the gospel to a crowd.[15]

Sankey served with Moody for more than 30 years. He directed music at Moody's church in Chicago and accompanied the evangelist as soloist and music director in crusades and special revival efforts. In 1872, Moody invited Sankey to travel with him to England. Moody and Sankey, along with their wives, spent two years in England.

Sankey is generally referred to as the "father of gospel music." Together, he and Moody became the first evangelistic preacher-singer team. The extraordinary response to the two-year Moody Crusades in Great Britain brought the duo to the attention of the entire Protestant world.

Music was an important part of Moody's campaigns. In mass meetings, Sankey often introduced gospel hymns as he accompanied himself on a portable reed organ.[16] On one occasion, he gave a concert at Exeter Hall, London, to an estimated congregation of 20,000 people, playing his organ and singing without amplification.[17]

By the late 1870s, a new genre of music appeared, called the gospel song or gospel hymn. Sankey combined the European approach of singing German lieder with this new gospel song genre. Other musicians such as Philip Phillips and P. P. Bliss had utilized the method, but Sankey was the one who popularized it during his journey to England with Moody.

Music and Worship Innovations

Sankey and Moody were among the most important shapers of evangelical worship during the latter half of the nineteenth century.

Moody's Innovations

Moody's approach to "worship evangelism" was akin to that of Finney. His commitment to preaching and simple gospel presentations made his ministry accessible to the average layperson. His use of personal testimony and presentation of "the gospel in song" combined the emotional with the intellectual.

Moody never forgot that he was at heart a layman-evangelist. That reality produced a love for people and affected his evangelistic methodology in at least seven ways: (1) He was less theological than notable ministers of previous eras, and his preaching was less refined. (2) He resisted the emotional extremes, which characterized earlier revival movements. (3) His services began with a full hour of singing and engaging entertainment, sprinkled with personal testimony. (4) The order of his evangelistic services was: congregational singing, special music by a soloist and/or choir, prayers, Scripture reading, sermon, and invitation. (5) There was significant use of choirs. These choirs were often very large, sometimes numbering several hundred. (6) Great attention was given to "creating an atmosphere." (7) The larger revival campaigns were held in "secular buildings" (tabernacles or exhibition halls) or temporary structures.

Moody's attempts to create a "revival atmosphere" for his services drew criticism. In one critic's words, "His unusual surroundings and general attitude of the crowds attending his meetings did not contribute to feelings of reverence or spirituality."[18] For Moody, the building was an important part of creating this atmosphere. He wanted the service to flow in an entertaining fashion. A newspaper reporter described a song at one of Moody's meetings as the combination of "a circus quick-step, a negro minstrel sentimental ballad, a college chorus, and a hymn all in one."[19]

Sankey's Innovations

Just as the rural camp meetings of the early 1800s produced popular hymnody, the urban revivals of the 1870s produced gospel songs, popularizing a type of music previously associated with the Sunday school movement. The genre was termed "gospel" songs because its message centered on core ideas of the salvation message—sin, grace, redemption, and the experience of conversion.[20]

The gospel song was a new musical style. Its poetry was simpler than that of a hymn—limited in theological scope, more repetitive, and with a refrain. According to William Reynolds, the distinguishing characteristics of the American gospel hymn are: (1) emotional rather than than intellectual emphasis, (2) simple phrases repeated over and over, (3) evangelistic emphasis, (4) simple tunes based on popular melody—camp or marching songs and parlor piano music, (5) an easy-to-learn refrain, (6) words and melodies that can be memorized easily, and (7) a melodic line supported by simple harmonic structure with infrequent changes of chords.[21]

Sankey was personal friends with many composers of gospel hymns. They enjoyed singing others' songs and freely exchanged ideas. Philip

Phillips, P. P. Bliss, George Stebbins, James McGranahan, and Fanny Crosby were among the well-known personalities to partner with him.

Strategic Personalities of This Awakening

From 1857 to 1900, God used an army of men and women to usher in innovations that still impact the way we express corporate worship. This brief study highlights a few.

The 1857 awakening actually began at the home of **Phoebe Palmer** in Canada. Palmer was no stranger to revival. In 1840, she began a Tuesday prayer ministry for the promotion of holiness in New York City. In 1850, Palmer and her husband, Walter, a homeopathic physician, helped establish The Five Points, an urban outreach center with a chapel, a school, and rent-free housing for the needy in one of New York's poorest sections. That same year, Palmer embarked on a four-year evangelistic tour of Great Britain. During her time overseas, she often taught large audiences about the need for holy living. By their influence, the Palmers spawned hundreds of social ministries.[22]

Twenty-three-year-old **George Williams** went to London to work in a draper's shop in 1844. Williams and several of his colleagues were concerned by the lack of "healthy activities" for young men in London.[23] Apparently, temptation toward brothels, taverns, and raucous nightlife was acute. On June 6, 1844, Williams joined 12 other men in establishing the first YMCA to improve the "spiritual condition of young men engaged in the drapery and other trades."[24] Moody and Sankey were actively involved in the YMCA. In fact, they met at a YMCA convention. Williams was a major supporter of the Moody-Sankey campaign in England.

The Salvation Army was launched by **William and Catherine Booth**. Pastor-teacher *Charles Haddon Spurgeon* filled his tabernacle each week with capacity crowds. Missionary *Hudson Taylor* started the China Inland Mission. The Open Air Mission was started by *Gawin Kirkham*. *Gypsy Smith, Reuben Torrey,* and *A. J. Gordon* were evangelists who preached to thousands with great international successes. African work was championed by *David Livingstone* and *Mary Slessor*.

Many musicians contributed to the revival and pioneered innovations in worship:

Composer and writer **William Howard Doane**[25] was born in 1832 in Preston, Connecticut. He attended the Woodstock Academy and at age 14 conducted the school choir. He was Sunday school superintendent of a very large group of children and adults at the Mount Auburn Baptist Church in Cincinnati. Doane wrote more than 2,000 gospel songs and tunes, many with his friend *Fanny Crosby*.[26]

Fanny Crosby[27] (1820–1915) was probably the most famous American hymn writer associated with this Great Awakening. Born in Putnam County, New York, she was blinded at six weeks of age by a doctor's error in treating an eye infection. Later in life she wrote about her blindness, "I verily believe that it was God's intention that I should live my days in physical darkness, so as to be better prepared to sing His praise and incite others so to do. I could not have written thousands of hymns if I had been hindered by the distractions that would have been presented to my notice." Crosby only wrote lyrics. She collaborated with scores of musicians, music publishers, and music educators, including Doane, Sankey, Robert Lowry, Charles Converse, George Root, Phoebe Knapp, Philip Phillips, James McGranahan, E. O. Excell, Elijah Hoffman, and George Stebbins.

Major Daniel Webster Whittle[28] (1840–1901) was a Bible teacher, hymn writer, businessman, and evangelist. Having lost his right arm in combat as a Union soldier during the Civil War, he was influenced and encouraged by Moody. He worked closely with Bliss, McGranahan,

Crosby, Sankey, and Moody. Whittle wrote more than 200 hymns that are still used and sung among evangelicals.[29]

Philip Phillips (1834–95) was a well-known and highly influential singing evangelist. In 1868 he held services in the principal cities of England. He also wrote the music book *The American Sacred Songster*, which sold more than one million copies. He traveled extensively with Whittle and was a favorite musician of Moody and Crosby.[30]

Philip P. Bliss[31] (1838–76) and his wife, Lucy Young Bliss (1841–76), were considered the leading duo in American gospel music during the 1860s and 1870s. Married on June 1, 1859, Philip was a songwriter and soloist while Lucy played the piano. Aside from Sankey and Crosby, Philip and Lucy Bliss are perhaps more responsible than anyone else for establishing the role of music evangelist in evangelical worship. Between 1865 and 1873, they held musical conventions, sacred concerts, and singing schools. Philip Bliss's contribution to evangelical worship practices cannot be overstated.

He was best known for his work with Whittle. Together, on March 25, 1874, Bliss and Whittle committed their lives to full-time evangelistic ministry. They had an enormous impact on the propagation of the gospel in England and America. From January to April 1876 alone, they traveled to Illinois, Missouri, Alabama, Mississippi, Georgia, and Louisiana, holding evangelistic campaigns and revival services.

Philip Bliss was one of Moody's favorite singers. In fact, Moody asked Bliss to join him on his famous journey to England. When Bliss declined the opportunity, Sankey went in his place. Whittle and Bliss later traveled to England and enjoyed great success as an evangelistic team.

The Blisses died in a train accident in Ashtabula, Ohio, on December 29, 1876, when a bridge gave way during a severe winter snowstorm and their train plunged into the ravine below. Within minutes the train burst into flames. Philip was able to climb out of the train but died when he went back in to rescue his wife. Ninety-two of the 150 passengers perished. The Blisses were en route from New York to Chicago to sing in special New Year's Eve services with Moody.[32]

James McGranahan[33] (1840–1907) was an American gospel song and hymn writer. He was educated as a voice teacher and performer before answering the call to full-time singing ministry. One week before Philip and Lucy Bliss were killed, McGranahan received a letter from Philip encouraging him to leave his secular employment and enter full-time music evangelism. In response to the letter, McGranahan became song leader and soloist for Whittle. McGranahan and Whittle traveled extensively in England and America.[34]

George Stebbins[35] (1846–1945) was a trusted friend of Sankey and an American gospel hymn writer. In 1870, he accepted a position as music director at the First Baptist Church in Chicago. During his time in Chicago, he befriended Philip Bliss, Whittle, Sankey, and Moody. He helped develop large choirs for the Moody-Sankey team for more than 30 years. At one point, he joined evangelist Dwight Pentecost in a series of evangelistic endeavors among the English-speaking people of India.[36]

Francis "Fanny" Havergal[37] was born on December 14, 1836, at Astly, Worcester, England. Her father was Anglican pastor, hymn writer, and composer William Havergal. She could read by age four and wrote prose at seven. Her mother died when Francis was eleven. She was fluent in Latin, Greek, and Hebrew and memorized books of the Bible, including Psalms, Isaiah, the Minor Prophets, and much of the New Testament. She said that she never wrote a hymn or prose without asking for God's guidance:

> I believe my King suggests a thought, and whispers to me a musical line or two, and then I look up and thank Him delightedly and go on with it. That is how my hymns come.[38]

Her songs were used extensively by Sankey and became popular at the Keswick Conference in the early twentieth century. Of her many hymns and songs, she is best known for "Take My Life and Let It Be," "Lord Speak to Me," "Like a River Glorious," and "Who Is on the Lord's Side?" Havergal died at age 42 on June 3, 1879.

Lina Sandell-Berg (1832–1903) rose to prominence during the 1870s European revivals led by lay-preacher Carl Rosenius. Often characterized as the Fanny Crosby of Sweden, she wrote more than 650 hymns. Sandell-Berg is known by American evangelicals for penning the lyrics to "Children of the Heavenly Father" and "Day by Day and with Each Passing Moment." Music for her hymns was most often composed by Oscar Ahnfelt, a guitarist and composer who traveled throughout Scandinavia singing her songs. Sandell-Berg once said of Ahnfelt, "[He] has sung my songs into the hearts of the people."[39] Contralto Jenny Lind helped popularize Sandell-Berg's hymns by performing and publishing them along with other "Pietist hymns." Considered the "sweet nightingale of Sweden," Lind was known for her ministry to the working class in Europe.[40]

Summary

The Moody-Sankey contribution to "worship evangelism" included five innovations: (1) By moving worship services outside a traditional church sanctuary, Moody made his gatherings accessible to the unchurched. (2) Moody's focus in services was evangelism, not corporate worship. His commitment to successful communication of the gospel superseded any desire for reflective, public, God-focused corporate worship. (3) Moody focused on God's love and provision of Jesus to redeem people from their sins. (4) Like Finney, Moody adapted worship to its cultural context. He embraced popular styles of communication. Most notably, music played a significant role in his evangelistic services. While he did not put Christian words to secular tunes, he endorsed the use of music stylistically familiar to the masses. (5) Sankey established the use of gospel songs and hymns as a hallmark of Christian worship.

The Chicago Fire of 1871 was a defining moment for evangelism. In its wake, ministers organized revolutionary evangelistic campaigns and placed increased emphasis on coming to salvation during a moment of decision. While not radical to today's thinking, this was radical in Moody's day. Donald Hustad rightly observes that Moody "brought his gifts of analysis and planning to the ministry of evangelism and developed policies and procedures which have influenced revivalism to the present day."[41] Yet the impact of the Laymen's Prayer Revival extended far beyond Moody's ministry. It sparked revival that swept around the world—to western Russia, Australia, the South Seas, South Africa, and India.[42]

In our next chapter, we will discover how God uses one college-age student in Wales to impact the world for the kingdom of God. In the process, a new paradigm for worship is established, and men, women, boys, and girls experience and express worship in new, innovative, and heartfelt ways.

Notes

1. Robert McNamara, "The Great Chicago Fire of 1871 Essentially Destroyed the Entire City: A Long Drought and a City Made of Timber Led to a Major 19th-Century Disaster," http://history1800s.about.com/urbanconditions/a/chicagofir.html; accessed July 15, 2011.

2. Ibid.

3. Elmer Towns and Douglas Porter, *The Ten Greatest Revivals Ever: From Pentecost to the Present* (Ventura, CA: Vine Books, 2000), 122.

4. Wesley Duewal, *Revival Fire* (Grand Rapids: Zondervan, 1995), 99–105.

5. Ibid.

6. Beth Moore, *Believing God* (Nashville: LifeWay, 2002), 171.

7. William R. Moody, *The Life of Dwight L. Moody* (New York: Fleming H. Revell, 1900), 39 and 41.

8. Ibid., 55–104.

9. Moody, *The Life of Dwight L. Moody*, 55.

10. Towns and Porter, *The Ten Greatest Revivals Ever*, 131.

11. Winkie Pratney, *Revival: Its Principles and Personalities* (Lafayette: Huntington House, 1994), 114.

12. Towns and Porter, *The Ten Greatest Revivals Ever*, 133.

13. Ibid.

14. Ibid., 133–34.

15. Pratney, *Revival*, 125.

16. Harry Eskew and Hugh T. McElrath, *Sing with Understanding* (Nashville: Church Street Press, 1995), 199.

17. Ira Sankey, *My Life and the Story of the Gospel Hymns* (Philadelphia: The Sunday School Times, 1907), 46.

18 Donald P. Hustad, *Jubilate II: Church Music in Worship and Renewal* (Carol Stream: Hope Publishing, 1993), 235.

19. Ibid., 236.

20. Ibid., 235.

21. William Reynolds and Milburn Price, *A Survey of Christian Hymnody* (New York: Holt, Rinehart and Winston, 1963), 102–6.

22. *Phoebe Palmer: Mother of the Holiness Movement*, http://www.christianitytoday.com/ch/131christians/moversandshakers/palmer.html; accessed July 15, 2011.

23. Ronald Wolf, "Sir George Williams and the YMCA," *Canadian Free Press* (December 9, 2009), http://www.canadafreepress.com/index.php/article/21198; accessed July 15, 2011.

24. Ibid.

25. According to Stephen Ross of WholesomeWords.org, Doane composed more than 2,000 tunes, most for Fanny Crosby—including "Rescue the Perishing," "I Am Thine, O Lord," "Near the Cross," and "Safe in the Arms of Jesus." He was a well-respected editor of music books, including the Sunday school songbooks *Sabbath Gems* (1861), *Little Sunbeams* (1864), *Silver*

Spray (1869), and *Songs of Devotion* (1864). He joined Robert Lowry (also a songwriter for Fanny Crosby) in publishing the songbooks *Pure Gold, Royal Diadem, Temple Anthem, Tidal Wave, Brightest and Best, Welcome Tidings, Fountain of Song, Good as Gold, Glad Hosanna, Joyful Lays, Glad Refrain,* and others. Doane also connected with Lowry to publish *The Gospel Hymn and Tune Book* and *The Baptist Hymnal* for the American Baptist Publication Society. In 1877, he wrote *Memoirs of Philip P. Bliss.*

26. Reynolds and Price, *A Survey of Christian Hymnody,* 104, 107.

27. According to Rodney D. Whaley in *Companion to Free Will Baptist Hymn Book (1964), Vol. III: Study of the Authors, Composers, and Contributors* (MDiv Thesis, Luther Rice Seminary, 1980), 35, the following titles represent the more than 8,000 hymns by Fanny Crosby: "Blessed Assurance," "He Hideth My Soul," "I Am Thine, O Lord," "Praise Him, Praise Him," "Rescue the Perishing," "Saved by Grace," "My Savior First of All," "Tell Me the Story of Jesus," "Redeemed," "Will Jesus Find Us Watching?" "All the Way My Savior Leads Me," "Safe in the Arms of Jesus," "Close to Thee," "Near the Cross," "Pass Me Not," and "To God Be the Glory."

28. According to Stephen Ross, WholesomeWords.org, Whittle wrote lyrics to about 200 hymns, including "The Banner of the Cross," "By Grace Are Ye Saved," "Christ Liveth in Me," "The Crowning Day," "I Know Whom I Have Believed," "Moment by Moment," "There Shall Be Showers of Blessing," and "Why Not Now?"

29. David J. Beattie, "Hymn Writers of America," in *The Romance of Sacred Song* (London: Marshall, Morgan and Scott, 1931), submitted September 9, 2010, http://www.plymouthbrethren.org/article/4931; accessed July 15, 2011.

20. *The National Cyclopaedia of American Biography,* vol. 7 (New York: James T. White, 1897), 531.

31. In 1875, Philip Bliss joined Sankey in compiling the songbook series, *Gospel Hymns and Sacred Songs No. 1* and *No. 2* for the Biglow and Main Company of New York. He wrote scores of gospel songs that are still widely used, including "Hold the Fort," "Jesus Loves Even Me," "Almost Persuaded," "Hallelujah, What a Savior," "The Light of the World Is Jesus," "Wonderful Words of Life," "I Gave My Life for Thee," and the lyrics to "My Redeemer" ("I Will Sing of My Redeemer"). He wrote the music to H. G. Spadford's

song "It Is Well with My Soul" and several tunes for use with Fanny Crosby's gospel hymns.

32. Edward Reese, "The Life and Ministry of Philip Bliss," http://www.wholesomewords.org/biography/biorpbliss.html; accessed July 15, 2011.

33. According to Whaley in *Companion to Free Will Baptist Hymn Book* (100), McGranahan wrote the music for "My Redeemer," "There Shall Be Showers of Blessing," "I Know Whom I Have Believed," "The Banner of the Cross," "Christ Returneth," "Christ Receiveth Sinful Men," "Hallelujah for the Cross," "Hallelujah, Christ Is Risen," and about 60 more gospel songs. He also worked with Sankey and Stebbins on the *Gospel Hymns* series for the Biglow and Main Company.

34. Stephen Ross for WholesomeWords.org. from Jacob Henry Hall, "James McGranahan: Gospel Song and Hymn Writer," in *Biography of Gospel Song and Hymn Writers* (New York: Fleming H. Revell, 1914), http://www.wholesomewords.org/biography/biorpmcgran.html; accessed July 15, 2011.

35. According to Ross, Stebbins wrote the well-known gospel hymns "There Is a Green Hill Far Away," "Ye Must Be Born Again," "Savior, Breathe an Evening Blessing," "Saved by Grace," "In the Secret of His Presence," "Take Time to Be Holy," "The Homeland," "O, House of Many Mansions," and "Have Thine Own Way, Lord!"

36. Jacob Henry Hall, *Biography of Gospel Song and Hymn Writers* (New York: Fleming H. Revell, 1914).

37. The following are the most familiar of the more than 80 hymns and songs by Frances Havergal: "Another Year Is Dawning," "God Will Take Care of You," "Golden Harps Are Sounding," "The Half Has Never Been Told," "I Am Trusting Thee," "I Bring My Sins to Thee," "I Could Not Do Without Thee," "I Gave My Life for Thee," "Is It for Me?" "Jesus, Blessed Savior," "Jesus, Master, Whose I Am," "Like a River Glorious," "Lord, Speak to Me," "Take My Life and Let It Be," "Tell It Out," "Thou Art Coming, O My Savior," and "Who Is on the Lord's Side?"

38. Paul Lusher, *Find Songs and Hymns: Frances Havergal* (Grand Haven, MI: Center for Church Music), http://songsandhymns.org/people/detail/frances-havergal; accessed July 16, 2011.

39. Ernest Edwin Ryden, *The Story of Our Hymns* (Rock Island, IL: Augustana Book Concern, 1930), 171–83.

40. Ibid.

41. Hustad, *Jubilate II,* 234.

42. Tony Cauchi, "Overview of Revival," http://www.prayer2000.org/Teachings/Public/Tony_Cauchi-Revival_Overview.pdf; accessed July 16, 2011.

CHAPTER 11

The Welsh Revival (1904–1906)

Following the prayer movement of 1857 and the powerful Moody-Sankey, Whittle-McGranahan, and Torry-Alexander revivals, manifestations of God's presence began to spread around the world. Bermuda, Africa, Japan, Australia, and New Zealand all experienced notable revivals. What many have considered the greatest revival occurred in Wales from 1904 to 1906.[1] Revival historian J. Edwin Orr[2] called it "a blaze of evening glory at the end of the great century." By some estimates, more than five million people came to faith in Christ within two years.[3]

One of the first Welshmen to experience the flames of revival was Joseph Jenkins, pastor of a church in New Quay, Cardiganshire. He organized a special preaching conference in January 1904, and many of his members began experiencing personal revival.

Then, evangelist Seth Joshua preached in the town of Blaenannerch, with a group of students from a nearby Methodist Bible school in attendance. Evan Roberts, a former coal miner and a twenty-three-year-old student, heard Joshua cry out, "Lord, bend me." The prayer so struck Roberts that he began praying, "Oh Lord, bend me." At nine o'clock the following morning, Roberts knelt at an early meeting with arms outstretched, perspiration soaking his shirt as he agonized over committing himself to God. He prayed aloud, "Bend me! Bend me! Bend me!" Later, Joshua made an entry in his journal recalling the young man's cry.

Roberts did not realize that he was about to become God's agent to carry a spirit of revival throughout his homeland, and ultimately the world. Later, he wrote the following:

> One Friday night last spring, when praying by my bedside before retiring, I was taken up to a great expanse—without time and space. It was communion with God. Before this I had a far-off God. I was frightened that night, but never since. So great was my shivering that I rocked the bed, and my brother, being awakened, took hold of me thinking I was ill. After that experience I was awakened every night a little after one o'clock. This was most strange, for through the years I slept like a rock, and no disturbance in my room would awaken me. From that hour I was taken up into the divine fellowship for about four hours. What it was I cannot tell you, except that it was divine. About five o'clock I was again allowed to sleep on till about nine. At this time I was again taken up into the same experience as in the earlier hours of the morning until about twelve or one o'clock.[4]

Such experiences continued for three months. Roberts spent long hours in personal Bible study, prayer, and worship of God. In addition, he experienced visions of large numbers of people coming to Christ. He felt that revival was coming to his native Wales and that he had to prepare for a special ministry.

At the end of October, Roberts took the train home to be with his family and conduct a week of meetings among the young people at his church. He told his pastor at Loughor that God had given him a message for the church and asked if he could deliver it. The pastor agreed.

When Roberts attended church, though, he was disappointed to hear the pastor say, "Young Evan Roberts is home from Bible school and has a word from God. He will give it at a later time." Again that evening, the pastor delayed Roberts's message again, "Young Evan Roberts has a word from God and will give it tomorrow night, on Monday." Monday evening the pastor announced, "Young Evan Roberts will deliver a word after the meeting." Only seventeen young people remained to hear him. Nevertheless, for almost three hours, the zealous evangelist led the group in prayer, worship, and calling on God to send revival. During the meeting, almost all of the young people were visited by the convicting power of the Holy Spirit, confessed their sins, and called on God for mercy. The revival continued each evening, and by Friday people were attending from all the other congregations in town.

The meeting continued to grow in number, and Roberts never returned to Bible school. The gathering continued a second week, without formal publicity. People crowded the church, standing in the vestibule and near open doors just to hear the Word of God. Soon, people went straight to the church from work to make sure they got a seat.

A journalist attended the meeting on Friday, November 12, 1904, and reported:

> The meeting at Brynteg congregational church on Thursday night was attended by those remarkable scenes which have made previous meetings memorable in the life history of so many of the inhabitants of the district. The proceedings commenced at seven o'clock and they lasted without a break until 4.30 o'clock on Friday morning. During the whole of this time the congregation was under the influence of deep religious fervor and exaltation. There were about 400 people present in the chapel when I took my seat at about nine o'clock. . . . There is nothing theatrical

about his preaching. He does not seek to terrify his hearers, and eternal torment finds no place in his theology.

Rather does he reason with the people and show them by persuasion a more excellent way. I had not been many minutes in the building before I felt that this was no ordinary gathering. Instead of the set order of proceedings to which we were accustomed at the orthodox religious service, everything here was left to the spontaneous impulse of the moment. The preacher too did not remain in his usual seat. For the most part he walked up and down the aisles, open Bible in hand, exhorting one, encouraging another, and kneeling with a third [person] to implore blessing from the throne of grace.[5]

Seven and a half hours after the meeting began, the newsman wrote,

> In the gallery a woman was praying and she fainted. Water was offered her, but she refused this, saying the only thing she wanted was God's forgiveness. A well-known resident then rose and said that salvation had come to him. Immediately a thanksgiving hymn was sung, while an English prayer from a new convert broke in upon the singing. The whole congregation then fell upon their knees, prayers ascending from every part of the edifice, while Mr. Roberts gave way to tears at the sight.[6]

When people claimed that Roberts's preaching and influence drove the revival, he went on a forty-day fast from speaking. He stayed in his room to pray and study the Scriptures, secluded from the public. The revival continued to grow and spread to other churches. According to Orr:

> Drunkenness was immediately cut in half, and many taverns went bankrupt. Crime was so diminished that judges were presented with white gloves signifying that there were no cases of murder, assault, rape or robbery or the like to consider. The police became unemployed in many districts. Stoppages occurred

in coal mines, not due to unpleasantness between management and workers, but because so many foul-mouthed miners became converted and stopped using foul language that the horses which hauled the coal trucks in the mines could no longer understand what was being said to them.[7]

Music and Worship Innovations

As with many Great Awakenings and revivals, much of the ministry associated with the Welsh Revival was carried out by college students. It was a student-led awakening in the truest sense and came to be known as a "singing, prayer, and worship revival." According to one revival chronicler:

> [Evan Roberts's] meetings were not typical for those times. They were more akin to what we would call worship and prayer meetings or, as it is often called today, "harp and bowl" gatherings. In a very real sense, the Welsh revival was a worship revival. Great singing abounded. The Welsh people have a rich and abundant hymn singing tradition. Great hymns and other worship songs grew out of this world-impacting revival.
>
> Intercessory prayer was a central focus to Roberts' meetings. In a typical gathering, he would have the first person stand and pray, "Send the Spirit now for Jesus Christ's sake." That person would sit down and the next person would stand and pray the same prayer: "Send the Spirit now for Jesus Christ's sake." Roberts would go from one person to the next and each would stand and pray the same way. Even people who had never prayed publicly stood and called to the Lord to send His Spirit now![8]

Roberts brought enormous and strategic innovations to worship. First, he changed the structure of corporate worship, shifting away from the patterns of revivalists from the previous two decades. While he retained the concept of musical solos from the Moody-Sankey model, little else resembled their approach to "revival services." In contrast with Sankey's forty-five-minute music program (complete with congregation, choir, and solo) and Moody's thirty-minute sermon, Roberts' meetings often included an hour or two of praying, singing, confessing, and repenting of sins before the evangelists even entered the building. The invitation was not necessarily reserved for the end of the service, as in Moody's evangelistic meetings. Rather, the entire service, from start to finish, included an open invitation for people to confess sin, seek forgiveness, and reconcile themselves to one another in Christian love.

Previously, the model for services had been fairly predictable: congregational music, prayer, solo, and Scripture for 45 minutes, and sermon for 30 minutes, followed by an invitation. The Welsh Revivals, however, were not governed by the clock. It was not uncommon for a type of pre-service to begin at 6 p.m. before the official service would commence at 7 p.m. and continue three or four hours. A reporter with the *Pall Mall Gazette* in London, William Stead, witnessed the revival and described the services:

> In Mardy I attended three meetings on Sunday—two and a half hours in the morning, two and a half hours in the afternoon, and two hours at night, when I had to leave to catch the train. At all these meetings the same kind of thing went on—the same kind of congregations assembled, the same strained, intense emotion was manifest. Aisles were crowded. Pulpit stairs were packed and two-thirds of the congregation were men, and at least one-half young men. "There," said one, "is the hope and the glory of the movement." Here and there is a grey head. But the majority of the congregations were stalwart young miners, who gave the meeting all the fervour and swing and enthusiasm of youth.[9]

Second, worship included significant lay participation. Frequently, young men and women assumed leadership roles. Teenagers and college students often broke out in spontaneous prayer and confession. Sometimes, this would be followed by other lay leaders praying, confessing sins, seeking God, and repenting. Stead noted:

> The most extraordinary thing about the meetings which I attended was the extent to which they were absolutely without any human direction or leadership. "We must obey the Spirit" is the watchword of Mr. Evan Roberts, and he is as obedient as the humblest of his followers. The meetings open—after any amount of preliminary singing, while the congregation is assembling—by the reading of a chapter or a psalm. Then it is go-as-you-please for two hours or more. And the amazing thing is that it does go and does not get entangled in what might seem to be inevitable confusion.[10]

Third, sermons were simple with a strong emphasis on public prayer. Roberts was not an expositor or Bible teacher-preacher in the Keswick or scholarly traditions. His sermons were direct and delivered with great emotion and conviction. Revival campaigns and services were often preceded by extended times of fasting and prayer. Then during the services, Roberts would often stand and pray for an hour. Sometimes prayers were interrupted by songs and seasons of confession. At times, confession, prayer, and repentance continued so long that the evangelist never had opportunity to preach. According to Stead:

> The prayers are largely autobiographical, and some of them intensely dramatic. On one occasion an impassioned and moving appeal to the Deity was accompanied throughout by an exquisitely rendered hymn, sung by three of the Singing Sisters. It was like the undertone of the orchestra when some leading singer is holding the house. The praying and singing are both wonderful, but more impressive than either are the breaks which occur when utterance can say no more, and the sobbing in the silence momentarily heard is drowned in a tempest of melody. No need

for an organ. The assembly was its own organ as a thousand sorrowing or rejoicing hearts found expression in the sacred psalmody of their native hills.[11]

Fourth, the services were focused and intense. Congregations and individuals often were given four admonitions: (1) confess all known sin to God, receiving forgiveness through Jesus Christ; (2) remove anything from your life of which you are in doubt or feel unsure; (3) be totally yielded and obedient to the Holy Spirit; and (4) publicly confess the Lord Jesus Christ.

Fifth, services were not conducted according to a predetermined order. The participants simply "waited on the Holy Spirit" to incite public repentance, confession of sins (including jealousy, anger, hatred, and immorality), and admission of need for Christ.

Sixth, worship music changed. Songs and hymns were often improvised, and extended times of "singing in the spirit" were the norm:

> The Welsh are . . . a very musical people, and worshipful singing was a feature of the revival. As the Holy Spirit moved, it was common to find part of the congregation singing a hymn in rapturous awe, while others were on the floor crying in agony for God's mercy. An eye-witness recalls: "Such marvelous singing, quite unrehearsed, could only be created by the Holy Spirit. No choir. No conductor, no organ—just spontaneous, unctionised [sic] soul-singing. Once the first hymn was given out, the meeting ran itself. There was no leader, but people felt an unseen control. Singing, sobbing, praying intermingled without intermission."
>
> Singing was a fruit of the revival. Many of those powerfully filled by the Holy Spirit recorded their experience, especially of how they trembled, laughed and sang for hours afterwards.
>
> Evan Roberts himself felt singing to be of massive importance for the release of God's power. When a Londoner asked him

one day if the revival could ever reach the capital, he smiled and asked, "Can you sing?"[12]

The Welsh services were spontaneous. This included extemporaneous singing, testimonies, and one-on-one ministry. Stead described the scene:

> Three-fourths of the meeting consists in singing. No one uses a hymnbook.... The last person to control the meeting in any way is Mr. Evan Roberts. People pray and sing, give testimony, exhort as the Spirit moves them.... As a student of the psychology of crowds, I have seen nothing like it. You feel that the thousand or fifteen hundred persons before you have become merged into one myriad-headed but single-souled personality.... You can watch what they call the influence of the power of the Spirit playing over the crowded congregation as an eddying wind plays over the surface of a pond. If anyone carried away by his feelings prays too long, or if anyone when speaking fails to touch the right note, someone—it may be anybody—commences to sing. For a moment there is a hesitation as if the meeting were in doubt as to its decision, whether to hear the speaker or to continue to join in the prayer, or whether to sing. If it decides to hear and to pray, the singing dies away. If, on the other hand, as it usually happens, the people decide to sing, the chorus swells in volume until it drowns all other sound. A very remarkable instance of this abandonment of the meeting to the spontaneous impulse, not merely of those within the walls, but of those crowded outside, who were unable to get in, occurred on Sunday night. Twice the order of proceeding, if order it can be called, was altered by the crowd outside, who, being moved by some mysterious impulse, started a hymn on their own account, which was at once taken up by the congregation within. On one of these occasions Evan Roberts was addressing the meeting. He at once gave way, and the singing became general.[13]

Frequently, a singer (usually Roberts or his soloist) improvised worship songs. Sometimes only the lyrics were improvised and set to a folk tune or familiar hymn tune. At other times, both the melody and lyrics were improvised.

Strategic Personalities of the Welsh Revival

Six personalities emerged as leaders of and major contributors to the revival movement. First, **Evan Roberts** was the undeniable leader of the movement. He avoided a celebrity role. He was persistent in his commitment not to take credit for what happened in the nightly revival services—giving glory to the "working of the Holy Spirit." He reminded those around him to "take not the glory that belongs *only* to God."

Roberts grew up in the home of a coal miner. He worked the mine in his late teenage years before becoming a blacksmith. At age 26 he felt the call of God to enter full-time Christian ministry. During his years at Bible school, he felt an "overwhelming move of God" to go back to his home church at Loughor, Wales, where the revival began. For 18 months following that initial meeting, Roberts traveled Wales preaching, praying, and singing the gospel. He was almost always accompanied by a group of young female soloists who took an active and strategic role in the nightly services.[14] Thousands of people came to a saving knowledge of Christ through his efforts.

Annie Davies was one of the "preferred soloists" on the Roberts team. She played a strategic role in his early revival ministry and remained with him until he discontinued active public work in 1906. Davies was especially gifted in providing improvised songs between times of prayer and testimony. Roberts often preached or led in long prayers following her spiritually perceptive solos. It was said that "her ability as a singer and sensitivity to the atmosphere of revival services very often moved congregations to tears."[15] She is best known for her presentation of the "love song" of the Welsh revival, "Here Is Love Vast as the Ocean."[16]

Evan Roberts's brother, **Dan Roberts**, also played a strategic role in the Welsh Revival. According to one source, Dan "took an active role in the endeavor after his eyes were healed in response to the words of his brother." He traveled with his brother around Wales, holding revival meetings.

A teenager named **Florrie Evans** made a public confession on February 14, 1904, that she loved the Lord Jesus Christ with all her heart. The response was an outpouring of revival that had major impact on the western part of Wales. Upon meeting Evans, Roberts noted the godliness she and her friends exhibited in ministry. Later, she and her New Quay youth group were able to join the Joseph Jenkins revival team to hold meetings in northern Wales.[17]

Seth Joshua, the minister who influenced Roberts, was an evangelist with the Forward Movement of the Calvinistic Methodist Church. He prayed that revival would begin among the working class. Roberts and Joshua met each other in Newcastle Emlyn, where Joshua's prayer inspired Roberts and became a driving theme of the Welsh Revivals.[18]

Sidney Evans married Roberts' sister, Mary. He was a close friend of Evan Roberts and was used powerfully during the revival days. He traveled with a group of college students all over Wales conducting revival services and encouraging working class people to seek a deeper walk with Christ. Eventually, Evans entered full-time missionary service and became principal of the Theological College of India.

Worldwide Influence

The 1904 revival shook the world. In Great Britain, it resulted in a reduction of crime, drunkenness, and gambling, along with increased honesty and chastity. Most policemen in Great Britain still do not carry guns, perhaps due in part to the respect for law and order produced by this revival.

News of the Welsh Revival encouraged those praying for revival throughout Great Britain to intensify their efforts. The archbishop of Canterbury called for a national day of prayer. When one bishop told of confirming 950 converts in a single country parish church, 30 others declared their support for the revival. Outside the Anglican Church, Protestants in England increased by 10 percent between 1903 and 1906. Revival swept through Ireland and Scotland as well.

F. B. Meyer, G. Campbell Morgan, William Booth, and Gypsy Smith all witnessed the work of God in revival meetings. When R. A. Torrey and Charles Alexander arrived in the British Isles, offerings for missions increased and thousands were brought into the kingdom through their preaching.

Continental Europe also experienced spiritual renewal in response to news of the Welsh Revival. According to historian Paul Dienstberger, "Scandinavia was especially moved after the 1904 earthquake took place in Norway."[19] The awakening that began under the ministry of evangelist Albert Lunde in Norway was described by Norwegian Bishop Eivind Berggrav as "the greatest revival of his experience."[20]

France experienced an awakening of unity among its one million evangelicals. Thousands were saved in Germany through evangelistic meetings held in tents. Revival spread through Sweden, Finland, and Denmark. Lutherans described the revival as "the greatest movement of the Spirit since the Vikings were evangelized." Germany, France, and other European nations were also touched. Portions of politically troubled Russia experienced revival as thousands turned to Christ. Mission agencies were established to reach the Slavic people, with great success.

Latin America experienced a 180 percent increase in conversions to Protestant Christianity over a seven-year period. Valparaiso, Chile, long known as a wicked city, became a center for spiritual renewal after an August 17, 1906, earthquake. Revival spread through major portions of Brazil through the distribution of Bibles.

In Asia, prayer meetings and Bible studies turned into extended times of confession, and baptisms increased as many Buddhists and Muslims turned to Christ. Missionaries in Burma reported an "ingathering surpassing anything known in the history of the mission." Among the Burmese ethnic group known as the Karen, there were 2,000 baptisms in 1905, ten times the usual number. In a single church, 1,340 of the Shan, another ethnic group, were baptized in one month.

In India, people converted to Christianity at a rate 16 times greater than the rate of conversions to Hinduism. At one point, 96 percent of the nurses in the country were Christians.

In 1907, John R. Mott held the first World's Christian Student Federation conference in Asia. Six years earlier, an aggressive program of house-to-house evangelism yielded large numbers of conversions in Tokyo, and the effort spread to other big cities. News of the revival in Wales helped renew this evangelistic thrust. The preaching of Kimuri and Nakada by two Moody Bible Institute graduates led to the formation of the Japanese Evangelical Alliance.[21]

As a final note on these extraordinary workings of the Lord, in 1908 and 1909, following the Boxer Rebellion and evil slaughter of missionaries by the hundreds in China, people throughout Asia experienced revival once again. The impact on Asian culture was profound.

Impact on the United States and Canada

News of the Welsh Revival provoked a revival in America in 1905. In Philadelphia, Methodists reported 6,101 new converts. The pastors of Atlantic City churches claimed there were only 50 unconverted adults left in the entire city.

The revival also swept through the South. First Baptist Church in Paducah, Kentucky, added more than a thousand members in 1905. Across the Southern Baptist Convention, baptisms increased by 25 percent in a single year.

In the Midwest, Methodists reported "the greatest revivals in their history." Every store and factory in Burlington, Iowa, closed to allow employees to attend prayer meetings. When the mayor of Denver declared a day of prayer in that city, churches were filled by ten o'clock. At 11:30, virtually every place of business in the city closed as 12,000 gathered for prayer meetings in downtown theaters and halls. Every school in town, and even the Colorado State Legislature, closed for the day.

In the West, interdenominational meetings attracted 180,000 attendees. One evening in Los Angeles, the Grand Opera House was filled with drunks and prostitutes seeking salvation. In Portland, Oregon, the entire city virtually shut down between 11:00 a.m. and 2:30 p.m. for noon prayer meetings.

Similar phenomena swept Canada. Urban and rural churches alike organized prayer meetings and evangelistic campaigns. Thousands gathered nightly during Torrey/Alexander campaigns in major Canadian cities, including Winnipeg and Toronto. Among the converts of Torrey's Toronto meetings was a young man named Oswald J. Smith, who would one day become known as "the greatest missionary statesman of the twentieth century."[22]

After the Welsh Revival, many young people went as student volunteer missionaries to foreign fields, where they established schools, hospitals, and churches. Many new Christian schools were founded in North America as well, including Toronto Bible College, Winnipeg Bible Institute, Toccoa Falls College, Nyack Missionary College, and Columbia Bible College.

The Welsh Revival had worldwide impact indeed. Christianity, which previously had been perceived as largely a Western religion, gained its largest international harvest in history.[23] Throughout the world, Christian missionaries began building hospitals and training doctors and nurses. There was a groundswell of humanitarian work, as believers cared for the sick, and of ministerial education, as schools trained future pastors, evangelists, and missionaries.

In the next chapter, we will see how the Welsh Revival set the stage for the great revival campaigns of the early twentieth century at Azusa Street in Los Angeles. We will see how God continues to use strategic men and women as worship leaders, musicians, evangelists, and preacher-teachers of the gospel. In the process, entire communities were changed and thousands of lives were transformed by the power of the Holy Spirit.

Notes

1. A survey of 13 national leaders who were authorities on revival was done for Elmer Towns and Douglas Porter, *The Ten Greatest Revivals Ever* (Ann Arbor: Servant Publications, 2000). It determined that the greatest revival in human history was the 1904 revival that began in Wales. These 13 authorities represented a wide variety of denominations and theological perspectives and include: Bill Bright, founder, Campus Crusade for Christ, Orlando, Florida (deceased); Gerald Brooks, Grace Outreach Center, Plano, Texas (Pentecostal, Word of Faith); David Yonggi Cho, the Full Gospel Church, Seoul, Korea (Assemblies of God); Robert Coleman, Gordon-Conwell Theological

Seminary, South Hamilton, Massachusetts; James O. Davis, national evangelism director, Assemblies of God, Springfield, Missouri; Lewis Drummond, Beeson Divinity School, Birmingham, Alabama (Southern Baptist) (deceased); Dale Galloway, Asbury Theological Seminary, Wilmore, Kentucky (Nazarene, Independent); Eddie Gibbs, Fuller Theological Seminary, Pasadena, California (Episcopal-Anglican); Jack Hayford, the Church on the Way, Van Nuys, California; Charles Kelly, New Orleans Baptist Theological Seminary, New Orleans, Louisiana (Southern Baptist); D. James Kennedy, pastor and founder, Coral Ridge Presbyterian Church, Fort Lauderdale, Florida (Presbyterian) (deceased); Ron Phillips, pastor, Central Baptist Church, Hixson, Tennessee (Southern Baptist-Charismatic); Alvin Reid, Southeastern Baptist Theological Seminary, Wake Forest, North Carolina (Southern Baptist); Chuck Smith, Calvary Chapel Costa Mesa, Santa Ana, California; Tommy Tenney, evangelist, Pineville, Louisiana (Pentecostal); C. Peter Wagner, Global Spheres, Denton, Texas (New Apostolic Reformation); Steve Wingfield, evangelist, Harrisonburg, Virginia (Wesleyan).

2. According to Paul Dienstberger, only J. Edwin Orr, the great English revival writer, discerned the global effects in his 1973 work *The Flaming Tongue*. Most students of the era favored the glorification of the numerous evangelists and their big-business, revivalism methods rather than the widespread God-inspired renewal. However, Orr documented how all six of the populated continents experienced a noticeable, and a spontaneous, spiritual awakening around 1905. See Paul R. Dienstberger, *The American Republic: A Nation of Christians* (Ashland, OH: Paul R. Dienstberger, 2000), chap. 8 (np), http://www.prdienstberger.com/nation/Chap8wpr.htm; accessed August 6, 2011.

3. Towns and Porter, *The Ten Greatest Revivals Ever,* 23–44.

4. Ibid., 30.

5. Ibid., 31–32.

6. Ibid., 32.

7. J. Edwin Orr, *The Flaming Tongue: Evangelical Awakenings, 1900* (Chicago: Moody, 1975), 192–93.

8. Jim W. Goll, *The Seer: The Prophetic Power of Visions, Dreams, and Open Heavens* (Shippensburg, PA: Destiny Image, 2004), 180–81.

9. "Revival Swept Across Wales," http://www.christianity.com/11630678/page2/; accessed August 3, 2011.

10. Ibid.

11. Ibid.

12. "Glory, Glory, Hallelujah! Music, Song and Worship Were at the Heart of the 1904 Welsh Revival," http://www.jesus.org.uk/ja/mag_revival fires_wales.shtml; accessed August 3, 2011.

13. "Revival Swept Across Wales."

14. "The People of the 1904 Revival," http://www.welshrevival.com/lang-en/1904thepeople.htm; accessed August 3, 2011.

15. Ibid.

16. Ibid.

17. Ibid.

18. Ibid.

19. Dienstberger, *The American Republic,* chap. 8, (np).

20. Towns and Porter, *The Ten Greatest Revivals Ever,* 15–17.

21. Dienstberger, *The American Republic,* chap. 8, (np).

22. Towns and Porter, *The Ten Greatest Revivals Ever,* 21.

23. Dienstberger, *The American Republic,* chap. 8, (np).

CHAPTER 12

The Azusa Street Revival (1906–1908)

April 18, 1906, 5:12 a.m. The morning breeze normally flowing from the Pacific Ocean across the California hillside was mysteriously absent. The stillness of the moment was atypical for this giant of a city. The silence was deafening. Everything was strangely peaceful and in order. The sun's daily wake-up call had not even greeted the sleeping residents when the earth moved. The ground buckled. Large portions of pavement began to separate. Buildings crumbled. Bricks bounced from the sides of big, tall buildings to the ground like popcorn in a pan of hot oil. Power lines snapped like toothpicks in the hands of a little child. San Francisco bore the brunt of a forty-second earthquake more powerful than the energy, force, and intensity of an atomic bomb.

Eyewitness accounts reported that

> The quake sounded like "the roar of the sea," to police officer Jessie Cook, who was at Washington and Davis streets. It was "a low, rumbling noise like the fluttering of wings of steel," said Pierre Berlinger. It was like "an uncanny mezzo forte . . . like the roll of a cymbal or gong," said Alfred Hertz, principal conductor of the Metropolitan Opera who was staying at the Palace Hotel.[1]

Businessman Jerome B. Clark of Berkeley describes what he saw when stepping off the ferry on that morning:

> The street car tracks were bent and twisted out of shape. Electric wires lay in every direction. Streets on all sides were filled with brick and mortar, buildings either completely collapsed or brick fronts had just dropped completely off. Wagons with horses hitched to them, drivers and all, lying on the streets, all dead, struck and killed by the falling bricks, these mostly the wagons of the produce dealers, who do the greater part of their work at that hour of the morning.[2]

Almost immediately, fire broke out everywhere. The network of underground gas pipes—important to the infrastructure of this grand city—were snapped, broken, and rendered useless. The least little spark set strong, invincible buildings ablaze. Water—normally available for firefighters and emergency personnel—gushed from broken fire hydrants and could not be sequestered or commandeered for battle. In minutes, the entire 410,000 inhabitants of San Francisco were held in bondage to one of the most feared acts of nature.

In his book *The Barbary Coast,* Herbert Asbury called San Francisco the "wickedest city on the continent." Some thought the event was truly the judgment of God on a sinful city. G. A. Raymond, eyewitness to the event, certainly believed many people thought it was the end of the world. Raymond describes what he saw when escaping through the hotel entrance:

> Outside I witnessed a sight I never want to see again. It was dawn and light. I looked up. The air was filled with falling stones. People around me were crushed to death on all sides. All around the huge buildings were shaking and waving.
>
> I asked a man standing next to me what happened. Before he could answer a thousand bricks fell on him and he was killed. . . .

All around me buildings were rocking and flames shooting. As I ran people on all sides were crying, praying and calling for help. I thought the end of the world had come.[3]

Fire wreaked havoc on the city for three days before large, God-sent thunderstorms intervened. When it was over, the devastation included the destruction of 490 city blocks and 25,000 buildings. Two-hundred fifty thousand were left homeless[4] and between 700 and 3,000 were killed in and around San Francisco city itself. Another 189 lives were lost in cities and towns to the north and south.[5] Cost estimates by professionals were in excess of $350 million.[6]

Ironically, according to the *San Francisco Chronicle*, "the National Board of Fire Underwriters had warned of fires as recently as 1905. San Francisco has violated all underwriting traditions by not burning up," the report said. Surrounding the downtown city were wooden houses crowded close together.[7] Like the Chicago Fire 35 years before, San Francisco was ready for *the perfect fire*.

Dennis Sullivan, city fire chief, who lost his life in the blaze, predicted such a catastrophic event just months before:

> "This town is in an earthquake belt," he said in a speech. "One of these fine mornings, we will get a shake that will put this little water system out, and then we'll have a fire. What will we do then? Why, we'll have to fight her with dynamite."

Sure enough, dynamite is exactly what the military used in trying to contain the fire. However, because the use of dynamite was poorly managed by seriously untrained men at the time, the effort proved futile, further fueled the fire, and increased the devastation.

A total of 290 miles of the earth's surface, from northwest of San Juan Bautista to the triple junction at Cape Mendocino, was ruptured. The 7.9 Richter scale quake was felt from Oregon to Los Angeles.[8]

It took millions of dollars from the American treasury, thousands of volunteers, multiple thousands of military professionals, scores of architects, thousands of carpenters, aggressive city leadership, and better than 10 years for the community to fully overcome ravages of the Great San Francisco Earthquake.

Four days prior to the 1906 San Francisco Earthquake, on April 14, another event occurred 400 miles south at 321 Azusa Street in Los Angeles. The San Francisco quake rocked the city and surrounding communities. The earthquake on April 14th rocked the world. This was a quake of spiritual dimension that still shapes the landscape of the evangelical community around the globe.

Beginning on April 14, 1906, the Azusa Street Revival forever changed the landscape of Christianity. In fact, when the Associated Press noted the 100 most important events in the twentieth century, it only included one religious event—the Azusa Revival.

The Azusa Revival marked the beginning of a new "brand" of Christianity.[9] It sparked the creation of many new denominations. Among them were the Church of God in Christ, the Pentecostal Holiness Church, the Assemblies of God, the International Church of the Foursquare Gospel, the Open Bible Standard Church, Apostolic Churches, and the Church of God. International organizations, missions initiatives, Bible colleges, and parachurch organizations were also influenced by the Azusa Revival. By 1998, approximately 500 million people in more than 100 nations called themselves Pentecostal or Charismatic—descendants of the Azusa Street Awakening.[10]

Overview of the Great Awakening

William Joseph Seymour was born to recently freed slaves in Centreville, Louisiana. He taught himself how to read and write, and by age 30 he had been saved through the ministry of an evangelistic team known as the Evening Light Saints in Cincinnati.

This group believed that history was coming to an end and anticipated Christ's imminent return to establish his kingdom. Citing Hos 6:3, they taught that just before Christ returned, there would be a fresh outpouring of the Holy Spirit known as "the Latter Rain." They were on a mission to prepare Christians for the return of Christ.

Following his encounter with the Evening Light Saints, Seymour went to Houston and attended an African American church. There he witnessed a phenomenon he had never seen before: a woman praying in another language. The Evening Light Saints taught him that such phenomena would usher in the return of Christ.

Seymour met with Lucy Farrow, the woman whom he witnessed speaking in tongues, and learned of a man in Topeka, Kansas, named Charles F. Parham, a white preacher who ran a Holiness Bible school, Bethel College. Parham had introduced her to an experience called the "baptism of the Holy Ghost."

Seymour headed for Topeka to seek Parham and admission to his Bible school. Seymour faced racial barriers. Parham welcomed Seymour's zeal, but he was not ready to welcome a black student into his school. So they arrived at a compromise. Seymour was allowed to listen to lectures from a chair outside an open window. In the event of rain, he could move his chair into the hallway, and a door would be left ajar for him to hear. Earnestly, Seymour sought the baptism of the Holy Spirit, but without success.

In 1902, Seymour moved to Houston and began preaching in African American mission churches. On one occasion, a visitor from Los Angeles heard him and recommended him to her pastor in California. Soon he was invited to preach on Santa Fe Avenue in Los Angeles at a little storefront church that started as a split from a local black Baptist church over the so-called "second blessing" of the Holy Spirit. Seymour saw this opportunity as his own "Macedonian vision" calling him to a new place of ministry. He borrowed train fare from Parham and traveled west to Los Angeles.[11]

When Julia W. Hutchins, the California church's pastor, met Seymour, she recognized a significant difference between her teaching and that of Seymour. She considered him extreme, even heretical. So, when Seymour arrived at the church to preach, he found the doors locked. He was no longer welcome. Undaunted, he agreed to preach at the home of Richard and Ruth Asberry at 214 Bonnie Brae Avenue.[12]

Many came from Hutchins's church to hear Seymour preach. Most of the congregation were domestic servants, and it was an interracial meeting of blacks and whites. They came to hear the preacher, who had never spoken in tongues, tell how God would bless them if they could speak in tongues.

On April 9, 1906, Edward Lee told Seymour he had received a vision that they would receive the gift of tongues that evening. Together, Lee, Seymour, and seven others prayed and made their way to the meeting. That night, "the power fell" on those assembled and they began speaking in other languages. Three days later, Seymour began praising God in an unknown tongue.[13]

News spread throughout the community, and the little home on Bonnie Brae Avenue was too small to hold the crowds. The weight of the crowd on the front porch was so great that it collapsed. An abandoned church building near Bonnie Brae Avenue was available and quickly secured—even though it had been used as a warehouse and livery stable and was in much need of repair.

Seymour's Apostolic Faith Gospel Mission moved into its new home at 312 Azusa Street East on Saturday, April 14, 1906. Seymour warned his listeners that the end of the world was at hand. He said that Jesus was coming soon to judge the world and establish his kingdom. Prior to the coming of Jesus there would be "Latter Rain," an outpouring of the Holy Spirit, which included speaking in tongues. In response, men and women began confessing sin. People were healed. Day and night for weeks on end people came from around the globe to experience the outpouring of the Holy Spirit. Historian Estrelda Y. Alexander described the phenomena:

> Men and women, adults and children, black, white, yellow, and red freely worshiped God and admonished each other to holiness of life through speaking in tongues and interpretation, prophecy, testimony, song, prayer, miraculous signs and preaching. Each one, in order, as they felt directed by the Holy Spirit, gave vent to the fire that was shut deep within their bones and glorified God for their newfound freedom and empowerment. Women and men freely participated as they felt God leading them. Even children who felt inspired by God had a voice in the worship and received Pentecostal Holy Spirit baptism.[14]

A skeptical reporter from the *Los Angeles Times* heard about the meeting and attended. The next day, he reported "wild scenes," a weird babbling of tongues, the prediction of coming judgment. His negative report was the first of many.

On the morning of April 18, four days after Seymour's prediction of the Lord's coming judgment, the earth shook in the infamous San Francisco Earthquake of 1906. For some months a spike in attendance at the Azusa Street Mission was attributed to the San Francisco disaster. Some said the earthquake gave credibility to Seymour's prediction.

Revival continued. Soon, Seymour published *Apostolic Faith,* a four-page tabloid that was sent across America. He used the paper to describe and explain the manifestation of tongues in his meetings. It was sent free of charge to nearly 50,000 readers and was often filled with testimonials from people who experienced "Holy Spirit Baptism, healing, deliverance, and other miraculous occurrences."[15] The world began to hear about the Azusa Street Revival.

Within a few months, more than 300 people crowded into the 40-by-60-foot wood-framed building, forcing many worshippers to gather in doorways and around the windows on the outside. Many who had come to investigate were touched. They continued to meet in daily, camp-meeting-style gatherings for more than seven years. Often services would run from 10 a.m. until midnight or later.[16]

Seymour did most of the preaching. He was a man of discipline who did not speak with a loud, boisterous tone. He simply encouraged worshippers to seek a Savior who could meet every need—emotional, physical, spiritual, and intellectual.

> Though many gave impromptu sermons as prompted by the Spirit, Seymour was the main preacher. He apparently did not fit the Bible thumping caricature often ascribed to Pentecostal preachers, but his messages were powerful enough that the altars of the mission were regularly filled with those seeking repentance, sanctification, Holy Spirit baptism or healing.[17]

Seymour advised worship leaders to speak to outsiders about their need for Jesus Christ as Savior and not about the mystery of glossolalia (speaking in tongues).[18] Everything was spontaneous at Azusa Street. Sermons were unannounced. There was no platform or stage on which the preacher stood. Rather, all were considered equal in the sight of God, so everyone was placed on the same level.[19]

The crowd at Azusa Street was multiracial. People of different ethnicities and cultures worshipped side by side. There was no segregated seating. Seymour preached that the dissolution of racial barriers was the surest sign of the Spirit's Pentecostal presence and the approach of a New Jerusalem. According to one historian:

The degree of racial harmony led Frank Bartleman to report in his later memoirs that the "color line was washed away in the blood [of Jesus]" . . . it was something very extraordinary . . . white pastors from the south were early prepared to go to Los Angeles to Negroes [sic], to fellowship with them and to receive through their prayers and intercessions the blessings of the Spirit. And it was still more wonderful that these white pastors went back to the south and reported that they had been together with Negroes [sic], that they had prayed in one Spirit and received the same blessing.[20]

Not everyone in the new Pentecostal movement appreciated Seymour's interracial methods. Parham, Seymour's mentor, came to Los Angeles in October 1906 to investigate the revival. Parham had preached for many years the need for a new dispensation of the Holy Spirit, so he came to Azusa Street with great expectations. What he saw was different from what he had anticipated. Parham shuddered to see blacks and whites praying at the same altar.

When Parham saw a white woman who was "slain in the Spirit" fall backwards into the arms of a black man, he was horrified. In his preaching he rebuked the crowd for their disregard of racial distinctions. The elders at the Azusa Street mission, both black and white, rejected Parham's condemnation, and he was asked to leave and barred from returning.

Parham was not the only white holiness preacher who was sympathetic to Seymour's message but unable to break from racist attitudes. Within a few years, segregated Pentecostal denominations began to arise. Even though they broke with Seymour's vision of racial integration, they embraced the speaking in tongues experienced on Azusa Street.

Strategic Personalities

William J. Seymour (1870–1922) was the most influential and strategic personality of the Azusa Street Revival. Reared Baptist, he left home for Memphis, Tennessee, at age 20. He worked as a waiter in some relatively high-end establishments in Memphis, Indiana, Ohio, and Illinois before meeting Daniel S. Warner and Martin Wells Knapp, both of Cincinnati. Knapp was founder of God's Bible school and the God's Revivalist movement. He believed in premillennialist eschatology and advocated divine healing, holiness revivals, preaching, and missionary endeavors. Warner's Church of God Reformation movement believed that interracial worship was a sign of the end times. They practiced multiethnic worship on a regular basis and, according to Alexander, testified that they were "saved, sanctified, and prejudice removed."[21]

While in Cincinnati, Seymour contracted smallpox. He did not know any cure for the dreaded disease. Then, one night he dreamed that "God told him he would heal him if he would preach the gospel."[22] Seymour answered the call to preach, and the only damage to his body from the disease was the loss of sight in his left eye.

In 1902, Seymour moved to Houston and was highly influenced by Lucy Farrow, the woman who introduced him to speaking in tongues. She also introduced him to the doctrine of Pentecostal Spirit baptism and other holiness doctrines.

Among the associates of Seymour after he moved to Los Angeles were *Neely Terry, Hiram Smith, Phoebe Sargeant, Jennie Moore* (whom he married in 1908), *Clara Lum, Florence Crawford,* and *G. W. Evans.*[23] This team of men and women captured the vision of the Azusa Street Revival and helped launch the Pentecostal movement.

William Durham, a prominent Chicago pastor, was deeply impressed by Seymour and the events at Azusa Street. Durham maintained a close friendship with the Azusa Street organization for years.

He influenced *Eudorous Bell*, who was instrumental in establishing the *Assemblies of God*, Springfield, Missouri.[24] The Pentecostal Assemblies of Canada recognized their spiritual indebtedness to Seymour and the Azusa Street vision as well, especially the early manifestations of charismatic phenomena in Winnipeg and Toronto.

Bell encouraged *Howard Goss*, who helped establish the *United Pentecostal Church*. *Aimee Semple,* supported and encouraged by Azusa Street participants, established the *International Church of the Foursquare Gospel*. *Charles Harrison Mason* considered Seymour his "father in the faith." Mason established the predominantly black *Church of God in Christ*.

Another Church of God denomination, this one white, became Pentecostal when *G. B. Cashwell*, an Azusa Street convert, described the revival at a national convention. During the meeting, the denomination's general overseer, *A. J. Thomlinson,* listened attentively. Then suddenly he fell out of his chair and began speaking in tongues at Cashwell's feet. While a few churches left the movement, most of them embraced the Pentecostal message. Soon, the *Church of God of Prophecy*[25] was another fast-growing denomination.

John G. Lake visited the Azusa Street meetings and then took the Pentecostal message to South Africa in 1908.[26] Within five years, he established 500 black and 125 white Pentecostal churches in that nation. Others took the Pentecostal message to Europe and Asia. *Apostolic Faith* reported:

> Pentecost has crossed the water on both sides to the Hawaiian Islands on the west, and England, Norway, Sweden and India on the east. . . . We rejoice to hear that Pentecost has fallen in Calcutta, India. . . . We have letters from China, Germany, Switzerland, Norway, Sweden, England, Ireland, Australia and other countries from hungry souls that want their Pentecost. . . .

> In Stockholm, Sweden . . . the first soul came through tonight, receiving the baptism with the Holy Ghost with Bible evidence. . . . In Christiana, Norway—God is wonderfully demonstrating His power.[27]

Innovations to Worship during the Great Awakening

Historian Robb Redman defined the Azusa Street Revival as a singing revival.[28] Edith Blumhofer explains that:

> Pentecostals sang the gospel songs of their day, some of the better-known hymns of the church, and choruses billed as "given" by the Holy Spirit. In many places, they kept singing songs they had sung before, adding some to express new dimensions of religious experience.[29]

Innovations to worship practices during the Azusa Street meetings were numerous. First, the services included impromptu sermons by clergy and laypeople alike. Second, the congregation sang in English and in tongues. Third, prophesying, divine healing, and exorcisms were common. Fourth, anyone and everyone could freely share testimony as the Spirit led. Fifth, there was a mixture of singing newly composed songs (sometimes improvised) and older hymns. Sixth, the Azusa Street meetings included anointing with oil, laying on of hands, and praying over material objects. These included prayer cloths, which were used as points of contact for those in pain, sorrow, anguish, suffering, grief, and distress. Seventh, women took on a new, active role in leading worship. They preached, taught, exhorted entire congregations, prayed, gave prophetic utterances, spoke in tongues, and interpreted.[30]

Clara Lum worked closely with Seymour from 1906 to 1908. She was a gifted editor and helped with the publishing of his *Apostolic Faith*. At one point, she wrote about the singing at the Azusa Street meetings:

> There is singing in the Spirit . . . the music is not learned. No one can join in unless it is given to them [by the Spirit]. They sing in different tongues at the same time, and the different parts are songs. Sometimes, one is singing in English, thus interpreting while the others are singing [in tongues].[31]

In 1915, Seymour developed the *Doctrine and Disciplines of the Azusa Street Mission*. The publication articulated foundational doctrines of the congregation and included "orders of worship for ordination, Communion, weddings and funerals, extending fellowship to new members and other special services."[32]

Summary of the Great Awakening

The Azusa Street Revival impacted Christian doctrine and practice. The Pentecostal movement traces its roots back to Seymour, including his emphasis on Holy Spirit baptism and glossolalia. During the Azusa Street Revival, more than 20 denominations and hundreds of congregations in the United States embraced the doctrine of glossolalia.

The worship at Azusa Street was largely a continuation of what Evan Roberts did in the Welsh Revivals—including long services, unstructured orders of worship, and spontaneous testimonies and singing. Among the practices Azusa Street helped introduce to evangelicals:

1. Services focused on personal worship, knowing Jesus more deeply, and repentance from sin
2. Emphasis on holiness and sanctification in worship services
3. Singing newly composed worship songs in English and in tongues
4. Impromptu sermons from laymen and clergy
5. Fully improvised services without any planned agenda
6. Camp-meeting-style worship sometimes lasting 10 to 12 hours—extended times for singing, confession of sin, foot washing and communion, prayer, and healing

7. Public practice of glossolalia with appropriate interpretation
8. Prophesying in public, divine healing, anointing with oil, and praying over material objects
9. Increased expression of emotions during worship services by men and women
10. Racial integration in services

Alexander summarized the importance of the Azusa Street worshippers for Christianity in the decades to come:

> They were at the forefront of shaping the theology, worship and music styles of a movement that would forever change the face of American and global Christianity. . . . Once their tongues were touched by the fires of Azusa Street and they felt themselves empowered by the Spirit of God, they left Los Angeles with others of every race and culture to take the message of the in-breaking of the Spirit in a powerful new way across the nation and the world, serving as missionaries both at home and abroad.[33]

Indeed, the Christian world is different today because of the worshippers at 321 Azusa Street in 1906.

The next chapter tells the story of how great men and women experienced revival in the eastern parts of the United States. Revivalists led large evangelistic campaigns with the help of dynamic song leaders.

Notes

1. "The San Francisco Earthquake, 1906," EyeWitness to History (1997), www.eyewitnesstohistory.com; accessed July 22, 2011.
2. Ibid.
3. Ibid.
4. Ibid.
5. See http://earthquake.usgs.gov/regional/nca/1906/18april/index.php; accessed July 22, 2011.
6. "The San Francisco Earthquake, 1906."

7. See http://www.sfgate.com/cgi-bin/article.cgi?f=/c/a/2006/04/09/BAGQ09QUAKE; accessed July 22, 2011.

8. Jennifer Rosenberg, "1906 San Francisco Earthquake," www.About.com; accessed July 22, 2011.

9. "Survey: 1 in 4 U.S. Christians Identify as Pentecostal," *Prophecy News Watch*, http://www.prophecynewswatch.com/2010/April08/0881.html; accessed April 1, 2011.

10. Michael Collins and Matthew A. Price, *The Story of Christianity: 2000 Years of Faith* (Wheaton: Tyndale House, 1999), 225.

11. Estrelda Y. Alexander, *Black Fire: One Hundred Years of African American Pentecostalism* (Downers Grove: IVP Academic, 2011), 114–16.

12. Ibid., 118.

13. Ibid., 118–19.

14. Ibid., 121.

15. Ibid., 120.

16. Ibid., 119.

17. Ibid., 128.

18. Paul R. Dienstberger, *The American Republic: A Nation of Christians* (Ashland, Ohio: Paul R. Dienstberger, 2000), np, http://www.prdienstberger.com/nation/Chap8wpr.htm; accessed August 6, 2011.

19. Ibid.

20. Alexander, *Black Fire*, 122.

21. Ibid., 113.

22. Ibid., 114.

23. Ibid., 128.

24. Ibid., 39–40.

25. Ibid.

26. Ibid., 40.

27. Ibid., 40–41.

28. Robb Redman, *The Great Worship Awakening* (San Francisco: Jossey-Bass, 2002), 28.

29. Ibid., 28–29.

30. Alexander, *Black Fire*, 48–49.

31. Ibid., 146.

32. Ibid., 129.

33. Ibid., 392.

CHAPTER 13

The Revivalists and Great Evangelistic Campaigns, Part 1 (1890–1935)

One would think that the revival fires witnessed by Evan Roberts in Wales (1904–1905) would have little, if any, impact on the churches of America. After all, those episodes of Holy Spirit blessing seemed to be localized and the winds of God appeared, at least on the surface, random and unfocused. One of the characteristics of a "Great Awakening" is that the working of the Holy Spirit has vast, most-often international, implication and impact. Such is the case of the revival of 1904 in Wales. During the first two months of 1905, churches from Philadelphia to Pittsburgh began to experience revival.

Large groups of people met to confess sins. They restored relationships with one another and reached out to unsaved neighbors and friends. The Methodists of Philadelphia saw more than 10,000 converts by late spring 1905. Pennsylvania Baptists announced that every part of the state was experiencing some type of awakening. Not since the days of the Moody-Sankey campaigns had Christians witnessed such a work of God. One historian wrote that "the northeast was ablaze."[1]

New York City witnessed its greatest harvest of souls since the 1858 Laymen's Revival. Schenectady, New York, newspapers ran stories about "the power of prayer," "Great Moral Liftup," "Pentecostal Fires," and "Yesterday's Conversions." Local ministers reported that large, multi-denominational groups were meeting for prayer at noon, in the afternoon, and in the evening.[2] In New York's Mohawk River Valley region, infidels, alcoholics, fornicators, and prostitutes were saved. People of various ethnicities and nationalities worshipped together and responded to the gospel message.

In New Jersey, Christian societies for youth and young adults reported a 300 percent increase in membership. In Newark, "Pentecost was literally repeated,"[3] and a significant percentage of the 60,000 people in Atlantic City came to a saving knowledge of Jesus Christ.

By April, the awakening reached New England. In Boston, the church pastored by A. C. Dixon witnessed 150 conversions on one Sunday. Daniel Shepardson, the well-known "wheelchair evangelist," experienced great success at Danbury, Connecticut. The YMCA had such a harvest in Rutland, Vermont, that it called on Dixon to assist with the 450 people seeking discipleship training.

In Northfield, Massachusetts, people confessed and repented when told of the Welsh Revival. In Forest City, Maine, famous for its drunkenness and immorality, churches that usually closed for the winter months stayed open.

In the Southern states, Methodists, Baptists, Presbyterians, and Episcopalians partnered in revival campaigns. In Atlanta, nearly 1,000 businessmen agreed to pray for an outpouring of the Holy Spirit. On November 2, 1904, they organized a midday prayer service. So successful was their effort that "stores, factories, offices, saloons, amusement places and even the Georgia Supreme Court closed operations during the noon time prayer."[4]

In Norfolk, Virginia, churches coordinated their efforts to win people to Christ. In Tennessee, Georgia, North and South Carolina, and Florida, God moved through unexpected waves of revival. Mordecai Ham, one of the most prominent evangelists in the South during those days, experienced a huge harvest of souls.[5]

More than 4,000 conversions were recorded in March 1905 at citywide noonday prayer meetings in Louisville, Kentucky. At least 58 businesses closed for the meetings. J. J. Checks, pastor of the First Baptist Church in Paducah, Kentucky, received more than a thousand new members in 1905.

In Michigan, Ohio, Indiana, Illinois, and Iowa, news of the Welsh Revival caused sensational response among Baptists and Methodists. Sometimes, as with Evan Roberts, a simple summons to prayer was enough to spark revival. Meetings were unstructured. People spontaneously confessed sin and responded to the call of God in their lives. Chicago, St. Louis, and Kansas City witnessed unexpected response at noonday prayer meetings. Gambling establishments and brothels were closed in Houston and Dallas. Churches were packed, and the Baylor University student body experienced revival.

So successful was J. Wilbur Chapman's 1905 ministry in Denver that the Colorado Legislature adjourned for a day of prayer. More than 12,000 people filled churches, theaters, and school auditoriums for midday prayer and evangelistic meetings. Chapman had similar results when preaching a series of services in Seattle.

Pastors in Oregon called the move of God a "Portland Pentecost." More than 200 shop owners decided to close their businesses from 11 a.m. to 2 p.m. so that people could attend noontime prayer services. In

Los Angeles, more than 100 churches partnered in a series of revival meetings and more than 180,000 people attended.

Student organizations across America experienced revival as young men and women answered the call to missions in unprecedented numbers. In 1896, 2,000 students declared intentions for missionary studies. By the end of 1905, an impressive 11,000 pursued missions on one level or another.

In February 1905, during a winter blizzard, God moved in an unexpected way in Wilmore, Kentucky. It began when a student from Maryland named E. Stanley Jones[6] answered the call to missions at a dormitory prayer meeting. Students began confessing sin and making decisions to follow Christ in full-time ministry service. Relationships between students were reconciled and lives restored. Revival chronicler Wesley Duewel told the story:

> Four of the young male students were having a prayer meeting in a private room. To their surprise, at about 10:00 p.m., the Holy Spirit seemed to enter the room, and suddenly they were all swept off their feet. Other students heard them and came running. For hours they continued in the Lord's presence and none of them slept the rest of the night.
>
> In the morning they went to college chapel service. . . . People were on their knees throughout the chapel seeking God. . . . Revival spread throughout the college and town, and people began to flock in from the surrounding area. . . . For three days there were no classes. "At the end of three days I think every student was converted and many people from outside," said Stanley Jones.[7]

God sent revival to universities, colleges, and seminaries in all parts of America. Awakenings were reported at Wheaton College in Illinois; Taylor University in Indiana; Stetson University in Florida; Seattle Pacific College on the West Coast; Bethel College in Minneapolis;

Baylor University in Texas; Yale, Cornell, Princeton, Rutgers, and Trinity in the Northeast; Drake University in Missouri; and Northwestern College in Minnesota.[8]

In 1905, the five largest Protestant denominations in America increased by a total of 264,253 members. Methodists surged to 102,000. Baptists reported a 10-percent increase in baptisms.

Revivalists

It was in this atmosphere of spiritual awakening that an army of professional revivalists and evangelistic preachers made their mark on America. J. Wilbur Chapman, R. A. Torrey, and Gypsy (Rodney) Smith were perhaps the most successful of these. Many felt they picked up the mantle of Moody and Sankey.

From 1912 to 1918, some 650 full-time and 1,200 part-time revivalists crossed the United States holding more than 35,000 campaigns in every major city and town. It was patriotism, prohibition, and social gospel all wrapped up into one mixture of old-time religion and hard-hitting preaching. Some revivalists attacked theater and carnival attendance, dancing, drinking, and gambling.

The Story of Billy Sunday and Homer Rodeheaver

Billy Sunday may have done more than anyone else to help spread revival in the United States during the 1910s and 1920s. A major league baseball player,[9] Sunday and a group of teammates stumbled into the Pacific Garden Mission on State Street in Chicago in 1886. Sunday was persuaded to stay and listen to the preaching. At the end of the sermon, he made his way to the altar and gave his heart to Christ.

Later, he became one of the greatest revivalists in America. During nearly 40 years of ministry, he preached more than 300 evangelistic campaigns in every major city in the country, and more than 593,000 made decisions for Christ as a result of his preaching.

Church buildings and auditoriums in most cities were not large enough for Billy Sunday crusades. Businessmen would pool their money, rent empty lots, and build pole buildings that came to be known as "Billy Sunday Tabernacles."[10] These buildings provided ample space for people to hear Sunday's preaching.[11]

The most impressive of all his campaigns stretched from April to June 1917 in New York City. By the end of this campaign, 98,264 people made professions of faith. It took more than 50,000 volunteers to run the event—including between 5,000 and 10,000 attending "cottage prayer meetings."

No other evangelist was as flamboyant or charismatic as Sunday. Called a "leather-lunged evangelist," 10,000 people could hear him preach without electronic amplification. He would often leap from his platform and cry out to the people, "If your heart is as my heart, then take my hand." In dramatic gesture, he offered his hand to anyone who would come forward and grab it, indicating a commitment to follow Christ.

Sunday also championed moral and ethical causes. He called for the end of child labor, supported women's suffrage, and included blacks in his revivals—even in the Deep South. He was known for his fights against evolution, card playing, movie attendance, and dancing. His favorite attack was against "Mr. Booze," and many say his preaching was instrumental in securing congressional approval of the Eighteenth Amendment.

Sunday was famous for his folksy wit:

> "I'm against sin," he once said. "I'll kick it as long as I have a foot. I'll fight it as long as I have a fist. I'll butt it as long as I have

a head. I'll bite it as long as I've got a tooth. And when I'm old and fistless and footless and toothless, I'll gum it till I go home to glory."[12]

In 1909, Sunday partnered with musician-businessman Homer Rodeheaver. Affectionately called "Rody" by Sunday, Rodeheaver used his gifts as a trombonist, choir director, and master of ceremonies to charm audiences before the preaching. One historian quipped that his services were "more for the circus than for worship."[13]

Rodeheaver was famous for leading enthusiastic congregational singing and large choirs.[14] He explained:

> Platforms were built to seat as many as two thousand singers. The chorus in Philadelphia, organized by Mr. H. C. Lincoln, that veteran master organizer, had a membership of considerably over five thousand. We divided them into three groups, No. 1, No. 2 and a male chorus, each of about two thousand [singers]. No. 1 chorus sang on Tuesday, No. 2 on Wednesday, and the male chorus on Thursday night. No. 1 chorus came again on Friday, and No. 2 on Saturday. They alternated Sunday morning and Sunday night, and usually the male chorus sang on Sunday afternoon.... Because of the large number of churches co-operating it was never difficult to keep our chorus platform filled with good singers.[15]

The choir was integral to the music portion of services. Rodeheaver choirs mesmerized audiences with marked contrast between loud and soft passages of music—often singing "Master the Tempest Is Raging" and ending with Handel's "Hallelujah Chorus." Like Sankey before him, Rodeheaver used gospel songs for evangelistic purposes, for which he drew criticism. One historian noted:

> These songs [were] not written for prayer meetings, but to challenge the attention of people on the outside who [had] not been

interested in any form of church work or worship. They [were] used simply as a step from nothing to something.[16]

Rodeheaver took credit for influencing the development of choirs at many important churches and schools:

> The outstanding example of this is the famous Westminster Choir, with its magnetic director, Dr. John Finley Williamson. He was the chairman of our music committee in the city of Dayton, Ohio. During that meeting . . . the Westminster Choir was organized. . . . Sometime after this I brought the great choir into the studio of the RCA Photophone Company in New York. . . . Dr. Charles R. Erdman, of Princeton Theological Seminary, read the Scripture. It was this meeting of Dr. Williamson and Dr. Erdman in this studio that opened the way to bring the Westminster Choir School to Princeton as a part of that institution.[17]

Rodeheaver and Sunday worked together for more than 20 years. A brilliant businessman, music publisher, and recording artist,[18] Rodeheaver was best known for his work with Sunday. His half-hour songfest was much like a political rally, combining patriotic and religious themes. According to Rodeheaver's own testimony, the goal of his music was always to encourage public professions of faith during Sunday's evangelistic invitations.

As wonderful and elaborate as Rodeheaver's presentations were, people came to see Sunday. His colorful, flashy, and at times gaudy preaching style was an attraction for believers and unbelievers alike. According to Rodeheaver:

> He was an overpowering speaker using 300-words a minute that kept every eye riveted on him. He ran, walked, skipped, bounced, and gyrated around the platform. Every story included some physical action that transfixed the observers. He would use

a chair to fend the Devil, and then smash it over something on the stage. He portrayed a believer's entrance into heaven with a baseball slide, and ended with "Safe in the Arms of Jesus." He did handstands. He pounded the podium and jumped off the pulpit. Throughout the sermon he'd shed his coat, pull off his tie, roll up his sleeves, and leave the audience emotionally drained.[19]

Sunday's preaching helped bring about political reform throughout the nation. Indeed, corrupt political leaders—mayors, governors, senators, and assembly delegates—were replaced with those who were perceived as honest. In Texas, J. Frank Norris, pastor of First Baptist Church, Fort Worth, joined with Sunday in preaching against horse racing. So successful were their efforts that the Texas State Assembly voted to outlaw the practice.[20]

The Bible-Teaching Movement

Beginning in 1876 there was a "Believers' Meeting for Bible Study" held annually in Niagara-on-the-Lake, Ontario, Canada, at the Queen's Royal Hotel and its pavilion.[21] Believers vacationed there during the summer months to hear outstanding teachers proclaim the Scriptures. They were drawn from churches primarily in large Northern cities of the United States and Canada.

To follow up on the revivalist campaigns of Moody, Whittle, and others, many felt that time had come for a greater emphasis on discipleship training. In America, many people attended mainline Protestant churches that had grown indifferent to the gospel message. Some were in churches more committed to liturgy than discipleship. They looked for spiritual food and freedom of worship expression. Others were in churches with pastors deeply influenced by European concepts of "higher criticism." In some cases, pastors attempted to convince their congregations that biblical stories were myth and that the Word of

God could not be trusted. Many members of these congregations were hungry to know truth. Also, by the end of the nineteenth century, some Methodists focused on emotionalism more than teaching Scripture (they were called "shouting Methodists"). Believers from all these groups attended Bible conferences to learn Scripture.

Most of the speakers at these conferences and Bible-study meetings were dispensationalists who emphasized the Holy Spirit, premillennialism, prophecy, Paul's epistles, and the fundamentals of the faith. The leading Bible teachers of the movement included James McGranahan, George Stebbins, Ada Habershon, C. I. Scofield, James H. Brookes, Charles Erdman, Adoniram Judson Gordon, James Hudson Taylor, G. Campbell Morgan, and William Eugene Blackstone.[22]

The Bible-teaching conference at Niagara-on-the-Lake had a significant impact on American Christianity. First, many summer Bible conferences began across the United States and Canada, often using the same speakers.

Second, a new group of independent foreign mission organizations were supported largely by Bible-teaching churches with close connections to these conferences.

Third, the Bible-conference movement contributed to the rise of Bible institutes and colleges to train ministers for the growing number of Bible-teaching churches.

Fourth, the movement precipitated a vast amount of literature defending the fundamentals of the faith and explaining prophecy. In 1904, Scofield released the New Testament version of the *Scofield Reference Bible*. The entire Scofield Reference Bible was released in 1916. This reference Bible influenced Bible interpretation for the next 100 years.

Fifth, many Bible-teaching local churches were founded, primarily across the Northern states, that emphasized expositional preaching.

Sixth, Bible "centers" were founded in large Northern cities where well-known Bible teachers held Sunday afternoon conferences.[23] In time, conference centers were established in Montrose, Pennsylvania; Winona Lake, Indiana; Montreat, North Carolina; Northfield, Massachusetts; and Stony Brook, Long Island, New York.

A new expression of Christian music arose among Bible-teaching churches. In response to the perceived deadness of the European music in mainline churches, they added modern American hymns and gospel choruses to their worship repertoire.

Strategic Personalities

J. Wilbur Chapman (1859–1918) was an American evangelist, pastor, and hymn writer. Moody called him the "greatest evangelist in the country." He wrote the words to the hymns "One Day," "Jesus, What a Friend for Sinners (Our Great Savior)," and "'Tis Jesus."

Chapman began his work as a full-time evangelist in 1893. His friend John H. Converse, a wealthy Presbyterian layman, set up a trust fund in 1905 to underwrite Chapman's ministry expenses. This allowed the evangelist opportunity to focus exclusively on his preaching, teaching, and revival ministries.

One of Chapman's most important innovations to large evangelistic campaigns was his method of simultaneously holding several meetings in a city. In the 1904 Pittsburgh campaign, the city was divided into nine districts with nine meeting places. An evangelist and song leader were sent to each location.

Charles Alexander, a well-known song leader long associated with evangelist R. A. Torrey, partnered with Chapman in 1907. Together, they launched the "Chapman-Alexander Simultaneous Campaign" emphasis, which enlisted evangelists and musicians to assist with citywide campaigns.[24]

The first such campaign was a three-week stint from March 12 through April 19, 1908, in Philadelphia. Twenty-one two-man teams went to forty-two districts. About 8,000 professed Christ during this campaign. From January 26 to February 17, 1909, teams of evangelists and musicians went to Boston. This time, the city was divided into twenty-seven districts. More than 7,000 prayed to receive Jesus Christ at these meetings.

On March 26, 1909, Chapman and Alexander launched their first "worldwide campaign." Together, they held revival services in Vancouver, British Columbia, Canada; Sydney and Melbourne, Australia; Hong Kong, Shanghai, Peking, and Canton, China; Kyoto, Tokyo, and Yokohama, Japan; and Seoul, Korea. They returned to America on November 26, 1909.

In 1910, Chapman-Alexander efforts focused on Chicago and Europe. On their trips to Scotland, Ireland, India, New Zealand, and Australia, Chapman preached as many as three to five sermons a day. Chapman's career as an evangelist spanned more than 25 years (1893–1918).[25] The following statement by Chapman articulated the spirit of his ministry:

> Anything that dims my vision for Christ, or takes away my taste for Bible study, or cramps me in my prayer life, or makes Christian work difficult, is wrong for me; and I must, as a Christian, turn away from it.[26]

Reuben A. Torrey (1856–1928) was an American evangelist, pastor, scholar, and author. He studied and rejected "higher criticism" in Europe.[27] Handpicked by Moody to head the Moody Bible Institute in Chicago, he later became dean and president of the Bible Institute of Los Angeles (called BIOLA University today). Torrey participated in numerous worldwide evangelistic campaigns with musician Charles Alexander. Author of more than 40 books, he was instrumental in establishing the Montrose Bible Conference, Pennsylvania, and held pastorates at churches in Chicago and Los Angeles.

Charles Alexander (1867–1920) was an American evangelistic song leader and preacher. A graduate of the Moody Bible Institute, he partnered with M. B. Williams, Torrey, and Chapman in evangelistic campaigns in scores of American and international locations. Hustad credits Alexander with being the first evangelistic song leader to use a piano in Christian worship—an instrument long associated with barrooms and saloons.[28] Alexander was fascinated by the percussive quality of the piano and used it to accompany lively evangelistic singing.

In his ministry with Torrey, Alexander established himself as a choir conductor of significant skill. Hustad explained Alexander's method of conducting revival services:

> A "Festival of Song"—shared equally by congregation, choir and soloists—was expected to last for three hours. . . . Torrey preached for about 45 minutes and the rest of the time was consumed by song. . . . It was apparent that the revival choir was expected to share the prophetic-evangelistic ministry of the evangelist. Its materials were simple—four-part settings of hymns, gospel songs, and chorus choir selections emphasizing the basic gospel and Christian life experiences. Further, the choir was seated with the evangelists behind the pulpit and facing the congregation, not in a "divided chancel" or in the balcony in the tradition of "worship centered" churches.[29]

Oswald J. Smith (1889–1968) was a versatile minister who served as pastor of the largest church in Canada. He traveled the world as an evangelist, missionary statesman, and hymn writer. Smith was born above a train station in Odessa, Ontario, in 1889; his father was a telegraph operator for the Canadian Pacific Railway. At age 13, he heard a Sunday school teacher say, "Any of you boys might be a minister." Smith never got that idea out of his mind.

On January 28, 1906, at age 16, Smith heard about a great evangelistic campaign led by the Torrey-Alexander team at Massey Hall in Toronto, Ontario, with more than 3,000 people in attendance. During the seventh meeting, he was converted.

Smith did undergraduate studies at Toronto Bible College and pursued graduate education at McCormick Theological Seminary in Chicago. Early in his career, he held the pastorate in several small churches in Toronto, Chicago, and Kentucky.

In 1908 he worked in St. Rupert Island, British Columbia, selling Bibles and preaching in local churches. During the winter of 1908 he spent time in Port Essington ministering to the Indians at Hartley Bay. With only a few supplies, deep snow, and barren living conditions, it was the most difficult winter of his life. That experience drove him closer to the Lord and helped him empathize with missionaries and their problems. He developed a deep sensitivity for missionaries that lasted the rest of his life.

On December 8, 1910, he testified of surrendering completely to God, writing,

> The great struggle is over, I surrendered completely to God. I now trust that He will send me out to the foreign field. I do not care if my life is hidden away, unknown by the civilized world, as long as it is known to Him.[30]

During the next few years, he pastored several churches in and around Toronto. He moved to Chicago and later on to New York. But his love for Toronto and the ministry challenge there brought him back to his roots, and he assumed the pastorate of the People's Church there.

The best evangelists and singers in North America often visited the People's Church. This gave Smith freedom to travel to other churches for campaigns, take many tours to foreign mission fields, and preach around the world.

His church was innovative, not following the liturgical worship patterns of most Canadian churches. Rather, he emphasized gospel singing, evangelistic preaching, and special sermons for children. He used props and object lessons in teaching children long before the practice became popular among children's pastors. The church sponsored Wednesday and Friday Bible teaching, with a great emphasis on the Second Coming of Christ.

Smith's hymn writing was an outlet for his emotions in the early, difficult days of his ministry. His gospel song "Saved," written in 1917, became his first hymn to gain broad circulation. He also wrote "Jesus Only" and "Jesus Is Coming Back Again."

B. D. Ackley, George Stebbins, Robert Harkness, D. B. Towner, and the famed composer Charles M. Alexander wrote melodies to Smith's lyrics. In all, Smith wrote more than 1,200 songs, with many published by the Rodeheaver-Hall-Mack Company. Between 1931 and 1946, Ackley and Smith published more than 73 hymns; among them: "Joy in Serving Jesus" (1931), "The Saviour Can Solve Every Problem" (1932), "A Revival Hymn" (1933), "The Glory of His Presence" (1934), "Take Thou O Lord" (1935), "His Love Is All My Plea" (1936), "God Understands" (1937), and "The Song of the Soul Set Free" (1938).

As a missionary statesman, Smith supported more than 350 missionaries representing 35 organizations in 40 countries. He published more than 35 books that sold more than a million copies. For more than 36 years he published a monthly magazine, *The People's Magazine*, which circulated worldwide. His church services were broadcast on more than 40 radio stations across Canada. And as a world traveler, he preached in 72 countries. Some of his missionary mottos became popular:

- "You must go or send a substitute."
- "Attempt great things for God; expect great things from God."
- "Why should anyone hear the gospel twice before everyone has heard it once?"
- "Give according to your income lest God make your income according to your giving."
- "The church which ceases to be evangelistic will soon cease to be evangelical."
- "The light that shines farthest shines brightest nearest home."
- "If God wills the evangelization of the world, and you refuse to support missions, then you're opposed to the will of God."[31]

Smith was long a favorite speaker at Bible-study meetings and conferences. His emphasis on missions and evangelism set him apart from many of the Bible scholar-preachers of the day.

Thomas A. Dorsey (1899–1993) was born in Villa Rica, Georgia, on July 1, 1899, to Etta and Thomas Dorsey. His father was an itinerant preacher and sharecropper. His mother was a respected musician who taught her son to play organ and piano at a very young age. Dorsey, an African American, learned *shape-note singing* and traditional *shouting spirituals* as a child—skills that he later used as a professional musician.

In 1908, Dorsey and his family moved to Atlanta where he was influenced by secular music and musicians. By the beginning of the 1920s, he had established himself as a skilled blues, jazz, and ragtime piano player.[32]

One of his first encounters with *traditional gospel music* occurred when evangelist Billy Sunday and his revival team visited Atlanta. Dorsey was impressed by the music of Rodeheaver. At this meeting, Dorsey made a public profession of faith and committed his musical talent to the Lord.[33]

Soon after his decision at the Sunday-Rodeheaver meeting, at the height of his career as a blues musician, Dorsey turned his attention to composing music for the church. In 1921, after hearing W. M. Nix sing at the National Baptist Convention, he decided to devote himself exclusively to ministry.

Dorsey studied at the Chicago School of Composition and Arranging and worked as a "house arranger" for J. Mayo Williams's Chicago Music Publishing Company. During his time at the publishing company, he worked as a music coach and producer for Paramount and Vocation Records.

In 1922, he became director of music at the New Hope Baptist Church of Chicago, where he fused worship music with blues technique. Dorsey called his new music genre *gospel blues*.[34] In 1931, Ebenezer Baptist Church in Chicago secured Dorsey to organize the first-ever "gospel choir." In 1932, he accepted a position as choir director at Pilgrim Baptist Church, also in Chicago. There he "invented" what became known as the "black gospel choir sound," a technique still used in the evangelical community today.

In 1932, Dorsey had an experience that reinforced his commitment to ministry. While he was away from his Chicago home leading music at a revival service, his wife, Nettie Harper, went into labor with their son. She died in childbirth, and their infant son died the next morning. In the days that followed, Dorsey wrote what is perhaps his most famous song, "Precious Lord, Take My Hand."[35]

This experience prompted Dorsey to forsake his blues music career and give himself to writing, performing, and promoting music for the Lord. He told others, "I was doing alright [sic] for myself but the voice of God whispered, 'You need to change a little.'"[36]

Dorsey's contribution to gospel music—black gospel in particular—and evangelical worship was monumental. He introduced to worship hand clapping, percussion instruments, vamping via repeated chord progressions over which a soloist improvises, and the 16-bar blues. He is known as the "father of black gospel song," a title he once explained:

> In the early 1920s, I coined the words "gospel songs" after listening to a group of five people one Sunday morning on the far south side of Chicago. This was the first I heard of a gospel choir. There were no gospel songs then, we called them evangelistic songs.[37]

He drew from oral tradition, melodic and harmonic patterns of blues music, and his experience as a blues/jazz pianist to establish a genre of music easily accessible to singers and successful in communicating the gospel.

In 1932, he cofounded the National Convention of Gospel Choirs and Choruses. This organization met annually to offer workshops and provide a showcase for singing groups. He also established the Dorsey House of Music, the first music publishing house organized solely to sell the music of black gospel composers.[38]

In all, Dorsey composed nearly 1,000 songs and published more than half of them himself. His music was popular with black and white audiences. Among his most famous songs was "Peace in the Valley."

Innovation in Worship

Evangelical worship changed vastly between 1850 and 1930. Congregational singing shifted from worship led by a vocal soloist accompanied by a small organ to a song leader directing the congregation with a large, well-rehearsed choir. The music itself also changed. Sunday school songs and hymns, once used only in the homes for private devotion, were used in public worship. Because of the camp meeting awakenings, there was greater acceptance of emotional expression in public worship. From 1890 to 1910, a strong emphasis on Bible teaching developed—in part to counter the influence of European higher criticism.

Between 1910 and 1920, there was less emphasis on the theological content of songs and more emphasis on free expression of personal feelings about God. Additionally, much greater attention was given to the music itself. Previously, music was seen primarily as a means to communicate the message of gospel lyrics. In the early twentieth century, however, believers began to describe worship according to its musical style.

By 1920, three distinct subgenres of gospel music emerged in American evangelical worship. In many ways, these genres reflected the cultures in which they were used. These genres were: (1) Traditional Gospel Song and Hymns, used primarily in the North and Midwest; (2) Southern Gospel Song, reflecting the folk music of the camp meeting and used primarily in the South; and (3) African American Gospel Song, used predominantly in African American churches from Atlanta, over to New Orleans, and up to Chicago. All three gospel genres, generally referred to as *gospel song,* reflected popular music of the broader culture. These songs were distributed through a growing music publishing industry.[39]

Traditional Gospel Song and Hymns

There are actually two types of music identified in this area: First, the *Traditional Gospel Song* found its origin in the Sunday school movements of the citywide revivals of the 1840s and 1850s. The text is often a simple expression of a personal, intimate relationship and commitment to God. *Traditional Gospel Song* is generally characterized by one or two verses or a short refrain repeated over and over. The *Traditional Gospel Song* is musically less sophisticated and usually demonstrates a commitment to one theological thought. An example of this kind of writing is seen in the gospel song "Jesus Loves the Little Children" by C. H. Woolston, with music by George F. Root:

> Jesus loves the little children;
> All the children of the world;
> Red and yellow;
> Black and white;
> They are precious in His sight;
> Jesus loves the little children of the world.

Second, the *Traditional Gospel Hymn,* sometimes referred to as "Northern gospel song," is essentially patterned in form and style after the German art song, popular during the latter part of the nineteenth century. The *gospel hymn* found its origin in the urban revivalism of the 1870s.[40] At first glance, it looks like a traditional hymn. The first half of the song is usually strophic in form—usually a series of verses communicating an important gospel thought. What sets it apart from the hymn is the inclusion of a chorus or refrain that drives home the message of the verse in summary. This section may be repeated over and over.[41]

The gospel hymn is most often theologically conservative, with strategic attention given to one or two important biblical thoughts—often told over the expanse of several verses. An example of this practice is seen in the gospel hymn "One Day." This lyric by evangelist J. Wilbur Chapman contains the complete story of redemption. Verse one demonstrates how Jesus left heaven to be born of a virgin. Verses two and three deal with the crucifixion and death of Christ. Verse four describes the resurrection. Verse five proclaims the truth of the second coming of Christ. A refrain proclaiming the story in summary is repeated after each verse:

> Living, He loved me;
> Dying, He saved me;
> Buried, He carried my sins far away;

Rising, He justified freely forever:
One day He's coming—
Oh glorious day![42]

The difference between traditional gospel song and gospel hymns has more to do with the focus of the text and appropriateness of the tune to that lyric than anything else. The gospel hymn "One Day" is a straightforward exposition about God's plan for redemption with an earnest expectation of the return of Christ in the clouds.

"Jesus Loves the Little Children" is a popular gospel song for children written during the great Sunday school movement. The tune and lyric affirm the loving relationship one may have with Jesus. There is no commitment on the part of the singer to holiness, godliness, or Christian service. There is simply an expression of gladness because "Jesus Loves the Little Children."

Southern Gospel or Singing Convention Style

Southern Gospel style is most commonly associated with the gospel male quartet and music in the fa-sol-la singing school tradition. In contrast with *Traditional Gospel music,* Southern Gospel, or as some refer to it "shaped-note gospel hymnody," is largely a rural or small-town phenomenon of the South.

There are two approaches to performing Southern Gospel music—(1) with a quartet and (2) with a choir or congregation. *Southern Gospel-style music* usually is sung by quartets and small ensembles. *Southern Gospel Singing Convention-style* music is usually associated with one- or two-day events featuring quartets, trios, other ensembles, and some congregational music.[43] As one musician put it:

> One of the first styles of Christian music that I ever heard was the Southern singing convention style of music. There was something exciting about the optimism, the counterpoint tech-

nique, the rhythm, the strong altos, the low basses and the hope contained in those songs. . . . To be honest with you, I still get excited when I hear a big choir singing a good "Southern Singing Convention Song"[44]

The method of publishing and distributing Southern Gospel Singing Convention music contributed to its popularity. Southern Gospel music publisher Robert MacKenzie explains:

> What developed was a vibrant, dynamic song publishing industry—an incredible industry—now called the Stamps-Baxter Industry. Ten, twelve, fifteen major companies were established. They all had their singing schools that grew out of their publishing house. Their salesmen and their singers traveled through the South with these twice-a-year books. That became what the singing convention sang for the next four months or six months, or whatever it was. It was a huge industry, and to have that many books there had to be song writers and there had to be staff songwriters. There were a lot of people in the South who made their living printing music.[45]

Connected with each singing convention was some type of singing school. These singing schools were usually held for a one- or two-week period at a local church. Monthly "class singing" sometimes grew out of these singing schools, and congregations soon began singing the newly published songs in their worship services. It was not at all unusual for a church to rotate their songbooks out of the pews every 6 to 18 months, when the publishers produced another song book. According to legendary Southern Gospel performer William Gaither:

> They published them [small soft-back songbooks] for the purpose of what they would call "class singing." They would get together on Sunday afternoons and sing these new songs that had been written and read . . . them from the book. It was amazing

... all these kids reading through these songs and singing the parts off—first with [fa-sol-la] syllables and then with words. It sounded great . . . I mean, they would come together and sing with emotion and energy. It was really teaching a tradition and culture from past generations.[46]

The undisputed leader in the publication of Southern gospel music from 1900 on was the Stamps-Baxter Company of Dallas, Texas. Its sales were so successful that the company's name became shorthand for the entire industry—like "Kleenex" is used to reference any tissue today.[47]

Black Gospel Song

Singers of traditional Black Gospel followed the African concept of using a *Griot*—a ceremonial leader who stimulated audience participation through spoken word, song, or drama.[48] Depending upon their location, nineteenth- and early twentieth-century African American congregations adapted their music from either Northern revival songs or Southern shaped-note singing. Their literature was the same as that of white congregations, but their method of singing was entirely African American in style and origin.

By the end of the 1930s an emotional, solo-driven African American Gospel style had developed. At first, African American Gospel Music mirrored music of the great revival campaigns. While blacks maintained their uniqueness in presentation, Sankey's gospel hymns, the Sunday school songs, and the Watts hymns remained popular with black congregations. However, during the first 30 years of the twentieth century, an African American Gospel Music genre emerged. Stylistically it was influenced by spirituals, jazz, rhythm and blues, and the singing associated with the Pentecostal Holiness tradition. Its theological heritage traced back to the Azusa Street Revival. The music was based on the gospel song tradition of Sankey and Bliss but was performed with hand clapping, bodily movement, shouts, and ornamentation of the melody.

Summary of the Great Awakening

The twentieth century began with a spiritual awakening—first in Wales, then in the United States. Two-man teams dominated the Christian landscape, with one man leading music and the other preaching. These revival teams established a musical style that lasted for better than 100 years.

In our next chapter, we will see how revivalists helped change the way evangelicals worshipped. We will also see how revival in the World War II era spawned the Bible-college movement, Christian radio, the Youth for Christ Movement, and hundreds of parachurch organizations.

Notes

1. Paul R. Dienstberger, *The American Republic: A Nation of Christians* (Ashland, OH: Paul R. Dienstberger, 2000), http://www.prdienstberger.com/nation/Chap8wpr.htm#II.%20The%20American%20Phase; accessed July 15, 2011.

2. Ibid.

3. Ibid.

4. Ibid.

5. Ibid.

6. After graduation from Asbury College, Stanley Jones became the best-known twentieth-century missionary to India.

7. Wesley Duewel, *Revival Fire* (Grand Rapids: Zondervan, 1995), 331–33.

8. Dienstberger, *The American Republic*, chap. 8 (np).

9. "Sunday had an eight-year major league baseball career as an outfielder for the Chicago (White Stockings), Pittsburgh, and Philadelphia teams. His speed and base stealing gained him fame, and he was the first major leaguer to

circle the bases in fourteen seconds." Taken from Dienstberger, *The American Republic,* chap. 8 (np).

10. I (Elmer Towns) saw two of these tabernacles before they were destroyed. The first in Indianapolis, Indiana, which had been owned by a man named Cadle, became a famous church called Cadle Tabernacle. However, the night I saw Cadle Tabernacle, it had been turned into a roller rink, and young people were skating to organ music. The second Billy Sunday Tabernacle was at Winona Lake, Indiana, the permanent home of Billy Sunday. Every summer it was filled with 10,000 worshippers who came to Winona Lake Campground to escape the heat of cities in the Midwest and Northeast.

11. Bert H. Wilhoit, *Rody: Memories of Homer Rodeheaver* (Greenville, SC: Bob Jones University Press, 2000), 4. Rodeheaver was an American music evangelist, music publisher, composer of gospel songs, pioneer in the recording of sacred music, and musical director for revivalist Billy Sunday.

12. Elmer L. Towns, *Masters of the Faith* (Lynchburg, VA: Liberty Home Bible Institute, 1971), 63.

13. Dienstberger, *The American Republic,* chap. 8 (np).

14. Vernon M. Whaley, "Trends in Gospel Music Publishing (1940–1960)" (Ph.D. diss., University of Oklahoma, 1992), 53–54.

15. Homer A. Rodeheaver, *Twenty Years with Billy Sunday* (Winona Lake, IN: Rodeheaver, 1936), 75–76.

16. D. J. Howard, "A Profile of the Current State of Music Used in Worship in the Churches of the Northwest Yearly Meeting of Friends (Quaker)," (Ph.D. diss., the Southern Baptist Theological Seminary, 1988), 366.

17. Rodeheaver, *Twenty Years with Billy Sunday,* 83–84.

18. Taken from http://www.gracyk.com/rodeheaver.shtml: "Rodeheaver was one of the first to record on the early versions of the record player. In late 1920 [Rodeheaver] founded his own record company. It was evidently headquartered in Chicago, at first at 440 South Dearborn Street. From the beginning the new company had recording labs in Winona Lake, Indiana [later in New York City as well and perhaps Chicago], and branch offices were established on the East Coast. Page 138 of the January 1921 issue of Talking Machine World announced the new venture: 'The Rodeheaver Co., 440 South Dearborn Street [Chicago], is out with the announcement of the first release of "Rainbow Sacred Phonograph Records." These consist of selections

by famous evangelistic speakers and singers. . . . The recording laboratories are situated at Winona Lake, Ind., which has long been famous as a center of evangelistic effort. The company has also an eastern branch at 814 Walnut Street, Philadelphia.' Rodeheaver recorded on Edison Cylinders and Disc, Early Victor Records' 78, 33, and 45 speed disc. He recorded and produced for Decca, Columbia House, and WORD Music."

19. Rodeheaver, *Twenty Years with Billy Sunday*, 84.

20. Ibid., 85.

21. See Niagara Bible Conference, http://en.wikipedia.org/wiki/Niagara_Bible_Conference; accessed June 23, 2011.

22. Ibid.

23. These centers included North Side Gospel Center, Chicago; Midwest Bible Center, St. Louis; Paul Rader Tabernacle, Minneapolis; and Cadle Tabernacle, Indianapolis. Some of them became Bible colleges and/or headquarters of mission organizations. Speakers in the summer conferences also traveled to speak there.

24. Anonymous, *J. Wilbur Chapman, 1859-1918: Evangelist and Pastor*, 2012, truthfulwords.org, http://www.truthfulwords,org/biography/chapman tw.html; accessed July 31, 2012.

25. Ibid.

26. Steven Ross, "Echoes from Glory: J. Wilbur Chapman," Wholesomewords, 2012, www.wholesomewords.org/biography/biorpchapman.html; accessed May 17, 2012.

27. Donald P. Hustad, *Jubilate II: Church Music in Worship and Renewal* (Carol Stream: Hope Publishing, 1993), 247.

28. Ibid., 248–49.

29. Ibid., 249.

30. "Oswald Jeffery Smith, Pastor, Evangelist," *Believer's Web*, March 17, 2003; http://www.believersweb.org/view.cfm?ID=130; accessed August 8, 2011.

31. Ibid.

32. Ian Hill, "Georgia Tom Dorsey (1899–1993)," Georgia Humanities Council and the University of Georgia Press, University of Georgia, March 11, 2005, http://www.georgiaencyclopedia.org/nge/Article.jsp?id=h-1603; accessed August 5, 2011.

33. Anthony Heilbut, *The Gospel Sound* (New York: Proscenium, 1985), 23.

34. Ian Hill, "Georgia Tom Dorsey (1899–1993)"; accessed August 5, 2011.

35. "During the late 1930s and early 1940s, Dorsey worked extensively with Mahalia Jackson, establishing Jackson as the preeminent gospel singer and Dorsey as the dominant gospel composer of the time. His work with Jackson and other female singers, including Della Reese and Clara Ward, ensured Dorsey's continued prominence." Ian Hill, "Georgia Tom Dorsey (1899–1993)"; accessed August 5, 2011.

36. Jacquie Gales Webb, "Thomas A. Dorsey: From 'Barrelhouse Tommy' to the Father of Gospel Music," Honky Tonks, Hymns and the Blues, http://www.honkytonks.org/showpages/tadorsey.htm; accessed May 17, 2012.

37. Heilbut, *The Gospel Sound,* 27.

38. Eileen Southern, *The Music of Black Americans: A History* (New York: W. W. Norton, 1983), 453.

39. Music publishing has always been related to singing in the evangelical tradition. In the 1700s, William Cowper joined with John Newton, Isaac Watts, and others to produce printed hymnbooks. The early singing schools, which began around 1727, promoted and sold songbooks–especially as written notation became more accepted. Several companies were publishing Sunday school songs and camp meeting hymns by the end of the 1820s. Lowell Mason was publishing his songs and books for church and school by 1832. By 1890, millions of copies of the Ira Sankey-D. L. Moody gospel songs and hymns had been sold. A proliferation of music publishers developed between 1890 and the Great Depression, with many producing music unique to one of the three gospel styles.

40. Harry Eskew and Hugh McElrath, *Sing with Understanding* (Nashville: Church Street Music, 1980), 177–78.

41. M. R. Wilhoit, "Ira Sankey: Father of Gospel Music," *Rejoice: The Gospel Music Magazine* (June/July, 1991): 13.

42. "One Day" is in the public domain. Words are written by J. Wilbur Chapman. The music is by Charles H. Marsh.

43. Whaley, "Trends in Gospel Music Publishing (1940–1960)," 42–46.

44. William J. Gaither, E. H. Knight, V. Polk, J. Taylor, C. Williams, and P. J. Zondervan, *Great Gospel Songs and Hymns* (Dallas: Stamps-Baxter Music of the Zondervan Corporation, 1976), 2.

45. Robert MacKenzie, interview by Vernon M. Whaley, October 3, 1991, Nashville, Tennessee, author's notes.

46. William J. Gaither, interview by Vernon M. Whaley, October 9, 1991, Alexandria, IN, author's notes.

47. Whaley, "Trends in Gospel Music Publishing (1940–1960)," 46.

48. Southern, *The Music of Black Americans,* 9–10.

CHAPTER 14

The Revivalists and Great Evangelistic Campaigns, Part 2 (1935–1960)

In November 1934, Kentucky evangelist Mordecai Ham preached an evangelistic campaign in a temporary tabernacle on Pecan Avenue on the outskirts of Charlotte, North Carolina. Ham was known across the Southeast as a hard-hitting Southern Baptist gospel preacher who stood unapologetically against alcohol, gambling, envy, greed, prostitution, and lying. God had used him to lead many people to faith in Christ. This campaign seemed ineffective, though. For days, it felt as if the Spirit of God would not bless the meeting. Few were responding to the invitations. Ham was troubled. During a morning time alone with the Lord, he scribbled on a sheet of hotel stationary, "Lord, please grant another Pentecost—do it tonight."

Little did Ham realize that attending the meeting that night was a cynical, self-consumed, sixteen-year-old farm boy who one day would preach the gospel to millions around the globe. At the encouragement of his mother, the teenager attended the evangelistic campaign with his trusted friend, Grady Wilson.

The tent was packed with more than 5,000 curious onlookers. All the seats in the congregation were taken. Many were making decisions to serve Christ. It made this teenager very nervous. He was not sure of his own salvation. So, to get away from the pressure of the crowd and what he perceived as the wrath of a fireball evangelist, he and Wilson sat in the choir loft, behind the preacher.

Ham's first words that night were, *"There's a great sinner in this place tonight."* The teenager looked at his friend, Grady, and said, *"Mother's been telling him about me."* Before the evening was over, the teenager turned to his friend and said, *"I can't stand it anymore, let's go!"* He walked forward and received Christ as savior.

During that November campaign, more than 6,400 people made public professions of faith. This one proved particularly significant, for the teenager was Billy Graham—the man who became the greatest evangelist of his generation.[1]

Events and Changing Landscape Leading Up to the Great Awakening

The nation was ready for another Great Awakening. Billy Graham's decision was just one of thousands during those days. Several factors led to the awakening.

First, colonialism began to collapse around the globe, and formerly subjugated peoples felt new freedom to seek answers to life's deepest questions. Following World War I, nations threw off the yoke of Britain, France, the Netherlands, Spain, Belgium, Portugal, and the United States. No longer could a few nations control the world.

Second, an improved world economy led to materialism. This left many unsatisfied and willing to consider Christ as the source of ultimate happiness.

Third, the expanded mass media allowed evangelists to communicate the gospel to more people in a shorter period of time than ever before. During the 1920s, American newspaper chains were standardized with central offices in New York, San Francisco, and Chicago. The movie industry advanced from silent pictures to spectacular productions involving color, sound, and sophisticated musical scores. By 1940, radio had emerged as the communication media of choice.[2]

Third, World War II ended with a prominent United States general issuing a call to prayer. When Japan signed a surrender document on September 2, 1945, aboard the USS Missouri, General Douglas MacArthur, who officiated the ceremony, called the world to prayer: "Let us pray that peace be now restored to the world, and that God will preserve it always."[3]

Fourth, liberal theology was growing in influence and left many craving a return to orthodox, biblical teaching. Liberal theologians de-emphasized gospel preaching. They did not believe in the supernatural. Many liberal theologians believed God dwelled in heaven but did not intervene in modern life. In a sense, these religious leaders embraced the deism introduced by French philosophers and theologians 150 years earlier. They treated God as though he were no longer needed. The spiritual needs of the world were great, and the stage was set for an awakening.

The Great Awakening of World War II

From 1930 to 1945, God used the Great Depression and the horrors of war to bring men and women to repentance. During World War II, God used Christian nurses, doctors, officers, enlisted men, chaplains, teachers, and others to bring people to himself. Thousands of men told of God's convicting power upon them the night before they were deployed to the Far East or to Western Europe.[4]

During those dark days of war, revival spread across America. Four areas of influence from this revival affected the development of worship practices: (1) mass evangelistic campaigns, (2) the Youth for Christ movement, (3) evangelistic radio programs, and (4) the Bible College movement.

The Great Evangelistic Campaigns

The Story of Mordecai Ham

Mordecai Ham (1878–1959) descended from eight generations of Baptist preachers. He attributed his conversion as an eight-year-old boy to his daily devotional habits. In 1901, Ham went with his father to a meeting of the District Association of Baptists in Bethlehem, Pennsylvania, where he was put on the spot and asked to preach. As a result, God called him to ministry. He accepted the call and borrowed money to get started in gospel campaign work.[5]

From the beginning of his career, he announced that he sought to convert the most notorious sinners. During his first meeting, Ham was directed to a cornfield where an atheist had been working. The evangelist found him hiding in a stack of cornstalks.

"What are you going to do with me?" the atheist asked. Ham answered, "I am going to ask God to kill you! You don't believe God exists. If there is no God, then my prayers can't hurt you. But if there is a God, you deserve to die because you are making atheists out of your children and grandchildren."[6] The atheist begged Ham not to pray that way. So Ham replied, "I shall ask God to save you." The atheist was saved, and before the meeting was over, all 40 of his family members were saved and baptized.[7]

Opposition followed Ham wherever he went, especially when he preached against liquor.[8] Early in his ministry he held a campaign at

Mount Zion, Kentucky. A pro-liquor crowd surrounded the church, threw rocks at the preachers, and threatened to kill Ham. The evangelist told the group's leader, "Put up the knife, you coward . . . now I'm going to ask the Lord either to convert you and your crowd or kill you." The crowd laughed. The leader of the group died the next morning before Ham had opportunity to witness to him again. Later that day, the town sawmill blew up and killed three others in the pro-liquor group. During that campaign, Ham announced that everyone had to return everything that they had stolen or God would kill them. The town was inundated with people returning stolen properties.[9]

In July 1910 in Gonzales, Texas, a murderer who had killed four men sat in Ham's audience listening to him preach. Midway through the sermon, the man jumped from his seat, shouting, "I'm SAVED! SAVED! SAVED!" So inspired was Jack Scofield, director of the choir, that the next afternoon he sat outside a hotel and composed the hymn, "Saved, Saved." That night, the tabernacle choir sang:

> Saved by His pow'r divine!
> Saved to new life sublime!
> Life now is sweet and my joy is complete,
> For I'm saved, saved, saved![10]

In 1912, W. J. Ramsay joined Ham as his music director, choir leader, and business manager. Ramsay served until 1945. Many thought his gentle spirit and sense of humor complemented Ham's sternness.

In 1926 and 1927, more than 4,000 people made professions of faith at meetings held by Ham and Ramsay in Danville, Virginia. By the end of 1927, the number of professions included 8,737 in Oklahoma, 12,043 in Kentucky, 10,013 in Tennessee, 9,500 in South Carolina, 4,385 in Virginia, 26,475 in North Carolina, and 33,650 in Texas.

In one year of ministry, there were more than 33,000 conversions. It is estimated that as a result of hearing Ham's preaching, more than

300,000 new converts joined Baptist churches in Georgia, Alabama, Mississippi, Tennessee, Kentucky, the Carolinas, and Texas.

In 1940, Ham joined the Mutual Broadcasting Network and preached over some 50 stations across the nation. His remarkable ministry schedule continued even as America launched into a war in Europe and Asia. In 1941, at age 65, he began a series of tent and tabernacle campaigns in Decatur, Alabama; Murfreesboro and Nashville, Tennessee;[11] and Denver, Colorado.[12] During the final 20 years of his life, he continued a vigorous preaching schedule, speaking on the radio and making appearances in more than 600 cities, often preaching three or four times a day. Some say that more than one million souls were converted under Ham's ministry.[13]

The Story of Billy Graham

In the wake of Ham's notable evangelistic campaigns, his convert, Billy Graham, closed the decade with perhaps the most notable campaign of all. Graham was president of Northwestern College in Minneapolis, Minnesota, in 1949 when he accepted an invitation to speak at a Los Angeles crusade.[14] The invitation came from a group of businessmen representing an association of 200 churches called "Christ for Greater Los Angeles." Graham wrote in his autobiography, "I burned with a sense of urgency . . . that if revival should break out in Los Angeles . . . it would have repercussions around the world."[15]

Before the crusade, Graham as a college president attended the annual conference for Christian colleges at Forest Home, a Christian retreat in the San Bernardino Mountains outside Los Angeles.[16] He met three significant people at that gathering.

First, there was Chuck Templeton, an evangelist of great notoriety. While studying at Princeton University, he adopted the theological approach of Karl Barth. Templeton questioned the inspiration and authority of God's Word and told Graham, "Billy, you're 50 years out of date. People no longer accept the Bible as inspired. The language is out of date. You're going to have to learn a new jargon if you're going to be successful in your ministry."[17]

Second, Graham met Henrietta Mears, a dynamic Christian leader who headed the educational program at the First Presbyterian Church in Hollywood, California. Under her leadership, the Sunday school grew from 175 students to more than 4,500. More than a Sunday school director, she was a developer of evangelical leaders, including Bill Bright of Campus Crusade, Dawson Trotman of the Navigators, Robert Pierce of World Vision, and Donn Moomaw, who pastored First Presbyterian Church of Beverly Hills, California. Mears talked with Billy Graham about his commitment to Christ and the fact that Jesus could change the world through his preaching.

Third, revivalist and revival chronicler J. Edwin Orr was also at the meeting. He was known for leading great revivals in New Zealand and Australia. Orr challenged Graham with the possibility that God might spark a national revival through his preaching in the Los Angeles crusade.

One night during the conference, Graham went into the hills to pray and seek God. Under a full moon, he prayed with open Bible in hand: "O Lord, there are many things in this book I do not understand. . . . Are there contradictions? . . . I can't answer the philosophical or psychological questions Chuck [Templeton] and others are raising. . . . Father, by faith I am going to accept this as Thy Word. . . . I will believe this is Thy inspired Word."[18] Graham looked back on this as the defining moment of his life. Afterward, he filled his sermons with the phrase, "The Bible says."

Emboldened in his faith, Graham insisted that the Los Angeles crusade committee include all Christian denominations in its efforts, that it raise the budget from $7,000 to $25,000, and that it erect a tent for 5,000 rather than 2,500, as originally proposed. Graham maintained that God would do a great work. The committee agreed to the requests, and the crusade was set to run for three weeks beginning the last week of September.

At the beginning of the crusade, Mears asked Graham to lead a series of Bible studies for Hollywood stars and songwriters in her home on Hollywood Boulevard. The studies touched the life of Stuart Hamblin, a popular West Coast radio personality. Hamblin was a legend, and quipped that he could fill the tent if he endorsed Graham.

The day before the crusade, Graham conducted a news conference with the local media, something he had never done before. The next day there was nothing in the newspaper except for a paid advertisement announcing the crusade. Hamblin interviewed Graham on his radio show and told the audience, "Go down to Billy's tent and hear the preaching," adding, "I'll be there."

That night crowds followed Hamblin into the tent. Yet during the message Hamblin angrily stomped out, a practice he repeated in subsequent services. Finally, after struggling with conviction over sin, Hamblin and his wife, Suzie, came to Graham's hotel at 4:30 a.m. They met Billy and Ruth Graham, and Hamblin gave his heart to Christ. Later, Hamblin wrote the well-known songs "It Is No Secret What God Can Do" and "This Ole House."

Graham believed Hamblin's conversion was confirmation that the crusade should be extended. When he arrived at the tent that night, it was teeming with reporters. William Randolph Hearst, owner of the two newspapers in Los Angeles and a string of newspapers across the country, had famously told his employees, "Puff Graham."[19] Later, Graham responded to criticism that the crusade was just an ordinary tent revival made popular by Hearst, saying, "If God were not doing something supernatural, and if souls were not being transformed, there would be nothing to 'puff.'"

The crusade committee planned on 50 converts over the three weeks, but more than 50 people made professions of faith *every night*. Stories ran in newspapers from Detroit to Miami to New York and Chicago, as well as in *Time* magazine, sparking Graham's long and successful evangelistic ministry.

While leading a series of meetings in Modesto, California, Graham's team agreed to what became known as the Modesto Manifesto. According to one chronicler:

> They agreed to live lives of integrity; being truthful in their speech and conduct; being consistent at home and on the crusade platform. They agreed to be accountable to God and to each other, and to those overseeing the ministry, particularly in finances. They each agreed to maintain personal calendars of where they were going, the purpose for their trip or activity, and who they were with. They also agreed to lives of purity, vowing never to be alone with a woman and to have the company of others in the presence of women not their wives. Finally, they agreed to act in humility, to speak carefully about the success of their meetings, and to be careful to give God the glory. They called this agreement the Modesto Manifesto, and it has guided their lives and ministry since that day.[20]

From the beginning of Graham's ministry, George Beverly Shea and Cliff Barrows were the nucleus of his music team. Barrows served as choir director and platform emcee for meetings. He also served as music director and radio-television program director for *The Hour of Decision*.[21]

New Hebrides Awakening

In the same year that God blessed Graham's evangelistic campaign, revival fires also burned in the Presbyterian churches of New Hebrides, off the coast of Wales. Peggy Smith, an eighty-four-year-old blind prayer warrior, and her sister Christine were no longer able to attend services in the Parish of Barvis, so they prayed! As they did, Peggy had a vision of churches crowded with young people. In short order she sent for her minister.

Reverend James Murray MacKay visited the two shut-ins and listened to their account of the vision. He was not surprised because his own wife had a similar dream only a few weeks earlier. He called for his leaders to pray. For three months they met two nights a week in a farmer's barn, praying for God to send revival.

One evening, after about a month of praying, a young deacon arose in the meeting and began reading from the Scriptures: "Who may ascend into the hill of the LORD? Or who may stand in His holy place? He who has clean hands and a pure heart" (Ps 24:3–4 NKJV). He closed his Bible and said, "It seems to me so much humbug to be waiting and praying, when we ourselves are not rightly related to God." Then, lifting his hands toward God, he prayed, "O God, are my hands clean? Is my heart pure?"[22] With the words barely out of his mouth, he fell to his knees and went into a trance. Many observers mark that night as the beginning of the New Hebrides Awakening.

Pastor MacKay knew he needed help and thought of a young street preacher named Duncan Campbell. About the same time, MacKay received word from Peggy Smith that she wanted to see him again. At their meeting, she told him to invite Duncan Campbell to preach, saying, "God is sending revival to our parish." She insisted, "He has chosen Mr. Campbell as his instrument."

MacKay promptly invited Campbell for ten days of meetings. Campbell had been raised in the Highlands of Scotland, spoke fluent Gaelic, and had a burden for the Gaelic-speaking people of the Highlands and the islands. He had been invited earlier to speak at the prestigious Keswick Bible Conference, so he turned down the invitation to New Hebrides.

MacKay did not know what to do when he received Campbell's negative response. He went to Smith and delivered the disappointing news. "That's what man says," she replied. "God has said otherwise! Write him again!"

God was indeed preparing Campbell for the revival. At home he was in his study preparing a sermon for the Keswick Conference when his granddaughter interrupted him, "Why doesn't God save souls today, like you talk about in your sermons?" The question brought deep conviction on Campbell. He shut the study door, fell on his face before God, and prayed, "Lord, if you'll do it again, I'll go anywhere to have revival."

As time came for the meeting at New Hebrides to begin, Campbell sat in the front row at the Keswick Bible Conference, ready to preach. The Holy Spirit spoke to his heart and instructed him to "immediately leave the Keswick meeting and go to New Hebrides." Turning to the moderator, Campbell said, "Something has come up. I must leave immediately." He left the building and caught the next ferry to New Hebrides.

By faith, the congregation had gone ahead with plans for the revival. Posters were placed throughout the island announcing that Duncan Campbell was speaking. The crowd had already assembled.

A solemn hush came over the congregation as he preached. At the conclusion of the sermon, as the people began to leave, a young deacon raised his hand and said, "God is hovering over us. He is going to break through. I can hear the rumbling of heaven's chariot-wheels."[23]

At that moment, the door opened and the clerk of the session beckoned Campbell, "Come and see what's happening!" He discovered that another congregation was waiting outside the church, drawn from their homes by an irresistible force. They could not explain it. The faces of more than 600 people in the churchyard were marked by deep distress.

The crowd quickly streamed into the church, filling the building beyond capacity, and Campbell preached again. Soon revival spread to neighboring districts.[24]

During the days of revival, Campbell traveled to other churches, which he found filled with people eager for him to preach the gospel. When people could not get into the church buildings, they prayed in nearby fields. One villager said, "The power of God swept through the town, and there was hardly a house in that village that didn't have someone saved in it that night." On Sundays, the rural roads on the island were crowded with people walking to church. Drinking houses, which were common before the revival, remained closed for a generation following the New Hebrides Revival.

On one occasion, a prosperous factory worker brought Campbell to his factory to impress the revivalist with his manufacturing prowess. However, Campbell's mere walking through the rows of mills brought conviction, and workers fell to the floor begging for salvation. Some factory owners shut down their machines and gathered their employees in a common area so Campbell could preach. As a result, thousands were saved in factories, businesses, and plants.[25]

Evangelistic Radio Programs

By 1927, there were more than 600 radio stations in America. By 1930, one in three homes in America owned a radio. As the Great Depression eased and America went to war, Bible-believing churches and denominations launched effective radio ministries.

Radio provided a forum for airing songs that expressed Christian doctrines. So effective were radio ministries that local churches often modeled their worship after the format of popular weekly broadcasts.

Mass communication became a tool for evangelism and building Christian community.

In 1924, Walter A. Maier, representing the Lutheran Church–Missouri Synod, started a radio ministry from the attic of his home in St. Louis, *The Lutheran Hour*. Indeed, Lutherans were the first denomination to take advantage of the new technology. During his life, Maier preached to more than 20 million people on 1,200 stations in 36 different languages.

Among the other radio ministries established during the 1930s and 1940s were: *The Old Fashioned Revival Hour, The Radio Bible Class* with M. R. DeHann, *Revivaltime* with C. M. Ward, *Young People's Church of the Air* with Percy Crawford, *The Hour of Decision* with Billy Graham, *Word of Life* with Jack Wyrtzen, *The Abundant Hour* with Oral Roberts, and *The Southern Baptist's Laymen's Hour*.

Perhaps the most successful independent radio ministry of the era was *The Old Fashioned Revival Hour* (*OFRH*) with Charles E. Fuller, the son of a wealthy Southern California produce farmer. Born on April 15, 1887, Fuller graduated from Pomona College and the Bible Institute of Los Angeles (BIOLA). He married Grace Payton, and together they worked in his father's produce business until the Lord called him to preach.

The *OFRH* aired its first broadcast over the 13 stations on the Mutual Network on October 3, 1937. In 1941, Fuller's nationwide broadcast was moved from a Hollywood studio to the Long Beach Municipal Auditorium. Each week thousands of servicemen en route to the Pacific attended the broadcast. Fuller and his *OFRH* musicians also traveled throughout North America, holding citywide rallies that were often broadcast live.

By the end of the 1940s, *OFRH* was heard on 650 radio stations affiliated with the ABC radio network. During its peak years in the 1940s and 1950s, an estimated 20 million people listened to the weekly broadcasts. Each week, Fuller's wife, Grace, shared letters from listeners. As one historian put it:

> Thousands of letters received each week told of people who listened in brothels, gambling dens, cocktail lounges and prisons. People who wouldn't dream of opening their doors to a local pastor or priest couldn't wait for another broadcast of the Old Fashioned Revival Hour.[26]

At least four factors contributed to the success of Fuller's broadcasts. First, he was an expository preacher and evangelist. His homespun, relaxed approach to preaching was much different from that of most evangelists.

Second, Fuller gathered a team of highly motivated and talented musicians. His music director, H. Leland Green, directed the chorus, had an earned doctorate in music, and was coordinator of music for the Pasadena school system.

The ministry included innovative and inspiring music. More than half of Fuller's hour-long program was devoted to music by a choir and male quartet. Green, Rudy Atwood, and George Bradbent provided evangelicals with fresh approaches to performing traditional gospel music.[27] Ralph Carmichael, a well-known Hollywood arranger and former publisher of gospel music, described the significance of the *OFRH* Choir:

> It was a wonderful choir. Leland Green and I always had a good friendship. That choir really had a secular feel. In the secular world there was Fred Waring. In the gospel field there was the Old-Fashioned Revival Hour Choir.[28]

Green's theme song, "Heavenly Sunshine," became the trademark of the ministry. Atwood's piano improvisations fueled the broadcast's fast-paced, spirited, and enthusiastic atmosphere.

Bradbent used a Hammond B-3 organ to accompany soloists and provide invitation music at the conclusion of Fuller's sermons. The OFRH Quartet included Bill MacDougall, Jack Coleman, Ken Brown, and Arthur Jaissle. The group sang a wide variety of literature, including Southern gospel, traditional gospel, Western European hymns, and African American spirituals. The *OFRH* was one of the first organizations in the evangelical community to fully embrace the use of popular musical genres to proclaim the gospel.

Third, the location of the live program played an important role in its success. In Southern California, the *OFRH* had access to a vast pool of evangelical musical talent.

Fourth, the format of the program played a significant role in its success.[29] It was broadcast live from Long Beach's Municipal Auditorium with a regular audience of 5,000 people. Fuller and his associates appeared in that auditorium for the last time on January 12, 1958.[30]

Though the *OFRH* has been off the air for more than a half century, it continues to have an influence. Jerry Falwell, a popular twentieth-century television evangelist, was converted as a result of listening to an *OFRH* broadcast in his home during the early 1950s. Falwell's television and radio ministries were influenced by what he heard on the *OFRH* in his youth. Many church pianists emulated Atwood's playing, and his piano arrangements are still available.[31]

Out of the radio ministry, Fuller established Fuller Theological Seminary in Pasadena, California. He died on March 18, 1968.[32]

Other significant Christian radio personalities included: (1) Paul Rader on WJBT, (2) Wendell Loveless on WMBI, (3) James Vaughn on WOAN, (4) Homer Rodeheaver on KDKA, (5) Paul Myers and the Haven of Rest in Los Angeles, (6) Virgil Stamps and the Stamps Quartet in Dallas, (7) Torrey Johnson and Youth for Christ in Chicago, (8) Al Smith and Singspiration in Montrose, Pennsylvania, and (9) The

Blackwood Brothers and the Statesmen Quartet in Memphis. Each radio program produced its own "brand of music for the evangelical community" based on a secular music genre.[33]

Most radio ministries developed some type of songbook. In some cases, radio ministries hired arrangers and musicians, collected copyrights, and established music publishing companies. *Back to the Bible* with Theodore Epp and *Young People's Church of the Air* were two of the most successful radio ministry groups to print music for evangelical churches. Radio programs gave worship leaders opportunities to hear what they were going to teach their churches to sing.[34]

Of the many influential radio stations operating prior to and during the war years, none was more important than *WMBI Radio*. A ministry of Moody Bible Institute in Chicago, WMBI served as a catalyst for gospel music development well into the 1960s and 1970s. Vocalist George Beverly Shea, organist Don Hustad, pianists Harold DeCou and Ted Smith, trombonist Bill Pearce, the Melody Four Quartet, gospel composer and vocalist John Peterson, and a host of other musicians made WMBI's live radio broadcasts a staple of Christian radio. Programs like *Songs in the Night* with Billy Graham, and later Bill Pearce, helped establish evangelical personalities as household names across the country.

Two radio ministries that targeted the growing high school and college-age markets of the 1940s and 1950s were Percy Crawford's *Young People's Church of the Air* and Jack Wyrtzen's *Word of Life*. Both were instrumental in promoting the use of popular musical genres in evangelical churches.

Crawford and his wife, Ruth, made a conscious effort to stay familiar with the popular music of their day. They brought swing into Christian music, especially through the new gospel choruses that came out regularly in their Pinebrook Praises chorus books, named for a camp in East Stroudsburg, Pennsylvania. Crawford also developed the Saturday night rally as a new style of Bible conference. Other youth organizations were inspired by the Crawfords' ministries: Youth for Christ, Word of Life, Singspiration, Song Time, High School Born-Againers, and New Life Boys Ranch.

Near the end of the war, Jack Wyrtzen established the highly successful Saturday night program *Word of Life Hour.* His broadcast, live from Times Square in New York City, was an enthusiastic, fast-paced, East Coast counterpart to the OFRH. Over the years, Wyrtzen mentored hundreds of young people going into full-time ministry. He published songs by hundreds of young musicians and encouraged them to market their work through his radio program. Norman Clayton, Dick Anthony, Harold DeCou, and Merril Dunlap were all associated with *Word of Life.* Because of the success of his radio ministry, Wyrtzen was able to establish Bible institutes in New York, Florida, Brazil, and Hungary, and thousands of Word of Life Clubs around the world.

The impact of radio on evangelical worship practices from the 1940s through the 1960s was significant. It blazed a trail for the Christian music artist industry of the 1970s and 1980s. These radio programs, with their commitment to providing print music for listeners, laid the groundwork for music publishing over the next half century.

Youth Meetings—Youth for Christ

Following the war, evangelicals experienced success in reaching high school and college-age students. As the World War II baby boomers grew into teenagers and adults, parachurch organizations established youth camps, Bible study groups, youth evangelism teams, Christian athletic organizations, radio ministries for youth, youth music teams, vacation Bible schools, Bible institutes, and youth music training institutes.

Among the parachurch organizations formed during this era were Inter-Varsity Christian Fellowship, Campus Crusade for Christ, AWANA Clubs International, Child Evangelism Fellowship, and the Navigators.

Perhaps the most significant new organization, though, was Youth for Christ, a coalition of ministries across America that launched evangelistic endeavors among American young people—especially returning servicemen. Typically, Youth for Christ rallies occurred on Saturday evenings, often in large municipal auditoriums, and involved a mixture of entertainment, fellowship, and preaching. According to one observer, the music was "dynamic, rhythmic, flashy, and energetic."[35] Youth for Christ represented the twentieth century's first attempt to adapt worship and evangelism to a specific age group.

The Bible College Movement

During the 1940s and 1950s, many denominations and parachurch groups established Bible and Christian liberal arts colleges. At first, these institutions served as trade schools, providing much-needed workers for the fast-growing evangelical movement. Some institutions, such as Fuller Seminary, Word of Life Bible Institute, and the King's College, were started as educational extensions of popular radio ministries. Other institutions, like Houghton College, Wheaton College, Taylor University, John Brown University, Eastern College, and the Bible Institute of Los Angeles (BIOLA), arose independently of radio ministries. During this period, the American Association of Bible Colleges was organized as an accrediting agency for the Bible college movement.

The Bible college movement impacted worship practices in at least two ways. First, colleges served as a training ground for evangelical music directors. Previously, musicians and worship leaders were educated in traditional conservatories or university music programs.[36]

Second, Bible colleges often published gospel music. For example, Moody Bible Institute developed its own gospel music publishing house to produce print products for evangelical churches. The organization employed a team of music editors, copyists, composers and arrangers, and office managers.[37]

Other evangelical colleges were also associated with music publishing companies. For example, *Young People's Church of the Air*, a popular program during the 1940s and 1950s, was affiliated with the Percy Crawford Evangelistic Association, which founded the King's College in Wilmington, Delaware. Crawford owned a publishing company and used musicians from his college to disseminate music originally heard on the broadcast. Traveling teams representing the college in churches around the country performed this music and modeled new approaches to worship. Other schools and publishing houses similarly employed traveling teams to publicize their music offerings in local congregations.

Strategic Personalities

Six people stand out for their contributions to evangelical music and worship during this awakening:

Cliff Barrows (1923–) was born in Ceres, California, the son of a farmer. He began an evangelistic partnership with Billy Graham in 1945 at a Youth for Christ rally in the hills of western North Carolina. When Graham discovered that the song leader scheduled for an evening service was absent, he asked if anyone in the crowd could help lead the singing. Barrows and his wife, Billie, volunteered to help. She played the piano and he led the singing and played the trombone.

Today, Barrows is best known as the choir and music director for the Billy Graham evangelistic campaigns. He traveled the world preaching the gospel and leading singing, and served as producer and emcee of the *Hour of Decision* radio program, a ministry based in Atlanta, since November 5, 1950.[38] Barrows was inducted into the Gospel Music Hall of Fame in 1988 and the National Religious Broadcasters Hall of Fame in 1996.[39]

Ralph Carmichael (1927–), arranger, composer, conductor, publisher, and owner of Lexicon Music Inc. and Light Records, was born in Quincy, Illinois, on May 27, 1927.[40] Classically trained as a violinist, Carmichael played in the San Jose Symphony before beginning his career as an arranger for Stan Kenton, Nat King Cole, Roger Williams, Andy Williams, and others. He wrote numerous movie and television sound scores, arranged for renowned performers, and ghost wrote for well-known pop arrangers including Nelson Riddle. He composed more than 200 original songs and arranged music for hundreds of recordings, film scores, and choral and instrumental publications. Carmichael introduced at least five innovations to evangelical worship music: (1) He brought the sound of 1940s big bands and commercial jazz to gospel music. (2) He merged musical innovations from Hollywood studios with music for the Youth for Christ movement. (3) He raised the quality of gospel music recordings to match that of secular record labels. (4) He is best known for integrating pop styles of the 1950s and 1960s, especially rock 'n' roll, into gospel recording and publishing for youth. (5) He mentored and inspired hundreds of aspiring evangelical arrangers.[41]

Percy Crawford (1920–1960) was born in Minnedosa, Manitoba, Canada, on October 20, 1902, to Thomas and Margaret Crawford. His father was pastor of a Wesleyan church, and his mother was a gifted musician. He was saved in 1923 during a revival campaign preached by Bill Nicholson at the Church of the Open Door in Los Angeles. R. A. Torrey was pastor at the church and president of

BIOLA. Crawford attended BIOLA from 1923 to 1926, and in 1928 he transferred to Wheaton College in Illinois.

Crawford began holding Saturday night youth rallies at the Barnes Memorial Presbyterian Church of Philadelphia and launched the *Young People's Church of the Air* radio ministry in 1931. It was fast-paced radio targeting American teenagers. In 1933, he organized Pinebrook Bible Camp, Shadowbrook Camp for boys, and Mountainbrook Camp for girls. In 1938, he opened King's College in Belmar, New Jersey. Finally, on October 9, 1949, he premiered the *Youth on the March* television ministry, the first coast-to-coast evangelistic television program. The impact of Crawford's radio and television ministry was massive:

> Tens of thousands heard [his] message, and accepted and believed. They encountered a life-changing challenge from the head and heart of one of the world's most powerful preachers. No one then or since was able to say more in fifteen short minutes about life's most important things. The combined power of the message and the man was mesmerizing.[42]

Henrietta C. Mears (1891–1963) was born in Fargo, North Dakota, to the family of a Baptist banker. She graduated from the University of Minnesota in 1913 and taught science at Central High School in Minneapolis.

In 1927, she left Minnesota for Los Angeles, where she accepted the job as director of Christian education at First Presbyterian church in Hollywood. In 1933, she established the Gospel Light Publishing Company to provide affordable curriculum to conservative Protestant congregations. The company published Vacation Bible School literature, graded Sunday school literature, and books by well-known Christian leaders, including Billy Graham. Mears was known for mentoring Christian celebrities and rising leaders.[43]

John W. Peterson (1921–2009), a Swedish-American born in Lindsborg, Kansas, was a composer of gospel songs, arranger, soloist, and member of the Gospel Music Hall of Fame. Following service in World War II, he attended Moody Bible Institute and the American Conservatory of Music, both in Chicago. Peterson is best known for creating the gospel cantata, a choral genre closely resembling the baroque cantata but utilizing the style of the post-World War II Broadway stage. By 1975, Peterson's cantatas sold more than 8.6 million copies.[44]

George Beverly Shea (1909–) was born on February 1, 1909, in Winchester, Ontario, Canada. The son of a Wesleyan Methodist pastor, he attended Houghton College and sang in many early-twentieth-century professional recording choirs.

Bev Shea is best known as the soloist affiliated with the Billy Graham Evangelistic Association. He first sang for Graham in 1943 on the live, Chicago-based broadcast *Songs in the Night*. In 1947, he joined Graham's inaugural revival campaign in Charlotte, North Carolina. In 1949, at the famous tent revival in Los Angeles, Shea became a permanent part of the Graham team. Graham said of him: "I've been listening to Bev Shea sing for more than 50 years, and I would still rather hear him sing than anyone else I know."[45]

In addition to his ministry with the Graham evangelistic team, Shea sang hundreds of concerts and recorded nearly eighty albums. At age 23, he wrote the music to Rhea H. Miller's song, "I'd Rather Have Jesus." Later, he wrote the words and music to "The Wonder of It All."[46]

Innovations to Worship

While popular musical genres were accepted by evangelicals as legitimate means of promoting the gospel, some resisted using secular-sounding music in worship.[47] So a host of publishing companies emerged after World War II to market a new style of worship music to churches.

Models for Worship from Radio Influences

Radio ministries played a major role in persuading evangelicals to accept Christian music written in popular styles. In the 1940s and 1950s, worship music in the evangelical tradition was significantly affected by the harmony, rhythm, and form of jazz, rhythm and blues, bebop, big band, and ragtime. Additionally, the song forms and harmonies used on Broadway were emulated by writers of traditional gospel song.[48] Techniques of such composers as Irving Berlin, George Gershwin, Cole Porter, Leonard Bernstein, and Rogers and Hammerstein were studied by traditional gospel songwriters.[49]

Commercial soloists like Ella Fitzgerald, Dinah Shore, Debbie Reynolds, Frank Sinatra, Bing Crosby, Perry Como, and Nat King Cole introduced new approaches to singing ballads that evangelicals adapted to gospel music. Ladies' trios and male quartets were popular among evangelicals, and composers like Carmichael copied the styles of such famous groups as the McGuire Sisters, the Andrews Sisters, the Modernaires, the Hi-Lows, the Mills Brothers, the Golden Gate Quartet, and the Ink Spots.[50]

Gospel songwriters associated with the youth movement of the 1940s and 1950s listened to and embraced the form, harmonies, rhythms, and ensemble sound of the big bands. Stan Kenton, Glenn Miller, Harry James, Benny Goodman, and Les Brown all served as unofficial mentors to gospel songwriters.[51]

Arrangers and composers of traditional gospel choral music were influenced by such groups as the Pennsylvanians, the Fred Waring Chorale, the Ringwald Group, and the Norman Luboff Chorale. These groups not only illustrated choral adaptation of pop genres, they also established a standard of excellence for musicians in the evangelical movement.[52]

Worship services in thousands of evangelical churches across the country were modeled after popular radio ministries. Emphasizing a theme in worship became popular—the blood of Jesus, love of God, peace of God, salvation, the Spirit of God, etc. The transition between elements of a worship service was timed to achieve a seamless presentation—just like on radio. Indeed, producers did not want any "dead" time. Though this seamless approach was new for the church, it met with broad acceptance.

Radio ministries also served as a marketing tool, enticing worship leaders to use songs they heard on the air. In 1947, for example, John Peterson joined the staff at WMBI, the Moody station, where he interviewed hundreds of well-known gospel musicians, wrote songs, and helped compile songbooks for the Melody Aire gospel music series published by Moody Press.[53]

Models for Worship from the Evangelistic Campaigns

As with radio, evangelistic campaigns provided a model for worship in evangelical congregations. Each revivalist-musician partnership had a unique style of worship. For example, Graham's campaigns were characterized by spirited congregational singing, large choral presentations, testimonies by celebrities, high-quality vocal presentations by soloists with large or small singing groups, and evangelistic preaching. Churches around the world began to use these elements in their own services.

Graham's notoriety afforded him and his team significant influence on evangelical worship. So he introduced the Billy Graham songbooks as spiral-bound publications that included 75 to 100 gospel hymns and choruses. The books were congregational songbooks easily adaptable for choirs, solos, duets, ladies trios, and quartets. A significant number of pages included photographs of the Graham team, notes about important crusade events, and a variety of interesting facts related to the organization.[54]

Graham crusades and songbooks impacted the worship ministry of local churches in three important ways. First, they established a pattern for publishers to use the evangelistic campaigns as platforms for presenting new music. Graham's organization gave publishers an opportunity to submit songs for performance in crusades.

Second, the songbooks provided local congregations immediate access to crusade songs. With the availability of songbooks at crusade meetings, worship leaders were able to take the music back to their churches.

Third, the crusades helped raise performance standards for local church choirs and music ministries. Crusade music was always well rehearsed and professional in presentation. This provided worship leaders and choir members opportunities to experience firsthand the work of highly trained, professional musicians.

Models for Worship Found in the Youth Meetings

Youth for Christ International (YFC) helped change the way evangelicals worship. They introduced short, easy-to-sing, highly popular gospel choruses to the evangelical culture—precursors of the praise and worship choruses of the 1990s.

Some of the composers, musicians, and arrangers associated with this movement were John Peterson, Harold DeCou, Ralph Carmichael, Tedd Smith, Norman Clayton, Cliff Barrows, Ethel Waters, George Beverly Shea, Alfred Smith, the Ohman Brothers Trumpet Trio, and a variety of ladies trios and male quartets. In a sense, YFC songs were a return to the music of early-nineteenth-century camp meetings. Harmonically diatonic and melodically predictable, they were generally little more than a refrain about some aspect of Christian experience. YFC taught evangelism and discipleship through these short, energetic compositions. Several publishers, including Percy Crawford's company, produced songbooks devoted almost exclusively to these choruses.

Summary of the World War II Awakening

Four phenomena in the post-World War II era affected worship practices in evangelical churches: (1) mass evangelistic campaigns, (2) the Youth for Christ movement, (3) evangelistic radio programs, and (4) the Bible College movement.

A large and successful youth movement introduced into the evangelical culture a body of songs based on popular music that were easy to sing and play. They were promoted by radio and crusade ministries and had an enormous impact on the way evangelicals organized their worship services. A proliferation of new music publishing companies emerged to meet the needs of worship leaders and congregations. Printed music gave churches access to the musical arrangements sung on radio and presented at the great evangelistic campaigns.

New organizations grew out of the revival endeavors. The National Association of Evangelicals was established in 1945. International agencies such as Youth for Christ, the Navigators, and Campus Crusade for Christ were established. A vast number of new colleges were established.

In our next chapter, we will discover how God moved in the heart of one man to reach out to a disillusioned culture called the Hippie Movement. We will also discover how the musical influences and personalities associated with one outreach movement still impact the way evangelical congregations worship.

Notes

1. J. J. (Dark) Di Pietro, quoted in http://www.canecreekchurch.org/index.php/what-is-your-legacy/33-mordecai-ham; accessed August 6, 2011.

2. Paul R. Dienstberger, *The American Republic: A Nation of Christians* (Ashland, Ohio: Paul R. Dienstberger, 2000), np, http://www.prdienstberger.com/nation/Chapter10.htm#II.%20The%20Turbulent,%20Tempestuous,%20; accessed August 6, 2011.

3. Ibid.

4. My father (Vernon) answered the call to ministry the night before he was deployed from San Francisco to fight the Japanese on the New Hebrides Islands. He told of having a vision and seeing Jesus. During the restlessness of the evening, he promised God that in exchange for safe return from war he would become a preacher. At the end of WWII, he enrolled in a Bible college in Nashville, Tennessee, and prepared himself for ministry.

5. "Mordecai Ham, 1878–1959, Baptist Evangelist," *Believer's Web,* http://www.believersweb.org/view.cfm?ID=128; accessed August 8, 2011.

6. Ibid.

7. Ibid.

8. "Mordecai Ham," *Higher Praise.com,* http://www.higherpraise.com/preachers/ham.htm; accessed August 8, 2011.

9. Ibid.

10. "Saved, Saved" by Jack P. Scholfield, © Public Domain. Mike Harland, *The Baptist Hymnal* (Nashville: LifeWay Worship Resources, 2008), 469.

11. During the 1941 Mordecai Ham Campaign at the Ryman Auditorium in Nashville, Tennessee, Ethel Pike Whaley, mother of one of the authors of this book, committed to full-time missionary service. At the time, her husband was in the Army and stationed overseas.

12. See http://soamc.org/tfh/FILES/Christian%20Testimonies/Biographical%20Sketch%20Of%20Mordecai%20Ham; accessed August 6, 2011.

13. Di Pietro, quoted in http://www.canecreekchurch.org/index.php/what-is-your-legacy/33-mordecai-ham; accessed August 8, 2011. "Mordecai Ham," *Higher Praise.com;* accessed August 8, 2011.

14. Taken from Dienstberger, *The American Republic,* 150–55.

15. Ibid.

16. Ibid.

17. Ibid.
18. Ibid.
19. Ibid.
20. Chuck Warnock, "Cliff Barrows: A Living Legend." http://chuckwarnockblog.wordpress.com/2009/05/13/cliff-barrows-a-living-legend/; accessed August 16, 2011.
21. "George Beverly Shea." http://www.billygraham.org.uk/Groups/171100/Billy_Graham_Evangelistic/Who_We_Are/Biographies/George_Beverly_Shea/George_Beverly_Shea.aspx; accessed August 20, 2011.
22. Elmer Towns and Douglas Porter, *The Ten Greatest Revivals Ever* (Ann Arbor: Servant Publications, 2000), 145.
23. Ibid., 147.
24. Ibid.
25. Ibid.
26. Read G. Burgan, "Charles E. Fuller's Old Fashioned Revival Hour," http://www.rgbdigitalaudio.com/Old_Fashioned_Revival_Hour_.htm; accessed August 20, 2011.
27. See http://www.biblebelievers.com/OFRH/history.html; accessed August 20, 2011.
28. Ralph Carmichael, interview by Vernon M. Whaley, October 17, 1991, author's notes.
29. Burgan, "Charles E. Fuller's Old Fashioned Revival Hour"; accessed August 20, 2011.
30. See http://www.biblebelievers.com/OFRH/history.html; accessed August 20, 2011.
31. Burgan, "Charles E. Fuller's Old Fashioned Revival Hour"; accessed August 20, 2011.
32. "Charles E. Fuller, 1887–1968, Preacher, Broadcaster,:" http://www.believersweb.org/view.cfm?ID=64; accessed August 20, 2011.
33. Vernon M. Whaley, "Trends in Gospel Music Publishing (1940–1960)" (Ph.D. diss., The University of Oklahoma, 1992), 67–72.
34. Ibid.
35. Quoting interview with John W. Peterson by Vernon M. Whaley, October 18, 1991, Scottsdale, Arizona.
36. Quoting interview with Robert MacKenzie by Vernon M. Whaley, January 10, 1992, Nashville, Tennessee.

37. Quoting interview with John W. Peterson by Vernon M. Whaley, October 18, 1991, Scottsdale, Arizona.

38. "Cliff Barrows Wants 'One More Goal for God,'" http://www.billy graham.org/articlepage.asp?articleid=1968; accessed August 20, 2011.

39. "Cliff Barrows," http://www.billygraham.org.uk/Groups/171099/Billy_Graham_Evangelistic/Who_We_Are/Biographies/Cliff_Barrows/Cliff_Barrows.aspx; accessed August 20, 2011.

40. William Reynolds, *Companion to the Southern Baptist Hymnal (1975)* (Nashville: Convention Press, 1976), 277.

41. Whaley, "Trends in Gospel Music Publishing (1940–1960)," 67–72.

42. See http://www.ruthandpercycrawford.com/; accessed August 20, 2011.

43. "Henrietta C. Mears," http://isae.wheaton.edu/hall-of-biography/henrietta-c-mears; accessed August 20, 2011.

44. Whaley, "Trends in Gospel Music Publishing (1940–1960)," quoting interview by Vernon M. Whaley with John W. Peterson, October 18, 1991.

45. "George Beverly Shea," http://www.billygraham.org.uk/Groups/171100/Billy_Graham_Evangelistic/Who_We_Are/Biographies/George_Beverly_Shea/George_Beverly_Shea.aspx; accessed August 20, 2011.

46. Ibid.

47. Whaley, "Trends in Gospel Music Publishing (1940–1960)," 72, quoting interview by Vernon M. Whaley with Bob MacKenzie, January 10, 1992, Nashville, Tennessee.

48. Ibid., 71, quoting interview by Vernon M. Whaley with Ralph Carmichael, October 17, 1991, Ventura, California.

49. Ibid., quoting interview by Vernon M. Whaley with John W. Peterson, October 18, 1991, Scottsdale, Arizona.

50. Ibid., quoting interview by Vernon M. Whaley with Ralph Carmichael, October 17, 1991, Ventura, California.

51. Ibid., 72.

52. Ibid., 71, quoting interview by Vernon M. Whaley with Bob MacKenzie, October 3, 1991.

53. Ibid., 101, quoting interview by Vernon M. Whaley with John W. Peterson, October 17, 1991, Scottsdale, Arizona.

54. Ibid., 75.

CHAPTER 15

The Baby Boomer Revival, Part 1 (1965–1985)

The evening prayer meeting had been over for about an hour. Students of Liberty University and members of Thomas Road Baptist Church in Lynchburg, Virginia, were milling around the front of the sanctuary. It was late—10:30 on a Wednesday night—so most of the ushers, members, and pastors had gone home.

Suddenly a lone student rose and walked to the pulpit, weeping, to confess sins. The microphone and pulpit lights were off, but God was in the building. That student's passionate repentance captured the attention of those who were still in the auditorium.

A student began singing. Someone else scooted over to the piano and began playing softly. There was the sacred sound of weeping. People dropped to their knees beside the altar and front pews.

Shortly, another student approached the pulpit and confessed sins, broken. Soon there were others. Two hours later at 12:30 a.m., frantic phone calls went out to the pastor and deacons: *"Revival's hit the church!"*

Church members, awakened from sleep, hurriedly dressed, rushed to their vehicles, and drove through the dark streets of Lynchburg. They returned to the church building expecting to experience God. No neckties, no Sunday morning dresses, just believers seeking a divine touch. Soon the glory of the Lord flooded the church. It had become a sanctuary of praise.

People stayed at the church around the clock from Wednesday night until Saturday morning. All normal activities ceased. Classes were canceled. Those involved did not leave for work; some did not eat. When drowsiness overtook them, students slept on the pews in the back of the auditorium, or even under the pews. No one wanted to leave the sanctuary for fear of missing a mighty act of God.

Some people loudly and publicly confessed sins. For others, confession and prayer were quieter. They prayed privately around the altar. The Holy Spirit's presence and work were evident.[1]

This revival, which occurred in the fall of 1973 at Liberty University, was not an isolated incident. God was orchestrating something much bigger. Between 1965 and 1980, revival fires burned in England, Canada, Europe, and the Far East. God moved in the hearts of young men and women in Southern California, the southeastern United States, at colleges and universities, on the beach, and on the Caribbean Islands:

> It was a movement amongst alternative youth culture in America which soon overflowed into Europe. . . . It was a spontaneous, humanly unorganized awakening which reached a culture far removed from the white Anglo-Saxon respectability of the contemporary church. . . . This movement began to experience a new brand of Christianity which was Bible-based, Spirit baptized, focused on community and missional.[2]

This "baby boomer revival" occurred amid a particularly interesting cultural milieu, especially in America.[3]

The Changing Landscape Leading Up to the Great Awakening

For nearly two decades following World War II, prosperity abounded in America. The quintessential symbol of these years was the nation's youthful president, John F. Kennedy, and his elegant wife, Jacqueline. They reigned over the United States much like a king and queen, likening the period to the fairytale kingdom of Camelot.

As in Camelot, the prosperity ended. The U.S. Supreme Court removed Bible reading and prayer from public schools, and abortion was legalized. Cohabitation and homosexuality gained broad public acceptance. Church attendance began to decline as North Americans abandoned the faith of their fathers, and humanism, liberalism, and hedonism increased. By the end of the 1960s, political turmoil helped spark social unrest.

Deep hurt and disillusionment became evident. Demonstrations against the "establishment" by America's youth erupted into abusive, hateful, disruptive, costly, and often deadly riots and protests. By the end of the 1960s at least three types of demonstrations against the American government could be identified: civil rights protests, anti-Vietnam War demonstrations, and protests of a youth counterculture known as the Hippie Movement.

The latter was perhaps most surprising and significant to sociologists, pastors, and educators. Hippie culture was characterized by a commitment to nontraditional values. Hippies gave themselves to promiscuous sex, illicit drugs, and "free living." Many claimed to be antimaterialism, antitechnology, antieducation, anti-Christian, antisocial, and antibusiness success. In an effort to calm inner turmoil, many sought answers in ancient and modified versions of the occult, Eastern mysticism, and other fringe religious practices. According to historian Paul Baker:

When it came to spiritual values, the young people were more disillusioned than ever. The motto "In God We Trust" seemed to them not a creed but a mockery. The youth were convinced that there must be a better way to do things.[4]

The famous 1969 Woodstock Music Festival in White Lake, New York, epitomized the Hippie Movement. Thirty-two musical acts performed during four days, including: Sweetwater; Tim Hardin; Arlo Guthrie; Joan Baez; Santana; the Grateful Dead; Creedence Clearwater Revival; Janis Joplin; the Who; Jefferson Airplane; Joe Cocker; Blood, Sweat and Tears; Crosby, Stills, Nash and Young; and Jimi Hendrix.[5] One historian described the event as "almost unanimous in the use of marijuana and hallucinogenic drugs like LSD."[6]

Christians lamented their perceived inability to remedy the restlessness of this rising generation. Even the noted minister Norman Vincent Peale, not known for firm biblical convictions, recognized the spiritual neediness of the Hippies:

> For years we watched a spiritual vacuum growing in our young people. All the signs were there: dissatisfaction with a materialistic and affluent society; impatience with old forms of worship; a groping for fulfillment—first in rock music, then in various kinds of mysticism, finally in drugs. . . . We saw all this happening. But did we reach out eagerly and offer the seekers a solution they could accept—in terms they could understand? I'm afraid many didn't.[7]

Yet the Hippie Movement provided fertile soil for the Holy Spirit to usher in the next great awakening, the Jesus Movement.

The Great Awakening: The Jesus Movement

The Jesus Movement was part of a revival that swept across America and circled the globe in the late 1960s and early 1970s. Like awakenings of the past, there was great emphasis on confession of sin, repentance, and commitment to full-time Christian ministry and missionary service. Many of the early "Jesus People"—as they were called by the mainstream media—were former hippies who turned to Christianity and away from drug addiction, occult influences, Eastern religions and mysticism, and atheism. These young people maintained the style of hippies, listened to rock-'n'-roll music, lived communally, and adopted an unconventional view of the church. According to historian Larry Eskridge:

> The Jesus People impacted both great numbers of young people in the counterculture as well as many young evangelical church youth who adopted the Jesus People persona and made it their own. Just as the lives of a significant number of Baby Boomers were shaped by the countercultures, the Jesus People movement was another of the major formative forces among American youth who came of age in the late 1960s and 1970s.
>
> Moreover, its influence remained significant within the American evangelical subculture in the decades that followed.... It is clear that the Jesus People movement played an important role in the resurgence of American evangelicalism in the late twentieth and early twenty-first centuries.[8]

The Jesus Movement originated in the Hippie-dominated Haight-Ashbury district of San Francisco. Jack Sparks, a statistics professor and Campus Crusade associate, established Christian World Liberation Front (CWLF) as a counterculture organization aimed at reaching the radical left wing of American culture, the students and street people of the Haight-Ashbury district. In 1967, Hubert Lindsay opened the first Christian coffeehouse as an affiliate of CWLF on the streets of Berkeley, California, the Living Room Coffee House. Lindsay made a deliberate attempt to reach the disillusioned hippies, homeless people, drug addicts, and derelicts walking by his building every day. Through this and other ministries, young people began to embrace the teachings of

Christ and become worshippers of the Most High God. In short order, the Jesus Movement took hold, and a generation was changed for the kingdom of God.[9] Historian Paul Dienstberger explains:

> When they were converted, their long hair, bell-bottoms, and barefoot appearance was overlooked because of their smiling faces, emotional joy, and bold, unabashed words of praise for Jesus. They were referred to as Jesus People, Jesus Freaks, Jesus Kids, and Street Christians. . . . While the movement originated in Southern California, spontaneous ministries sprang up in many places and in many forms. These new Christians made a fanatical effort to know the Scriptures and to quote chapter and verse . . . spread the gospel in the streets, coffee houses, rescue missions, communes, [and] rock festivals. . . . Bible studies were the central emphasis in every segment of the new Jesus culture.[10]

On June 21, 1971, *Time* put a portrait of Jesus on its cover and said that a "Jesus revolution" was gripping youth across the nation:

> Bibles abound: whether the cherished, fur-covered King James Version or scruffy, back-pocket paperbacks, they are invariably well-thumbed and often memorized. . . . There is an uncommon morning freshness to this movement, a buoyant atmosphere of hope and love along with the usual rebel zeal. Some converts seem to enjoy translating their new faith into everyday life. . . . But their love seems more sincere than a slogan, deeper than the fast-fading sentiments of the flower children; what startles the outsider is the extraordinary sense of joy that they are able to communicate. . . . If any one mark clearly identifies them it is their total belief in an awesome, supernatural Jesus Christ, not just a marvelous man who lived 2,000 years ago but a living God who is both Savior and Judge, the ruler of their destinies. Their lives revolve around the necessity for an intense personal relationship with that Jesus, and the belief that such a relationship should

condition every human life. They act as if divine intervention guides their every movement and can be counted on to solve every problem.[11]

The "Jesus People" embraced Christ as Savior but did not abandon aspects of their subculture, including informal dress, rock music, casual speech, and simple living. While they rejected the sins of Hippies, they adapted some aspects of the counterculture to a Christian context.[12]

One ministry that had a notable impact on the Hippie and Jesus Movements was Calvary Chapel in Costa Mesa, California. On one occasion, Chuck Smith, pastor of Calvary Chapel, took his wife out for coffee on the Palisades overlooking Huntington Beach in Southern California. Stretched out on the beach for miles in each direction were baby boomers, soaking in the sun and enjoying the water. Smith's wife said to him, "Why don't you go down there and preach Jesus to them?"

"You don't do that," he replied, and promptly forgot about her suggestion—until that night, when during prayer Smith said he heard the Holy Spirit say to him, "Why don't you go down there and preach Jesus to them?" Again, he put it out of his head. The next morning, he felt the Holy Spirit's prompting again. So that afternoon, he took off his suit, tie, and white shirt and donned a golf shirt, khakis, and tennis shoes. He took a Bible to the beach and began to preach Jesus.

After about an hour, one of the young people said, "Here is water. Can we be baptized?" Smith took off his shoes, waded into the Pacific Ocean, and began baptizing young people. Youth from all over the beach began running to see the "religious experience." So with an even larger crowd, Smith began preaching Jesus again. That day more than 200 young people confessed Jesus Christ as Lord and were baptized in the Pacific Ocean. The next day, the same thing happened. Smith preached on the beach and again hundreds received Christ and were baptized in the Pacific Ocean.

Smith invited them to his church in Costa Mesa, and on Sunday morning, the "Jesus People" showed up. These new Christians—men with long hair and jeans, women in unapologetically simple attire—seemed out of place among the traditional Pentecostal audience of smartly dressed Christians.[13]

Their Sunday morning worship service remained traditional. But, on Sunday night, Monday night, and other times during the week, large numbers of "Jesus Worshippers" met at Calvary Chapel to sing newly composed songs for three and four hours, to pray, and to devote themselves to serious Bible study.

Smith's preaching was uniquely suited for the Jesus People. He started at Genesis 1:1 and preached chapter by chapter through the Bible, Sunday morning, Sunday evening, and Wednesday evening. When he finished Rev 22:21, he began again in Gen 1:1. At times, the preaching and music were coordinated. According to Calvary Chapel worshipper Chuck Fromm:

> I remember we'd just finished a song and all of a sudden Chuck jumped up and started preaching on the subject we'd been singing about. It was incredible. These songs were just personal to us and I never thought of somebody taking the lyrics and turning them into a sermon. Afterwards he gave an altar call and a lot of people were saved. That sort of thing started happening over and over again.[14]

At one point, the church was winning more than 200 to Christ each week. As many were baptized in the Pacific Ocean weekly. On one occasion, more than 3,000 came to watch a baptism, after which Smith presented the gospel and saw even more come to Christ.

> It was not unusual for young people to line up . . . at 4:00 p.m. waiting in line for a 7:00 p.m. . . . evening Bible study. They would share Scriptures with each other. . . . Many would bring

unsaved friends and loved ones. Every Bible study had a musical group or solo artist that would share in song and testimony of the life-changing power of Jesus Christ. Many would respond to the invitation to come forward and receive Jesus into their hearts and lives. The pews were filled with longhaired youth, others in suits and ties. There were young people, middle-aged people, and elderly folks—there was no generation gap.[15]

Smith's church spawned other similar congregations, and the Calvary Chapel phenomenon became a movement. When his disciples built churches, typically they began as home Bible studies, grew with solid congregations of influence, and emerged as beacons of hope in the community. In some cases, the Calvary Chapel congregations have developed into megachurches with international outreach and appeal.

One of the most significant contributors to the early Jesus Movement, and disciple of Smith's expository preaching, was a free-spirited young man named Mike MacIntosh. Living on the beaches of Southern California during the 1960s, he was divorced, emotionally and spiritually broken, and miserable. On his twenty-sixth birthday, he was invited by friends to attend a music service at Calvary Chapel in Costa Mesa. That night the gospel was preached, and he embraced Jesus Christ as his Savior.

Under Smith's guidance, MacIntosh moved into a "commune" for training in the Christian life. It was a boarding house with *Christian standards and fellowship* that required Bible study, discipline, and hard work. In this spiritual boot camp, MacIntosh and his colleagues spent time in the Bible morning, noon, and night. They learned how to follow Jesus, how to get along with others, how to witness, and how to earn a living. This commune, which they dubbed "Mansion Messiah," proved effective in discipleship training. Later, MacIntosh joined the Calvary Chapel staff and was ordained. As he grew in his Christian faith, he saw his marriage restored and pursued graduate-level ministry training at Azusa Pacific University.

Soon after his conversion, MacIntosh began recording "Jesus music."[16] His songs were introduced to American Christianity through Maranatha! Music, a new record label affiliated with Calvary Chapel.

In 1974, he was invited by friends to teach a weekly Bible class. It began with 12 people in a home on Point Loma and soon expanded to 45 enthusiastic young converts. In August of that year, they moved to the Ocean Beach Women's Club. Soon, more than 100 were studying the Bible together. They moved to Balboa Park, where they began holding Sunday services.

In 1975, the young congregation moved to an unused church facility in the Linda Vista area of San Diego. In addition to young people, families began attending.

MacIntosh's vision continued to expand. During the fall of 1976, the congregation's first mission church was planted in San Diego's North County. By 1980, nine churches had grown out of the original fellowship. They were planted in the communities of Encinitas, El Cajon, Escondido, Chula Vista, Poway, Pacific Beach, Point Loma, and Alpine.

Explo '72

One of the most significant events of the Jesus Movement was "Explo '72," a meeting organized by Bill Bright and Campus Crusade for Christ (CCC). Billy Graham served as honorary chairman. More than 80,000 students from all over the country met during the week of June 17–22, 1972, at the Cotton Bowl in Dallas. As one historian explained,

The preaching came from Billy Graham and other renowned speakers, and the music came from perhaps the widest array of musicians ever to gather to worship the Lord at one time.[17]

Explo '72 was historic for its integration of Bible preaching, Bible study, discipleship training, and contemporary Jesus music. Concerts were presented each night at the Cotton Bowl, various parks, churches around Dallas, and on the Woodall Rogers Parkway. More than 180,000 Christians and non-Christians gathered at a day-long concert. Paul Baker contends it was the most diverse program of Christian music in America's history:

> The program of performers and speakers that sultry June day was overwhelming: Billy Graham, Johnny Cash, Randy Matthews, Larry Norman, Danny Lee and the Children of Truth, Katie Hanley (star of the Broadway production of *Godspell*), country singer Connie Smith, Andrae Crouch and the Disciples, Willa Dorsey, the Armageddon Experience, Reba Rambo, Barry McGuire, Vonda Kay Van Dyke (former Miss America) . . . and many others, including an appearance by Kris Kristofferson and Rita Coolidge. Gospel music would never be the same again. . . . For several music groups and solo musicians, Explo '72 was their springboard to national prominence.[18]

The climax of the six-day celebration was a candlelight service in the Cotton Bowl. Participants lit candles and sang "Pass It On"[19] at the end of a sermon on the Great Commission. "As each person lit the candle of a person [seated next to them], the entire stadium sparkled with strikingly beautiful light."[20]

Campus Crusade and Explo '72 helped integrate the Jesus Movement into mainstream American Christianity.[21] Previously, traditional evangelical church leaders feared that the Jesus Movement was "pulling young people away from the church," but they trusted Bright and Campus Crusade.[22]

The Jesus Movement lasted less than ten years, but in that time its effect on evangelicalism was momentous. During the decades that followed, thousands of Jesus Movement converts assumed leadership in local churches, parachurch organizations, and denominations. The Calvary Chapel churches, Hope Chapel churches, Horizon Christian Ministries, Vineyard churches, and Jews for Jesus trace their roots to the Jesus Movement.[23] A multimillion-dollar contemporary Christian music industry—with global influences, implication, inspiration, and impact—was birthed by the Jesus Movement. Thousands of congregations secured full-time youth pastors to manage and nurture their growing youth populations. According to historian Robb Redman, the Jesus Movement preserved "the substance of Christian worship . . . in a new format, especially in their emphasis on biblical preaching, prayer, and congregational participation."[24]

One might be tempted to think that the Great Awakening of the Baby Boomers was limited to America. Not so. God was also pouring his Spirit out around the globe—in Indonesia, on college campuses, and in Canada.[25]

The Great Awakening: The East Timor (Indonesia) Revival 1965

During the mid-1960s, revival swept Indonesia. Some suggest that more than 100,000 people were won to Christ during this revival, and a vast number of nominal Christians recommitted themselves to biblical Christianity.

Before the revival, promiscuity and drunkenness were common, even among confessing Christians. Many professing believers used the services of Shamans, participated in a type of *fettish worship* and embraced *magic and sorcery*.

Early in 1965, a member of the pastoral team at the Soe church began conducting a series of evangelistic meetings. The preacher, Benjamin Manuain, delivered Christ-centered messages, calling people to repent of sin and trust Jesus alone for salvation. According to J. M. E. Daniel, pastor of the Soe church, the evangelistic campaign in January and February marked the beginning of the revival.

A revival team visited the town of Niki-Niki in early October 1965. In a two-week campaign, 9,000 people professed conversion. Prior to the Niki-Niki campaign, many pastors had been indifferent, or even hostile, toward the revival movement. At Niki-Niki, most began assisting revival teams. Within two years, more than 100 teams had been organized and commissioned to take the gospel around the nation.

The Great Awakening: The College Campus Revival

While secular colleges and universities were experiencing unprecedented protests, marches, riots, and sit-ins during the early 1970s, students at Christian schools were experiencing spiritual renewal. Perhaps the most profound awakening began on February 3, 1970, at Asbury College in Wilmore, Kentucky. The college dean began chapel with a personal testimony. At the conclusion of his presentation, he invited others to come to the front of the auditorium and share their own testimonies. Students began giving personal testimony of the changing power of the Holy Spirit in their lives. At the conclusion of the chapel time, the dean invited students to come to the front of the auditorium and pray. Immediately students moved forward from all parts of the building. Revival chronicler Wesley Duewel tells the story:

> Those who had come forward and knelt at the . . . Asbury altar joined those on the platform to make humble and tearful confessions of their needs. Some went to individuals in the congregation, asked forgiveness, and became reconciled. A long line of students began to form, each waiting to tell what God had done. As confessions were made, other students came forward. . . . Intense divine manifestation continued into the noon hour.[26]

Classes were adjourned. The 1,550-seat building was filled to capacity. Faculty and students shared testimonies and sang praise to the Lord in duets or solos. The revival continued for six days.

Soon, news of the happenings at Asbury College spread to Asbury Theological Seminary across the street. Students and faculty met for an all-night prayer meeting. The next morning, seminary chapel turned into a time of revival. When the bell rang for classes to begin, most students and faculty remained in the chapel. Classes were officially canceled the next morning as married students knelt with their spouses in times of confession, repentance, prayer, and praise to God.

By the weekend, the undergraduate college and seminary merged their times of worship. The revival continued around the clock. As late as 2:30 a.m., more than 300 students gathered for prayer in the chapel. Then at sunrise, the chapel was full again with students seeking revival.[27] Duewel explained the impact of the revival on other universities and colleges:

> Appeals began coming from other campuses across the United States . . . asking for student delegations to come and share the news of the revival. By the end of May 1970, at least 130 colleges, seminaries, and Bible schools had received some revival blessings through the witness of the Asbury students.[28]

"Witness teams" from Asbury College traveled to scores of Christian colleges, universities, and Bible institutes across the country.[29] The night before a team arrived at Azusa Pacific University in Los Angeles, faculty met for an all-night prayer meeting. At chapel the next morning, the "witness team" told about the events at Asbury. Before the team finished speaking, Azusa students made their way to the front of the room to confess sins and pledge repentance. The time of revival was so powerful that afternoon classes were called off. A student prayer meeting continued in the dorm rooms that night and through the next week, and spread to other secular schools and Christian institutions in the Pasadena area.

In Kankakee, Illinois, at the Olivet Nazarene University, hundreds of students repented of their sins when they heard the testimony of the Asbury students. Again, classes were canceled and hundreds of students dispersed across the nation to their homes and churches with the revival news.

In Greenville, Illinois, students from Asbury drove through sleet and snow to share their testimonies at the Free Methodist Greenville College. According to Duewel,

> They shared the revival and immediately individuals were humbled before God, public confessions of wrong attitudes began, and revival continued through early Saturday morning hours. Numerous teams went out from Greenville College to most of the churches of the Free Methodist conferences, and the spiritual tone of those churches was transformed.[30]

In Fort Worth, Texas, students at Southwestern Southern Baptist Theological Seminary had been praying for two years that God would move on their campus. When the Asbury Awakening was reported, students began confessing sin and repenting. All the students in one class fell on their knees in repentance. Prayer meetings continued through the night. The next morning, more than 1,200 students stayed in the chapel after Founder's Day activities to hear testimonies, pray, and ask God for revival.

In Georgetown, Kentucky, six Asbury students shared their testimonies. More than 700 students, faculty, and administration experienced revival at Georgetown College.

Revival spread to the University of Tennessee, Texas A & M, the University of Texas at Arlington, and institutions in Oklahoma.[31] By 1971, revival fires were burning in Troy, New York, and at the Rensselaer Polytechnic Institute. As Asbury College and Seminary "witness teams" shared their stories, students repented and turned to Christ at Harvard University, Stanford University, Eastern Illinois University, Northern Baptist Theological Seminary, and North Park College in Chicago, and at more than 30 other colleges and universities in the United States and Canada. The campus revivals lasted about three years.[32] In all, about 2,000 "witness teams" from Asbury College told their stories:

> Hundreds of other teams went out from other colleges and local churches that were impacted by the [Asbury] revival. The little town of Wilmore, Kentucky, became the center of a network of revival that touched and brought new spiritual life and blessing to thousands of individuals in several thousand towns and villages in the United States and in other countries.[33]

The Great Awakening: The Canadian Prairie "Restitution" Revival

Duncan Campbell, leader of the New Hebrides revival in Wales, went to Winnipeg, Canada, and in a meeting asked, "If God could do it in Scotland, why not Canada?"[34] That question made a deep impression on many, including Bill MacLeod, pastor of a General Conference Baptist church in Saskatoon, Saskatchewan, who asked, "Why not Saskatoon?"

Saskatoon was a quiet prairie town in the heart of Western Canada's Bible Belt. Families often attended the same church for generations. As students graduated from high school, it was customary for them to spend at least a year in one of the many Bible schools that dotted the prairie landscape.

At the invitation of MacLeod, twin evangelists Ralph and Lou Sutera were invited to conduct revival meetings at the Ebenezer Baptist Church. MacLeod had been praying for revival for some time, and the Sutera twins shared his desire. Recent meetings caused them to believe that God was preparing to accomplish a powerful work. As preparations for the Saskatoon Crusade were finalized, expectations were high. Very early in the crusade it became clear that expectant believers would not be disappointed.

Though the meetings lasted longer than typical Saskatoon church services, no one seemed in a hurry to leave. When the preaching concluded, people flocked to the prayer room in response to the invitation of the evangelists. "What is God pointing his finger at in your life?" they asked.

People were encouraged to examine their lives in light of the Scriptures. If in doing so God "pointed his finger" at something, they were encouraged to repent, confess their sin, and make restitution when appropriate. One oft-quoted verse during the meetings became a theme Scripture of the revival: "Turn at my rebuke; Surely I will pour out my spirit on you; I will make my words known to you" (Prov 1:23 NKJV).

The revival meetings soon outgrew the facilities at Ebenezer Church, filled the larger United Church, and finally moved to the city auditorium. Shortly, revival spread across the Canadian prairies.[35]

The Saskatoon Revival proved a challenge for business in a strange way. As people repented of their sins, they began offering to pay for merchandise they had stolen years earlier from local businesses. Businessmen had already written off the losses, so most simply forgave the debt. Then people began returning the things they had stolen to store owners. This action was so widespread that many stores became overstocked.

One person touched by that revival was Henry Blackaby. Based on his encounter with the Lord, he wrote the best-selling book *Experiencing God*, which brought renewal to many churches in America, including many in the Southern Baptist Convention.

In our next chapter, we will introduce strategic personalities used by God to bring innovations to worship during this baby boomer awakening. We will also document those innovations and how they shape our worship services today.

Notes

1. Elmer Towns and Douglas Porter, *The Ten Greatest Revivals Ever* (Ann Arbor: Servant Publications, 2000), 13–14.

2. Tony Cauchi, "Twentieth Century Awakenings," http://www.revival-library.org/catalogues/20thcentury/index20thcentury.html; accessed August 6, 2011.

3. Porter and Towns, *The Ten Greatest Revivals Ever*, 13–14.

4. Paul Baker, *Contemporary Christian Music: Where It Came From, What It Is, Where It's Going* (Westchester, IL: Crossway Books, 1985), 4.

5. "The Woodstock Festivals: Woodstock 1969," http://www.woodstock.com/themusic.php; accessed August 6, 2011.

6. Paul R. Dienstberger, *The American Republic: A Nation of Christians* (Ashland, OH: Paul R. Dienstberger, 2000), np, http://www.prdienstberger.com/nation/Chapter10.htm#II.%20The%20Turbulent,%20Tempestuous,%20; accessed August 6, 2011.

7. Norman Vincent Peale, "The Surging Spirit," *Guideposts,* November 1971, 4, quoted in Paul Baker, *Contemporary Christian Music,* 5; accessed July 29, 2011.

8. Larry Eskridge, "God's Forever Family: The Jesus People Movement in America (1966–1977) (Ph.D. diss, the University of Stirling, 2005), abstract.

9. Baker, *Contemporary Christian Music,* 6.

10. Dienstberger, *The American Republic,* n.p.

11. "The Alternative Jesus: Psychedelic Christ," http://www.time.com/time/magazine/article/0,9171,905202-1,00.html; accessed August 6, 2011.

12. I (Elmer) wrote a cover story for *Christian Life* magazine in 1968 on hippie Christianity. I drove to a picnic area in the Palisades of Huntington Beach, California, and found seven Jesus freaks who were all dressed in long, sky-blue tunics, each wearing rubber thongs for shoes. They told me that they lived in an abandoned house that had been boarded up, but it had no bathing facilities or running water. They used the bathhouse on the beach. The boys slept on plastic floats on the floor in one room, the girls in another. They had no use for toiletries, makeup, or the other things that fill the cabinets of standard bedrooms across America. When asked how they ate, they said they witnessed in local restaurants, and when people had compassion on them, they gave them food. When no food was given, they fasted. They spent all day witnessing for Christ, studying their Bibles, fellowshipping, and composing and singing Christian music.

13. When I (Elmer) was there on a Sunday evening, I was amazed at two things: First, young people were sitting on the floor, flooding the aisles. Second, the platform was small and there was no choir. I was told, "We don't have a choir to sing to the people; the entire congregation is a choir that sings to God."

14. Chuck Fromm, "New Song: The Sound of Spiritual Awakening," presented at the meeting of Oxford Reading and Research Conference, Oxford, England, July 1983, 2.

15. David Burgin, "Calvary Chapel," http://www.one-way.org/jesusmovement; accessed August 2, 2011.

16. Sherwood Eliot Wirt, *For the Love of Mike: The Mike McIntosh Story* (Nashville: Thomas Nelson, 1984). This is a biography about the early days of Pastor Mike McIntosh, Horizon Christian Fellowship, San Diego, California.

17. Baker, *Contemporary Christian Music*, 53.

18. Ibid.

19. "Pass It On" is a song written by Ralph Carmichael and Kurt Kaiser. It was included in the youth musical "Tell It Like It Is" and became a popular song of the entire Jesus Movement.

20. Baker, *Contemporary Christian Music*, 55.

21. According to Paul Baker, Chuck Fromm, and others, as a result of Explo '72, more than 3,000 youth signed up for missionary service with Campus Crusade for Christ. The event was one of the most important moments in Bright's ministry with college students. Baker, *Contemporary Christian Music*, 53; accessed July 29, 2011.

22. Ibid., 54.

23. These church groups developed into large, influential associations with hundreds of congregations around the globe. Combined membership exceeded one million.

24. Robb Redman, *The Great Worship Awakening: Singing a new Song in the Postmodern Church* (San Francisco: Jossey Bass, 2002), 54.

25. Towns and Porter, *The Ten Greatest Revivals Ever*, 13–14.

26. Wesley Duewel, *Revival Fire* (Grand Rapids: Zondervan, 1995), 343.

27. Ibid., 345.

28. Ibid., 345–46.

29. During the spring of 1970, a team from Asbury College came to the Bible college I (Vernon) attended in Nashville, Tennessee. They told about the events taking place in Wilmore and at the conclusion of their testimony extended an invitation for students to make commitments to the Lord. Scores of students responded.

Prior to that, our college had already been experiencing revival, so much so that I joined with classmate Jonathan Thigpen to form the Conquerors Evangelistic Team. I led the music and Jonathan preached. Jonathan and I had been meeting nightly for prayer in the storage closet of our dormitory for more than six months. Jonathan was inspired to "do something for Christ" after reading Leonard Ravenhill's "Why Revival Tarries." Together, we agreed to form the team and devote ourselves to evangelism, discipleship, worship singing, and preaching. Suddenly, we began receiving invitations to lead revivals, preach and sing at youth camps, make presentations at large youth meetings, and host weekend retreats. By late April 1970, the executive director of the Home Missions Department of our denomination asked if we would do evangelistic work among America's youth culture. We accepted the 12-week assignment and held 15 revivals and youth camps. Almost always, our meetings were preceded by a Friday-to-Saturday, twenty-four-hour prayer time. On Tuesday and Friday nights of our weeklong meetings, we would present a drama-music-preaching program called "Teenspiraction." We preached and sang everywhere— -on the back of tobacco trucks at a Hardees parking lot in Grifton, North Carolina; at scores of public and Christian schools in the southeastern part of the country; in tabernacles, tents, shelters, and metal buildings at more youth camps than one could imagine; in hotel banquet rooms; and before a high school dance at a public high school in Illinois. God always seemed to bless and yield fruit. Jonathan continued with my brother, Rodney Whaley, in 1971. Over the 24 months or so that the team traveled, thousands of young people made commitments to Christ. Hundreds answered the "call into full-time Christian work." The three of us were forever changed by the experience.

30. Duewell, *Revival Fire,* 347.

31. Ibid.

32. Dienstberger, *The American Republic,* n.p.

33. Duewell, *Revival Fire,* 351.

34. Duncan Campbell was the preacher of record at the New Hebrides Revival, Scotland, 1949.

35. Erwin Lutzer, *Flames of Freedom* (Chicago: Moody Press, 1976).

CHAPTER 16

The Baby Boomer Revival, Part 2 (1965–1985)

God uses strategic personalities to accomplish his work during every awakening. What follows is a list of strategic men and women from the Jesus Movement, significant because of their (1) roles as preachers, leaders, or musicians; (2) roles as decision-makers within the revival movement; and (3) enduring contributions to evangelical culture.

Arthur Blessitt was born on October 27, 1940, in Greenville, Mississippi. In the late 1960s, Blessitt began an evangelistic ministry to the hippies, prostitutes, flower children, and runaways on Sunset Strip of Hollywood, California.[1] He opened His Place, a Christian coffee house next door to a topless go-go club, in 1968. His early influence on hippies was unparalleled. He coined the phrases "turn on to Jesus" and "eternal rush"—describing his salvation experience.[2]

Lonnie Frisbee (1949–1993) was an early evangelist to the drug culture associated with the Hippie Movement. Chuck Smith, pastor of Calvary Chapel in Costa Mesa, California, discipled Frisbee and gave him opportunities to preach to and teach the growing youth population coming into the church. Frisbee was an early supporter of the Jesus Movement and a gifted preacher. During his time at Calvary Chapel, it was not uncommon for more than 1,000 Jesus People to attend his weekly Wednesday night Bible lessons. Frisbee had a profound influence on Greg Laurie and Mike MacIntosh. Frisbee was instrumental in helping to establish the Vineyard churches and the Calvary Chapel churches.

Bill Gaither was born on March 28, 1936, in Alexandria, Indiana. He attended Anderson College (BA) and Ball State University (MA), where he received his degrees in English. He is a composer, concert and recording artist, publisher, and entrepreneur. Gaither played a major role in gospel music publishing and performing beginning in the early 1970s. Working with his wife, Gloria, he published a large body of literature that is now part of the worship hymnody of Christians around the world. Their 1971 song "Because He Lives" is included in every major denominational hymnal.[3] Gaither, his sister Mary Ann, and brother Danny, formed a trio in 1956. Later, his wife, Gloria, joined Bill and Danny and together recorded more than 30 albums.[4]

Edwin Hawkins was born in Oakland, California, on August 18, 1943, into a family of musicians and began playing piano at age five. He served as the music director and organist for the Ephesians Church of God in Christ in Berkeley, California. He is known as a singer, songwriter, producer, vocalist, organist, and choir director. His "Edwin Hawkins Music and Arts Seminar" is an annual workshop that has trained young worship leaders, musicians, and artists for the ministry. His seminar features classes on song writing, keyboards, gospel music ministry, choir decorum, fashion design, the business of music and communications, vocal techniques, and drama. At the end of each workshop, participants help present and record a mass choir concert.[5]

Billy Ray Hearn, born in 1939 in Honeygrove, Texas, and a graduate of Baylor University, served Southern Baptist churches as minister of music before moving to Waco, Texas, to work with Word Inc. In 1967, while serving as minister of music at the First Baptist Church of Thomasville, Georgia, Hearn joined Bob Oldenburg and Cecil McGee[6] to write the first youth musical, *Good News*. Beginning in 1968 and continuing through 1975, Hearn worked for Word Inc., identifying Christian artists who utilized pop and rock styles. He promoted and developed the gospel youth musicals by Ralph Carmichael and Kurt Kaiser, *Tell It Like It Is* and *Natural High,* along with *Come Together* by Jimmy Owens. He championed contemporary Christian music by creating a record label devoted exclusively to the production of Jesus Music, Myrrh Records. In 1976, he founded Sparrow Records with Second Chapter of Acts, John Michael Talbot, Terry Talbot, Barry McGuire, Keith Green, and the Agape Force among his artists. It was an immediate success.

Glenn Kaiser (1953–) joined the Jesus Movement during the early 1970s. An accomplished blues guitarist, lead vocalist, songwriter, back-up singer, and producer, he was influential in establishing the group Resurrection Band. Kaiser was an important theological influence within the Jesus People Movement, providing spiritual guidance to musicians and fans of the emerging Contemporary Christian Music industry. Kaiser pastors the Jesus People USA community in downtown Chicago, Illinois.[7]

Kurt Kaiser (1934–) was born on December 17, 1934. Having earned the BM and MM degrees from the Northwestern University School of Music in Chicago, he joined Word Inc. in 1959 as director of artists and repertoire and later became vice president and director of music. Kaiser arranged and produced recording projects for Kathleen Battle, Tennessee Ernie Ford, Larnelle Harris, Burl Ives, George Beverly

Shea, Joni Eareckson Tada, Ethel Waters, and others. In 1992, he was awarded a Lifetime Achievement Award by the American Society of Composers, Authors and Publishers (ASCAP). He is an accomplished pianist, having recorded 16 instrumental albums of his own and served for more than 20 years as accompanist for Shea. His youth musicals *Tell It Like It Is* and *Natural High,* written with Carmichael, were considered the first rock-'n'-roll musicals for the church. *Tell It Like It Is* featured his most famous song, "Pass It On," which became the unofficial anthem of the 1960s Jesus Movement.[8] It was used on the final night of "Explo '72," when more than 80,000 students participated in a candlelight ceremony at the Cotton Bowl in Dallas, Texas.[9]

Love Song was one of the first music groups from Calvary Chapel. Original members of the ensemble were Chuck Girard, Tommy Coomes, Jay Truax, and Fred Field.[10] Initially a secular rock-'n'-roll group in the late 1960s, the entire group was converted to Christianity through Calvary Chapel and asked if it could sing for worship services. When the pastor asked to hear a song or two, they played an original composition by Girard, "Welcome Back":

> Welcome back to the things you once believed in,
> Welcome back to what you knew was right all along,
> I'm so happy now to welcome you back,
> Welcome back to Jesus.

Not only were they welcomed into services at Calvary Chapel, they also went on to become leaders in the contemporary Christian music industry. According to music historian Chuck Fromm:

> Love Song went on to become one of the most popular groups of the Jesus Movement, traveling the country, doing concerts in churches and schools, often as part of an anti-drug program. By the time they disbanded in 1974, they had inspired dozens of

imitators who identified not so much with their particular sound as with the sincerity of their expression.[11]

Robert "Bob" R. MacKenzie (1938–2000) was one of Christian music's most prominent "behind-the-scenes" personalities from 1965 to 2000. MacKenzie moved to Nashville, Tennessee, in 1964 where he served as general manager of the Nashville Symphony. He left the symphony in 1966 to become artist and recording director for the John T. Benson Company of Nashville.[12] During his tenure at the Benson Company, MacKenzie helped develop the gospel music publishing industry. He produced hundreds of gospel music recordings and books in all musical styles and genres for the company.

MacKenzie was an innovative producer and avid student of the Christian music market. He was the first person to use full orchestrations with a Southern gospel quartet. In his highly acclaimed *Alleluia: A Praise Gathering for Believers*,[13] he merged the traditional choir with Southern and Black Gospel music. He also created a method for promoting new copyrights through radio, television, and other media and mentored scores of young artists in the industry.[14]

MacKenzie was a longtime associate of Bill Gaither. In the mid-1970s, they established Paragon and Associates, a music publishing and recording company devoted to developing new products for evangelical churches. In the late 1970s, they created the groundbreaking hymnal *Hymns for the Family of God*. Gaither said of MacKenzie:

> Bob MacKenzie came into the gospel music field in the early 1960s at a time when we desperately needed a breath of fresh air and a visionary with the courage to take us into daring new territory. Bob was that sort of visionary. The list of artists and music-related business talent that he brought to this field is endless. He acted as a catalyst and motivator for us all, to move us to new and

higher levels of excellence. Still today his fingerprints remain on what we now know as the broad Christian music field.[15]

To Bob MacKenzie, the "why" question was the most important . . . Bob's blunt honesty with his artists was his strongest suit. . . . Before long, he was one of the leading proponents of a new style of gospel music that became known as "Contemporary Christian Music."[16]

Mac was one of the greatest representatives of Christian music that we've had in the past fifty years. When the definitive history of Christian music is written, Bob MacKenzie must be included as a key player during the 20th century.[17]

MacKenzie was inducted into the Gospel Music Hall of Fame in 2001, a year after his death, because of his extensive work mentoring and inspiring young musicians.[18] Singer Michael W. Smith credits MacKenzie as the first one to give him work in Nashville.[19]

Martin Meyer "Moishe" Rosen (1932–2010) was born to Ben Rosen and Rose Baker, both Orthodox Jews from Austria, during the Great Depression. While at the University of Colorado, he met Ceil Starr, a young Jewish student, and they married in 1950. Three years later, she was converted through the ministry of an evangelical Christian preacher, and her husband, at age 21, soon trusted Jesus too. He enrolled in a Bible college in New Jersey and was ordained to preach.

In September 1973, Rosen founded Jews for Jesus, an organization dedicated to teaching Jews that Jesus is the Messiah. With more than 200,000 members, it became the largest messianic Jewish organization in the world. Rosen has been dubbed "the godfather of Jewish evangelism."[20]

Larry Norman (1947–2008), often called "the father of Christian rock music,"[21] was a Christian singer, songwriter, record producer, and record label owner. He used abrasive humor and sarcasm in his music as a means of presenting truth to non-Christians. Norman compared his harsh lyrics to a "street fight" for Jesus and told fellow believers, "This album is not for you."

Norman's 1969 release "Upon This Rock" became an anthem for the Jesus Movement. "I Wish We'd All Been Ready" was another popular Norman song. He was a pioneer in using rock music as a tool for evangelism.[22] His 1972 album *Only Visiting This Planet* is often cited as the most influential Christian rock project of the Jesus Movement era.[23]

As author and speaker Mike Duran noted:

> Perhaps it's the plight of artistic pioneers, but Norman's albums received lots of flack. He pushed the envelope of what Christian music should be, tackling themes of racism, drugs, and homelessness when Christian music was still a musically-challenged, antiseptic sing-along.[24]

Second Chapter of Acts was one of the first music groups to engage the Hippie Movement. The trio Annie Herring, Matthew Ward, and Nelly Griesen ministered to the Jesus People with a new "gospel rock" style that bridged the gap between pop and sacred music.[25] By the end of the 1970s, the group's audience had grown to include the broader evangelical culture. Second Chapter of Acts is best known for its 1974 "Easter Song," which is included in many hymnals today and is still sung during Easter celebrations at many churches.

Chuck Smith (1927–) was one of the most important leaders in the Jesus Movement. As pastor of Calvary Chapel in Costa Mesa, California, he encouraged hundreds of young musical artists to use their talents for the Lord. His church was a pioneer in evangelism to the youth counterculture during the mid- to late 1960s. Calvary Chapel pioneered an informal and contemporary approach in its worship and public meetings. Much of Contemporary Christian Music (CCM) has its roots in Calvary Chapel worship music. The church grew in weekly attendance and helped start scores of daughter congregations.[26]

Jack Sparks (1928–2010), a former statistics professor at the University of Colorado, was an associate with Campus Crusade for Christ and one of the early evangelicals to minister to the street people of the Hippie Movement. He founded the Christian World Liberation Front (CWLF) in the fall of 1968 as a ministry to hippies, street people, and students in Berkeley, California.

Sparks was one of a few evangelists to hippies and Jesus People who strongly encouraged membership in and accountability to a local church. He and his followers partnered with the Billy Graham Evangelistic Association in evangelistic endeavors.

Innovations to Worship

Economic, political, social, and ecclesiastical changes from the mid-1960s through the mid-1980s prompted significant innovations in worship. Some have suggested that Christian worship changed more between 1965 and 1985 than it did between the Reformation and the mid-1960s. Most of the changes in worship practices during the sixteenth to nineteenth centuries were gradual in nature. Their introduction to the broader evangelical community was relatively slow, usually over a twenty-five- to fifty-year time span, or more. Not so with changes in worship practices from 1965 forward.

The advent and influence of mass communication on the evangelical community was profound. The introduction of popular music genre as a primary tool for communication by the Jesus People only expedited an already inevitable process of cultural infiltration on the evangelical community. The impact postmodern culture had on "the way churches worshipped" from the mid-1960s through the mid-1980s is almost immeasurable. What follows is a summary of some of the changes and innovations to worship that took place from 1965 to 1985.

Jesus Music

One important aspect of the Jesus Movement was its music. In fact, the "baby boomer awakening" may have been driven by music more than any previous awakening. Music was a tool for evangelism, and it provided an outlet for Jesus People to express deep emotions. Most of the Jesus music was derived from a form of folk music—primarily because that was a popular genre among the broader culture.

Early Jesus music reflected the commercial folk music of popular groups like the New Christy Minstrels and Peter, Paul and Mary. Heavily driven by guitar, the songs were harmonically simple and lyrically straightforward. Platform presentations were deliberately unpretentious. What emerged was a mixture of pop, folk, soft rock, country, and rock-'n'-roll. Musicians did not want to call their new genre "gospel music." So they used the phrases "Jesus music" and "praise music." Larry Eskridge explained that the new style "was an amalgamation of simple Scripture songs and choruses" and was aimed "primarily at creating a corporate worship experience" rather than creating music for performance.[27]

Use of Radio, Television, and Other Media

Between 1965 and 1970, songs about Jesus entered the rotation of music for secular radio stations. These songs were not generally overtly Christian, but they made some mention of Jesus and the need for wholesome values. Music historian Paul Baker gave three reasons for this Christian intrusion into secular markets:

> First, the Jesus movement was gaining momentum, and the Jesus theme was a little more acceptable than it had been in years past.

Secondly, the youth of the "generation gap" were opening up to *any* possible religion. They were considering each faith's claims and experimenting with each, searching for spiritual fulfillment. To these youth, Jesus represented just another religious possibility.

A third reason [was that] the lyrics seemed to appeal to the masses.[28]

In 1969, Andrew Lloyd Webber's rock opera *Jesus Christ, Superstar* became a hit on Broadway. "Jesus Is a Soul Man," "Put Your Hand in the Hand of the Man from Galilee," and "Amazing Grace" (performed by Judy Collins) were number-one hits on the *Billboard* record charts. Radio stations all over the world played them, prompting *Billboard* magazine to note that religious themes were catching on in popular music.[29]

Television. Television had a profound impact on the worship practices of evangelical churches during the 1970s and 1980s. Three programs were particularly important:

1. *Oral Roberts and the World Action Singers.* From the early days of television, Oral Roberts used it as a means of proclaiming the gospel. At first, he had a syndicated broadcast that highlighted his tent crusades, preaching, and healing ministries. With the advent of color television in the early 1970s, he changed his weekly televised ministry to a studio-based format. He featured his son Richard as soloist, singing with the World Action Singers.[30] Although Oral Roberts University and his evangelistic headquarters were in Tulsa, Oklahoma, his new television program was based in Los Angeles. Ralph Carmichael wrote all the music and produced the shows. He published arrangements from the shows in book form and made recordings available through his Light Records. These products had a profound impact on the evangelical community.

2. *Day of Discovery* was an extension of the Radio Bible Class ministry in Grand Rapids, Michigan. Filmed on location at Cypress Gardens in Florida from the early 1970s through the 1990s, the weekly thirty-minute broadcast featured an eight-to-ten voice ensemble singing in various parts of the garden followed by a ten- to twelve-minute sermon. The music was widely accepted by fans of traditional gospel music. Among the early arrangers for these programs were Dick Anthony, John Peterson, Don Wyrtzen, and Larry Mayfield.

3. *The Old Time Gospel Hour* was presented by Jerry Falwell Ministries in Lynchburg, Virginia. It was a rebroadcast of the Sunday morning worship services of Thomas Road Baptist Church and included all the singing and preaching. Heavily influenced by the Southern Gospel and revivalist music of the 1950s and 1960s, artists on the program included Doug Oldham, the Old Time Gospel Hour Trio, and college ensembles from the young Liberty Baptist College. Publishers provided composers and arrangers for the ministry to produce music that could be used on the broadcasts and subsequently in churches across America.

Infusion of New Copyrights

Country stations played Southern Gospel. Middle-of-the-road stations often played the more pop-sounding Christian singers. In time, rock-'n'-roll stations played the new Christian rock—especially during the hours devoted to religion. New Christian music stations sprang up all over the country. The Moody Radio Network, Salem Broadcasting, and Crawford Broadcasting developed huge followings.

Christian music publishers and record companies used the growing Christian radio market as an opportunity to promote their artists and new copyrights directly to local churches. Many songs made popular through airplay on radio or television were included in hymnals for the church during the 1970s and 1980s. These songs were then assimilated into the weekly worship of the evangelical community.

The Demand for Full-Time Professional Worship Pastors

Ministers of music and worship pastors had been an important part of many large church staffs. With the development of new music and worship resources, churches of all sizes began to feel a need for full-time ministers of music and worship. Church choirs grew at a startling rate. Many churches, especially large Southern Baptist churches, boasted choirs and orchestras of 200 to 300 members. The growing need for music leadership in local churches created a demand for skilled musicians with a heart for worship.

Publishers were the first to respond to this need. They established partnerships with bookstores, music dealers, distributors, and local churches to provide training programs for musicians and church workers in all areas of worship. Regional workshops were developed to demonstrate new worship materials, seasonal musicals (and cantatas), youth musicals, and children's musicals. Thousands of worship leaders across America took part in these workshops.

Youth Musicals

During the late 1960s, there were very few youth choirs. In general, the evangelical community had not adapted to the lifestyle, dress, or music of the Jesus People. According to Ralph Carmichael:

> We discovered that there was a great gulf developing between the youth and the traditional church . . . and the gulf was growing wider and wider. There were a lot of influences, but the result was that we decided to try something for the kids.[31]

Popular during those days were humanitarian music groups like Up with People. These were large choirs that sang newly written folk songs with guitar accompaniment. Billy Ray Hearn, minister of music at First Baptist Church, Thomasville, Georgia, and a group of music leaders in the Southern Baptist Convention decided to attempt a similar venture with Christian music. As Hearn recounted:

> A bunch of us got together during Recreation Week at the Baptist Assembly in Glorieta, New Mexico, and asked ourselves why we couldn't develop our own "Up with People" music. We decided to write some music like that by the next annual Recreation Week.
>
> Meanwhile, we got together a bunch of kids who were there at Glorieta, and some guitars. We started working on some known spirituals and folk songs, and doing some hymns in a folk style. There were about eighty kids, about twenty guitars and a bass, but no drums. *That* was still a little far out.[32]

By 1967, Hearn, Cecil McGee, and Bob Oldenburg had completed a new youth musical, *Good News*. It was published by the youth division of the Baptist Sunday School Board in Nashville, Tennessee, and premiered at both Glorieta and the Ridgecrest Baptist Assembly in North Carolina.

The musical was an instant success. Small "campfire" versions of the songbooks were made available for youth, and the work sold an estimated 2 million copies. In 1968, *Good News* was presented to the Southern Baptist Convention in Houston by 1,300 students and a fifty-piece orchestra. Kurt Kaiser, a composer and executive with Word Music in Waco, Texas, flew to Houston to see the performance. While in Houston, Kaiser and Hearn phoned Ralph Carmichael and discussed the possibility of developing another folk musical through Word Music. That conversation was the genesis of a youth musical by Kaiser and Carmichael, *Tell It Like It Is*.

Later that year, Hearn accepted a position at Word and moved to Waco. His main job initially was to promote the new youth musical to Southern Baptist churches. Recalling the experience, Carmichael explained:

> Different choir directors started to see the potential, and youth choirs started growing. I think we ultimately sold something over a half million of that $2.98 music folio, *Tell It Like It Is*.[33]

The partnership between Carmichael and Kaiser proved a success. They moved on to write *Natural High* in the same quasi-rock, folk style. Based on the success of *Tell It Like It Is,* Carmichael started his own company, Light Music, in California. Other publishers produced youth musicals by Jimmy Owens, Otis Skillings, and Don Wyrtzen.

By 1985, four streams of gospel music emerged: Contemporary Christian Music, African American Gospel Music (also called Black Gospel), Traditional Gospel Music, and Southern Gospel Music. Each genre of music was identified by and associated with its own unique culture, style of performance, publishing house and/or record company, and regional following.

Advent of Contemporary Christian Music (CCM)

The Jesus Movement pioneered a new genre of music called "Contemporary Christian Music," introducing to evangelicals an integration of rock-'n'-roll, rhythm and blues, classical music, folk music, country-western, and nineteenth-century gospel song. The Jesus People sang new songs, in a new style, and created a new type of rock-'n'-roll. It was unlike anything previously accepted by evangelical churches. John Styll, former editor of *CCM Magazine,* explained why the Jesus People did not adopt the term "gospel music" for their songs:

> I wouldn't say it was deliberate in the sense of wanting to distance it [Jesus Music] from anything, but "gospel" meant black or southern. What went out of the Jesus movement had never been called *gospel music*. We have just called the music [and all that surrounds it] *Contemporary Christian Music*. . . . By the way, the term "CCM" had never been used until we started using it out in California. . . . In 1979, CCM began. As the whole thing escalated, we saw this is really getting large.[34]

By the turn of the century, CCM had grown into a multibillion-dollar industry.

During the 1970s, CCM radically changed the way evangelicals perceived the relationship between worship and music. For the first time in church history, worship and music were seen as synonymous. By the beginning of the 1990s, a new paradigm for worship was in place.

Contemporary Christian Music Artists

Within the Jesus Movement, a large number of itinerate musicians emerged. Reaction to these groups and soloists by the broader church, especially the evangelical community, was mixed. Thus, it took more than two decades for the evangelicals to embrace the use of rock music in worship.

Several early record labels helped establish CCM musicians and opened doors of ministry for Christian musicians of many styles. By the mid-1980s, scores of full-time, itinerate artists traveled to churches to participate in weekly worship ministry. They were often perceived as guest worship leaders.

From the 1940s through the 1960s, Southern Gospel quartets performed largely in high schools or civic auditoriums. Rarely did a quartet perform in a church on Sunday morning. By the 1980s, though, Southern Gospel quartets were more involved in the weekly Sunday morning worship at large churches. Saturday night "sings" were being phased out.

A host of artists using "middle-of-the-road," "country-gospel," "traditional," and "black gospel" styles emerged. Churches clamored to have them take part in weekly worship services. Several artists secured agents to manage their schedules. By the end of the 1980s, a core of pop Christian artists developed. Bob MacKenzie explains:

> People that were artists identified with a specific stylistic culture: rock, folk, black, rhythm and blues, etc. . . . We started moving out into the enormous stylistic possibilities that we found in the pop world. And what happened is that it just opened the market broadly. And, because people had all these diverse interests, each found a hearing. Once somebody got the idea, "Oh we can use the current, commercial music culture to communicate our faith," then the barn door was open. Then, everything was fair game.[35]

It was the first time in history that a group of musicians initially devoted to developing and creating music for the church "crossed over" to secular markets.[36] In the past, secular artists had been converted to Christianity and became "Christian artists." Keith Green, Larry Norman, Randy Matthews, and Barry McGuire were notable examples of this. By 1985, Christian artists entered the secular marketplace. MacKenzie explains:

> We have created artists of Christian persuasion who are at the front edge of what's happening in pop music, and so they are accepted. They are accepted for two reasons. One, because they bring the whole body of subculture [the evangelical worshipping community] to the table with them, as far as sales go. And two, the culture likes their music and doesn't mind the message.[37]

Many of the changes in worship by the end of the 1980s were driven by Christian music publishers and record companies. For example, the Benson Company, according to MacKenzie,

> believed these songs needed to be in print because the church needed them. As we go through the 1970s and hit the 80s, the big significant thing is that a whole songwriting enterprise comes along to create what I would call special material for the soloists . . . instead of being a reflection of what the congregation did, it became something that the congregation could not do so that the congregation became spectators to what the artist/singer/songwriter did. And that then started spawning the whole artist enterprise.[38]

As CCM matured, the quality of music in evangelical circles increased and the music became more viable as a commercial product. By the end of the 1970s, a strong Christian music industry developed which paralleled the secular music industry.

African American Gospel Music

In 1968, Edwin Hawkins recorded a "live" album, *Let Us Go into the House of the Lord,* with his forty-six-member Northern California State Youth Choir, a group of seventeen- to twenty-five-year-old student singers from his church. Having pressed only 500 copies of the album, Hawkins wanted to sell enough to recoup his expenses and sponsor his group to attend a conference in Washington, DC.[39]

Abe "Voco" Kesh at KSAN-FM radio station in San Francisco somehow got a copy of the release and played cut number 8, a rhythm-and-blues arrangement of a hymn written in 1755 by Phillip Doddridge, "Oh Happy Day."[40] It became an overnight sensation. Radio stations across the country began playing the song. It entered the mainstream market, and in the end, nearly 2 million copies were sold. The group was renamed the Edwin Hawkins Singers, took a U.S. tour, and appeared on *The Ed Sullivan Show*. Hawkins received a Grammy for his efforts.

This became a model for a new type of gospel music merging gospel and hymn singing. The arrangement of "Oh Happy Day" introduced to evangelicals an innovative way to sing praise that remains a part of their worship culture.[41]

Traditional and Southern Gospel Music

By 1985, changes emerged in the worship of many churches associated with "Traditional Gospel Music." These churches were often conservative in their music preferences and worship practices. Worship services were led by a song leader, soloist, choir, organ, and piano, not a band. They changed to emulate the Broadway musical style of the 1950s and 1960s, with soloists and choirs singing songs of testimony in a quasi-Broadway music style.

Composers such as Bill and Gloria Gaither, Mosie Lister, and Dottie Rambo helped drive this shift in the worship of traditional churches through publication of quartet or singing convention style music.[42]

Role of the Choir, Ensemble, and Special Groups. The first innovation in Traditional and Southern Gospel Music involved the use of choir in worship.

Previously, choral presentation during worship at many churches featured a classical music style. It included the choir and an occasional vocal soloist. Choirs in many evangelical churches performed songs by classical composers, and soloists sang in a manner resembling the German lieder art song.

Before 1970, choral literature was only available from a small number of publishers. These publishers generally focused on printing choral arrangements based on classical literature, spirituals, and established hymns. For the most part, Traditional Gospel Music was not available for choirs. Indeed, not many music publishers saw a need for choral music targeted toward evangelical churches.

In 1971, a radical change occurred in the way publishers of worship resources viewed the choir. According to MacKenzie:

> We got with this young guy named Bob Harrington, who was called the Chaplain of Bourbon Street. He was a phenomenal preacher—an absolutely amazing high-powered kind of guy. He came into our life through [Harrington's song leader Jack Price]. . . . We got involved with him and [said], "Hey, you've got this choir every single night in this crusade—thousands of people and I say you need some music. Come, we'll create a book for you and you sell it." The first book really . . . reflects my old 1956 to '60 Youth for Christ days [big choirs, big endings to songs, high notes for the sopranos, etc.]. That was new to where these guys were going because they come from a tradition that wasn't that flamboyant . . . but it was part of my psyche. . . . When it was done, the book sold between 250,000 and 300,000 copies.
>
> That also started the tradition where—because Jack [Price] was moving around the country in major crusades North and South—we provided books for his meetings.[43]

Bob Harrington crusades resembled the meetings of revivalists half a century earlier. In some respects they followed in the tradition of Billy Graham crusades in the 1950s and 60s, but their use of a dynamic musician-preacher team resembled Billy Sunday crusades. Just as Homer Rodeheaver served with Sunday, Jack Price served with Harrington. According to the notes on one Harrington crusade choir recording:

> Part of the excitement of a Bob Harrington crusade meeting is the ministry of music—conducted and supervised by exciting song leader, soloist, conductor Jack Price. . . . The tone for music ministry in the crusades is set by one of Bob Harrington's favorite songs, "Let's Talk About Jesus!" The great songs—wonderfully

arranged by W. Elmo Mercer—are all geared, as is the entire ministry of Bob Harrington, to introduce people to the life-changing gospel of Christ.[44]

Innovations in recording and publishing made it possible for traditional choirs to sing in worship services the gospel music they heard on the radio or television. In fact, they could sing the very arrangements performed by their favorite music groups. Orchestrations were written to accompany these choral arrangements. Recordings of well-known artists served as a means to demonstrate presentation for local church choirs and soloists. Publishers sold the arrangements and their "demonstration recordings" to local church choirs and congregations. As MacKenzie noted, "The demo recording became indispensable to the marketing and promotion of a choral book."[45]

Sound tracks (accompaniment music without the singers) created in professional recording studios were made available for use by local choirs. Publishers created a new sound track product line. Soloists and choirs could use these sound tracks as accompaniment during worship services. The idea was an immediate publishing and marketing success.

As Contemporary Christian Music developed and matured, the quality of musical presentation at evangelical churches improved. As a result, a strong, aggressively visionary Christian music industry developed, which paralleled the secular music industry. By the end of the 1970s, publishers of traditional gospel music were established in Grand Rapids, Nashville, Los Angeles, Kansas City, and Dallas—with each publisher employing a group of composers and arrangers.[46]

The second innovation in traditional and Southern Gospel music was the use of small vocal ensembles in worship services. Churches adapted the musical arrangements of groups like the World Action Singers, Day of Discovery, and the Old Time Gospel Hour singing teams. Soon, small ensembles replaced soloists in many evangelical worship services. Another new genre of evangelical music for worship was created.

The third innovation was the publication of children's musicals. Southern Baptists had long been proponents of music education for children, using a program known as "the graded choir." Many Southern Baptist congregations had large and well-developed children's choir ministries complete with full-time, paid staff. Music for these groups was published by the Baptist Sunday School Board. Other publishers began to develop Christmas, Easter, and patriotic musicals specially written for children. As the choral print industry developed, so did the emphasis on children's songs and programs for evangelical worship. The concept of developing children as worshippers became extremely popular among evangelicals.

Summary of the Baby Boomer Revival Awakening

The Baby Boomer revival between 1965 and 1985 changed Christian worship in important ways. Key individuals developed the Contemporary Christian Music industry and marketed to churches music that could be heard on the radio and the concert stage. Music publishers and record companies were established by the end of the 1970s that provided churches with musical resources not previously available for local congregations. This included new songs for weekly worship.

Radio, television, and recordings helped introduce new worship styles to congregations quickly. By the 1980s, evangelicals moved toward less formal services, compartmentalization of music styles (Traditional, Southern Gospel, Black Gospel, and Contemporary Christian Music), and the use of large choirs along with large volunteer orchestras.

Because many Christian colleges did not offer training in these new areas of worship and music, music publishers, music dealers, and ministers of music at local congregations began training programs for church musicians. These workshops served as a primary training venue for ministers of music and worship pastors well into the 1990s.

In our next chapter, we will discover how God continues to move in the hearts of people who praise him with song. We will discover how one music publisher's emphasis on teaching children how to praise impacted the broader evangelical community and, in the process, paved the way for an awakening called the Worship and Praise Movement.

Notes

1. Annie Young Frisbie, review of *The Cross: The Arthur Blessitt Story,* http://www.christianitytoday.com/ct/movies/reviews/2009/crossarthurblessitt story.html; accessed on May 21, 2012.

2. David di Sabatino, "History of the Jesus Movement," http://www.allsavedfreakband.com/jesus_movement.htm; accessed on August 31, 2011.

3. Ibid.

4. "Year of 1999: The Gaither Trio," http://www.gmahalloffame.org/site/?page_id=84; accessed on May 21, 2012.

5. See http://www.myspace.com/edwinhawkins; accessed on May 21, 2012.

6. Billy Ray Hearn, interview by Vernon Whaley, October 3, 1991.

7. Di Sabatino, "History of the Jesus Movement."

8. "Year of 2001: Kurt Kaiser," http://www.gmahalloffame.org/site/?page_id=88; accessed September 4, 2011.

9. Paul Baker, *Contemporary Christian Music: Where It Came From, What It Is, Where It's Going* (Westchester, IL: Crossway Books, 1985), 53–54.

10. "Love Song: The History," http://one-way.org/lovesong/history2.htm; accessed July 29, 2011.

11. Ibid.

12. Vernon M. Whaley, "Trends in Gospel Music (1940–1960)," (Ph.D. diss., University of Oklahoma, 1992), 6–7.

13. The first gold record in Christian music was for a landmark work produced by MacKenzie, *Alleluia: A Praise Gathering for Believers.*

14. The musicians mentored by Bob MacKenzie include the Imperials, the Cathedrals, Dottie Rambo, the Oak Ridge Boys, the Gaither Trio, Doug Oldham, the Speers, Truth, Joshua, Roger Breland and TRUTH, Robert Hale and Dean Wilder, Buddy Greene, and Michael W. Smith.

15. "Bob MacKenzie: 1938–2000," http://www.crossrhythms.co.uk/articles/news/Bob_MacKenzie_19382000/30333/p1/; accessed September 3, 2011.

16. Bill Gaither with Ken Abraham, *It's More Than the Music: Life Lessons on Friends, Faith and What Matters Most* (New York: Warner Faith, 2003), 96–97.

17. Ibid., 107.

18. "Year of 2000: Bob MacKenzie," http://www.gmahalloffame.org/site/?page_id=86; accessed September 3, 2011.

19. "Bob MacKenzie: 1938–2000."

20. Phil Davidson, "Moishe Rosen: Evangelist Who Founded the Jews for Jesus Movement," *The Independent* (24 August 2010), http://www.independent.co.uk/news/obituaries/moishe-rosen-evangelist-who-founded-the-jews-for-jesus-movement-2060054.html; accessed September 4, 2011.

21. Sarah Pulliam, "Larry Norman, 'Father of Christian Rock,' Dies at 60," http://www.christianitytoday.com/ct/2008/februaryweb-only/109-22.0.html; accessed September 5, 2011.

22. Di Sabatino, "History of the Jesus Movement."

23. "Jesus Movement," http://www.conservapedia.com/Jesus_Movement; accessed August 30, 2011.

24. Mike Duran, "The 'Father of Christian Rock' Dies," http://mikeduran.com/2008/02/the-father-of-christian-rock-dies; accessed on September 4, 2011.

25. "Year of 1999: Second Chapter of Acts," http://www.gmahalloffame.org/site/?page_id=84; accessed September 4, 2011.

26. Chuck Fromm, "New Song: The Sound of Spiritual Awakening," presented at the meeting of Oxford Reading and Research Conference, Oxford, England, July 1983, 21.

27. Ibid., 26.

28. Baker, *Contemporary Christian Music*, 21–22.

29. Paul R. Dienstberger, *The American Republic: A Nation of Christians* (Ashland, OH: Paul R. Dienstberger, 2000), n.p., http://www.prdienstberger.com/nation/Chapter10.htm#II.%20The%20Turbulent,%20Tempestuous,%20; accessed August 6, 2011.

30. Tal Davis, http://www.4truth.net/fourtruthpb.aspx?pageid=8589951926&terms=Oral%20Roberts, North American Mission Board, 2007; accessed September 12, 2011.

31. Baker, *Contemporary Christian Music*, 14–15.

32. Ibid.

33. Ibid.

34. John Styll, interview by Vernon M. Whaley, January 10, 1992, Nashville, Tennessee.

35. Bob MacKenzie, interview by Vernon Whaley, November 16, 1991, Brentwood, Tennessee.

36. Among the Christian musicians who signed with secular pop music record labels were Take Six, Russ Taff, Bee Bee and Cee Cee Winans, Amy Grant, and Michael W. Smith.

37. Bob MacKenzie, interview by Vernon Whaley, January 10, 1992, Nashville, Tennessee.

38. Ibid.

39. Baker, *Contemporary Christian Music*, 21–22.

40. "Oh Happy Day by the Edwin Hawkins Singers," http://www.songfacts.com/detail.php?id=2032; accessed September 3, 2011.

41. "Year of 2000: Edwin Hawkins," http://www.gmahalloffame.org/site/?page_id=86; accessed September 3, 2011.

42. These resources were made available about every six months by music publishers that specialized in printing songbooks with shaped-music notation. Several companies published music for Southern Gospel quartets and convention style singing. The three most notable sources for Southern Gospel music were: the Stamps-Baxter Music Publishing Company, Dallas, Texas; the Benson Company, Nashville, Tennessee; and the Vaughn Music Publishing Company, Cleveland, Tennessee. The Stamps-Baxter Music Company was purchased in the early 1980s by Zondervan Music in Grand Rapids, Michigan. Later, the Benson Company bought the music publishing

division from Zondervan, Inc. The Vaughn Music Publishing Company was purchased by the Church of God of Cleveland, Tennessee, in the early 1990s.

43. Bob MacKenzie, interview by Vernon Whaley, January 10, 1992, Nashville, Tennessee.

44. Bob MacKenzie, back liner notes to *Bob Harrington Crusade Choir* record (Nashville: Impact Records, 1971).

45. Bob MacKenzie, interview by Vernon Whaley, January 10, 1992, Nashville, Tennessee.

46. At Singspiration Inc. in Grand Rapids, John Peterson and Don Wyrtzen were the best-known composers. Among the Singspiration composers and arrangers were Dick Bolks, David Culross, David Clydesdale, Larry Mayfield, and Don Wyrtzen. At the Benson Company in Nashville, primary composers were Bill and Gloria Gaither, Dottie Rambo, Elmer Mercer, and a host of new musicians writing Jesus Music-type materials. Other Benson composers and arrangers included Ronn Huff, Rick Powell, Don Marsh, Lari Goss, Derric Johnson, and Bill Purcell. Among the composers and arrangers at Tempo, in Kansas City, were Otis Skillings, Dave Williamson, and Mark Hayes. At Light, Manna, and Sparrow companies in Los Angeles were Ralph Carmichael, Jimmy Owens, Michael Omartian, Andre Crouch, Second Chapter of Acts, Phil Keaggy, and a host of others.

CHAPTER 17

Moving toward a Twenty-First-Century Great Worship Awakening

In 1978, twenty-eight-year-old Chuck Fromm organized and directed one of the first worship festivals in America at the Anaheim Convention Center in Anaheim, California. Hosanna USA was an evening of celebration as scores of new artists proclaimed biblical truth through new songs. The program was televised across the nation live via satellite. A mobile multitrack recording studio captured the event on three-inch analog tape and delivered a "live album project" for distribution through Word Music. Michael Omartian led the platform band and orchestra. Major artists were joyously received by an army of fans. Pastor Chuck Smith preached a short gospel message, and more than 400 people came forward during the altar call. In the minds of industry personnel, Hosanna USA was a smashing success.[1]

However, during the early morning hours, God began working in Fromm's heart. He went to bed but sleep escaped him. All night, he wrestled with God. "Maranatha is one of five words for worship in the Bible," thought Fromm, who served as CEO of Calvary Chapel's Maranatha!

Music. "But, we are missing the mark. Yes, God was gracious and people were introduced to the kingdom, but something is wrong."

"Are we caught up in a spirit of greed? Are we primarily focused on using our publishing as a means for making money?" he wondered.[2] "We've gotten really well organized and commercial. In the process, our company has moved from a folk culture of sharing the gospel to a selling thing . . . making money." Fromm asked the Lord for wisdom. He thought to himself as he prayed:

> [I know] artists have a tendency to want to hijack the communication experience and turn it into . . . a mere performance. . . . To me, worship leading requires facilitators, not controllers. Only God deserves the glory. We are setting a program in motion so that artists, songwriters, producers and publishers get the glory. . . . It's an affirmation of their own ego through the experience on the stage. . . . They really want to be in the entertainment industry. Is this what God made [Maranatha! Music] for?[3]

The Lord continued to stir Fromm's heart. *Ministry is about teaching God's people how to praise the Living Lord*, he thought. *God created us to praise him, to be something different, to love him, to worship.*[4]

The following Monday, Fromm met with his board. After a few days and a series of intensely prayer-saturated meetings, they decided Maranatha! Music would be a company devoted to teaching God's people *how to worship*. They believed that non-Christians would turn to Christ when believers praised God with newly created songs.[5]

They adopted as their company mission two verses from the Bible:

> O Lord, our Lord, how majestic is your name in all the earth! You have set your glory above the heavens. From the lips of children and infants you have ordained praise, because of your enemies, to silence the foe and the avenger. (Ps 8:1–2 NIV)

Much to the surprise of the Christian music industry, Maranatha! immediately changed its focus and began publishing worship songs for children. True to its word, the Maranatha! board changed its emphasis back to teaching worship, and Fromm released all the company's artists from their contracts. He explained, "We turned the focus on creating worship song . . . the folk music of the church . . . the new hymns."[6]

In short order, Maranatha! began sending worship songs to the church. By the mid-1980s, simple tunes with simple lyrics were being sung by congregations all over the world. Among the company's many songs were: "Father, I Adore You," "Seek Ye First," "Glorify Thy Name," "I Love You, Lord," "Give Thanks," and "In His Time."[7]

The story of Chuck Fromm and Maranatha! Music is documentation of one of many life-changing experiences Jesus Movement people had with God. Thousands of men and women who were spiritually changed during the Jesus Movement years serve today as pastors, denominational executives, missionaries, and lay leaders.

The Paradigm Shifts in Worship from 1985 to 2000

The last 15 years of the twentieth century were marked by isolated movements of God rather than in one global awakening, like those experienced by previous generations. Still, evangelicals published and recorded praise and worship songs, hosted worship conferences, and even organized large worship gatherings in stadiums. By the end of the twentieth century, Christian schools formally began to train students as leaders of praise and worship music, and the evangelical community began to embrace the new worship paradigm.

Influence of the Jesus Movement

In many ways, the Jesus Movement's legacy has endured. Thousands of church plants started by the 1970s Jesus People are known today for their commitment to biblical inspiration and inerrancy, expositional preaching, evangelism, meeting physical and social needs, global missions, and the use of rock-'n'-roll music in worship. They are deeply committed to church growth, church planting, and *seeker initiatives*.

Yet evangelical worship music is perhaps the area of the Jesus Movement's most profound and enduring influence. It introduced expressions of praise that were God-centered and biblically based. As historian Robb Redman notes:

> The Jesus movement felt strongly that if Christian worship were to be meaningful . . . the old music of their parents' church, both the classically oriented mainline church and the Billy Graham crusade clones of conservative evangelicalism, [had to go]. . . . The positive perspective was their high esteem for authenticity and simplicity. . . . It is remarkable how much of the substance of Christian worship they preserved in a new format, especially in their emphasis on biblical preaching, prayer, and congregational participation.[8]

Those convictions resulted in the production of new songs for worship. Most are songs of personal experience, private expressions of faith, and commitment to God. Usually written in the first person singular, the songs are short and repetitive. Their virtue lies in the "brevity and simplicity of the lyric and style."[9]

The role of musicians changed as a result of the Jesus Movement. An industry of traveling artists emerged, representing a variety of musical genres. Many Christian musicians moved to Nashville, Dallas, Atlanta, New York, Los Angeles, and other recording centers and assumed positions of leadership in the Christian music industry. Some continued to travel on the weekends to churches, music festivals, county fairs, and youth camps. By the end of the 1990s, many artists transitioned from the role of concert performer to that of worship leader.

Influence of Christian Music Publishing Companies

The enduring influence of Christian music publishers was enormous. For more than 20 years, publishers were the primary source of education in worship leading, music literature, and new songs for evangelical churches. Worship leaders, choir directors, lay musicians, children's music specialists, and instrumentalists attended publisher-sponsored workshops through which they received much of their training.

For years, secular companies sought to take advantage of the successes of the Christian music business. Most notable were ABC television's purchase of Word Music in the early 1980s and Rupert Murdoch, who held majority ownership in the Zondervan Corporation, merging his music publishing and recording divisions with the Benson Company. By 1981, Paragon, Benson, Stamps-Baxter, and Zondervan Music were reorganized as "The New Benson Company." By the end of the 1980s, the Christian Contemporary Music industry had developed into a multibillion-dollar business.

In the mid-1990s, secular companies began to buy major portions of Christian publishing companies. As the new millennium opened, most major Christian music publishing companies in America had been purchased by secular corporations. With each acquisition came a new and impressive level of influence on the broader music industry.

Influence of Church-Based Publishing and Recording Companies

Several groups emerged as significant influences in the new praise and worship movement: Calvary Chapel, with its Maranatha! Music; Vineyard Christian Fellowship, with its Mercy Music; and Hillsong Church of Sidney, Australia, with its lineup of world-class musicians; Lifeway Christian Resources, with its online publication of the *Baptist Hymnal* (2008) and praise and worship resources; Lillenas Music Publishers, with its commitment to worship choir; Integrity Music, with its commitment to teaching worship through song lyric; and Worship Together, with its emphasis on British composers and songwriters. All of these publishers specialize in producing songs for a new genre called "praise and worship music."

Three commonalities tie these praise and worship leaders together: (1) Each publisher began as an outgrowth of local church or denominational ministry. (2) All are devoted to providing "new song" for congregational worship and are at the heart of a relatively new industry known as Contemporary Worship Music (CWM). (3) Each organization is intensely interested in teaching the church *how* to worship through song. The combined impact of these production companies during the years leading up to the twenty-first century was massive. Any Great Awakening in the years to come will almost certainly include worship music from these groups.

Calvary Chapel and Maranatha! Music. The shift of Maranatha! from being an artist-driven company identified with the baby boomer Jesus People to producing the simple praise and worship music of Generation X proved a booming business success. During the 1990s, Maranatha! partnered with a newly organized men's ministry, Promise Keepers, to provide hundreds of songs for stadium events and regional discipleship gatherings. Promise Keepers events in turn influenced worship in thousands of evangelical churches.

Vineyard Christian Fellowship and Mercy Music. Vineyard Christian Fellowship began as a breakaway organization from Calvary Chapel in the early 1980s, led by founding pastor John Wimber. Mentored by Chuck Smith, Wimber was a former music arranger, sideman, and producer of the 1970s pop group, the Righteous Brothers. Because of his musicianship and love for praise and worship, he attracted hundreds of young musicians and songwriters to his church.[10] Together, they started

Mercy Publishing to disseminate praise and worship music from the nearly 800 Vineyard ministries around the world.

According to Redman, "Vineyard songs reflect the theology and philosophy of worship taught in the Vineyard."[11] Among the hundreds of copyrights owned by Mercy Publishing are "Draw Me Close to You," "Breathe," and "In the Secret (I Want to Know You)."

Hillsong Church and Hillsong Music. Hillsong Church is a twenty-one-thousand-member fellowship based in Sydney, Australia. With church plants and ministry offices in London, Paris, Berlin, Cape Town, Stockholm, and Kiev, the organization's growth can be attributed largely "to the success of its music in Australia, particularly the contribution of Hillsong Church and United Youth Bands."[12]

Beginning in 1996, worship leaders Geoff Bullock, Russell Fragar, Reuben Morgan, and Darlene Zschech made an enormous impact on the Contemporary Worship Music industry and evangelical church. Their songs "The Power of Your Love," "Worthy Is the Lamb," "Lord, I Give You My Heart," "Holy Spirit Rain Down," "The Potter's Hand," and "Shout to the Lord," have become standard repertoire for worshipping congregations around the world.

LifeWay Worship Resources is the music publishing arm of the Southern Baptist Convention. As such, they have led the evangelical community in providing graded choir music for children and music practical for contemporary, blended, and traditional worship.

Lillenas Publishing Company is the official music publishing division of the Church of the Nazarene in Kansas City, Missouri. They have long been an innovator in music for the evangelical community, having pioneered the use of sound tracks with solo and choir and introducing the first choral clubs in the early 1970s.

Integrity Music and Integrity Worship Institute. Integrity Music was chartered by a group of pastors in 1987 as an alternative to Contemporary

Christian Music publishers to promote "message music" to Christian bookstores. Initially, the company established itself as a producer of "praise and worship music" recorded in pop, country, Hebrew, gospel, and folk styles.[13] It launched a popular direct-mail subscription program that delivered to customers through mail the latest praise and worship songs on cassette or CD.

In 1997, Integrity Music established Integrity Worship Institute to offer "a concentrated curriculum in worship study" in partnership with strategic Christian colleges and universities around the world. In 1998, it forged a partnership with Liberty University of Lynchburg, Virginia, and launched an institute, Integrity Media Worship School, in Mobile, Alabama.[14]

Worship Together and EMI Christian Music Group. Worship Together began in the late 1990s with a group of worship leaders and songwriters from the United Kingdom. Stuart Townend, Matt Redman, Noel Richard, Martin Smith, and Graham Kendrick brought a new approach to praise and worship music by producing songs modeled after the music of secular pop music bands. Lyrics were generally focused on confession of sin, personal brokenness, forgiveness of sin, the cross, and biblical imagery.[15]

Influences from Christian Copyright Licensing Inc.

One of the most important influencers in worship since 1988 is Christian Copyright Licensing Inc. (CCLI). CCLI is not a church or a music publishing company. Rather, CCLI is a company that monitors the church usage of copyrighted songs. They collect fees from churches for the use of copyrighted songs and pay royalties to copyright holders.

> CCLI now serves more than 200,000 churches worldwide in worship. It was founded as a ministry of the church and a service to the church, to educate the church about copyright laws, to protect the church from the consequences of copyright infringe-

ments and to encourage greater utilization of copyrights in church services.[16]

The significance of this company and its influence on worship practices is enormous. Robb Redman says that CCLI as a company "democratized music publishing."[17] It developed a means whereby churches and worship pastors could easily gain access to newly copyrighted songs for congregational use. Their "Song Discovery" service provides for the worship pastor immediate access to new music for the worship service.

The music industry at large recognizes CCLI as a company of unequaled professional integrity. In this position of strength, CCLI has been able to assume a much larger role as media broker and agent for the entire evangelical community. Today, CCLI provides four strategic services for the local church: (1) Church Copyright License covers the use of over 200,000 worship songs for congregational singing; (2) Church Rehearsal License covers the legal sharing of commercial recordings of songs to be learned by choirs, ensembles, and praise teams; (3) Church Streaming and PodCast License provides a legal venue for churches to stream or podcast live-recorded worship music on their website or other streaming services; and (4) Church Video License (CVLI) provides a way for churches to use movies for ministry-related activities.[18]

Influence of Large Events and Mega Rallies

From 1990 to 2000, three parachurch organizations had a significant impact on the worship practices of evangelical churches: Promise Keepers, Passion Conferences, and Women of Faith. The major difference between the groups is seen in their commitment to intentional and strategic demographic mission: Promise Keepers—seeking to meet the spiritual needs of men; Passion—reaching out to the college-aged students of America; and Women of Faith—encouraging spiritual maturity in the lives of women of all ages.

Promise Keepers. On March 20, 1990, Bill McCartney, head football coach at the University of Colorado, expressed a vision to see men take seriously their responsibility to be faithful disciples of Jesus Christ. He talked of the need for a nondenominational, multiracial organization that would "call men to be responsible to Jesus, their wives and families, their church, and each other:"[19]

> I envision men coming together in huge numbers in the name of Jesus, worshipping and celebrating their faith together; I long to see men openly proclaiming their love for Christ and commitment to their families.[20]

Promise Keepers (PK) was officially launched in 1991 with 4,200 men at a rally in Boulder, Colorado. By 1996, the organization was hosting two-day stadium conferences at 22 locations with attendance in excess of 1.1 million men.[21] Chuck Fromm, former president and CEO of Maranatha! Music, says: "The most powerful and lasting legacy of the Promise Keepers movement is musical."[22]

Promise Keepers' influence on worship practices in local churches was almost immediate. Each year, new songs were written for the stadium events. Cassettes and CDs were sent to the participants three and four weeks prior to the gatherings. Men were encouraged to "practice worship." In turn, they introduced the new songs to their local church congregations. They came to the events with these new songs already on their lips and in their hearts.

In 1997, the organization achieved three watermark goals: First, more than 40,000 church leaders attended a PK-sponsored pastors' conference in Atlanta. Many believed this was the "largest single gathering of pastors in the history of the Christian Church."[23] Second, PK arena events were established in Canada, New Zealand, and Australia. Third, on October 4, 1997, nearly one million men met in Washington, DC, at the National Mall. The event was broadcast live on C-Span and called

"Stand in the Gap: A Sacred Assembly of Men."[24] Chuck Fromm was at the event with his seven-year-old son:

> For all of America's future it will be told, that one day one million men came together and spoke with a single prophetic voice at the symbolic center of American political culture and life.... Their goal was not political power as the media imagined.... The desire was the transformation of human lives; men who would return home to their communities filled with the Spirit of God and ready to engage in new forms of action as the Spirit guided them.[25]

Passion Conferences. Passion Conferences are gatherings of college students and young adults focused on spiritual awakening and renewal. Louie Giglio had the initial idea for the conferences in June 1995. In the fall of 1996, a meeting of campus ministry leaders resulted in plans for a large rally to be held in Austin, Texas.[26] They decided that Isa 26:8 would serve as a theme verse, and in January 1997 more than 2,000 students gathered for Passion's first four-day conference. In May 2000, more than 40,000 college students from every state in the Union gathered at Shelby Farms outside Memphis, Tennessee, for a solemn assembly of prayer, asking God for spiritual awakening in their generation.[27]

Modeled after the Cutting Edge and Soul Survivor events in the United Kingdom, Passion Conferences continue to have an enormous impact on the worship practices of young adults and college students. Through their Passion Worship CDs, "268 events," OneDay gatherings, and record label sixstepsrecords, songs such as "Better Is One Day" and "We Fall Down" have become standard repertoire for most evangelical congregations.[28]

Women of Faith. Organized in 1996, Women of Faith is a nondenominational agency dedicated to encouraging women in spiritual growth, faith, and discipleship. Women of Faith usually hosts between

25 and 30 annual conferences that feature Bible messages from well-known speakers, concerts by popular Christian music artists, original drama presentations, and extended times of worship.[29]

Influential College and University Degrees in Worship

One of the most significant influences on worship practices in evangelical churches during the years leading to the twenty-first century is seen in the establishment of college worship study degrees. Prior to 1990, most training in the disciplines of worship was imbedded in church history, church music, discipleship, or spiritual formation curricula. Certainly, there were not many worship study degrees and very little, if any, emphasis on the development or leading of contemporary worship. Students graduated as skilled musicians with degrees in church music. Several Catholic or mainline institutions offered degrees in liturgical studies or ancient worship but undergraduate and graduate curricula in worship in the evangelical traditions simply were not available at Christian institutions.

Realizing the need for further training in the disciplines related to worship, in 1995 Robert Webber, long-time professor of religion at Wheaton College of Wheaton, Illinois, and Northern Baptist Theological Seminary in Lombard, Illinois, designed two degrees in worship studies: the Master of Theological Studies in Worship (at Tyndale Seminary in Toronto, Canada), and the Doctor of Ministry (at Northern Baptist Theological Seminary).[30]

Throughout most of the 1990s, demand for qualified, skilled, and educated personnel to serve in local churches and parachurch organizations prompted serious discussion as to the need for innovative worship curricula. By 2000, and in response to these needs, worship studies degrees or special emphasis in worship were established at Liberty University in Lynchburg, Virginia,[31] Regent University in Virginia Beach, Virginia,[32]

Calvin Institute of Christian Worship at Calvin College in Grand Rapids, Michigan,[33] and a new Institute of Worship Studies (started by Robert Webber) in Orange Park, Florida.[34] Several seminaries and graduate colleges quickly followed their lead, and serious studies in the discipline began. While these degree programs meet the rigors of quality education required by the academic academy at large, there is an important emphasis on practitioner training at many of these institutions.

As of 2010, more than 85 institutions provide undergraduate degrees in worship studies or worship and music. Nearly 40 graduate degrees in worship are now available at evangelical universities, colleges, and seminaries. These are primarily vocational degrees that strategically equip students to lead worship in the evangelical community.

Influential Books on Worship

During the years following the Jesus Movement, several authors highlighted the biblical mandate for worship. Among them were Jack Taylor,[35] Henry Blackaby,[36] David Jeremiah,[37] and Jim Cymbala.[38] Three authors, however, became particularly important in the evangelical community: A. W. Tozer, Jack Hayford, and Robert Webber.

The writings of A. W. Tozer. **A. W. Tozer** was born on April 21, 1897, in the mountainous region of western Pennsylvania. He died from a heart attack on May 12, 1963, in Toronto. This twentieth-century prophet had a profound impact on the praise and worship movement of the 1990s and early twenty-first century—nearly 30 years after his death. Some call Tozer a C. S. Lewis for the twenty-first-century evangelical community. Through more than 40 books—most dealing with nurturing a worship relationship with God, Tozer was able to awaken the evangelical community to "the pursuit of God" through worship.[39] Three of his books, *The Pursuit of God, Whatever Happened to Worship?* and *Knowledge of the Holy,* are read today by thousands of college students and participants in worship classes at American and Canadian institutions.

The father of seven and pastor of Southside Alliance Church in Chicago for 30 years, Tozer wrote simply, elegantly, and forcefully. Though criticized by some as a "mystic," many viewed him as a twentieth-century prophet. Tozer gained a reputation for eschewing the trivial and challenging Christians to think deeply about their practice of spiritual disciplines and their relationship with God. A 1950 editorial for *Alliance Life,* the official publication of the Christian and Missionary Alliance denomination, typified his meditative style:

> It will cost something to walk slow in the parade of the ages, while excited men of time rush about confusing motion with progress. But it will pay in the long run and the true Christian is not much interested in anything short of that.[40]

The ministry of Jack Hayford. Pastor of the twelve-thousand-member Church on the Way in Van Nuys, California, for more than 30 years, **Jack Hayford** is author of more than 50 books and nearly 600 hymns. His involvement with Promise Keepers from its inception through 1998, along with his successful television and radio ministries, made him a significant evangelical voice on worship.

He emphasized issues of the heart more than methodology or song selection. Hayford famously said, "Worship changes the worshiper into the image of the One worshiped."[41] His chorus, "Majesty," was written in 1977 while on vacation with his wife in Great Britain. In his book, *Worship His Majesty: How Praising the King of Kings Will Change Your Life* (2000), Hayford wrote, "As we travel on the road of worship toward God, He travels back to us and manifests His presence when we worship Him." In providing vision for his church, Hayford wrote this statement on worship:

[Worship] is a transcendent priority—we will never sacrifice worship on the altar of conventionality nor convenience. We will be unhesitatingly joyful, refreshing, and unashamed in our worship. Yet, we'll also be tender and healing in our expressions. In being worshipers, we have nothing to prove, yet everything to give to God who has given us so much![42]

The writings of Robert Webber. **Robert Webber** (1933–2007) was born and raised in the Belgian Congo.[43] His parents were missionaries with the African Inland Mission.[44] Having earned the Th.D. from Concordia Theological Seminary, he served as professor of theology at Wheaton College from 1968 to 2000. Then, in the fall of 2000, Webber was appointed William R. and Geraldine D. Myers Professor of Ministry and Director of the M.A. in Worship and Spirituality at Northern Baptist Theological Seminary.[45]

Webber played a strategic role in the Convergence Movement in the United States, a movement devoted to blending charismatic theology with liturgies from the Book of Common Prayer. According to John Witvliet, director of the Calvin Institute of Christian Worship, "In many ways, Robert Webber paved the way for Protestants, especially evangelical Protestants, to take worship seriously as a primary occupation both in the church and in the academy."[46]

His work as founder of the Institute of Worship Studies (IWS) in Orange Park, Florida, in 1998 is perhaps his most significant legacy. IWS provides a graduate and postgraduate program of study and is the only accredited institution in the world solely devoted to equipping and training worship leaders.[47]

The author of more than 40 books on worship, Webber argued that evangelicals should appropriate ancient worship expressions in contemporary worship settings. He served as primary editor and author of the Complete Library of Christian Worship (1993–1995), an eight-volume reference series featuring contributions from more than 600 writers; resources from more than 150 publishers; and articles on such topics as contemporary applications of music and the arts, Sunday worship, special seasons of the Christian year, and activities for outreach ministry.[48]

What about Twenty-First-Century Worship?

During this study together, we've articulated the relationship between worship and the Great Awakenings. We've gathered data that demonstrate "where we've been" and "what we have done" in worship. So, it follows that we should ask, "Where are we going? What will be the driving forces, trends, and paradigm shifts in worship during the twenty-first century?

For certain, worship has become much more diversified in evangelical community since the beginning of this new millennium. We have already seen in our study that controversy over worship preferences is not new to the evangelical community. The division between old and new, liturgical and free, and experiential and intellectual models are much more pronounced.

The Center for Worship at Liberty University has identified five "Current Issues in Twenty-First-Century Worship" that the center believes will impact worship practices in the United States for the next decade. These include: *Missions and Evangelism, the Emerging Church and Postmodern Worship, the Charismatic Renewal, Reformed Theology and Intellectual Worship Influences,* and *Liturgical Influences.*

Each of these influences is identified within the context of evangelicals' continued commitment to *free worship*. Based on their research, the university has developed graduate curricula to meet the strategic and well-articulated needs of this century. Ironically, while these "trends" may be identified, there is crossover and overlap between many of the areas; they are not isolated from each other. The controversies usually accompanying change in Christian worship are no less prevalent when "trends are identified" than in any other moment in Christian history. What follows is a brief summary of the Center for Worship findings.

Missions and Evangelism: World Music, a Ministry Melting Pot

As the cultural landscape in America (and most of the world) has become more ethnically diverse, so have the worship expressions of God's people. There is a greater interest in ethnic and racial diversity in worship. African, Latino, and Asian influences on American culture have affected the way churches meet people's spiritual needs.

Twenty-first-century evangelicals emphasize world missions. They reach out to people of every nation and ethnic group. As diverse men and women are saved and enter local congregations, evangelicals attempt to incorporate worship influences from their diverse cultures. As Witvliet notes,

> Christian worship is shaped by culture. It all reflects a process of contextualization, indigenization, acculturation, and inculturation, whether self-conscious or inadvertent. All worship is shaped by local languages, communication styles and habits, patterns of dress, sense of time, and body language.[49]

There is renewed interest in discovering "how culturally relative some forms are and how transcultural the Christian gospel is."[50] Scholars and worship leaders are studying ethnomusicology and ethnodoxology. There is great emphasis on ensuring that the intended meaning of worship is understood by each participating ethnic group. This has provoked a movement toward contextualizing worship for each Christian community. An emerging consensus is that in order for corporate worship to be biblical, it must be ethnically diverse and culturally relevant.

Emerging Church and Postmodern Worship

The Emerging Church is a twenty-first-century movement that seeks to minister to postmodern culture through a three-dimensional strategy of worship, mission, and community.[51] Theologian Scot McKnight argued that five distinctives characterize the Emerging Movement:

First, the Emerging Church is *prophetic and provocative*. It deliberately seeks to change the standard "church" rhetoric and to use language that is more "friendly" to unchurched postmoderns.

Second, the Emerging Church is unashamedly *postmodern*, ministering not only to and with postmoderns, but as postmoderns.[52]

Third, the Emerging Church is *praxis-oriented*, intent on living out Christian faith through worship and missions.[53] In worship, Emerging Church groups seek to be creative, experiential, and sensory. As McKnight explains, "They wonder if there is another way to express—theologically, aesthetically, and anthropologically—what we do when we gather."[54]

Fourth, the Emerging Church is *post-evangelical*. It generally resists systematic theology and contends that God delivered his Word as a "storied narrative." Some Emerging Church leaders reject the exclusivity of the gospel.[55]

Fifth, the Emerging Church is *political*. Most Emerging Church leaders are staunchly committed to meeting social needs. Many tend to vote Democratic in national elections.

Charismatic Renewal in Twenty-First-Century Worship

The Pentecostal-Charismatic movement in the United States impacts corporate worship in virtually every Christian denomination. Some of the most significant worship songwriting, publishing, and media distributing firms have roots in charismatic traditions. Approximately one in ten people worldwide is a Pentecostal or charismatic, and more than 50 percent of Protestants have at least some affiliation with the movement.

Paul Rumrill of the Center for Worship at Liberty University points out four ways in which the charismatic movement is a "renewal movement." First, it has *renewed an emphasis on the Holy Spirit's role in personal and corporate worship.* In doing so it has usually encouraged a trinitarian view of God in worship. Second, it has *highlighted the reality of spiritual gifts and manifestations.* Third, it has *encouraged the emotional involvement of the Christ-follower in worship.* Fourth, it has *encouraged a wide range of external, physical, demonstrative expressions of devotion to the Lord*—lifting hands, shouting, dancing, bowing.[56]

The Charismatic-Pentecostal tradition has encouraged non-charismatic communities to express worship outwardly by singing, praying out loud together (sometimes called choral prayer), simultaneously and vigorously raising their hands in the air to the Lord, shouting "Hallelujah" or "Amen," and confessing sin.[57]

Jack Hayford explains:

> New Testament worship comprises a full array of expression. Biblical worship isn't a one dimension activity. It involves a combination of reason, spiritual intuition, and emotions . . . worship is neither an exercise of barren intellectualism or thoughtless emotion. Worship involves the total human being: spirit, mind, emotions, body.[58]

Reformed Theology: Intellectual and Biblically Based Worship Influences

With the resurgence of "Reformed theology" in the evangelical community has come a renewed emphasis on worshipping according to the Word of God.[59] According to D. A. Carson, the traits of Reformed corporate worship include three essentials: (a) simplicity, (b) transcendence, and (c) the gospel reenactment.[60] Reformed worship seeks to find a balance between "spectacle" and "sentimentality." There is strong emphasis on proclaiming the wonders of God—his greatness or transcendence.

Some liturgies in the Reformed tradition maintain a balance between "hearing the gospel" in the first half of the service, also called the "Service of the Word," and responding with gratitude in the second half of the service, also called the "Service of the Table"—the Eucharist. David Miller suggests that there are five aspects of corporate worship in the Reformed tradition: (1) gathering around the Word, (2) proclaiming the Word, (3) responding to the Word, (4) the sealing of the Word: sacraments, and (5) bearing and following the Word into the world.[61] Often, Reformed worship resonates with postmoderns because it eschews emotional manipulation but provides a forum in which to experience the transcendent God.[62]

Liturgical Renewal Influences: Sacramental Worship

The Liturgical Renewal Movement has its historical roots in the early Roman Catholic Church. Sweeping changes in worship were introduced into the Roman Catholic Church from 1962 to 1965 during the Second Vatican Council. These changes were quickly adopted by Anglican and Lutheran churches. According to Robb Redman, this means that "liturgy is 'inculturated' [and made] relevant to the cultural context in which it takes place."[63]

The goal of the Liturgical Movement is to help Christians appreciate and reinstitute the church's historical worship practices. The movement's objectives include: (1) restoration of Christ as the center of all worship, (2) promoting the Bible as the authority, center, and guide for all worship practices, (3) the promotion and practice of the sacraments, especially the Eucharist, (4) a commitment to the lectionary and Christian year, and (5) richer participation in congregational worship, especially music.

Today, many conservative evangelical churches incorporate these changes in their weekly worship services. The "convergence" between free worship, usually identified with evangelical traditions, and Catholic liturgy often includes the Eucharist, baptism, daily prayer, ordination, marriage, funerals, and a commitment to calendar and lectionary.[64]

Webber, an early leader in the Liturgical Movement, sought to maintain evangelical theology but incorporate the liturgies of the Catholic Church into worship. In general, he reasoned that every worship service should follow a simple order: the Gathering, the Word, the Table, and the Dismissal. According to Webber, adopting such a pattern for worship:

1. Restores commitment to the sacraments, especially the Eucharist, as part of the weekly worship event.
2. Satisfies the desire of many evangelicals to know more about the early church and captures the mystery and transcendence of God in a way that modern forms of Protestant worship do not.
3. Stresses the unity of the church and a desire to overcome division.
4. Embraces diversity and inculturation.
5. Seeks to integrate form and freedom in worship.
6. Provides a greater role for ritual gesture, symbol, and visual art in worship.[65]

Recovery of the arts in worship is at the center of this movement. Signs and symbols, he said, "point beyond themselves to a greater truth and serve as contact points for apprehending inward spiritual reality."[66]

Evangelical Tradition and Commitment to Free Worship

Worship in the evangelical tradition is in the midst of a paradigm shift. The influence of postmodern culture on evangelicals is greater now than it has ever been. In one sense, evangelical worship practices today are an amalgamation of all influences mentioned above. Evangelicals are more focused on missions. The emphasis on community encouraged by Emerging churches has greatly influenced evangelical congregational singing practices. More and more churches are emphasizing the arts in worship. There is an emphasis on sensory worship. There is greater sensitivity to adapting worship to the surrounding culture.

The Charismatic Renewal Movement has introduced to evangelicals greater freedom of expression in worship and emphasized spontaneity in presentation. It has also called greater attention to the diverse spiritual gifts in the body of Christ. The Reformed worship movement has focused the evangelical community on scriptural and intellectual integrity. Liturgical influences have reminded evangelicals to focus on Christ during worship and placed renewed emphasis on communion.

Changes in media also impact worship in the twenty-first century. There is a greater emphasis on lighting, technology, and creating atmosphere.

At the end of the day, worship practices will continue to change as the evangelical community becomes more culturally diverse, commits itself to communicating to the next generation with clarity and focus, and worship leadership continues to develop innovative ways for creative expression.

Notes

1. Chuck Fromm, interviewed by Vernon Whaley, October 4, 2011, Lynchburg, Virginia.

2. Ibid.

3. Ibid.

4. Ibid.

5. Ibid.

6. Ibid.

7. "Declare his glory among the heathen, his wonders among all people" (Ps 96:3 KJV).

8. Robb Redman, *The Great Worship Awakening: Singing a New Song in the Postmodern Church* (San Francisco: Jossey Bass, 2002), 53–54.

9. Ibid., 54–55.

10. Ibid., 56.

11. Ibid., 54.

12. Tanya Riches, "Shout to the Lord! Music and Change at Hillsong: 1996–2007" (MPh thesis, School of Arts & Sciences [Victoria], Australian Catholic University, Australia, 2010), 9.

13. Redman, *The Great Worship Awakening*, 57.

14. According to the website, http://www.answers.com/topic/integrity-mutual-funds-inc, education partnerships included Integrity Media Worship School (Mobile, AL; 1998–present); Integrity's Seminars4Worship (regional seminars; 1999–present); Liberty University (Lynchburg, VA; 1998–99); the University of Mobile (Mobile, AL; 2002–present); Regent University (Virginia Beach, VA; 2000–2008); and the King's College and Seminary (Van Nuys, CA; 2005–6). Additionally, IWI has hosted international worship training in Brazil, Armenia, Cyprus, Russia, Taiwan, Jordan, Italy, Egypt, Lebanon, Syria, and the United Kingdom.

15. Redman, *The Great Worship Awakening*, 57–58.

16. See http://www.ccli.com/WhoWeAre/CompanyProfile.aspx; accessed November 21, 2011.

17. Redman. *The Great Worship Awakening*, 62.

18. See http://www.ccli.com/WhoWeAre/CompanyProfile.aspx; accessed November 21, 2011.

19. "PK History," http://www.promisekeepers.org/about/pk-history; accessed November 21, 2011.

20. *From Ashes to Glory: Conflicts and Victories on and Beyond the Football Field* (1990), quoted in Chuck Fromm, "Textual Communities and New Song in a Multi-media Age" (PhD diss,, Fuller Seminary, 2006), 321.

21. "PK History."

22. Fromm, "Textual Communities," 326.

23. Paul R. Dienstberger, *The American Republic: A Nation of Christians* (Ashland, OH: Paul R. Dienstberger, 2000), n.p., http://www.prdienstberger.com/nation/Chapter10.htm#II.%20The%20Turbulent,%20Tempestuous,%20; accessed August 6, 2011.

24. Ibid.

25. Chuck Fromm, interview by Whaley.

26. See http://www.268generation.com/2.0/splash1.htm; accessed November 22, 2011.

27. Ibid.

28. "Passion Conferences," http://en.wikipedia.org/wiki/Passion_Conferences; accessed November 22, 2011.

29. See http://www.womenoffaith.com/about; accessed April 30, 2012.

30. See http://www.iws.edu/IWS/fla_history.html; accessed November 22, 2011.

31. See http://www.liberty.edu/worship; accessed November 23, 2011.

32. See http://www.worship.calvin.edu/about/mission.html; accessed November 25, 2011.

33. See http://www.integrityworshipinstitute.com/about/history; accessed November 25, 2011.

34. See http://www.iws.edu/IWS/fla_history.html; accessed November 22, 2011.

35. Jack Taylor wrote two books having significant impact on the evangelical community: *The Key to Triumphant Living* (Jacksonville, FL: Seedsowers, 1997) has sold more than 1.5 million copies and documents a spiritual awakening that took place in 1970 at the Castle Hills First Baptist Church in San Antonio, Texas. Taylor was pastor of the church for 17 years. The church membership doubled to more than 5,000 in four years from 1970 to 1974. *The Hallelujah Factor* (Mansfield, PA: Kingdom Publishing, 1983) discusses ten essential elements of praise. Pastors across the country used this book to help launch worship and praise in their churches.

36. Henry Blackaby has published several influential books and articles, most notably *Experiencing God: Knowing and Doing the Will of God* (Nashville: LifeWay Christian Resources, 1990), which has sold 4 million copies and has been translated into more than 45 languages.

37. David Jeremiah is pastor of Shadow Mountain Community Church in San Diego. His radio ministry, *Turning Point*, is heard around the world. His book, *My Heart's Desire* (Brentwood, TN: Integrity, 2002), documents his journey in personal worship.

38. Jim Cymbala is pastor of the Brooklyn Tabernacle in New York City. His *Fresh Wind, Fresh Fire* (Grand Rapids: Zondervan, 1997) documents the spiritual journey he and his wife followed in pursuing the will of God to build a church in Brooklyn through prayer. Other books by Cymbala include *Fresh Faith* (Grand Rapids: Zondervan, 1999) and *Fresh Power* (Grand Rapids: Zondervan, 2001).

39. See http://www.awtozerclassics.com/page/page/4891821.htm; accessed November 20, 2011.

40. "A.W. Tozer," http://www.eastwallingfordbaptist.com/a_w_tozer.htm; accessed November 20, 2011.

41. "Great Worship Quotes," http://www.experiencingworship.com/articles/general/2001-7-Great-Quotes-on.html; accessed November 26, 2011.

42. See http://www.tcotw.org/#/on-the-way/family-traits; accessed November 28, 2011.

43. "Robert E. Webber, Founder," http://iws.edu/about/who/robert-e-webber; accessed November 19, 2011.

44. "Robert E. Webber," http://en.wikipedia.org/wiki/Robert_E._Webber; accessed November 19, 2011.

45. "Robert E. Webber, Founder."

46. Tabby Yang, "Robert E. Webber, Theologian of 'Ancient-Future' Faith, Dies at 73," http://www.christianitytoday.com/ct/2007/aprilweb-only/118-12.0.html; accessed November 19, 2011.

47. "The Robert E. Webber Institute for Worship Studies: History," http://iws.edu/about/unique/history; accessed November 19, 2011.

48. The Complete Library of Christian Worship, 8 vols. (Peabody, MA: Hendrickson Publishers, 1993–95), includes: vol. I, *The Biblical Foundations of Christian Worship*; vol. II, *Twenty Centuries of Christian Worship*; vol. III,

Renewal of Sunday Worship; vol. IV, *Music and the Arts in Christian Worship*, books 1 & 2; vol. V, *The Services of the Christian Year*; vol. VI, *The Sacred Actions of the Christian Worship*; vol. VII, *The Ministries of Christian Worship*; and vol. VIII, *Comprehensive Indices*.

49. John D. Witvliet, *Inculturation, Worship and Dispositions for Ministry*. Included in Charles E. Farhadian, ed., *Christian Worship Worldwide: Expanding Horizons, Deepening Practices* (Grand Rapids: Eerdmans, 2007), 274.

50. Ibid., 276.

51. Ian Mobsby, *The Becoming of G-d* (Oxford: YTC Press, 2008), 15–18, 32–35, 37.

52. Scot McKnight, "Five Streams of the Emerging Church," http://www.christianitytoday.com/ct/2007/february/11.35.html; accessed November 27, 2011.

53. Ibid.

54. Notes from lecture in Graduate Worship course, "Current Issues in Worship," Liberty Baptist Theological Seminary, Lynchburg, Virginia, July 15, 2009.

55. Ibid.

56. Paul Rumrill, "Charismatic Influences on Evangelical Worship," July 2009, 1.

57. Ibid., 10–11.

58. Jack Hayford, "Charismatic Worship," in *Experience God in Worship* (Loveland, CO: Group, 2000), 145.

59. See http://www.reformedpraise.org; accessed November 26, 2011. Taken from the mission statement of Reformed Praise, a ministry founded by David Ward, director of worship ministries for Redeemer Bible Church in Minnetonka, MN (a suburb of Minneapolis).

60. Quoted in a presentation by John Kinchen III, "Current Issues in Reformed Worship," video presentation at Liberty University, July 15, 2010.

61. David A. Miller, *Contemporary Worship in the Reformed Tradition* (Pittsburgh: Vital Faith Resources, 2001), 103.

62. Kinchen, "Current Issues in Reformed Worship."

63. Redman, *The Great Worship Awakening*, 75.

64. Ibid., 77.

65. Robert Webber, "The Convergence Movement," *The Christian Century* 99 (1982), quoted in Redman, *The Great Worship Awakening*, 78–80.

66. Ibid., 80.

EPILOGUE

Worship through the Ages

We have taken an exciting and fascinating journey together. In the process, we have discovered that Christians from every generation are called to worship. Along the way, we have identified and articulated trends, cultural shifts, ecclesiastical developments, strategic personalities, great spiritual awakenings, and new paradigms for worship. *Eerdmans' Handbook to the History of Christianity* provides a wonderful overview of the changes in worship since the early church. It is amazing to see how many of these changes are brought about by truly Great Awakenings. What follows is a brief documentation of those changes and strategic paradigm shifts in worship:

AD 100–200: Many churches had daily worship services. One early practice was for Christians to rise and pray at midnight. Morning and evening prayer in church became customary through the fourth century, especially at centers of pilgrimage like Jerusalem.[1]

AD 200–300: Instrumental music was almost universally shunned because of its association with debauchery and immorality. Lyre (guitar) playing, for example, was associated with prostitution.[2]

AD 300–400: Ambrose of Milan (339–397), an influential bishop often called the father of congregational singing, introduced community hymn singing in the church.[3] These hymns were composed in metrical stanzas, unlike biblical poetry. They did not rhyme but were sometimes sung while marching.[4] Many of these hymns were based on tunes written by non-Christians, but with new lyrics and intent.[5]

AD 400–600: Congregations often sang psalms in a call and response manner. This probably involved the traditional Jewish practice of cantor and congregation singing alternate verses.[6]

AD 600–800: Monasteries, based on Ps 119:164 ("Seven times a day I praise you"), developed a worship schedule involving seven daily congregational gatherings. The services varied in content but included singing, mainly by a soloist, with the congregation repeating a refrain at intervals.[7] The services included the singing of all 150 psalms in a rotation that repeated each week.[8]

AD 800–900: Almost all singing was done in chant, based on scales that used only the white keys on today's piano. Monasteries played a vital role in sustaining and developing Christian music through the Dark Ages.[9]

AD 900–1100: Music notation gained wide usage in the church. This gave choirs opportunity to sing from written music. New types of music were created, printed on paper, and distributed to many congregations. The advent of music notation also provided a new way to document worship traditions and musical preferences.

AD 1100–1200: The refinement of new forms of Latin verse using rhyme and accent led to new mystical meditations on the joys of heaven, the vanity of life, and the suffering of Christ.[10]

AD 1200–1300: Beginning in France, musicians experimented with harmony. Choir music shifted from the lone and sinuous melody of the chant to two-, three-, and even four-part harmony. This did not please everyone. One critic complained that harmony "sullie[d]" worship by introducing "lewdness" into the church.[11]

AD 1300–1400: Worship in Gothic cathedrals and abbeys utilized professional choirs sealed off by screens from the congregation. Ordinary people played little role in church life, except perhaps in the giving of their finances.[12]

AD 1400–1500: Music became increasingly complex, prompting criticisms that only choirs were allowed to sing in worship. As reformer John Wycliffe complained, "No one can hear the words, and all the others are dumb and watch them like fools."[13]

AD 1500–1600: In England, a new prayer book, pushed by King Henry VIII, decreed that all services would be in English, with only one syllable to each note.[14]

Martin Luther set about reforming public worship from what he believed to be overly rigid forms. One way he did this was by putting stress on congregational singing.[15] As Harry Eskew and Hugh McElrath explained, "Although Luther led the revolt against the abuses of the Roman Catholic Church, he continued to make use of its texts and tunes. He modified Roman Catholic tunes and texts to fit his new theology. As a result, people recognized familiar hymns and chants and felt at home in the new church. Luther used music which was already familiar to the majority of the people in Germany."[16]

AD 1600–1700: The organ played an important role in Lutheranism, Anglicanism, and Roman Catholicism, while in the Reformed churches there was much opposition to it.[17] Initially the organ was not used to accompany congregational singing.[18]

AD 1700–1800: Isaac Watts, the father of Western hymnody, advanced the controversial practice of congregations singing "manmade" hymns by writing songs that freely paraphrased Scripture. Charles Wesley paraphrased the Anglican *Prayer Book* and versified

Christian doctrine and experience. Wesley's songs, it was said, "had at least as great an effect as his sermons."[19]

AD 1800–1850: William Booth, founder of the Salvation Army, used rousing melodies with a martial flavor to set the tone for his organization. He is credited with popularizing the question, "Why should the devil have all the good music?"[20] Worshippers at camp meetings adapted popular folk songs for use in worship.

AD 1850–1900: Churches adopted a new genre of music with verses and a chorus called "the gospel hymn." The gospel hymn became the standard music of evangelical worship. Evangelistic services moved from church buildings to large arenas and "tabernacles." Evangelistic meetings featured the worship leader as a soloist.

AD 1900–1950: Evan Roberts and William Seymour led revivals in Wales and Los Angeles respectively. Many called this awakening another Pentecost because of its renewed emphasis on the manifestation of spiritual gifts.

Christian radio pioneers such as Donald Grey Barnhouse and Charles E. Fuller began broadcasting gospel music and evangelistic teaching over the airwaves. Many Christians initially were skeptical about the usefulness of this new medium for evangelism and worship.

Revivalists, accompanied by song leaders, traveled around the world preaching the gospel. Millions came to a saving knowledge of Jesus Christ.

AD 1950–2000: Worship evangelism efforts moved beyond church buildings, tents, and "tabernacles" to football stadiums with the Billy Graham evangelistic meetings.

The Jesus Movement introduced folk music-type bands, recording technology, and the rock-'n'-roll genre for evangelical worship.

AD 2000– : Many evangelical churches abandoned the singing of hymns altogether (and the use of hymnals) in favor of short songs and choruses from the new "praise and worship" movement.

The Next Great Awakening

So is there another Great Awakening on the horizon? If so, will it bring major paradigm shifts in the way we worship? Secular commentator Lauren Sandler argues that "we are poised before the next Great Awakening in American History."[21] If this is correct, what lessons should we draw from the past to help usher in the next awakening?

1. Worship is at the heart of every Great Awakening and movement of God. It always includes recommitment to God, repentance of sin, and believers living in personal holiness. Such worship often is accompanied by a commitment to social ministry (feeding the poor, reaching out to the marginalized, etc.).

2. God always provides opportunity for people to understand and communicate worship in their own vernacular and culture.

3. God always uses people to proclaim his wonders. In great awakenings, highly energized, college-age students often have been God's chief instruments.

4. God is in the business of changing people, and worshipping him as sovereign is at the heart of this change.

5. Prepare for it. The next awakening will be met with serious criticism from within the church and the surrounding culture.

So, what about the next Great Awakening? Most biblical scholars believe God uses the times of great awakenings to make his glory known, draw people unto himself, and unify the body of Christ—the church. In the process, culture is changed, marriages are restored, thousands turn from sin, and people's lives are forever transformed. So, we need to continually ask the question: "Is there another Great Awakening on the horizon?" As we make inquiry into the next great awakenings, let's keep our eyes looking to the Eastern skies. Soon, the Lord Jesus Christ will himself return in the sky, and we will rise to worship him in the throne room of heaven.

While the secular humanist is threatened by the possibility of another awakening, those of us who worship Jesus Christ wait eagerly. God is moving in a mighty way to draw this next generation—the disciple generation—to himself. He is doing this through worship of Jesus. If he does bring another awakening, chances are good that it will be known as *the Great Worship Awakening*.[22]

Notes

1. *Eerdmans' Handbook to the History of Christianity* (Grand Rapids, MI: Eerdmans, 1977), 216.

2. Andrew Wilson-Dickson, *Story of Christian Music* (Minneapolis, MN: Fortress, 1996), 28.

3. *Eerdmans' Handbook,* 140.

4. Andrew Wilson-Dickson, *The Story of Christian Music* (Minneapolis, MN: Fortress, 1996), 36. See also Harry Eskew and Hugh McElrath, *Sing with Understanding* (Nashville, TN: Broadman/Church Street Press, 1995), 86–87.

5. Steve Miller, *The Contemporary Christian Music Debate* (Wheaton: Tyndale, 1993), 109.

6. Wilson-Dickson, *Story of Christian Music,* 30.

7. *Eerdmans' Handbook,* 216.

8. Wilson-Dickson, *Story of Christian Music,* 33. See also Donald Hustad, *Jubilate II,* 2nd edition (Carol Stream, IL: Hope Publishing Company, 1993).

9. Wilson-Dickson, *Story of Christian Music,* 34.

10. Eskew and McElrath, *Sing with Understanding,* 91–92.

11. Wilson-Dickson, *Story of Christian Music,* 52.

12. Ibid., 46.

13. Ibid., 56.

14. *Eerdmans' Handbook,* 363.

15. Ibid.

16. Eskew and McElrath, *Sing with Understanding,* 99.

17. J. D. Douglas, Walter Elwell, Peter Toon, *Concise Dictionary of Christian Tradition* (Grand Rapids, MI: Zondervan, 1989), 259.

18. Wilson-Dickson, *Story of Christian Music,* 76.

19. *Eerdmans' Handbook,* 426–27, 448.

20. Wilson-Dickson, *Story of Christian Music,* 139. Some sources attribute the concept to Martin Luther. See Richard Friedenthal Luther, *His Life and Times,* translated by John Nowell (New York, NY: Helen and Kurt Wolff Book, Harcourt Brace Jovanovich, Inc., 1967), 464.

21. Lauren Sandler, *Righteous: Dispatches from the Evangelical Youth Movement* (New York: Viking, 2006), 11.

22. Ibid.

Worship through the Ages
Old Testament

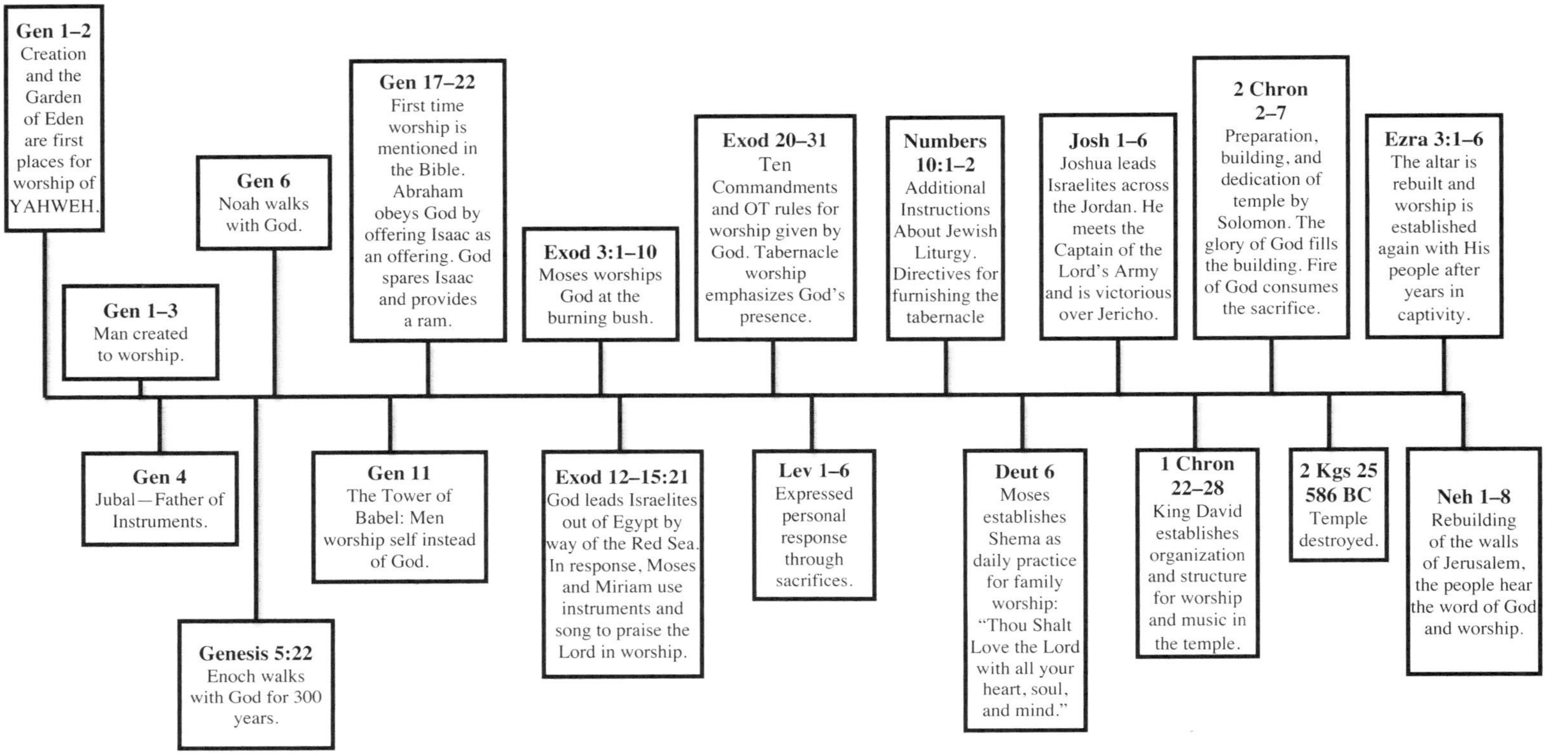

- **Gen 1–2** Creation and the Garden of Eden are first places for worship of YAHWEH.
- **Gen 1–3** Man created to worship.
- **Gen 4** Jubal—Father of Instruments.
- **Genesis 5:22** Enoch walks with God for 300 years.
- **Gen 6** Noah walks with God.
- **Gen 11** The Tower of Babel: Men worship self instead of God.
- **Gen 17–22** First time worship is mentioned in the Bible. Abraham obeys God by offering Isaac as an offering. God spares Isaac and provides a ram.
- **Exod 3:1–10** Moses worships God at the burning bush.
- **Exod 12–15:21** God leads Israelites out of Egypt by way of the Red Sea. In response, Moses and Miriam use instruments and song to praise the Lord in worship.
- **Exod 20–31** Ten Commandments and OT rules for worship given by God. Tabernacle worship emphasizes God's presence.
- **Lev 1–6** Expressed personal response through sacrifices.
- **Numbers 10:1–2** Additional Instructions About Jewish Liturgy. Directives for furnishing the tabernacle.
- **Deut 6** Moses establishes Shema as daily practice for family worship: "Thou Shalt Love the Lord with all your heart, soul, and mind."
- **Josh 1–6** Joshua leads Israelites across the Jordan. He meets the Captain of the Lord's Army and is victorious over Jericho.
- **1 Chron 22–28** King David establishes organization and structure for worship and music in the temple.
- **2 Chron 2–7** Preparation, building, and dedication of temple by Solomon. The glory of God fills the building. Fire of God consumes the sacrifice.
- **2 Kgs 25 586 BC** Temple destroyed.
- **Ezra 3:1–6** The altar is rebuilt and worship is established again with His people after years in captivity.
- **Neh 1–8** Rebuilding of the walls of Jerusalem, the people hear the word of God and worship.

Worship through the Ages
Old and New Testament

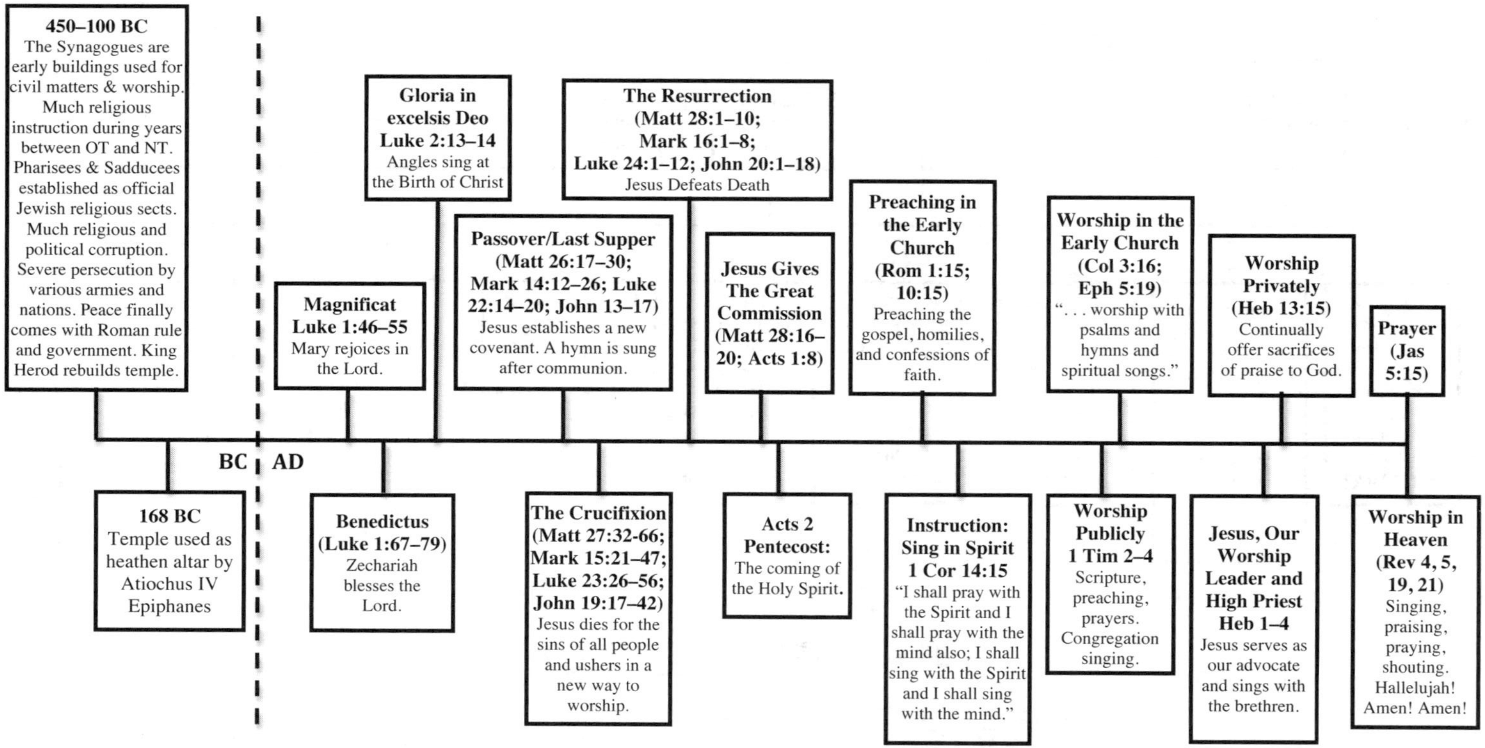

450–100 BC
The Synagogues are early buildings used for civil matters & worship. Much religious instruction during years between OT and NT. Pharisees & Sadducees established as official Jewish religious sects. Much religious and political corruption. Severe persecution by various armies and nations. Peace finally comes with Roman rule and government. King Herod rebuilds temple.

168 BC
Temple used as heathen altar by Atiochus IV Epiphanes

BC | AD

Magnificat Luke 1:46–55
Mary rejoices in the Lord.

Benedictus (Luke 1:67–79)
Zechariah blesses the Lord.

Gloria in excelsis Deo Luke 2:13–14
Angles sing at the Birth of Christ

Passover/Last Supper (Matt 26:17–30; Mark 14:12–26; Luke 22:14–20; John 13–17)
Jesus establishes a new covenant. A hymn is sung after communion.

The Crucifixion (Matt 27:32-66; Mark 15:21–47; Luke 23:26–56; John 19:17–42)
Jesus dies for the sins of all people and ushers in a new way to worship.

The Resurrection (Matt 28:1–10; Mark 16:1–8; Luke 24:1–12; John 20:1–18)
Jesus Defeats Death

Jesus Gives The Great Commission (Matt 28:16–20; Acts 1:8)

Acts 2 Pentecost: The coming of the Holy Spirit.

Preaching in the Early Church (Rom 1:15; 10:15)
Preaching the gospel, homilies, and confessions of faith.

Instruction: Sing in Spirit 1 Cor 14:15
"I shall pray with the Spirit and I shall pray with the mind also; I shall sing with the Spirit and I sing with the mind."

Worship in the Early Church (Col 3:16; Eph 5:19)
". . . worship with psalms and hymns and spiritual songs."

Worship Publicly 1 Tim 2–4
Scripture, preaching, prayers. Congregation singing.

Worship Privately (Heb 13:15)
Continually offer sacrifices of praise to God.

Jesus, Our Worship Leader and High Priest Heb 1–4
Jesus serves as our advocate and sings with the brethren.

Prayer (Jas 5:15)

Worship in Heaven (Rev 4, 5, 19, 21)
Singing, praising, praying, shouting, Hallelujah! Amen! Amen!

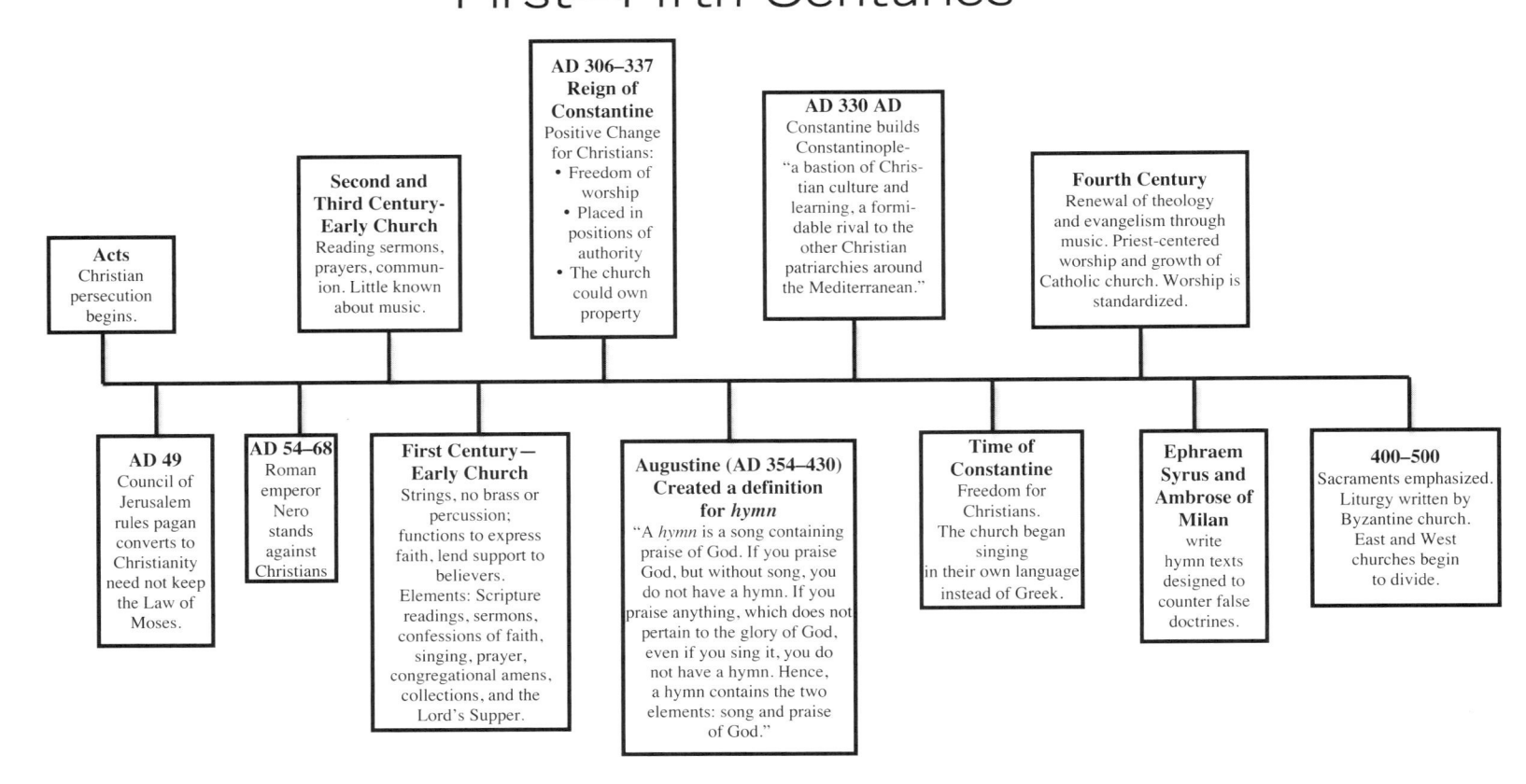

Worship through the Ages
First–Fifth Centuries

Acts
Christian persecution begins.

AD 49
Council of Jerusalem rules pagan converts to Christianity need not keep the Law of Moses.

AD 54–68
Roman emperor Nero stands against Christians

First Century—Early Church
Strings, no brass or percussion; functions to express faith, lend support to believers. Elements: Scripture readings, sermons, confessions of faith, singing, prayer, congregational amens, collections, and the Lord's Supper.

Second and Third Century-Early Church
Reading sermons, prayers, communion. Little known about music.

AD 306–337 Reign of Constantine
Positive Change for Christians;
- Freedom of worship
- Placed in positions of authority
- The church could own property

AD 330 AD
Constantine builds Constantinople-"a bastion of Christian culture and learning, a formidable rival to the other Christian patriarchies around the Mediterranean."

Augustine (AD 354–430) Created a definition for *hymn*
"A *hymn* is a song containing praise of God. If you praise God, but without song, you do not have a hymn. If you praise anything, which does not pertain to the glory of God, even if you sing it, you do not have a hymn. Hence, a hymn contains the two elements: song and praise of God."

Time of Constantine
Freedom for Christians. The church began singing in their own language instead of Greek.

Fourth Century
Renewal of theology and evangelism through music. Priest-centered worship and growth of Catholic church. Worship is standardized.

Ephraem Syrus and Ambrose of Milan write hymn texts designed to counter false doctrines.

400–500
Sacraments emphasized. Liturgy written by Byzantine church. East and West churches begin to divide.

Worship through the Ages
Medieval Period and the Reformation

The Medieval Period AD 500–1500
Created emphasis on services hours; sang psalms and select scriptures called Biblical canticles. Preaching becomes a focus.

Pope Gregory the Great AD 590–604 adopts Gregorian Chant.

Gregorian Chant
Sung in one of the eight modes which corresponds to the eight tones of the scale. Sung as a hymn.

Antiphon
A refrain sung in between each verse of Psalm.

Strategic Persons of Pre-Reformation
Patrick of Ireland (c. 389–461), Benedict of Nursia (c. 480–543), Anselm of Canterbury (c. 1033–1109), Bernard of Clairvaux (c. 1090–1153), Peter Waldo (c. 1140–1218), St Thomas Aquinas (c. 1225–1274), John Wycliffe (c. 1320–1384), Jon Huss (c. 1370–1415), Thomas a Kempis (c. 1380–1471), St Francis of Assisi (1182–1226), Girolamo Savonarola (1452–1498).

1054 Division between Western and Eastern Christendom.

Changes in Worship by Laymen 1100–1200
Congregation singing in common vernacular, not Latin. Preaching common for gatherings outside normal church service hours.

1163–1250 Cathedral of Notre Dame Built
Polyphony accepted and took root.

Pre-Reformation Issues
- Tradition valued more than Bible.
- Lord's Supper only available to priests.
- Transubstantiation adopted
- Prayer of thanksgiving morphed into long petitions w/little emphasis on praise.

1323 Pope John XXII issues Papal bull against polyphony.

1517 — The Reformation
Martin Luther Nails 95 Theses on a church door in Wittenberg, Germany.

1440–1452 Johannes Guttenberg invents printing press. Publishes Guttenberg Bible in c. 1455.

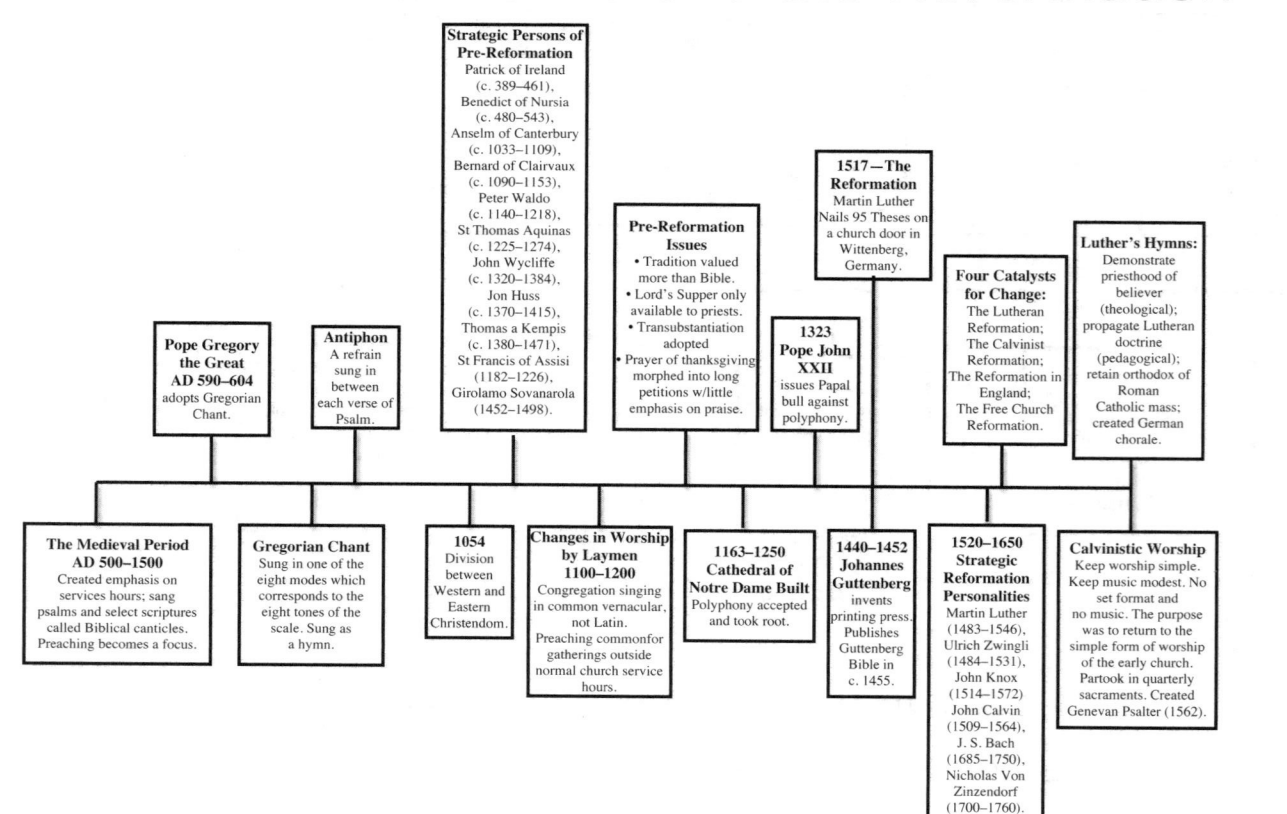

Four Catalysts for Change:
The Lutheran Reformation; The Calvinist Reformation; The Reformation in England; The Free Church Reformation.

Luther's Hymns:
Demonstrate priesthood of believer (theological); propagate Lutheran doctrine (pedagogical); retain orthodox of Roman Catholic mass; created German chorale.

1520–1650 Strategic Reformation Personalities
Martin Luther (1483–1546), Ulrich Zwingli (1484–1531), John Knox (1514–1572), John Calvin (1509–1564), J. S. Bach (1685–1750), Nicholas Von Zinzendorf (1700–1760).

Calvinistic Worship
Keep worship simple. Keep music modest. No set format and no music. The purpose was to return to the simple form of worship of the early church. Partook in quarterly sacraments. Created Genevan Psalter (1562).

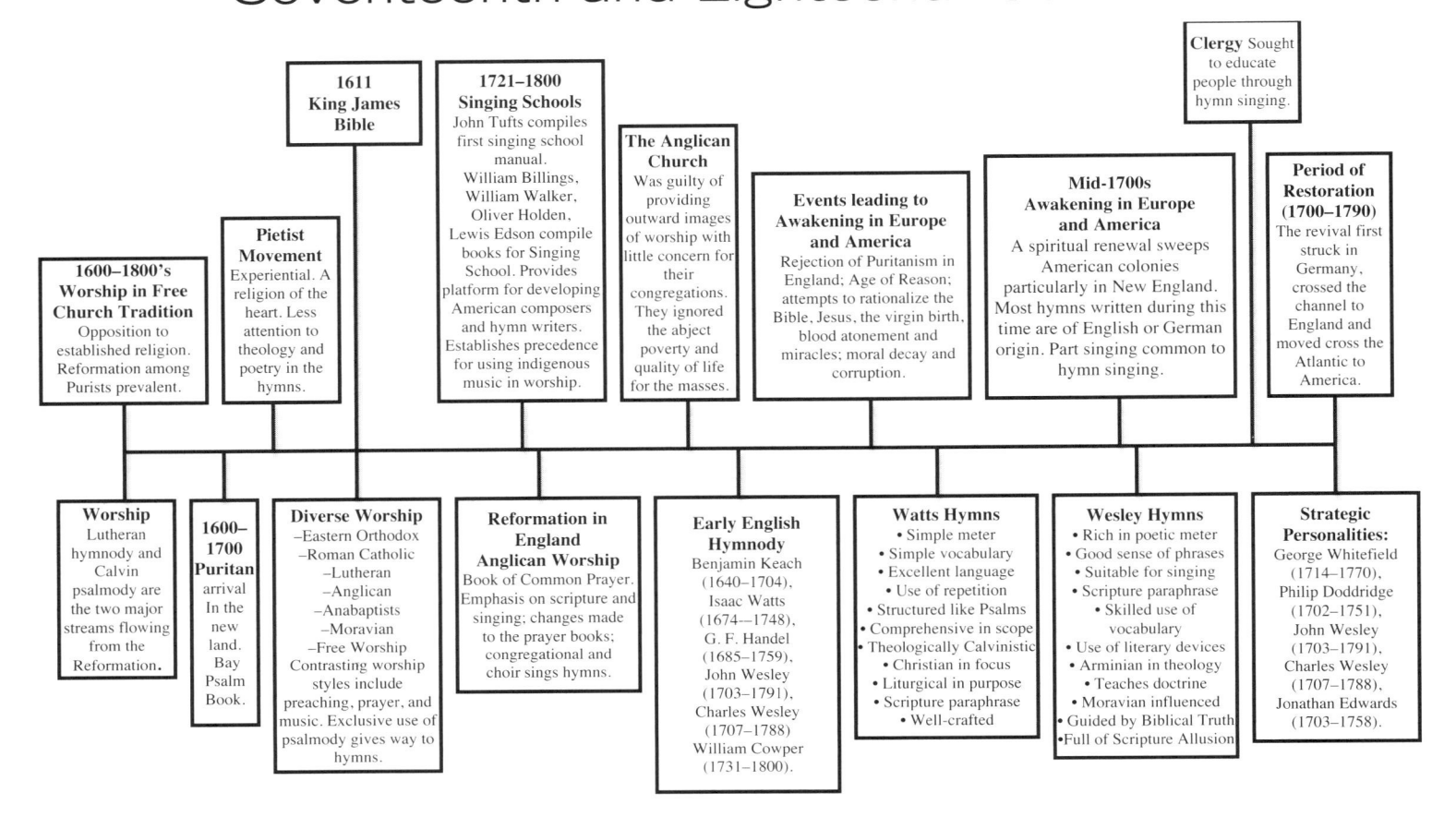

Worship through the Ages
Seventeenth and Eighteenth Centuries

1600–1800's Worship in Free Church Tradition
Opposition to established religion. Reformation among Purists prevalent.

Worship
Lutheran hymnody and Calvin psalmody are the two major streams flowing from the Reformation.

1600–1700 Puritan arrival In the new land. Bay Psalm Book.

Pietist Movement
Experiential. A religion of the heart. Less attention to theology and poetry in the hymns.

Diverse Worship
- Eastern Orthodox
- Roman Catholic
- Lutheran
- Anglican
- Anabaptists
- Moravian
- Free Worship

Contrasting worship styles include preaching, prayer, and music. Exclusive use of psalmody gives way to hymns.

1611 King James Bible

1721–1800 Singing Schools
John Tufts compiles first singing school manual. William Billings, William Walker, Oliver Holden. Lewis Edson compile books for Singing School. Provides platform for developing American composers and hymn writers. Establishes precedence for using indigenous music in worship.

The Anglican Church
Was guilty of providing outward images of worship with little concern for their congregations. They ignored the abject poverty and quality of life for the masses.

Reformation in England Anglican Worship
Book of Common Prayer. Emphasis on scripture and singing; changes made to the prayer books; congregational and choir sings hymns.

Early English Hymnody
Benjamin Keach (1640–1704), Isaac Watts (1674–1748), G. F. Handel (1685–1759), John Wesley (1703–1791), Charles Wesley (1707–1788), William Cowper (1731–1800).

Events leading to Awakening in Europe and America
Rejection of Puritanism in England; Age of Reason; attempts to rationalize the Bible, Jesus, the virgin birth, blood atonement and miracles; moral decay and corruption.

Mid-1700s Awakening in Europe and America
A spiritual renewal sweeps American colonies particularly in New England. Most hymns written during this time are of English or German origin. Part singing common to hymn singing.

Period of Restoration (1700–1790)
The revival first struck in Germany, crossed the channel to England and moved cross the Atlantic to America.

Clergy Sought to educate people through hymn singing.

Watts Hymns
- Simple meter
- Simple vocabulary
- Excellent language
- Use of repetition
- Structured like Psalms
- Comprehensive in scope
- Theologically Calvinistic
- Christian in focus
- Liturgical in purpose
- Scripture paraphrase
- Well-crafted

Wesley Hymns
- Rich in poetic meter
- Good sense of phrases
- Suitable for singing
- Scripture paraphrase
- Skilled use of vocabulary
- Use of literary devices
- Arminian in theology
- Teaches doctrine
- Moravian influenced
- Guided by Biblical Truth
- Full of Scripture Allusion

Strategic Personalities:
George Whitefield (1714–1770), Philip Doddridge (1702–1751), John Wesley (1703–1791), Charles Wesley (1707–1788), Jonathan Edwards (1703–1758).

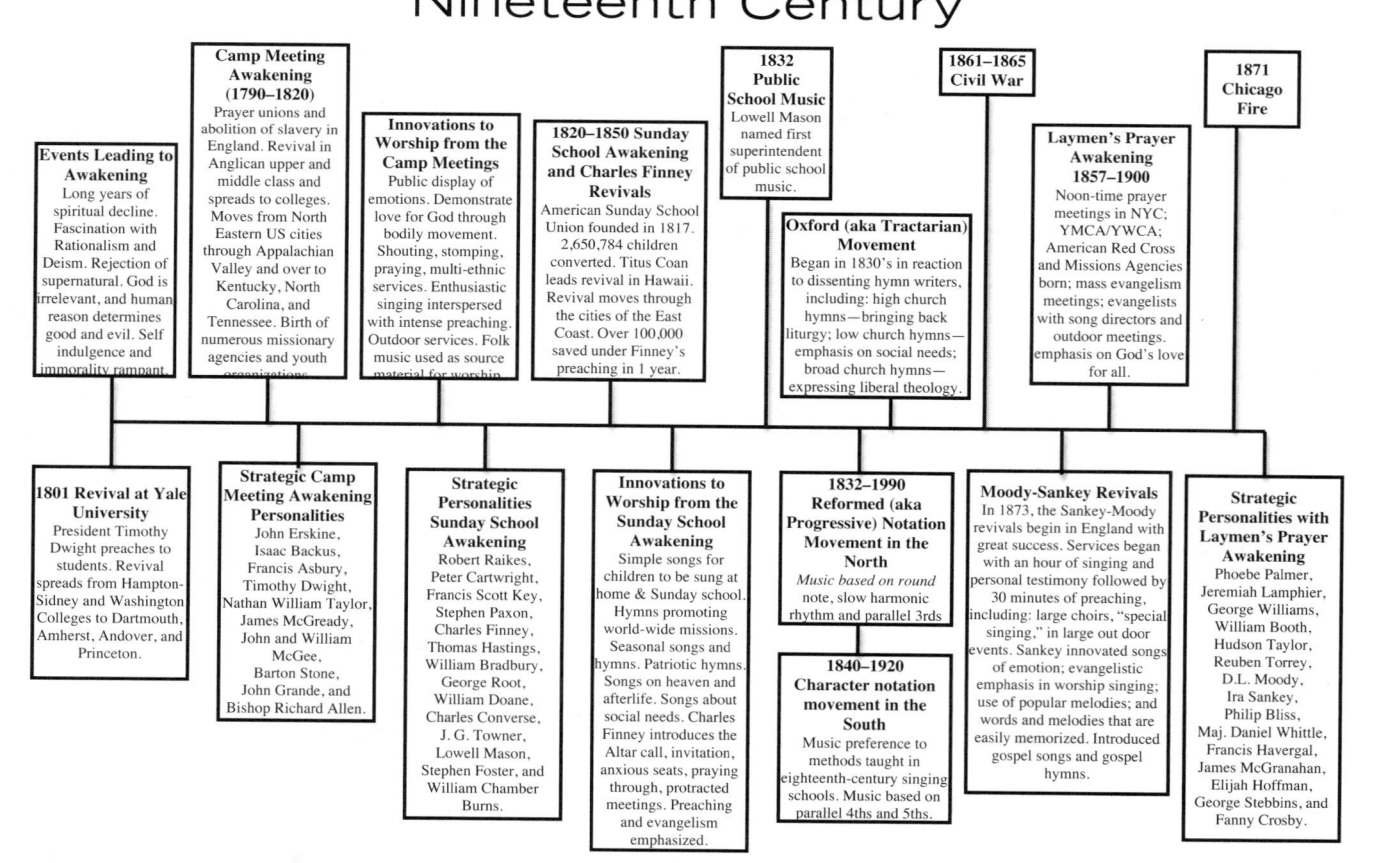

Worship through the Ages
Nineteenth Century

1832 Public School Music
Lowell Mason named first superintendent of public school music.

1861–1865 Civil War

1871 Chicago Fire

Events Leading to Awakening
Long years of spiritual decline. Fascination with Rationalism and Deism. Rejection of supernatural. God is irrelevant, and human reason determines good and evil. Self indulgence and immorality rampant

1801 Revival at Yale University
President Timothy Dwight preaches to students. Revival spreads from Hampton-Sidney and Washington Colleges to Dartmouth, Amherst, Andover, and Princeton.

Camp Meeting Awakening (1790–1820)
Prayer unions and abolition of slavery in England. Revival in Anglican upper and middle class and spreads to colleges. Moves from North Eastern US cities through Appalachian Valley and over to Kentucky, North Carolina, and Tennessee. Birth of numerous missionary agencies and youth

Innovations to Worship from the Camp Meetings
Public display of emotions. Demonstrate love for God through bodily movement. Shouting, stomping, praying, multi-ethnic services. Enthusiastic singing interspersed with intense preaching. Outdoor services. Folk music used as source

Strategic Camp Meeting Awakening Personalities
John Erskine, Isaac Backus, Francis Asbury, Timothy Dwight, Nathan William Taylor, James McGready, John and William McGee, Barton Stone, John Grande, and Bishop Richard Allen.

1820–1850 Sunday School Awakening and Charles Finney Revivals
American Sunday School Union founded in 1817. 2,650,784 children converted. Titus Coan leads revival in Hawaii. Revival moves through the cities of the East Coast. Over 100,000 saved under Finney's preaching in 1 year.

Innovations to Worship from the Sunday School Awakening
Simple songs for children to be sung at home & Sunday school. Hymns promoting world-wide missions. Seasonal songs and hymns. Patriotic hymns. Songs on heaven and afterlife. Songs about social needs. Charles Finney introduces the Altar call, invitation, anxious seats, praying through, protracted meetings. Preaching and evangelism emphasized.

Strategic Personalities Sunday School Awakening
Robert Raikes, Peter Cartwright, Francis Scott Key, Stephen Paxon, Charles Finney, Thomas Hastings, William Bradbury, George Root, William Doane, Charles Converse, J.G. Towner, Lowell Mason, Stephen Foster, and William Chamber Burns.

Oxford (aka Tractarian) Movement
Began in 1830's in reaction to dissenting hymn writers, including: high church hymns—bringing back liturgy; low church hymns—emphasis on social needs; broad church hymns—expressing liberal theology.

1832–1990 Reformed (aka Progressive) Notation Movement in the North
Music based on round note, slow harmonic rhythm and parallel 3rds

1840–1920 Character notation movement in the South
Music preference to methods taught in eighteenth-century singing schools. Music based on parallel 4ths and 5ths.

Laymen's Prayer Awakening 1857–1900
Noon-time prayer meetings in NYC; YMCA/YWCA; American Red Cross and Missions Agencies born; mass evangelism meetings; evangelists with song directors and outdoor meetings. emphasis on God's love for all.

Moody-Sankey Revivals
In 1873, the Sankey-Moody revivals begin in England with great success. Services began with an hour of singing and personal testimony followed by 30 minutes of preaching, including: large choirs, "special singing," in large out door events. Sankey innovated songs of emotion; evangelistic emphasis in worship singing; use of popular melodies; and words and melodies that are easily memorized. Introduced gospel songs and gospel hymns.

Strategic Personalities with Laymen's Prayer Awakening
Phoebe Palmer, Jeremiah Lamphier, George Williams, William Booth, Hudson Taylor, Reuben Torrey, D.L. Moody, Ira Sankey, Philip Bliss, Maj. Daniel Whittle, Francis Havergal, James McGranahan, Elijah Hoffman, George Stebbins, and Fanny Crosby.

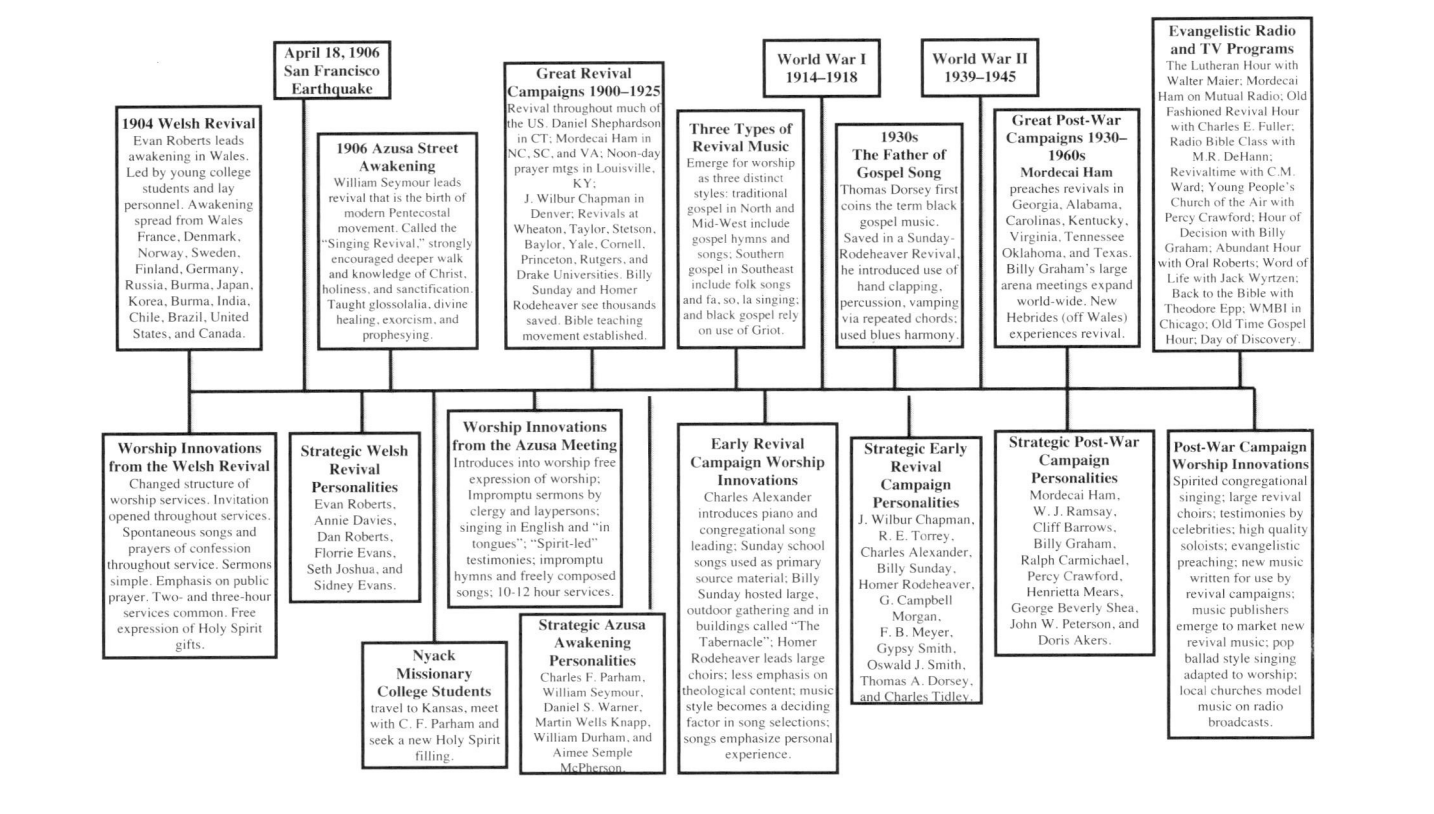

Worship through the Ages
Early and Mid-twentieth Century

Timeline markers: April 18, 1906 San Francisco Earthquake | World War I 1914–1918 | World War II 1939–1945

1904 Welsh Revival
Evan Roberts leads awakening in Wales. Led by young college students and lay personnel. Awakening spread from Wales to France, Denmark, Norway, Sweden, Finland, Germany, Russia, Burma, Japan, Korea, Burma, India, Chile, Brazil, United States, and Canada.

Worship Innovations from the Welsh Revival
Changed structure of worship services. Invitation opened throughout services. Spontaneous songs and prayers of confession throughout service. Sermons simple. Emphasis on public prayer. Two- and three-hour services common. Free expression of Holy Spirit gifts.

Strategic Welsh Revival Personalities
Evan Roberts, Annie Davies, Dan Roberts, Florrie Evans, Seth Joshua, and Sidney Evans.

1906 Azusa Street Awakening
William Seymour leads revival that is the birth of modern Pentecostal movement. Called the "Singing Revival," strongly encouraged deeper walk and knowledge of Christ, holiness, and sanctification. Taught glossolalia, divine healing, exorcism, and prophesying.

Nyack Missionary College Students
travel to Kansas, meet with C. F. Parham and seek a new Holy Spirit filling.

Worship Innovations from the Azusa Meeting
Introduces into worship free expression of worship; Impromptu sermons by clergy and laypersons; singing in English and "in tongues"; "Spirit-led" testimonies; impromptu hymns and freely composed songs; 10-12 hour services.

Strategic Azusa Awakening Personalities
Charles F. Parham, William Seymour, Daniel S. Warner, Martin Wells Knapp, William Durham, and Aimee Semple McPherson.

Great Revival Campaigns 1900–1925
Revival throughout much of the US. Daniel Shepardson in CT; Mordecai Ham in NC, SC, and VA; Noon-day prayer mtgs in Louisville, KY; J. Wilbur Chapman in Denver; Revivals at Wheaton, Taylor, Stetson, Baylor, Yale, Cornell, Princeton, Rutgers, and Drake Universities. Billy Sunday and Homer Rodeheaver see thousands saved. Bible teaching movement established.

Three Types of Revival Music
Emerge for worship as three distinct styles: traditional gospel in North and Mid-West include gospel hymns and songs. Southeast gospel in Southeast include folk songs and fa, so, la singing; and black gospel rely on use of Griot.

Early Revival Campaign Worship Innovations
Charles Alexander introduces piano and congregational song leading; Sunday school songs used as primary source material; Billy Sunday hosted large, outdoor gathering and in buildings called "The Tabernacle"; Homer Rodeheaver leads large choirs; less emphasis on theological content; music style becomes a deciding factor in song selections; songs emphasize personal experience.

1930s The Father of Gospel Song
Thomas Dorsey first coins the term black gospel music. Saved in a Sunday Rodeheaver Revival, he introduced use of hand clapping, percussion, vamping via repeated chords; used blues harmony.

Strategic Early Revival Campaign Personalities
J. Wilbur Chapman, R. E. Torrey, Charles Alexander, Billy Sunday, Homer Rodeheaver, G. Campbell Morgan, F. B. Meyer, Gypsy Smith, Oswald J. Smith, Thomas A. Dorsey, and Charles Tidley.

Great Post-War Campaigns 1930–1960s Mordecai Ham
preaches revivals in Georgia, Alabama, Carolinas, Kentucky, Virginia, Tennessee, Oklahoma, and Texas. Billy Graham's large arena meetings expand world-wide. New Hebrides (off Wales) experiences revival.

Evangelistic Radio and TV Programs
The Lutheran Hour with Walter Maier; Mordecai Ham on Mutual Radio; Old Fashioned Revival Hour with Charles E. Fuller; Radio Bible Class with M.R. DeHam; Revivaltime with C.M. Ward; Young People's Church of the Air with Percy Crawford; Hour of Decision with Billy Graham; Abundant Hour of Life with Oral Roberts; Word of Life with Jack Wyrtzen; Back to the Bible with Theodore Epp; WMBI in Chicago, Old Time Gospel Hour, Day of Discovery.

Strategic Post-War Campaign Personalities
Mordecai Ham, W. J. Ramsay, Cliff Barrows, Billy Graham, Ralph Carmichael, Percy Crawford, Henrietta Mears, George Beverly Shea, John W. Peterson, and Doris Akers.

Post-War Campaign Worship Innovations
Spirited congregational singing; large revival choirs; testimonies by celebrities; high quality soloists; evangelistic preaching; new music written for use by revival campaigns; music publishers emerge to market new revival music; pop ballad style singing adapted to worship; local churches model music on radio broadcasts.

Worship through the Ages
Late Twentieth and Early Twenty-First Centuries

1940–1965 Bible College Movement
Served as training organizations for musicians; some published music; some affiliated with radio ministries; traveling music and ministry teams featured at churches.

Worship Innovations by Youth and Bible College Movements
Introduced short, easy to sing, highly popular gospel choruses. Evangelism and discipleship where taught through short, energetic choruses. Produced songbooks. Traveling music teams modeled music and worship.

1940–1980 Youth for Christ Rallies
Parachurch organizations established youth camps, youth evangelism teams, Bible study groups, radio ministries for youth, athletic organizations, vacation Bible schools, Bible training institutes, youth music teams, and youth music training programs, including: Inter-varsity Christian Fellowship, Campus Crusade, Youth for Christ, AWANA, Word of Life, and Child Evangelism Fellowship.

Strategic Personalities By Youth & Bible College Movements
John Peterson, Harold DeCou, Ted Smith, Ralph Carmichael, Norman Clayton, Cliff Barrows, Alfred Smith, Ohman Bros. Trio Don Wyrtzen, Jack Wyrtzen, George Beverly Shea, Percy Crawford, and Ronn Huff.

1965–1985 Jesus Movement Awakening
Confession of sin, repentance, commitment to holiness, and full time Christian ministry or missions by former hippies turned Christian. Influx of newly converted and highly qualified rock-n-roll artists. Worship in coffee houses. Strong commitment to use of popular folk music for evangelism. Calvary Chapel and Chuck Smith baptized thousands of new converts. Expo '72 at Cotton Bowl in Dallas.

Worship Innovations By Jesus Movement
Informal dress, rock music, casual services, and simple living. Sang newly composed songs for 3-4 hrs, prayer, and bible study. Harmonically simple pop songs used for evangelism with drums, guitars, keyboards. Youth musicals. TV and radio promotion of new copyrights with artists and churches. Advent of CCM. Fulltime worship leaders at churches. Advent of CCM. New market for large evangelical choirs.

Strategic Personalities of the Jesus Movement
Chuck Smith, Mike MacIntosh, Arthur Blessitt, Lonnie Frisbee, Bill Gaither, Edwin Hawkins, James Cleveland, Billy Ray Hearn, Glenn Kaiser, Bob MacKenzie, Moishe Rosen, Chuck Fromm, Larry Norman, Jack Sparks, and Jack Hayford.

1970s College Revival Movement
Begins Feb 3, 1970, at Asbury College with days of confession, repentance, and commitment to Christian living. Asbury sends revival witness teams to BIOLA, Azusa Pacific, Olivet Nazarene, Seattle Pacific, Greenville Colleges and Universities, University of Tennessee, University of Kentucky, and Harvard. 1973 Revival at Liberty University.

Influential Artists of 1965–1985
Edwin Hawkins, Michael Card, Love Song, Honeytree, Pat Terry Group, Randy Stonehill, Larry Norman, JC Power Outlet, Phil Keaggy, Andrae Crouch, Chris Christian, Paul Clark, Lamb, Evie, Chuck Girard, 2nd Chapter of Acts, Steve Camp, Keith Green, and Jimmy and Carol

Emergence of Influential Music Publishers
The Benson Company; Word Music; Myrrh Hope Music; Tempo; Zondervan Music; Brentwood Music; Provident Music; Integrity Music!; Thank You Music!; Maranatha!; Vineyard Music; Hillsong; Hillsong United; Praise Charts.com; New

1990–2010 Great Worship Awakening
Revival of and commitment to biblical worship. Strong commitment to the local church. Influenced by charismatic theology. Commitment to new song and teaching how to worship. Strong emphasis on multi-ethnic worship. Revivals in Pensacola, FL; Toronto, Canada; Sidney, Australia; Great Britian; Large Youth Worship

1980–2000 Worship Innovations
Congregational singing becomes more and more important. Shift from evangelistic to worship and praise services. Use of multi-media as a main facilitator for worship. A merging of traditional, Southern gospel, black gospel, and charismatic music styles. Demand for fulltime, professional worship leaders and worship artists. Small choral ensembles give way to small rock-n-roll

Influential Artists of 1985–2010
Michael W. Smith, Dallas Holm, Steven Curtis Chapman, Twila Paris, Point of Grace, DC Talk, 4 Him, Amy Grant, Jeremy Camp, Petra, Sandy Patty, Babbie Mason, Avalon, Scot Wesley Brown, Steve Green, Keith & Kristyn Getty, Don Moen, Gaither Vocal Band, Ron Kenoly, Graham Kendrick, Lenny LeBlanc, Israel Houghton, The Winans, Richard Smallwood, David Crowder, Third Day, Natalie Grant, Mercy Me, Donnie McClurkin, Laura Story, Chris Tomlin, Darlene Zschech, Paul Balouch; Matt Redman; Rebecca St. James, Meredith Andrews, Casting Crowns, Shane and Shane; Charles Billingsley, Travis Cottrell,

Mega-Conferences
Passion! Conferences, Promise Keepers, Cutting Edge, Soul Survivor, and Women of Faith.

Twenty-First Century Influences
Missions and evangelism; emerging church and postmodern worship; charismatic renewal; Reformed theology; intellectual worship; liturgical worship; evangelical traditions; and free worship.

Worship Degrees
Robert Webber, IWS, Liberty University, SBC seminaries, BIOLA, Azusa, Spring Arbor University.

Name Index

Ackley, B. D. 249
Alexander, Archibald 147
Alexander, Charles M. 212, 245, 247, 249
Allen, Richard, Bishop 149
Anthony, Dick 279, 325
Asbury, Francis, Bishop 148
Atwood, Rudy 276

Bach, Johann Sebastian 106
Baker, Paul 295, 303, 310–12, 323, 336
Barnhouse, Donald Grey 370
Barrows, Cliff 271, 281–82, 287, 290–91
Battle, Kathleen 317
Beecher, Lyman 167
Bell, Eudorous 229
Bennett, George 181
Bianconi, Lorenzo 110, 112
Billings, William 127
Blackaby, Henry 310, 353, 365
Blackstone, William Eugene 244
Blessitt, Arthur 315, 336
Bliss, Philip P. 172, 188, 190, 192, 197

Booth, Catherine 190
Booth, William 190
Bradbent, George 276
Bradbury, William 168, 172–73
Brainerd, David 113
Brown, Les 285
Bullock, Geoff 347
Burns, William Chambers 175–76

Calvin, John 96, 104, 108–9, 115, 127, 353, 355
Campbell, Duncan 212, 244, 272–74, 308, 313
Carey, William 154
Carmichael, Ralph 276, 282, 285, 287, 290–91, 312, 317–18, 324, 326–28, 339
Cartwright, Peter 131–34, 148, 150, 155
Cash, Johnny 303
Cashwell, G. B. 229
Chalmers, Thomas 137
Chapman, J. Wilbur 237, 239, 245–47, 254, 260–61
Checks, J. J. 237

Claxton, Ecroy 144
Clayton, Norman 279, 287
Coan, Titus 159
Collins, Judy 324
Converse, Charles 172, 191, 245
Coomes, Tommy 318
Cowper, William 125, 261
Crawford, Florence 228
Crawford, Percy 275, 278–79, 281–82, 288
Crosby, Fanny 190–92, 194, 196–98, 285, 296
Crouch, Andrae 303
Cymbala, Jim 353, 365

D'Alembert 139
Davies, Annie 210
DeCou, Harold 278–79, 287
DeHann, M. R. 275
Diderot 139
Dienstberger, Paul 140, 156–57, 212, 216–17, 233, 258–59, 289, 298, 310–11, 313, 338, 364
Dixon, A. C. 236
Doane, William Howard 172, 191, 196–97
Dodderidge, Philip 125
Doddridge, Phillip 331
Dorsey, Thomas A. 250, 261
Durham, William 228
Dwight, Timothy 138, 148

Edson, Lewis 127

Edwards, Fanny V. 187
Edwards, Jonathan 114–15, 128, 137–38, 148
Epp, Theodore 278
Erdman, Charles 244
Erskine, John 137
Eskew, Harry 122, 128, 178, 196, 261, 369, 372
Eskridge, Larry 297, 311, 323
Evans, Florrie 211
Evans, G. W. 228
Evans, Sidney 211
Excell, E. O. 191
Falwell, Jerry 63–64, 277, 325
Fawcett, John 125
Field, Fred 318
Finney, Charles Grandison viii, 6, 159–60, 164—70, 172, 174–76, 188, 194
Ford, Tennessee Ernie 317
Foster, Stephen 172
Fragar, Russell 347
Franklin, Benjamin 146
Frisbee, Lonnie 315–16
Fromm, Chuck i, 300, 311–12, 318, 337, 341, 343, 350–51, 363–64
Fuller, Charles E. 216, 275–77, 280, 290, 364, 370

Gaither, Gloria 332, 339
Gaither, William (Bill) 256, 316, 319, 332, 337
Giglio, Louie 351

Girard, Chuck 318
González, Justo 52, 64, 76–77, 79–81, 111, 128, 157, 177–78
Goodman, Benny 285
Gordon, Adoniram Judson 244
Gordon, A. J. 191
Goss, Howard 229
Graham, Billy 264, 268–71, 275, 278, 281, 283–84, 286–87, 290–91, 302–3, 322, 333, 344, 348, 370
Grande, John A. 147
Green, H. Leland 276
Green, Keith 317, 330
Griesen, Nelly 321

Habershon, Ada 244
Haldane, James 137
Haldane, Robert 137
Hamblin, Stuart 270
Ham, Mordecai 237, 263, 266, 289
Harkness, Robert 249
Harrington, Bob 333–34, 339
Harris, Larnelle 317
Hastings, Thomas 168, 172–74
Havergal, Francis "Fanny" 193
Hawkins, Edwin 316, 331–32, 338
Hayford, Jack 216, 353–54, 359, 366
Hearn, Billy Ray 317, 327–28, 336
Hearst, William Randolph 270
Heinz, H. J. 183
Herring, Annie 321
Hoffman, Elijah 191

Holden, Oliver 127
Huntingdon, Lady 125
Hus, John 91, 96, 102, 116
Hustad, Donald P. 26, 42, 64, 80–81, 106–7, 111–12, 120–21, 129, 171, 177–78, 195–96, 199, 247, 260, 278, 372

Ives, Burl 317

James, Harry 285
Jenkins, Joseph 201, 211
!eremiah, David 353, 365
Jones, E. Stanley 238, 258–59
Joshua, Seth 201–2, 211
Judson, Adoniram 147, 154

Kaiser, Glenn 317
Keach, Benjamin 119–20
Kenton, Stan 282, 285
Key, Francis Scott 163
Kimball, Edward 183
Kirkham, Gawin 191
Knox, John 96, 104

Lake, John G. 229
Lamphier, Jeremiah 180
Laurie, Greg 316
Lee, Danny 303
Lindsay, Hubert 297
Lister, Mosie 332
Livingstone, David 99, 191
Loveless, Wendell 277
Lum, Clara 228, 230
Luther, Martin 84, 96, 102–4,

107–10, 115, 117, 127, 197, 369, 373
MacIntosh, Mike 301–2, 316
MacKay, James Murray 272–73
MacKenzie, Robert "Bob" R. 256, 262, 290–91, 319–20, 330–31, 333–34, 336–39
MacLeod, Bill 309
Maier, Walter A. 275
Manuain, Benjamin 305
Marsden, Samuel 154
Marshall, John, Chief Justice 136
Mason, Charles Harrison 229
Mason, Lowell 170, 172–73, 261
Matthews, Randy 303, 330
Mayfield, Larry 325, 339
McCartney, Bill 350
McElrath, Hugh 122, 261, 369, 372
McGee, Cecil 327
McGee, John 141–42
McGee, William 141
McGranahan, James 190–91, 193, 198, 201, 244
McGready, James 140–42, 145, 149–50, 156–57
McGuire, Barry 303, 317, 330
McMillian, James 149
Mears, Henrietta C. 269–70, 283, 291
Meyer, F. B. 212
Miller, Glenn 285
Mills, Samuel J. 147
Moody, Dwight L. 8, 42, 176, 180, 182–96, 201, 205–6, 216,

236, 239, 243, 245–47, 261, 278, 281, 284, 286, 313, 325
Moore, Jennie 228
Morgan, G. Campbell 212, 244
Morgan, Reuben 347
Mott, John R. 213
Myers, Paul 277

Newton, John 125, 151, 261
Nix, W. M. 251
Norman, Larry 303, 320–21, 330, 337

Oldenburg, Bob 317, 327
Omartian, Michael 339, 341
Orr, J. Edwin 136, 140, 155–56, 175, 201, 204, 216, 269
Owens, Jimmy 317, 328, 339

Palmer, Phoebe 190, 196
Parham, Charles F. 223–24, 227
Paxson, Stephen 163–64, 177
Payton, Grace 275–76
Pearce, Bill 278
Perronet, Edward 125
Peterson, John W. 278, 284, 286–87, 290–91, 325, 339
Phillips, Philip 188–89, 191–92
Price, Jack 333

Rader, Paul 260, 277
Raikes, Robert 137, 162–63
Rambo, Dottie 332, 337, 339
Rambo, Reba 303
Ramsay, W. J. 267

Redman, Robb 168, 177, 230, 233, 304, 312, 344, 349, 360, 363
Rippon, John 125
Roberts, Dan 211
Roberts, Evan 201–11, 231, 235, 237, 370
Roberts, Oral 275, 324
Rodeheaver, Homer 239, 241–42, 250–51, 259–60, 277, 333
Root, George 172–73, 191
Rosen, Martin Meyer "Moishe" 320, 337
Ross, Allen 40

Sandell-Berg, Lina 194
Sankey, Ira D. 180, 186–98, 201, 205–6, 236, 239, 241, 257–58, 261
Sargeant, Phoebe 228
Savonarola, Girolamo 84–85, 95–96, 102
Scofield, C. I. 244
Scofield, Jack 267
Semple, Aimee 229
Seymour, William Joseph 222–31, 370
Shea, George Beverly 271, 278, 284, 287, 290–91, 317
Shepardson, Daniel 236
Skillings, Otis 328, 339
Slessor, Mary 191
Smith, Alfred 287
Smith, Chuck 216, 299, 301, 315, 321, 341, 346

Smith, Gypsy (Rodney) 191, 212, 239
Smith, Hiram 228
Smith, Michael W. 320, 337–38
Smith, Oswald J. 214, 247
Smith, Ted 278
Spener, Philipp Jakob 106
Spurgeon, Charles Haddon 190
Stamps, Virgil 277
Stead, William 206
Stebbins, George 190–91, 193, 198, 244, 249
Stone, Barton 142, 149
Styll, John 328, 338
Sunday, Billy 239–43, 250, 259–60, 333
Sutera, Lou 309
Sutera, Ralph 309

Tada, Joni Eareckson 318
Talbot, John Michael 317
Talbot, Terry 317
Taylor, James Hudson 191, 244
Taylor, Nathaniel William 148
Templeton, Chuck 268–69
Terry, Neely 228
Thigpen, Jonathan 312
Thomlinson, A. J. 229
Toplady, Augustus 125
Torrey, Reuben A. 191, 212, 214, 239, 245–48, 277, 282
Towner, J. G. 172, 249
Tozer, A. W. 353
Truax, Jay 318

Tufts, John 126

Voltairé 135
von Zinzendorf, Count Nikolaus 91, 106, 116

Walker, William 127
Ward, C. M. 275
Ward, Matthew 321
Waters, Ethel 287, 318
Watts, Isaac 114, 120–23, 125, 151–52, 173, 257, 261, 369
Webber, Andrew Lloyd 324
Webber, Robert 71, 352–53, 355, 366
Wesley, Charles 117–18, 123, 369
Wesley, John 114, 116–19, 123–25, 129, 136–37, 152, 195, 238, 258, 305, 312, 369–70

Whaley, Rodney 313
Whitefield, George 118–19
Whittle, Major Daniel Webster 191
Williams, George 190, 196
Williams, M. B. 247
Williamson, John Finley 242
Williams, William 125
Wilson-Dickson, Andrew 42, 80, 92, 94, 96–97, 109–12, 115, 128, 129, 144, 152, 157–58, 372, 373
Wimber, John 346
Wycliffe, John 90–91, 96, 102, 369
Wyrtzen, Don 325, 328, 339
Wyrtzen, Jack 275, 278–79

Zschech, Darlene 347
Zwingli, Ulrich 96, 103–4, 115

Subject Index

Abel 12–13, 29
Abraham 15–18, 23, 29, 49, 149, 187, 337
absolute fast 114
Abundant Hour, The 275
Adam 11–12
African American Episcopal Church 149
African American Gospel Song 253
African Inland Mission 355
Age of Reason, the 116, 148
à Kempis, Thomas 89
Alleluia: A Praise Gathering for Believers 319, 336
"altar call" 166, 174, 300, 341
Altar of Incense 32
"Amazing Grace" 125, 324
Ambrose of Milan 78, 368
American National Anthem 163
American Revolution 135, 146
American Sunday School Union (ASSU) 162–64, 172
Amherst 131, 138
Amherst, Virginia 131
Anabaptist Movement 102

Ancient of Days 3
Andover 138
Andrae Crouch and the Disciples 303
Andrews Sisters, the 285
angels 10–11
Anglican Church (Church of England) 104, 115, 172, 212
Anglican clergyman 117
Anglicanism 369
Anglican *Prayer Book* 369
Anglicans 137–38, 146, 172
Annual Red River Communion 141
Anselm 89
Anthony 87
Antioch 61–62, 65–66, 100
anti-Vietnam War demonstrations 295
"anxious seats", the 166
Apostles' Creed, the 76
Apostolic Churches 222
Apostolic Faith Gospel Mission 224
Apostolic Faith, the 225, 229–30
Aquinas, Thomas 89
Asaph 35–36

Asbury College 258, 305–8, 312
Assemblies of God, the 215–16, 222, 229
Augustus 70
awakening 5
AWANA Clubs International 280
Azusa Pacific University 302, 307

Babel 14–15
baby boomer revival 294–95, 297, 299, 301, 303, 305, 307, 309, 311, 313, 317, 319, 321, 323, 325, 327, 329, 331, 333, 335, 337, 339
Back to the Bible 278
banners 28–29
Baptist Missionary Society 154
Baptist Sunday School Board 327, 335
Benedict of Nursia 87, 92–93, 96
Benson Company 319, 331, 338–39, 345
Bernard of Clairvaux 89
Berno of Baume 88, 96
Bethesda Orphanage 119
Bible College Movement 266, 288
Bible Institute of Los Angeles (BIOLA) 275, 280
Billy Graham Evangelistic Association 284, 322
"Billy Sunday Tabernacles" 240
Bithynia 72
Black Gospel music 80, 96, 111, 128, 157, 257, 319, 328, 335
Blackwood Brothers, the 278

Bonnie Brae Avenue 224
Book of Common Order, The (Knox) 105
Booth, William 212, 370
Boston Academy of Music 173
breaking bread 56, 60
Brethren of the Common Life, the 102, 116
British and Foreign Bible Society 154
broad church hymns 172
burnt offering 17, 30

Cain 12–14, 29
Calvary Chapel, Cosa Mesa, CA 216, 299–302, 304, 311, 315–16, 318, 321–22, 341, 345–46
Calvinistic theology 122, 150
Calvinists 107, 109–10, 114, 120, 126, 150
Camp Meeting revivals 127, 134, 149
camp meetings 145–47, 150–52, 154, 161, 189, 288, 370
Campus Crusade for Christ 215, 280, 288, 302, 312, 322
Canaan 15–16, 23
Canadian Prairie Revival 308–10
Cane Ridge Revival (Awakening) 131, 140, 142–44, 149–50
Celsus 67
Center for Worship at Liberty University 356, 359
"Chapman-Alexander Simultaneous Campaign" 245

SUBJECT INDEX

Character Notation 170
Character Notation Movement 170
Charismatic Renewal Movement, the 356, 362
Charles VIII 95
Chenaniah 35
Chicago Music Publishing Company 251
Child Evangelism Fellowship 280
chorale 108–9, 126
Christian Life magazine 311
Christian Synagogue 74
Christian World Liberation Front (CWLF) 297, 322
church growth 137, 344
Church Missionary Society 154
Church of England (Anglican Church) 104, 116, 119, 149
Church of God in Christ, the 222, 229, 316
Church of God, the 222, 228–29, 316, 339
circuit-riding preachers 127, 146–47, 151
civil rights protests 295
clapping of hands 27
Clovis 86
Colored Sacred Harp 153
Columba 88, 94, 96
Columbia Bible College 215
Come Together 317
common (communal) meal 74
Complete Library of Christian Worship, the 355, 365
Compline 92

Congregationalists 126, 146
Constantine 70, 71, 74, 78, 80, 86
Constantinus Chlorus 70
Contemporary Christian Music (CCM) 310–12, 317, 320–21, 328–29, 331, 334–38, 345, 347, 372
contextualizing worship 357
Convergence Movement, the 355, 361, 366
Crawford Broadcasting 325
Crossweeksung, New Jersey 113
Crusades, the 79, 83, 187
Cumberland Presbyterians 154
cup of blessing 53–54
cup of consummation 53, 55
cup of interpretation 53
cup of sanctification 53
Cutting Edge events 351
cymbals 27

Damascus 66
dance 29, 34, 41, 72, 133, 164, 313
Danny Lee and the Children of Truth 303
D'Arezzo, Guido 94
Dark Ages, the vii, 79, 83, 100, 368
Dartmouth 138, 156
Day of Atonement 32–33
Day of Discovery 325, 334
deism 135, 139, 148, 154, 265
Diocletian 68, 70
disciples 43–45, 47, 49, 51, 54–56, 86, 301, 350
Disciples of Christ 154–57

dissenting hymns 172
diversity 357, 361
Divine Office 93, 95
Doctrine and Disciplines of the Azusa Street Mission, the 231
Drake University 239
Duomo Cathedral 85

Eastern College 280
"Easter Song" 321
East Timor (Indonesia) Revival 304–5
Ebenezer Baptist Church (Chicago) 251
Edinburgh, Scotland 137
Edwin Hawkins Singers, the 332, 338
Elisha 26
Elohim 3, 8
Emerging Church and postmodern worship, the 356
Emerging Church, the 356, 358, 362, 366
empiricism 135
end times 50, 228
Enlightenment, the 148
Enoch 14
ethnodoxology 357
ethnomusicology 357
Eucharist 52, 107, 360–61
Euphrates valley 66
evangelical or low church hymns 172
evangelistic radio programs 266, 288

Eve 12
examine themselves 54, 99
Experiencing God 310, 365
Explo '72 302–3, 318
Ezra 22, 36

fast 114
fasting 32, 76, 84, 87, 141, 207
"father of American church music" (Mason) 173
"father of black gospel song" (Dorsey) 252
"father of English hymnody" (Watts) 120
"father of gospel music" (Sankey) 187
Feast of Firstfruits 32
Feast of Lights (Hanukkah) 32
Feast of Pentecost iv, vii, 6, 31, 33, 43–47, 49–50, 56, 59–60, 63, 66, 96, 111, 155, 176, 193, 195, 229, 236, 237, 263, 370
Feast of Tabernacles 33
Feast of Trumpets 28, 33
"Festival of Song" 247
Finney Songbooks 168
First Book of Discipline, The (Knox) 105
Florence 84–85, 95
Forest Home 268
formational 4
four-shape notation 170
Franciscan Order, the 89
Francis of Assisi 89
Fred Waring Chorale, the 286

free choice 10
Free Methodist Greenville College 307
free will 3, 148, 174
French Revolution, the 116
Fuller Theological Seminary 216, 277

garden of Gethsemane 55
Gasper River 141, 142, 149–50
Generation X 346
Genevan Psalter 109, 127
Georgetown College 308
Gideon 27
Glasgow University 104
Gloucester, England 137, 162
Gnostics 77
Golden Gate Quartet, the 285
Good News 317, 327
gospel blues 251
gospel cantata 284
Gospel Light Publishing Company 283
gospel rock 321
"Gospel Wagon, The" 183
Great Awakening(s) i, 6, 47, 49, 91, 102, 111, 113–18, 125, 127–28, 138, 147, 150–51, 154, 156, 160, 174, 180, 191, 222, 230–31, 235, 258, 264–65, 295–96, 304–5, 308, 346, 371–72
Great Chicago Fire, the (Oct. 8, 1871) 180, 184–85, 195, 221
Gregory ("the Illuminator") 67

Griot 257
guitar 28, 323, 327, 367

Haight-Ashbury 297
Hallel 53, 55
"Hallelujah Chorus" 241
Hampden-Sidney College 138
Harvard 126, 139, 308
Haven of Rest, the 277
"Heavenly Sunshine" 276
Hebrews 27, 34, 51, 54
hedonism 295
Hellenistic 40, 51, 66
Hellenists 51
Heman 35
Herrnhutt 116–17
high church hymns 172
High School Born-Againers 279
Hillsong Church 345, 347
Hillsong Music 347
Hi-Lows, the 285
Hippie Movement, the 288, 295–96, 315, 321–22
holiness 10, 38, 57, 190, 225, 227–28, 231, 255, 371
Holiness Bible school 223
Hosanna USA 341
Houghton College 280, 284
Hour of Decision, The 271, 275
humanism 101, 295
humility 54, 90, 271
Hussites, the 102
hymns 50, 55, 58, 74, 77–78, 80, 89, 93, 95, 108–10, 114,

119–23, 125–27, 143, 149,
151, 153, 170–74, 187, 189,
191–95, 197–98, 205, 208,
230, 245, 247, 249, 252, 255,
257, 261, 277, 287, 327, 332,
343, 354, 368–69, 371
Hymns for the Family of God 319

"I'd Rather Have Jesus" 284
Ignatius 65–66, 69
Illinois Sunday School Association 183
Immanuel 47, 183
incantations 26
incense 26, 32
inculturation 357, 361
Infidel Movement, the 140
Ink Spots, the 285
"Instantaneous Conversion" (Moody) 184
Institute of Worship Studies 353, 355
institutionalized 40, 115
Integrity Media Worship School 348, 363
International Church of the Foursquare Gospel, the 222, 229
Inter-Varsity Christian Fellowship 280
Introduction to the Singing of Psalm Tunes, An (Tufts) 126
Irenaeus 67
Isaac 17, 23, 29, 49, 120–23, 138, 151, 173, 261, 369
Isaiah 27
"Is the Bible the Word of God?" (Dwight) 139

itinerate musicians 152, 174, 329
Jabal 13
Jacob 23, 26, 29, 49, 198
James, the brother of John 62
James, the half brother of Jesus 51, 63
Jeduthun 35
Jehoshaphat 27, 36
"jerks" 134
Jerry Falwell Ministries 325
Jerusalem 22, 36, 41, 43, 45, 50–51, 60, 63, 66, 100, 104, 226, 367
Jesus Christ, Superstar 324
"Jesus Is a Soul Man" 324
"Jesus Loves Me" 168
"Jesus Loves the Little Children" 254–55
Jesus Movement, the (Jesus People, Jesus Freaks) 7, 296–304, 311–12, 315–18, 321–23, 326, 328–29, 336–37, 343–44, 346, 353, 370
Jesus music 302–3, 323
"Jesus revolution," a 298
Jews for Jesus 304, 320, 337
Job 10
John 50–51, 67
John Brown University 280
John T. Benson Company 319
Jonah 27
Joseph 29
Josephus 28
Joshua 20, 23, 27
Jubal 13

SUBJECT INDEX

Justin Martyr's Apology 74

Keren 28
Keswick tradition 194, 207, 273
King David 2, 20, 23, 27, 34–35
King Henry VIII 104, 369
king of Naples 95
King's College 280–81, 283, 363
King Tradt of Armenia 67
Knowledge of the Holy (Tozer) 353
Kurt Kaiser 312, 317, 327, 336

lamentations 26
Last Supper, the 47, 49, 53–55, 120
"Latter Rain," the 223, 225
Lauds 92
Laymen's Prayer Movement, the 181
Laymen's Revival 236
"leather-lunged evangelist" (Sunday) 240
lectionary 40, 52, 361
Lectures on Revival (Finney) 166
liberalism 295
Liberty University 155, 293–94, 348, 352, 356, 359, 363, 366
lifestyle 57, 62, 68, 73, 326
LifeWay Christian Resources 345
LifeWay Worship Resources 289, 347
Light Records 282, 324
Lillenas Music Publishers 345, 347
Liturgical influences 356, 362
Liturgical Renewal Movement 360–61

Living Room Coffee House 297
living sacrifice 53, 57
Logan County, Kentucky 140, 149
Lollards, the 91, 102
London Missionary Society 154
Lord's Supper 52, 54, 75, 104, 107, 117
Loughor, Wales 210
Love Song 318, 336
Lucifer 10–11
lute 28
Lutheran Hour, The 275
Lutheranism 369
Luther's German Chorale 108

making melody 27
Maranatha! Music 302, 341–43, 345–46, 350
Marcionites 77
"Master the Tempest Is Raging" 241
materialism 90, 139, 264
Matins 92
Maxentius 70
McCormick Theological Seminary 248
McGuire Sisters, the 285
meal offering 31
Melchizedek 16–17
Melody Four Quartet, the 278
Mercy Music 345–46
Messiah, the 37, 47, 53, 301, 320
metrical psalmody 126
Mills Brothers, the 285
Miriam 27

missional 4, 294
Missions and Evangelism 356–57
Mississippi Valley Enterprise, The 163
Modernaires, the 285
modes 93
Modesto Manifesto, the 271
Mohawk River Valley (New York) 236
monasteries 83, 88–89, 101, 368
monasticism 87, 96
Moody Bible Institute 213, 246–47, 278, 281, 284
Moody Radio Network 325
Moody-Sankey campaigns 236
Moravians 112–13, 117, 127, 138
Moses 18–20, 23, 27, 29, 34, 37, 64
Most High God 20, 23, 44, 46, 298
Mountainbrook Camp 283
Mount Moriah 17
Mount of Olives 55
Mount Sinai 18–19, 29
"mourners' benches" 165–66
"Mr. Booze" 240
multiethnic worship 151, 228
musicians 27, 323
music notation 152, 170, 368
Myrrh Records 317

National Baptist Convention 251
National Convention of Gospel Choirs and Choruses 252
Natural High 317–18, 328
"Nature and Danger of Infidel Philosophy, The " (Dwight) 139

Navigators, the 269, 280, 288
Nazareth 46, 184
Nehemiah 22, 36
Nero 50, 68–69
New Benson Company, The 345
new covenant 42, 47–49, 51–52, 54, 64
New Hebrides Awakening 271–72
New Life Boys Ranch 279
new song 127, 346
"New Song: The Sound of Spiritual Awakening" (Chuck Fromm) 311, 337
New Testament, the 6, 42, 47, 59–60, 63, 89, 110, 120–21, 193, 244, 359, 376
Niagara-on-the-Lake, Ontario, Canada 243
Noah 14, 29
None 92
Northern Baptist Theological Seminary 308, 352, 355
Northwestern College 239, 268
Nyack Missionary College 215

Ohman Brothers Trumpet Trio 287
Old Fashioned Revival Hour, The (OFRH) 275–77, 279, 290
Old Time Gospel Hour, The 42, 325, 334
Olivet Nazarene University 307
omnipotent 2
omnipresent 2
omniscient 2
"One Day" 245, 254–55, 261, 351

Open Air Mission, the 191
Open Bible Standard Church, the 222
Ottoman Turks 83, 101
Oxford (or Tractarian) Movement 171–72, 177
Oxford Reading and Research Conference 311, 337

Pachomius 87
Pacific Garden Mission 239
parachurch organizations 222, 258, 279–80, 304, 349, 352
paradigm 6–7, 42, 63, 113, 195, 329, 343, 356, 362, 367, 371
Paragon and Associates 319, 345
Passion Conferences 349, 351, 364
"Pass It On" 303, 312
Passover 32–33, 48, 53–55
Patmos 50–51
Patrick of Ireland 87–88, 96
Paul 50–51
peace offering 26, 31
Pentateuch, the 37
Pentecostal Assemblies of Canada, the 229
Pentecostal Holiness Church, the 222
People's Church, the 248–49
People's Magazine, The (Oswald Smith) 249
people's priest, the (Zwingli) 103
percussion 27
Period of Restoration 116
Peter 45–46, 50–51

Pharaoh 18
Pharisees 41
Pietists 102, 106–7, 114
Pilgrim Baptist Church (Chicago) 251
Pinebrook Bible Camp 283
Pinebrook Praises chorus books 278
Pliny the Younger 72
ploughboy preachers 114
Polycarp 69–70
polyphony 93, 95
Pontifex Maximus 71
Pontus 45, 72
Pope Alexander IV 95
Pope Gregory 91–92
Port Tobacco, Maryland 149
post-evangelical 358
postmodern 322, 358, 362
praxis-oriented 358
"prayed through" 165
Prayer Unions 137
praying together 56, 160
preaching 56
"Precious Lord, Take My Hand" 251
Prime 92
Princeton 138, 239, 242, 268
Promise Keepers 346, 349–50, 354
protracted meetings 166, 174
psallo 59
psalms 36–39, 50, 58, 77, 80, 92, 109, 122, 127, 368
Psalms, book of 36, 109
psalters 108–9, 121, 125, 127
psalterys 28

public invitation 13, 142, 165–66, 174, 176, 180, 184–85, 188, 206, 268, 273, 277, 301, 309, 312
"Put Your Hand in the Hand of the Man from Galilee" 324

Radio Bible Class, The 275
rationalism 135, 139
Red Sea 27
Reformation, the vii, 6, 64, 85, 90–91, 95, 99–100, 102, 104–8, 111–12, 114–16, 120, 128, 157, 171, 177, 216, 228, 322, 378
Reformed Branch (or Progressive Movement) 169
Reformed churches 369
Reformed Notation 170, 173
Reformed theology 360
Reformed theology and intellectual worship influences 356, 362
Regent University 352, 363
relational 4
Religious Tract Society 154
Renaissance, the 85, 95, 101
repentance 4, 29, 46, 102, 106, 142, 147, 150–51, 167, 207–8, 226, 231, 265, 293, 297, 306–7, 371
reproducible 4
Resurrection Band 317
revivalist theology 148
revivals 5, 60, 127, 140, 154, 160–61, 163, 165, 167–69, 171, 173, 175, 177, 181, 189, 194, 201, 205, 214, 228, 240, 253, 269, 308, 312–13, 370
Ridgecrest Baptist Assembly 327
Rodeheaver-Hall-Mack Company 249
"Rogues Harbor" 140
Roman Catholicism 369
Rule, The 92–93

sacraments 360–61
Sacred Harp, The 153
sacrifices 12–13, 18–20, 23, 29–30, 32–33, 36, 39, 41, 48, 57, 62–63
Sadducees 41
Salem Broadcasting 325
Salvation Army, the 370
Sarai 15–16
Saturday night rally 279
"Saved, Saved" 267, 289
scientific music 173
Scofield Reference Bible 244
Scots Confession of Faith, The (Knox) 105
Second Chapter of Acts 317, 321, 337, 339
Second Vatican Council 360
seeker initiatives 344
seven-shape notation 170
Sext 92
Shadowbrook Camp 283
sharing 56
Shophar 28
shouting 26–27, 41, 144, 147, 150,

244, 250, 267, 359
showbread 31
singing 26–27, 34, 53, 55, 57, 59, 78, 85, 89, 92, 94–95, 107–8, 110, 113, 119–21, 123–27, 144–45, 147, 152–53, 168, 170–73, 187–89, 192–94, 204–10, 230–31, 241, 247, 249–50, 252, 255–57, 261, 281, 285–86, 293, 300, 311–12, 324–25, 332, 334, 338, 349, 359, 362, 368–69, 371
singing schools 125–27, 152, 173, 192, 256, 261
Singspiration 277, 279, 339
sin offering 30
Sistrum 28
slums of Chicago 183
Solomon 23, 27, 34–36
Songs in the Night 278, 284
songs of "human composure" 120
Song Time 279
Soul Survivor events 351
Southern Baptist's Laymen's Hour, The 275
Southern Gospel Music 328, 332
Southern Gospel Singing Convention-style music 255
Southern Gospel Song 253, 255, 257, 277, 319, 338
Southwestern Southern Baptist Theological Seminary 307
Sparrow Records 317
spiritual gifts 58, 359, 362, 370

spiritual songs 50, 74, 77
Stamps-Baxter Company of Dallas, Texas 257
Stamps-Baxter Music Publishing Company 338, 345
Stamps Quartet, the 277
"Stand in the Gap: A Sacred Assembly of Men" 351
Statesmen Quartet, the 278
Stephen 62
strings 28
Sunday School Movement 137–38, 154, 162, 167, 174
Sunday school revivals 154
Swiss Brethren 102
synagogue 39–41, 49, 51–52, 55, 58, 61, 63, 74, 92

tabernacle 19–20, 23–24, 32, 34, 41, 49, 190, 263, 267–68
Tacitus 69
Taylor University 238, 280
teaching 56
Tell It Like It Is 312, 317–18, 327–28
temple 20, 22–23, 27, 34–36, 39, 41, 44–45, 48–49, 55, 57, 61, 63
temple worship 20, 35, 41
Terce 92
The Pursuit of God (Tozer) 353
"The Wonder of It All" 284
Third Presbyterian Church 165
Thirty Years' War (1618–1648) 105
Thomas Road Baptist Church i, 64,

293, 325
Tigris valley 66
Toccoa Falls College 215
Torah, the 26, 40
Toronto Bible College 215, 248
Traditional Gospel Hymn 254
Traditional Gospel Song 253, 255, 285
transcendence 106, 360–61
transformational 4
trespass (guilt) offering 30–31
tribe of Levi 23, 35–36
trinitarian view of God in worship 359
trumpet 28
Tubal-Cain 13

United Pentecostal Church 229
Up with People 326–27

vacation Bible schools 279
Valparaiso, Chile 213
Vespers 92
Vineyard Christian Fellowship 345–46
Vineyard churches 304, 316

Waldo, Peter 89
Washington College 138
Welsh Revival, the viii, 201, 205, 210–12, 214–15, 217, 236–37
Western European developments (1830–1850) 171
Whatever Happened to Worship? (Tozer) 353
Wheaton College 238, 280, 283, 352, 355
"Why Revival Tarries" (Leonard Ravenhill) 312
wind instruments 28
Winnipeg Bible Institute 215
Wittenberg 102
Women of Faith 349, 351
Woodstock Music Festival 191, 296, 310
Word Music 317, 327, 341, 345
Word of Life 275, 278–80
World Action Singers, the 324, 334
World War II 7, 87, 258, 265, 279, 284–85, 288, 295
worship before creation 9

Yahweh 18, 20, 23, 47, 53
Yale 114, 138–40, 148, 156–57
Yale Divinity School 114, 148
Young Men's Christian Association (YMCA) 184, 187, 190, 196, 236
Young People's Church of the Air 275, 278, 281, 283
youth camps 279, 312–13, 344
Youth for Christ International (YFC) 277, 279, 287–88
Youth for Christ movement 266, 282, 288
youth musicals 312, 317–18, 326–28

Zelzelim 28
Zondervan Corporation 262, 345
Zondervan Music 338, 345